KUMĀRADĀSA'S JĀNAKĪHARAṆA

JĀNAKĪHARANA

OF

KUMĀRADĀSA

A Study, Critical Text and English Translation of Cantos XVI-XX

By

Dr. C.R. SWAMINATHAN

Edited By

Dr. V. RAGHAVAN

MOTILAL BANARSIDASS

Delhi :: Varanasi :: Patna

Indological Publishers & Booksellers,
Head Office : BUNGALOW ROAD, JAWAHAR NAGAR, DELHI-7
Branches : 1. CHOWK, VARANASI-1 (U.P.)
2. ASHOK RAJPATH, PATNA-4 (BIHAR)

ISBN 0 8426 1028 6

First Edition : Delhi, 1977

–

PRINTED IN INDIA
BY SHANTILAL JAIN, AT SHRI JAINENDRA PRESS, A-45, PHASE-I, INDUSTRIAL AREA, NARAINA, NEW DELHI-28 AND PUBLISHED BY SUNDARLAL JAIN, FOR MOTILAL BANARSIDASS, BUNGALOW ROAD, JAWAHAR NAGAR, DELHI-7

FOREWORD

When, as Head of the Department of Sanskrit in the University of Madras, I started taking young Research Scholars and putting them on research projects for their Post-Graduate Degrees, there were some important subjects on which work was long due, particularly outstanding texts in different fields of which manuscripts had been known for a long time but work on which still remained to be undertaken, e.g. the *Jānakīharaṇa* of Kumāradāsa and the *Dīpikā* of Bhartṛhari on the *Mahābhāṣya*. There were also texts of the next order of importance, still in manuscripts, significant in the history of the branches to which they belonged, the *Gadyakarṇāmṛta* of Sakala Vidyācakravartin and Vidyācakravartin's commentary on the *Alaṁkārasarvasva*, the *Camatkāracandrikā* of Viśveśvara, the *Daśarūpakavyākhyā* of Bahurūpamiśra etc., some of which I had used in the course of my own work and brought to light through my introductory studies on them.

Although the *Jānakīharaṇa* was the first of such works taken up by my Research Students, the work done on this *Mahākāvya* has unfortunately taken the longest time to appear in print. At the time it was taken up, it was the first attempt to study this important *Mahākāvya* of the classical period on the basis of full manuscripts of the work discovered in South India. For long, all that was known or had been said of the poem was based on its Sinhalese *Sanna* and although original and full mss. of it had come to light, work on them had long remained a desideratum.

The nature of the work as planned and as finally done within the limitations of the time given, has been explained in the Preface. The judges of the Thesis observed that for the first time the unpublished portion of the poem had been presented from mss. and the work accomplished in accordance with the approved methods and standard textual criticism and editing. The study-part was also commended and the findings about the date of the poet approved. Had this work appeared in print soon after its approval, it would have been received with the importance due to it; but during the period of its long-delayed appearance, the full text of the twenty cantos of the poem had appeared in two editions, the one brought out by Sri Krishna Das from Allahabad in 1966 and the other by the Ceylonese scholars Paranavitana and Godakumbura from Ceylon in 1967. While the former edition had all the appearance of having been rushed through, the latter offered not only a better production, but in its Introduction, brought to light new information on Kumāradāsa.

In view of their highly interesting nature, the new data about Kumāradāsa placed before scholars by Paranavitana deserve to be mentioned here. An inscription of the 9th century A.D. on a pillar, discovered in Madilla, recounts the story of Kumāradāsa and his father. In the troubled political situation, Māna, who was Yuvarāja, was killed and his son, as a baby, was taken away to a place of safety on the mountains. This son who was named Kumāra Dhātusena had then to be taken to Śrīvijaya beyond the seas, for further safety. Kumāra Dhātusena studied Sanskrit in Śrīvijaya and then came to Kāñcīpuram and the Pallava Kingdom, along with his cousin Mānavarman for political assistance. Mānavarman was backed by the Śrīvijaya King whose daughter he had married.

At Kāñcī, Kumāra Dhātusena came under Brahmin influence, called himself Kumāradāsa, and entered the royal retinue for a time. He studied with Daṇḍin and began composing his poem *Jānakīharaṇa* at Kāñcī. With the help of the Pallava King Narasimhavarman II, Mānavarman then captured the Ceylonese throne and returned to the island. Kumāradāsa who accompanied Mānavarman completed his poem at Anurādhapura and was made Yuvarāja.

The tide again turned against Kumāradāsa when Agrabodhi V, son of Mānavarman, came to the throne and the poet left for Śrīvijaya. He was received there well and his poem rewarded. The local King, however, being a Buddhist, asked Kumāradāsa to compose a poem on a Buddhist theme and the poet accordingly wrote the *Śrighana-nanda* on the same theme as that of the *Saundarananda* of Aśvaghoṣa. Mss. of both poems of Kumāradāsa were extant in Śrīvijaya and also Ceylon and South Malabar. Kumāradāsa finally returned to Ceylon and had a tragic end.

In I. 17 of the *Jānakiharaṇa*, Kumāradāsa describes the prowess of the Indian King as scorching the East and making the ruler of *Kaṭāha* (*Kedah* in Malaya) uncomfortable. In the very next verse (I. 18) the capital city of Kāñcī and its affluence are described. In the light of the new data presented above, the two verses in *Jānakīharaṇa* cited above would gleam with new significance.

The *Jānakīharaṇa* is therefore of interest from many sides. It integrates not only India and Ceylon but also S.E. Asia, in Sanskrit and creative work in that language.

The information in the above chronicle that Kumāradāsa was a younger contemporary and pupil of Daṇḍin would reinforce the chronological position assigned to Kumāradāsa in the present Thesis.

The present work has been edited and seen through the Press by the undersigned from Madras. From time to time different former students had been assisting him in reading the proofs. In the last few years Dr. S.S. Janaki had assisted in this work. The Index of verses was compiled by another student, Smt. Prema Anantanarayanan.

Madras V. RAGHAVAN

PREFACE

In the years 1950-52 I had the privilege of working as a University Research Scholar under Dr. Raghavan, Head of the Department of Sanskrit, University of Madras. According to the regulations in force at that time in the Madras University the first Research Degree of M.Litt. was an essential precursor to Ph.D. and hence my research work on the *Jānakīharaṇa* was submitted in the form of a thesis for the M. Litt. Degree. The work comprised a critical edition of the then unpublished portion of the poem and a critical study of the entire Mahākāvya. This was the maiden attempt, at that time, to fix the text of the poem as well as to make a full study of the author on the basis of original manuscript material explored for the first time. Till then, all that was said about Kumāradāsa or his work was based on the Sanskrit rendering of the Sinhalese version of the poem. To that extent, it was a new attempt to study the author and his work from the original Sanskrit manuscripts. I must thank the authorities of the University of Madras and Dr. V. Raghavan for the opportunity that was made available to me to do this work.

The work as planned by my Professor comprised, in the section of the critical edition of the text, the whole of the twenty cantos of the poem. But the limitations of the time available to me under the University scholarship permitted me to complete only the edition of the last five cantos of the poem ; as the first fifteen cantos had appeared in print in some form, it was thought advisable to concentrate first on the last five cantos, which would be new to the world of scholars.

The manuscript material and the critical apparatus on which the edition is based are dealt with in the opening chapter of this Thesis, the Introduction. The portion edited contains some of the difficult parts of Kumāradāsa's composition and it was thought necessary to give an English translation of the Text.

At the end of the edition, there is an Appendix containing the extra verses found in the London manuscript and in the partial transcript in Adyar, together with a critical review on the admissibility of these extra verses. Detailed remarks on all the additional verses had been prepared, but owing to the exigencies of time and limit set to the page-number of the Thesis, such notes could be included only upto the end of the tenth canto.

In the section on the critical study of the author and the poem, the history and the date of the author have been reviewed completely on the basis of the fresh light from the new manuscript material. A detailed study of Kumāradāsa in relation to the other poets who preceded him, is then given. A collation and critical evaluation of citations of the *Jānakīharaṇa* in the anthologies and other works have been carried out.

An appreciation of Kumāradāsa as poet, his descriptions, treatment of Nature and ideals and an account of the varied learning of the poet and the references which he has made to diverse matters of cultural interest have also been given.

However, owing to the limitations of time, certain chapters and parts thereof which were planned and partially done, could not be included in the present Thesis. Firstly, in the edition of the last five cantos in the latter part of the Thesis, in canto XVII, which is devoted to difficult *Bandhas*, satisfactory presentation of a few verses with translation has not been possible. Similarly in cantos XVII and XIX, three verses particularly difficult had to be left over for future consideration. In the former part containing the critical account, data gathered on Kumāradāsa's relation with Māgha, a consideration of the figures of speech and of the grammatical and lexicographical peculiarities, on which Thomas (*JRAS*. 1901) had collected some data, could not be included in the Thesis.

Work was first started with the transcript of the poem available in the Government Oriental Manuscripts Library, Madras, for the loan of which and several other connected manuscripts and printed works, my thanks are due to the authorities of that Library and the University of Madras. This transcript was thoroughly checked with its own palm-leaf original, which I traced and secured from its owner, Sri Tuppan Nambudiripād of Ponnurkottumana, to whom I express my gratitude. For the third manuscript, a partial transcript, I am indebted to the late Pandit E. V. Raman Nambudiri of Trivandrum. The use, for the purpose of this work, of a palm-leaf manuscript of the whole poem in the London University Library, has added much value to this work ; this was made possible by the kindness of the authorities of the London University Library and Prof. C. A. Rylands of the School of Oriental and African Studies, London who sent to my Professor a micro-film copy of this manuscript, free of cost. I thank also the Adyar Library for the loan of its partial transcript of the *Jānakīharaṇa* and some other manuscripts which were required for my work like the *Padacandrikā* of Rāyamukuṭa on Amara. Prof. D. D. Kosambi of Poona was kind enough to send some data from the anthology *Subhāṣitaratnakośa* which he was editing at that time on the basis of two new manuscripts. My friend Śrī C. S. Sundaram, of the Sanskrit Department, helped me to use the material in some German articles.

My indebtedness to Dr. V. Raghavan, Head of the Department of Sanskrit then, under whom I have had the privilege of working, would extend beyond the present work. It was under him that I learnt the methods and discipline of scientific research and critical investigation. He was always kind and accessible to me and gave me, day to day, many hours of his precious time both at office and at home. Apart from the help he gave me at every stage and in every part of this work, he created in me an enthusiasm for research work and widened my scholarly interest.

In addition to the University Library and the personal Library of my Professor, I had to use the Sanskrit Departmental Library of the Presidency College, Madras, and the rich collection of books and periodicals in the Kuppuswami Sastri Research Institute, Madras ; I record here my gratitude to the late Dr. A. Sankaran, Professor of Sanskrit at the Presidency College, Madras, and to the authorities of the K. S. R. Institute for giving me free access to these libraries.

Dr. Raghavan had continued his interest in me and in my work. After my period of research, I became a Sanskrit Lecturer in the Madras Education Service and then joined the Ministry of Education, Government of India and became involved in administration and schemes for the promotion of

Sanskrit. In between I went to Kathmandu to work for a period in Bir Library of Sanskrit Mss., under the Indian Aid Mission scheme. During these years, my Professor had taken up the publication of my work with Messrs. Motilal Banarsidass and edited and seen it through the Press. For all this, I express my deep gratitude to him. My thanks are also due to Messrs Motilal Banarsidass for bringing out this publication.

New Delhi
1-12-76

C. R. SWAMINATHAN

CONTENTS

BIBLIOGRAPHY

A. *Articles* :

Apte, M. V., The Flora in Kālidāsa's Literature, *ABORI*, XXXII

Bandyopadhyaya, Kalipada, Preface to Haridasa Sastri's edition of *Jānakiharaṇa*, Calcutta, 1893.

Barnett, L. D., 'The *Jānakīharaṇa* XVI', *Bulletin of the School of Oriental and African Studies*, London, IV (1926-28).

Barua, B. M., Ājīvika—What it means, *ABORI*, VIII, 183.

Bendall, C.. Correspondence, *JRAS* (1888), 440.

Davids, T. W. Rhys, Kālidāsa in Ceylon, *JRAS* (1888), 148-49.

Davids, T. W. Rhys, A Review of the Calcutta edition of the *Jānakīharaṇa*, *JRAS* (1894), 623-24.

De, S. K., On the date of the *Subhāṣitāvalī*, *JRAS* (1927), 471-77.

De, S. K., Some readings of the *Jānakīharaṇa*, XVI, *Bulletin of the School of Oriental and African Studies*, IV 1926-28) 611-13.

Doraiswamayya, M., Kumāradāsa and *Jānakīharaṇa*, *TSV* I, 203ff.

Doraiswamayya, M., A Reply, *ibid.* I,386-92.

Hocart, A. M., the Mortuary use of the Bo Tree, *Ceylon Journal of Science*, Section G, II, 31.

Hopkins, W. E., Allusions to the Rāma story in the Mahābhārata, *Journal of the American Oriental Society*, Vol. 50.

Hultzsch, E., Ipur Plates of Govindavarman's son Mādhavavarman, *Epigraphia Indica*, XVII. 334 ff.

J. A., Three Traditional Tales, *Ceylon Literary Register*, IV (1935-36), 227-31.

Kaul, A. B., The Date of Kumāradāsa, *JRAS* (1901), 578-82.

Keith, Anand, Kashmiri Proverbs, *IA*, LXII (1933), 71-76.

Krishnamacharya, K., A Note on 'Kumāradāsa and *Jānakiharaṇa*', *TSV* I, 385.

Law, B. C., Ancient Indian Flora, *Indian Culture*, Barua Commemoration Volume.

Leumann, Earnest, Zum *Jānakīharaṇa* des Kumāradāsa *Vienna Oriental Journal*, VII (1893), 226-32.

Nandargikar, G. R., Introduction to the *Raghuvaṁśa*, 3rd edn., Poona (1897), pp. 121-27.

Paranavitana, S., Epigraphical Summary, *Ceylon Journal of Science*, Section G, II. 103-104.

Paranavitana, S., *Annual Report for the Archeological Survey of Ceylon* for 1890.

Paranavitana, S., Nagirikanda Rock Inscriptions of Kumāradāsa, *Epigraphica Cylonica,* IV. 115-28.

Paranavitana, S., Two Inscriptions of Vihara-Maha-Devi from Magul-Maha-Vihara, *ibid.*, pp. 161-68.

Peterson, P., *Aucityālaṅkāra* of Kṣemendra, with a note on the date of Patañjali, *JBBRAS*, XVI. 170.

Ramakrishna Kavi, M., Janāśraya School of Sanskrit Prosody, *TSV.* I. 133 ff.

Randawa, M. S., Progressive Desiccation of Northern India in Historical Times, *Journal of the Bombay Natural History Society*, Vol. 45.

Rao, Lakshmana, K. V., The Telugu Academy Plates of Vishnukundin Madhavavarman III, A. D. 594, *Journal of the Department of Letters*, Calcutta University, XI. 31-64.

Rao, Subba, R , Polumuru Plates of Vishnukundin Madhavavarman, *Journal of the Andhra Hist. Res. Soc.*, VI. 17 ff.

Rylands, C. A., Karṇikāra, *Indian Culture,* Barua Commemoration Volume.

Sastri, Ramaswamy, V. A., Jānāśrayī *Chandoviciti*, *Journal of Or. Res.*, XVIII (1947-48), 138 ff.

Sircar, D. C., Genealogy of the Vishnukundins, *IHQ*, IX (1933) 273-77.

Sircar, D.C., Chronology of the Vishnukundins, *ibid.* 957-66.

Sircar, D. C., Successors of the Satavahanas, *Journal of the Dept. of Letters*, Calcutta, XXVI. 113.

Thomas, F. W., The *Jānakīharaṇa* of Kumāradāsa, *JRAS* (1901) 253-80.

Thomas, F. W., Introduction to the *Kavindravacanasamuccaya* 1912, Bibliothica Indica, No. 1309.

B. *Books*:

Bandyopadhyaya, N. C., *Kauṭilya*,, Calcutta, 1327.

Basham, A. L., *History and Doctrines of the Ājīvikas*, London, 1, 1950.

Belvalkar, S. K., *Systems of Sanskrit Grammar*, Poona, 1915.

Codrington, S. W., *History of Ceylon*, London, 1926.

Fischer, C. E. C., *Flora of the Presidency of Madras*, London, 1928.

Geiger, W., *Sinhalese Language and Literature*, Strassburg, 1900.

Gopalachar, K., *Early History of the Andhra Country*, Madras University Historical Series No. 16, 1941.

Katre, S. M., *Introduction to Indian Textual Criticism*, Bombay, 1941.

Keith, A. B., *A History of Sanskrit Literature*, Oxford, 1928.

Krishnamachariar, M., *History of Classical Sanskrit Literature*, Madras, 1937.

Malalasekera, G. P., *Pali Literature of Ceylon*, London, 1928.

Majumdar, and Altekar, *A New History of Indian People*, Vol. VI, Lahore, 1946.

Mendis, G. C., *The Early History of Ceylon.*

Muller, E., *Ancient Inscriptions in Ceylon*, London, 1883.

Parker, H., *Ancient Ceylon*, London, 1909.

Raghavan, V.,*Bhoja's Śṛṅgāraprakāśa*, Bombay, 1940, 1942.

Raghavan, V., *The Number of Rasas*, Adyar Library, Madras, 1940.

Rao, Krishna, B. V., *Early Dynasties of Andhradesa.*

Sankaran, A., *Some Aspects of Literary Criticism in Sanskrit*, University of Madras, 1929.

Sirr, H. C., *Ceylon and the Cinghalese*, Vol. II.

Trimen, Henry., *A Hand-Book on the Flora of Ceylon*, London, 1898.

Upadhyaya, B. S., *India in Kālidāsa*,, Allahabad, 1947.

C. *Texts*:

Amarakośaṭikā of Vidyāvinoda-Nārāyaṇa, Manuscript, O.M.L., R. 3645.

Amarakośavyākhyā, Kāmadhenu of Subhūticandra, Manuscript, O.M.L., R. 2933.

Amarakośavyākhyā, *Padacandrikā* of Rāyamukuṭa, Manuscript, Adyar, 38. I. 4.

Arthaśāstra of Kauṭilya, Ed. by Mm. Dr. T. Ganapati Sastri, 3 Vols, 1921, 1924, 1925 (TSS 79, 80, 82).

Arthaśāstra of Kauṭilya, Ed. by Dr. R. Shama Sastri, Mysore, 1924.

Cūlavaṁsa, Translated into English by Mrs. C. Mabel Rickness, from the German Translation of W. Geiger, Pali Text Society, London, 1929-30, 2 Vols.

Dīpavaṁsa, Edited and Translated by H. Oldenberg, London, 1879.

Dhanvantarī Nighaṇṭu, Ānandāśrama Sanskrit Series, Poona.

Dhvanyāloka of Ānandavardhana, with the commentary of Abhinavagupta etc. by Mm. S. Kuppuswami Sastriar and T. R. Chintamani, Madras, 1944.

Gaṇaratnamahodadhi of Vardhamāna, Ed. by Julius Eggling, Sanskrit Text Society, London, 1879.

Jānakīharaṇa of Kumāradāsa, Ed. by Haridasa Sastri and published by Kalipada Bandyopadhyaya, Calcutta, 1893.

Jānakiharaṇa Ed. by G. R. Nandargikar, Bombay, 1907.

Jānāśrayī Chandoviciti, Ed. by P. K. Narayana Pillai, Trivandrum, 1949.

Jānāśrayī Chandoviciti, Ed. by M. Ramakrishna Kavi, Venkateswara Oriental Series, Tirupati.

Kambarāmāyaṇam, Ed. by V. M. Gopalakrishnamachariar, Madras.

Kavīndravacanasamuccaya, Ed. by F. W. Thomas, Bibliotheca Indica No. 1309, 1912.

Kāvyādarśa, Ed. by Rangacharya Reddy Sastri, Poona, 1927.

Kāvyālaṅkārasūtra of Vāmana, Ed. by N. N. Kulkarni, Poona, 1927.

Kāvyamīmāṁsā of Rājaśekhara, Baroda, 1934, GOS., 1.

Kāvyānuśāsana of Hemacandra, Bombay, 1901, Kāvyamālā 71.

Kāvyānuśāsana of Hemacandra, Ed. by Rasiklal C. Parikh, Sri Mahavira Jaina Vidyalaya, Bombay, 1938.

Kirātārjunīya of Bhāravi, N. S. Press, Bombay, 1885.

Kumārasambhava of Kālidāsa, N. S. Press, Bombay, 1927.

Mahābhārata, Kumbhakonam Edn., 1907.

Mahāvaṁsa, Translated by W. Geiger, Pali Text Society, London, 1912.

Medinikośa, Banares, 1916.

Meghadūta of Kālidāsa, N. S. Press, Bombay, 1881.

Nāmaliṅgānuśāsana of Amarasimha, with the commentary *Ṭikāsarvasva* of Sarvānanda, Ed. by T. Ganapati Sastri, TSS.

Nāṭya Śāstra of Bharata. Kashi Sanskrit Series, 60, Benares, 1929.

Nikāya Saṅgraha, Ed. by D. M. de Z. Wickremasinghe, Colombo, 1890, and Translated by C. M. Fernando, Colombo, 1908.

Nītisāra of Kāmandaka, Ed. by T. Ganapati Sastri, TSS 14, 1912.

Pañcatantra, N. S. Press, Bombay 1930.

Paryantapañcāśikā of Abhinavagupta, Ed. by Dr. V. Raghavan, Madras University, 1950.

Pratimānāṭaka of Bhāsa, Poona Oriental Book Agency, 1930.

Pūjāvali, Translated under the title "A Contribution to the History of Ceylon", by B. Gunasekera, Colombo, 1895.

Raghuvaṁśa of Kālidāsa, Benares, 1930.

Rāmacaritamānasa of Tulasidas, (Hindi), Ed. by Shyam Sundar Das, Kashi, 1948.

Rāmāyaṇa of Vālmīki, (Southern Recension), Ed. by T. R. Krishnamacharya, Bombay, 1905.

Rāmāyaṇa of Vālmīki (Eastern Recension), Ed. by G. Gorresio, Perigi, 1844.

Rāmāyaṇa of Vālmīki, (North Western Recension), Ed. by Visvabandhu Sastri, Lahore, 1928.

Śabdakalpadruma, Calcutta.

Saduktikarṇāmṛta, Punjab Oriental Series, No. XV, 1933.

Śākuntala of Kālidāsa, N. S. Press, Bombay.

Śaṅkaravijaya of Mādhavācārya, Ānandāśrama Series, Poona.

Sarasvatīkaṇṭhābharaṇa of Bhoja, Bombay, 1925, Kāvyamālā, 95.

Śārṅgadharapaddhati, Ed. by Peterson, Bombay, 1888.

Śiśupālavadha of Māgha, Benares, 1929.

Śṛṅgāraprakāśa of Bhoja, Manuscript, O. M. L., R. 3252 (4 vols).

Subhāṣitāvali of Vallabhadeva, Ed. by Peterson, Bombay, 1886.

Sūktimuktāvali of Jalhaṇa, Baroda, 1938, GOS. 82.

Uṇādisūtras with the commentary of Ujjvaladatta, Ed. by Vidyasagara, Calcutta, 1873.

Upavanavinoda, Ed. by G. P. Majumdar, Indian Positive Sciences Series No. 1, Calcutta, 1935.

Vṛttaratnākara of Kedārabhaṭṭa, Bombay, 1926.

ABBREVIATIONS USED

A.	Adyar Library Transcript of the *Jānakīharaṇa*
ABORI.	Annals of the Bhandarkar Oriental Research Institute.
GOS.	Gaekwad's Oriental Series.
H.	Printed text of the *Jānakīharaṇa*, Ed. by Pandit Haridasa Sastri, Calcutta.
IA.	Indian Antiquary.
IHQ.	Indian Historical Quarterly.
JBBRAS.	Journal of the Bombay Branch of the Royal Asiatic Society.
JH.	*Jānakīharaṇa* of Kumāradāsa.
JRAS.	Journal of the Royal Asiatic Society of Great Britain and Ireland.
L.	London Manuscripts of the *Jānakīharaṇa*.
MT.	Madras Manuscript of the *Jānakīharaṇa*.
N.	Printed text of the *Jānakīharaṇa*, Ed. G. R. Nandargikar, Bombay.
OML.	Govt. Oriental Manuscript Library, Madras.
R.	Trivandrum Transcript of the *Jānakīharaṇa*.
TSS.	Trivandrum Sanskrit Series.
TSV.	Tirumalai Sri Venkateswara Oriental Journal.
Vāl.	Vālmīki's *Rāmāyaṇa*.

INTRODUCTION

The *Jānakīharaṇa* of Kumaradasa is one among the earlier Mahākāvyas in Sanskrit literature, which had long remained in oblivion. Though early Ālaṅkārikas, prosody-writers, commentators on the *Amarakośa* and anthologists bear testimony to the importance and vogue of this poem, a complete text of it was not available till 1920. Regarding the author, traditional stories have come to this day remembering him as a king of Ceylon and a friend of Kālidāsa. The history of the work indeed shows close connection with Ceylon; for, it is through the Sinhalese that we came to have the first view of it. Thomas said in 1901—"The history of this little-known work is remarkable. No manuscript of it has yet been discovered, and on the continent of India the only traces of its existence consists in the facts that a few of its verses are quoted in two Sanskrit anthologies,......and that the author is coupled with Kālidāsa in a memorial verse of Rājaśekhara..... The Sinhalese literature, however, has preserved to us a Sanna or word for word gloss of the first fourteen cantos and of the fifteenth in part, from which gloss it has been found possible to piece together a text which cannot diverge very far from the original,"[1] The word for word gloss in the Sinhalese language is by one Rājasundara and it is incomplete. It goes only up to the middle of the 15th canto. A re-construction from this Sanna was first attempted by K. Dharmarama Sthavira in the year 1891. The text and the Sanna were published along with a valuable introduction by this author at Peliyagoda in Ceylon. Dharmarama did the most difficult and valuable task of re-constructing fourteen cantos and part of the fifteenth from the Sinhalese gloss. Greater is our indebtedness to this scholar when we realise that he was the first man to unearth this piece of literature and call our attention to the merits of this forgotten

1. Prof. F. W. Thomas, Jānakīharaṇa of Kumāradāsa, *J.R.A.S.*, 1901, p. 263.

poet. On the basis of Dharmarama's re-construction, Prof. Leumann wrote an article on the poem and the nature of the Sinhalese Sanna and the re-construction, in 1893, in the *Vienna Oriental Journal.*[1] This edition of the Sanna by Dharmarama contained "(with a few unimportant exceptions), each word of the poem, but in no particular order; the puzzle which had to be solved was to re-arrange those words in metrical order."[2] This task of rearranging the verses in metrical order was first undertaken by Pandit Haridasa Sastri of Calcutta who passed away before getting it published. In the year 1893, Kalipada Bandyopadhyaya of Jeypore published this re-construction prepared by the late Haridasa Sastri in Nagari Script, with the Sanskrit introduction of Haridasa Sastri and an English introduction of his own. A re-construction from the Sinhalese: this too stops with the fifteenth canto. It was reviewed by Prof. Rhys Davids in the *J.R.A.S.* for 1894 and was welcomed in the following words : "......scholars will be very glad to have the edition in the Nagari character and one prepared by so good a native scholar as the present editor."[3] Haridasa Sastri's edition is referred to as 'H' in the following pages.

The most important contribution to the study of the poem after the publication of Haridasa Sastri's edition was the valuable article which Prof. F.W. Thomas contributed to the *J.R.A.S.* of 1901[4] from which we have already quoted. In this article Prof. Thomas gave a short history of the work, collected the verses from Kumāradāsa cited in the anthologies then known, discussed the comparative merit of the readings of these citations with those of the Sanna and the re-constructions, dealt with grammatical and lexicographical peculiarities of the poet, dwelt on his style and indebtedness to the *Rāmāyaṇa* and the *Raghuvaṁśa* and appended a list of rare words and meanings and an abstract of the contents of the poem canto by canto.

1. *Zum Jānkīharaṇa Des Kumāradāsa*', Vol. VII, pp. 226-232.
2. Prof. Rhys Davids, Jānākīharaṇa by Kumāradāsa; *J.R.A.S.*, 1894 p.623.
3. P. 624.
4. Pp. 253-280.

Using Haridasa Sastri's edition, the Sinhalese edition and some manuscripts of the work from South India, G.R. Nandargikar brought out from Bombay another edition, but giving us only the first ten cantos of the work. The use of manuscripts of the work from South India is the advance registered by Nandargikar's work. Nandargikar's edition is mentioned as 'N' in the sequel.

According to his critical notice in his edition, he had used five manuscripts, the last of which was a fragment. The first manuscript which he calls 'A' is a palm-leaf manuscript in Telugu characters lent by T. Gopala Rao, Principal of the Government College, Kumbhakonam in 1885. It contained the first fourteen cantos and the first six verses of the fifteenth. In the beginning it started with the words 'ओं नमः सर्वज्ञाय' and had some marginal notes by a different hand. The age of the leaves is estimated by Nandargikar as 'more than sixty years.' The second one which he names as 'B' is another palm-leaf manuscript in Grantha characters, from the same source, beginning with the words 'ओं नमो रत्नत्रयाय'. At the end of the 8th canto of this manuscript it was stated: 'सिंहललिपिटीकातः समुद्धृत्य गुम्फितम्'. Its approximate age, according to the editor may be 50 years. It contained the first fourteen cantos and ten verses of the fifteenth. Manuscript 'C' which is the third one that Nandargikar refers to, came from the same source and was in thick country paper and in Devanagari script. It began with 'ओं नमो नमोऽर्हते' and at the beginning of the fourteenth canto it read सिंहलभाषातः उद्धृत्य श्रोत्रियेण पाप्पय्यदीक्षितेन पाठनार्थमलेखि. It contained the first fourteen cantos and five verses of the fifteenth. It was much worn out and Nandargikar estimates its age as hundred years. It too had some marginal notes but written in a different note-book. The history of these manuscripts is quite interesting. Gopala Rao sent them in response to a request for manuscripts of Raghuvaṁśa. 'B' and 'C' clearly mention their Sinhalese derivation. Regarding 'A', the editor admits that there was no clue to determine its independent character. The next one, manuscript 'D' was in thick blue-black foolscap paper with Devanagari writing. It was procured from Prof. Seshagiri Sastri in 1886. It was a recent copy made from an original in an unknown Jain Manuscript Library and began with 'ओं नमः श्रीघनाय'. It contained the first fourteen cantos and two verses of the fifteenth. There was no clue to trace the source of This too. From the same source Nandargikar got another manuscript which he names as 'Fr.' This was a fragment and had only some pages of the cantos except those of the eighth to the tenth and the thirteenth; and only one page of the fifteenth having two verses, 21st and 22nd; it contained also a solitary last verse of the 25th canto giving the name of the poet. While nothing is known about the source of this fragment too, its relation with the Sinhalese is clear.

The readings that these additional manuscripts give, vary so little from the direct Sinhalese re-construction, that we have to conclude that they are not original manuscripts of the poem and probably they too are re-constructions from the available Sinhalese Sanna. The variants that are given by Nandargikar in his foot-notes are mostly of the type of synonyms of equal syllabic character. For example : avanyām-dharitryām; niśāsu-kṣapāsu; samṛdhyā-vibhūtyā and so on, which would show that the so-called readings are but different possible restorations from the Sinhalese. The fact that these manuscripts do not progress beyond the extent of the Sinhalese Sanna and that 'B' and 'C' have express mention of their source, show that these are derived from the Sinhalese and they have little value as original sources. It is curious that under 'Fr.' Nandargikar says that it contains the solitary verse mentioning the author's name as occurring in the 25th canto of the poem; Haridasa Sastri also mentions the 25th canto in his Sanskrit preface. It is to the Sinhalese Sanna and its restoration by Dharmarama that this information ultimately goes; Leumann says in his article, referred to already, that this पञ्चविंशतितमः सर्गः occurs as a variant for 'पञ्चदशः सर्गः' and "that our epic (Jānakīharaṇa) had had not only 15 sargas as Dharmarama presumed but at least twenty-five". But it is clear that there is no canto of the poem beyond the twentieth, and the solitary colophonic verse mentioned by Nandargikar may be identified as the one beginning with 'कृतज्ञ इति .....' coming from Rajasundara and Dharmarama, about which however, we shall speak later at length. Thus, like the edition of Haridasa Sastri, Nandargikar's too is in effect an edition based on the Sinhalese Sanna.

The Indian editions in so far as they are based on the re-construction of the Sinhalese Sanna are not to be taken as genuine representations of the original text of the poem. Dharmarama had to introduce something of his own to make up the lacunae in the Sanna. Leumann presents the exact position regarding the Sanna and the re-construction as follows : "Numerous gaps resulted which the editor tried to fill up properly. The gaps which are present are only missing syllables on an average of ten to twenty in each sarga. Besides this, however, on the whole, about 40 supplimentations of more than one syllable were necessary; in some places even complete lines, (X-29d to 30b, III-80d). What Amṛtānanda has done for the Buddhacarita, Dharmarama has also done for this Jānakīharaṇa, though less completely .....he (Dharmarama) was scrupulous in putting them in brackets .....The syllables occurring in the text as well as in the revised Sanna can be nothing but conjecture." Hence the unreliability of the material handled by these editors makes their editions defective, these being based on an incomplete and defective Sanna, as a result of which the arrangement of lines in their respective verses, the arrangement of words in their respective lines and the readings themselves appear to be inconclusive in their nature.

The Madras Manuscript :

In the year 1920, the Peripatetic Party of the Government Oriental Manuscripts Library, Madras, came across a complete manuscript of this work in a Nambudiri family in Nortn Travancore. A transcript of this is now preserved in the Madras Oriental Manuscripts Library. Though the existence of this transcript has been known for quite a long time and various proposals had been, we understand, made from time to time for editing the *Jānakīharaṇa* afresh and making a fresh study of Kumāradāsa and his work on the basis of this transcript, nothing was done and it was fortunately given to us to undertake this work here.

When work was started with the help of this transcript and some progress had been made, it was found necessary that this transcript should be completely checked with its palm-leaf original. Accordingly effort was taken to trace the original and it proved successful. The original was lent to us through the kindness of the owner Sri Thuppan Nambudiripad of Ponnurkottumana near Alwaye in North Travancore. This manuscript is in Malayalam script and is 8″ long and 1″ wide. Each side of a leaf contains about seven lines. The letters are fairly legible and the whole work extends over 52 leaves. It is preserved in a very good condition, except for the fact that about 1/3rd of the tenth canto is missing and in other places, a few words and lines are found missing here and there. The age of the manuscript could be roughly estimated as more than hundred years, though the satisfactory condition in which it is found due to careful preservation would give the impression of lesser antiquity. It contains all the twenty cantos and has a definite ending in the coronation of Rāma and the colophon verses dealing with the life of the author. Compared to the London Manuscript which will be described below, this manuscript has 46 extra verses spread over cantos VIII, IX, XI, XIII, XIV, XV, XVII, XVIII, XIX and XX. Of these many are found in 'H' and 'N'. The advantage of securing this original was undeniable. For, when we carried out the collation we found that many improvements could be effected in the text as transcribed by the Peripatetic Party of the Madras Oriental Manuscripts Library. As we have used the Madras transcript as corrected by its palm-leaf original as one manuscript for purposes of noting the variants, we have adopted here, the designation, MT. to refer to this source.

Trivandrum Transcript :

At a further stage of our work it was brought to our notice,[1] that Sri E.V. Raman Nambudiri of Trivandrum had a transcript of the poem. He was kind enough to lend the transcript. This is in Devanagari script beginning with the

1. By Sri K. Venkateswara Sarma to whom our thanks are due for securing this manuscript.

words 'ओं नमः सर्वज्ञाय' and carries some variants noted by a different hand. It has also some gaps which had been later filled by a different hand. It contains too many scribal errors and Cantos XI, XII, XIII, XIV and XVIII are not to be found in it. With regard to the number and order of the verses in each canto and with regard to the readings, it is more or less in agreement with the Madras Manuscript. All the four colophon verses at the end of the poem are to be found in this transcript also. The source for this transcript is not known. Its original should have been in Malayalam script since the Devanagari transcription bears some of the peculiarities of Malayalam writing like 'ḷ' for 'l.' This transcript is referred to in our work as 'R'.

The London Manuscript :

In the *Bulletin of the London School of Oriental Studies* for 1946-41, Dr. L. D. Barnett reported the acquisition by the London School, of a Malayalam palm-leaf manuscript for the complete text of the *Jānakīharaṇa* and offered an edition of the XVIth canto of the poem[1]. According to the description of Barnett here, this manuscript is about 14″ long and 1½″ wide and was probably written in the 16th century or even earlier. But, from the scribal errors, he suggested that it might have been copied out from a Sinhalese original. My Professor then secured through the kind offices of Prof. Rylands of the London School and the authorities of the London University Library, a micro-film copy of this full manuscript of twenty cantos. On examination it was found that this manuscript comprised about 118 leaves with seven to eight lines on each side of a leaf. The owner of the manucript is given as 'Gartavana Sankara'. Gartavana is the Sanskrit equivalent for Kuzhikāḍu, a Bhattatiri estate near Kālaḍi in North Travancore. From oral tradition locally available, this Gartavana family is known to have had a Sankara about one and a half centuries back and probably this manuscript itself is not older than that time.

Regarding the specialities of this manuscript, the chief

1. Pp. 280-293,

characteristic is that it has many extra verses not found in the Madras manuscript or the Trivandrum transcript, but does not contain the four colophon verses dealing with the life of the poet. Instead it has at the end of the poem a small verse in the form of *Phalaśruti* which runs thus :

जानकीहरणं श्लक्ष्णं लक्षणैरुपलक्षितम् ।
रामायणसुधासारमास्वाद्यं मुक्तिदायकम् ॥

which is an obvious scribal addition. Another peculiarity of this manuscript is that, unlike the Madras manuscript, which mentions in the colophons to each canto the Sinhalese nativity of the poet—

इति सिंहलकवेः कुमारदासस्य कृतौ जानकीहरणे महाकाव्ये....सर्गः ।

this manuscript reads its colophons simply as जानकीहरणे.... ....सर्ग : Besides these two peculiarities, this manuscript exhibits also a good number of variants in the verses common to the Madras manuscript and the Trivandrum transcript. This London manuscript is referred to as 'L' in the following pages.

Adyar Transcript :

There is a transcript of part of the poem in the Adyar Library which contains cantos XI-XX. It is in Malayalm script and was prepared in 1926 from an original Malayalam palm-leaf Ms. It is found that this transcript was made by Pandit V. Venkatarama Sarma, who is probably also responsible for supplying the palm-leaf manuscript, described previously, to the London School of Oriental Studies. This has general agreement with 'L' so far as it goes. This also gives no colophon verses like 'L' and has, as in the latter, the Anuṣṭubh *Phalaśruti*.

If it had been copied from the original sent to London it is inexplicable how it displays so many differences from 'L'. We have separately used it as 'A', because of these differences.

It will be clear from the above account that the four available manuscript sources fall into two categories, one having no extra verses but having the four colophonic verses at the end of the work, and the other having extra verses but not the four colophon verses. "MT' and 'R' belong to the former and 'L' and 'A' to the latter.

The edition and the critical study of the poem offered here is based on these sources set forth above.

We shall now examine in detail the merits and importance of these sources in relation to the printed editions 'H' and 'N'.

MT' : While the number of verses in each canto of 'MT' does not generally agree with 'L' or with 'A', it agrees completely with 'H' and 'N'. Perhaps this is the only common feature between this and the printed texts. It is not possible to contend that 'MT' was only an earlier attempt at a re-construction from the Sinhalese Sanna and sails on the same boat as the so-called manuscripts used by Nandargikar. The re-construction of Dharmarāma, the Sinhalese Sanna itself, 'H' and 'N' and the manuscripts referred to by Nandargikar are uniformly incomplete.

In marked contrast to this, 'MT' has got all the twenty cantos with a definite conclusion to the poem at the end. While the single colophon verse at the end of 'H' appears to be most strange in that place, 'MT' contains the four colophon verses in the appropriate context at the end of the twentieth canto. In the printed texts, the arrangement of lines in their respective verses is very confused and artificial, making it difficult to discover the *anvaya* ; while in 'MT' lines appear in their natural order and yield themselves to interpretation more easily. There are no gaps in 'MT' to correspond to the gaps in the Sanna which the originality of the re-constructor had filled. 'MT' has also several variant readings affecting sometimes even the meanings of verses. Further, 'MT' has no express statement like two of the manuscripts used by Nandargikar about its being a re-construction from Sinhalese ; normally a re-constructor would be expected to make mention of his labour if he had resorted to that difficult process. Another note-worthy point is that 'MT' has got a long gap in the tenth canto which is not to be found in the other ones. The agreement in the number of verses between 'MT' on the one hand and the printed texts on the other, as also the absence from all these of the extra verses of 'L' and 'A' would show that the Sinhalese Sanna and 'MT' go ultimately to a common original.

L: Barnett says of 'L'—'A certain number of mistakes and omissions are to be found in the Ms., some of them perhaps due to the scribe and others certainly due to a faulty archetype. Some of the scribe's errors suggest that the original copied by him or, at least, a parent or ancestor of it, was in Sinhalese script'[1]. The scribal error can be ascribed to the peculiar idiosyncracies in the transcription of some of the Sanskrit words into Malayalam, or to the unconscious errors due to the writing material, or to the carelessness or ignorance of a copyist. Some of the differences may be traced to the mistaken reading of a Sinhalese original by the Malayalam copyist. But such a hypothesis, that the copy goes to a Sinhalese original requires more concrete proof.

Importance of the new manuscripts :

With only the Sanskrit restoration before them, scholars like Leumann, for instance[2], thought that these restored texts were to be relied upon. Leumann said that the insignificance of the variants proves for the text a greater degree of certainty than that could have been expected[3]. The discovery of the new manuscript material since known shows that it is no longer possible to consider the Sanna-text as representing the reliable version. These new manuscripts have not only numerous variants but also considerable difference in the order of the lines in most of the verses. The readings given by these two manuscripts are in agreement with the quotations given in the various anthologies, commentaries the *Amarakośa* and works of prosody, to a greater degree than those of the printed texts. The number and variety of these

1. *Bulletin of the London School of Oriental Studies*, 1946-8. p. 285.

2. Zum Jānakīharaṇa Des Kumāradāsa' *Vienna Oriental Journal*, Vol. VII, 1893, pp. 226-232.

3. See the article above referred to ; also F.W. Thomas, *J R.A.S.* 1901, p. 254.

variants do not warrant even the approval with reservation of Leumann's statement by F. W. Thomas[1].

Comparison of MT and L

The independent value of these two manuscripts cannot be denied in view of the fact that they differ widely between themselves both in quantity and in quality. 'L' contains a large number of verses in excess of 'MT'. These additional verses are distributed throughout the work. The disparity in number of verses per canto between these two manuscripts and the nature of distribution of the extra verses in 'L' can be well understood from the following table :

Canto No.	*No. of verses in each canto in 'MT'.*	*Extra verses in 'L'.*	*Extra verses in 'MT'.*
I	90	I	—
II	79	6	—
III	81	3	—
IV	74	16	—
V	61	33	1
VI	60	53	—
VII	59	26	—
VIII	100	21	19
IX	68	15	1
X	90	43	—
XI	100	—	2
XII	56	21	—
XIII	46	53	2
XIV	84	9	4
XV	64	10	2
XVI	74	9	—
XVII	43	51	—
XVIII	76	62	1
XIX	64	37	5
XX	60	39	7
	1428	508	45

1. Commenting on Leumann's remark, Thomas writes :-"This conclusion, based on a comparison of the seven cited verses..., seems beyond question, though complicated by the fact that four of these were known to the author of the re-construction". *J.R.A.S.*, 1901 p. 254

The total number of extra verses in 'L' is 508. As a natural result of this, we find that the order in which verses appear in these two is also different on many occasions.

Some verses belonging to one canto in 'MT' are found in a different canto in 'L'. 29 such instances could be traced as the following table will show :

'MT'			*'L'*	
V	38	—	XVII	73
V	39	—	XVII	71
V	40	—	XVII	64
V	41	—	XVII	75
V	42	—	XVII	78
V	43	—	XVII	80
V	44	—	XVII	82
V	46	—	XVII	84
V	47	—	XVII	87
V	48	—	XVII	91
VI	20	—	II	49
VI	22	—	II	46
VI	23	—	II	47
VI	25	—	II	45
VI	28	—	II	50
VIII	60	—	XIV	85
VIII	88	—	XIV	88
XIII	17	—	XII	67
XIII	18	—	XII	65
XIII	19	—	XII	69
XIII	20	—	XII	71
XIII	21	—	XII	73
XX	31	—	XII	78
XX	38	—	XII	74
XX	39	—	XII	68
XX	40	—	XII	72
XX	47	—	XII	80
XX	50	—	XII	82
XX	51	—	V	54

Whenever they have common verses they differ to some extent in their readings and they never differ at all in the matter of arrangement of lines within their respective verses, which is so common a feature with the printed texts.

With regard to the extra verses in 'L' which are found also in 'A', we are discussing them in detail in the Appendix at the end of this thesis, containing the extra verses. Here it may be mentioned in brief that there are sufficient grounds to reject them as interpolations. Some of the extra verses appear in the middle of the cantos in meters different from those that precede and succeed. Such metrical changes in the middle of a canto are not acceptable to poetic canon. Some other extra verses appear irrelevant and out of context and involve textual contradiction. Thirdly there are some extra verses which bear a marked contrast with Kumāradāsa's verses with regard to style and mode of expression. Fourthly, some of these bear too many marks of the well known verses of other poets. Fifthly, grammatical lapses are also found in these verses. A general consideration of all these verses would show two clear tendencies : 1. to insert greater elaborations and to make up for the brevity of treatment in the original ; and 2. to add further details and make up for supposed omissions and gaps. Hence we have to conclude that the Madras Manuscript is more dependable both from standpoint of quality and from that of quantity and 'L' and 'A' represent an inflated text.

However, two cases in these extra verses call for some special remarks : The London Manuscript has one extra verse in canto XVIII in which there is a *cakra bandha* design incorporating the names of the poet and the work. This would make the number of *cakra bandhas*, in this context, two, while normally poets compose only one *cakra bandha* in the *Sarga* devoted to the *Śabda citra*. We have therefore to accept the plain *cakra bandha* and doubt the authenticity of the one in 'L' and 'A'. When exactly these additions were made, is however, more difficult to decide. Because three of these additional verses in canto VII found in 'L' and 'A' and not in 'MT' are found in 'N' also, which would mean that these go to the time of the Sinhalese Sanna. 'MT' does show some clear gaps; in one place, in canto X, the manuscript itself mentions the *Grantha-pāta*. In cantos I, XIII, and XV, there are a few verses missing, without the scribe noting their absence. On this evidence it may be legitimately suggested that the absence of the verses in canto VII in 'MT' may be due to such omissions. As we shall see below, one of the extra verses in 'L' is cited by Bhoja in both his Alaṁkāra works. It seems therefore necessary to assume an antiquity for these extra verses.

THE DATE OF KUMĀRADĀSA

Much has been discussed in respect of the date and identity of Kumāradāsa, though no definite conclusion has yet been reached. A discussion on his date has become all the more important, since scholars believe that they could get at some clue out of it to solve some other problems in the history of Sanskrit Literature. Apart from those who are exclusively interested in this poet, those engaged in fixing the date of Kālidāsa also evince some interest in this, because of the traditional story that links the lives of these two poets.[1] Those who believe in the attribution of an oft-quoted line, वरतनु संप्रवदन्ति कुक्कुटा to Kumāradāsa, look for his date to find some clue to the periods of Patañjali and Ujjvaladatta.[2] All these discussions have ended only in some speculative and hypothetical statements. What warrants a fresh approach to the whole problem from us is the availability of a few more data

1. See Geiger –"Sinhalese Language and Literature".
   T.W. Rhys Davids—"Kālidāsa in Ceylon" *J.R.A.S.* (1888) pp. 148-149.
   A Review of the Calcutta Edition of the Jānkīharaṇa *Ibid* (1894) pp. 623-24.
   Pandit Anand Koul—'Kashmiri Proverbs"—*Indian Antiquary*, Vol. LXII, p. 73.
   Mrs. Higgins –"Stories from the History of Ceylon", pp. 147
   Kalipada Bandyopadhyaya-Preface to Haradasa Sastri's edition where he says about the tradition-'It is our opinion that it cannot be altogether fictitious.'
2. Peterson –"Auchityālaṅkāra of Kṣemendra with a note on the date of Patañjali"– *J.R.A.S.* Vol. XVI, pp. 170 ff.
   The discovery that Kṣemendra quotes this verse and assigns it to Kumāradāsa, will one day, I hope, prove a valuable datum for the Mahābhāṣya itself.'
   But as against this, see Bhandarkar, *Ibid*, pp. 199 ff. See also Introduction to *Subhāṣitāvali*, pp 24, 25.

in addition to those already used by scholars like Leumann,[1] F. W. Thoms[2], A. B. Keith[3], Nandargikar[4], and others who had discussed it before.

The most important additional datum is a group of colophon verses that we have got at the end of a manuscript that had subsequently been procured (in 1920) by the Government Oriental Manuscripts Library, Madras. These colophon verses contain a few details about the life-history of the poet. Secondly we have in the above as well as in another[5] manuscript, a complete text which expels many of the wrong premises on which former scholars had based their arguments. For example, the belief that the verse ending with the line वरतनु संप्रवदन्ति कुक्कुटा :belongs to Kumāradāsa, has been disproved once for all by its conspicuous absence in the available manuscripts. Some scholars were of opinion that Vāmana's censure of the use of the word 'Khalu' at the beginning of the line[6] is with reference to Kumāradāsa's usage[7]. This view is based on the rendering of a line given in Haridasa Sastri's printed edition which runs : खलु प्रजहती मुहुर्विरचिताञ्जलिर्विष्टरम् । The manuscripts of the poem do not have this line as found in the edition of the text. Instead, they read the corresponding verse as :

'विकल्पघटितं स्वयं दिशि भवन्तमालोक्य सा
चिरेण खलु निर्घृणः स्मृतिपथे कृतोऽयं जनः ।

1. Prof. Ernest Leumann—"Zum Jānakīharaṇa Des Kumārdāsa," *Vienna Oriental Journal*, Vol. VII pp. 226-232.
2. F.W. Thomas—"The Jānkiharaṇa of Kumāradāsa," *J.R.A.S.* (1901), pp. 253-268.
   Thomas—"Introduction to Kavīndravacanasamuccaya", p. 34.
3. A.B. Keith—"The Date of Kumāradāsa," *J,R.A.S.* (1901), pp. 578-582.
   A.B. Keith "A History of Sanskrit Literature", pp. 119 ff.
4. Nandargikar—"Introduction to Raghuvaṁśa, "pp. 121 to 127.
   Nandargikar—"Introduction to Jānakīharaṇa," Bombay (1907).
5. In the London University Library.
6. See Vāmana's *Kāvyālankārasūtravṛtti* न पादादौ खल्वादयः । V, 1-5.
7. A.B. Keith—"A History of Sanskrit Literature," pp. 149, 123.

So the reading of the Calcutta edition may be only due to the fault of the re-constructor. One of the verses[1] quoted by Vāmana in his *Kāvyālankārasūtravṛtti* is alleged to bear "too many marks of Kumāradāsa's style to leave any doubt of its authorship".[2] F. W. Thomas affirms that it belongs to the lost part of Kumāradāsa's poem. A. B. Keith also agrees[3] with this view. We have in the London and Adyar manuscripts many extra verses. But this particular verse is not to be found even in these manuscripts. Despite its supposed semblance with Kumāradāsa's verses, we have to discard it as not belonging to him. Hence Vāmana's date does not afford any clue to the date of Kumāradāsa.

Thirdly the citation of the verses of this poet in a prosody work called the *Jānāśrayī Chandoviciti*[4] has made possible the fixation of a lower limit to the date of the poet.

Almost all the commentators on the *Amarakośa* have quoted verses from the *J. H.* in their works.[5] Rāyamukuṭamaṇi, author of *Padacandrikā* (about A. D 1430), Sarvānanda the author of *Ṭīkāsarvasva* (1159 A.D.), and Subhūticandra, the author of *Kāmadhenu* (1010-1062 A.D), all quote verses from the *J. H.* and expressly mention the name of the author as well as that of the poem.

The evidence of the anthologies also proves the popularity of the poem of Kumāradāsa in the same age as indicated by the commentators of *Amarakośa*.[6] Thus the *Śārṅgadharapaddhati*, compiled in 1363 A.D., extracts three verses from

1. सपदि पङ्क्तिविहङ्गमनामभृत्तनयसंवलितं बलशालिना ।
विपुलपर्वतवर्षशितैश्शरैः प्लवगसैन्यमुलूकजिता जितम् ॥
Vāmana, II, 1-13.

2. F.W. Thomas—'The Jānakīharaṇa of Kumāradāsa", *J.R.A.S.* (1901), p. 266.

3. A.B. Keith—"A History of Sanskrit Literature," p. 119. '(Vamana).... and cites a stanza which in content and form proclaims itself as unquestionably a citation from the lost part of the Jānakiharaṇa.

4. Editions, Trivandrum Sanskrit Series and Sri Venkateswara Oriental Series, Tirupati.

5. For the actual citations, see below.

6. For the exact verses found in the anthologies, see below.

the *J. H.* mentioning the author's name. The Sūktimuktāvali of Jalhaṇa quotes the largest number of verses-fourteen-from Kumāradāsa's poem and it was compiled in 1258 A.D. The *Saduktikarṇāmṛta* of Śrīdharadāsa (1205 A.D., has two verses from the *J. H.* The *Subhāṣitāvali* of Vallabhadeva quotes nine verses from the *J.H.* and this anthology was earlier than Sarvānanda.[1]

As far as the so-called *Kavīndravacanasamuccaya* edited by Thomas[2] is concerned, this anthology which is the earliest of its class now available, is fragmentary in the edition of Thomas. In it only one verse बाले नाथे विमुञ्च etc. not belonging to our poem is found (No. 366) and that over the name of Kumārabhaṭṭa. A new edition of this work based on two complete manuscripts of it from Nepal and Tibet has been prepared by Prof. D. D. Kosambi[3]. According to the information supplied by him, this earliest anthology called in this manuscript *Subhāṣitaratnakośa* has the well-known eulogy on Kumāradāsa without the name of the author Rājaśekhara and with a few variants :

जानकीहरणं कर्तुं रघुवंशे पुरः स्थिते ।
कविः कुमारदासो वा रावणो वा यदि क्षमः ॥

Of actual quotations from the *J.H.*. Prof. Kosambi reports that शिशिरशीकरवाहिनि मारुते. etc. *J.H.* XI, 66, found also in *Subhāṣitāvali and Śārṅgadharapaddhati*, is found in this *Subhāṣitaratnakośa as* 34, 13 (Vātavrajyā) with the name of the author as Kumārī-dāśa (Kumāradāsa).

1. See S. K. De, on the date of *Subhāṣitāvali*, *J.R.A.S.* (1927), pp. 471 to 477.
   My professor agrees with Dr. De's contention that as Sarvananda's commentary on *Amarakośa* has reference to this anthology and its author, it is not possible to date the *Subhasitavali* in the 15th Century. My professor has verified the occurrence of the reference to Vallabhadeva and *Subhāṣitavali* in the manuscripts of Sarvānanda's commentary in the manuscript available in Govt. Oriental Manuscripts Library, Madras.
2. *Bibliotheca Indica*, 1309 (1912).
3. Prof. Kosambi was kind enough to send the required information to my Professor and I am thankful to him for his help. The work *Subhāṣitaratnakośa* of Vidyākara has since appeared in the *Harvard Oriental Series*.

Now turning to the Alankāra writers, we find that Hemacandra (1089 to 1173 A.D.) and Bhoja (1010 to 1055 A.D.) also quote from Kumāradāsa's work.[1] Next comes the important author, Rājaśekhara of *C.* 900 A.D., who makes some references to Kumāradāsa. In his *Kāvyamīmāṁsā* he refers to the poet as born blind[2]. He has also left a verse on Kumāradāsa and his poem[3]. While we shall discuss in detail the significance of this verse later, we can now push up the lower limit of our poet's date to 900 A.D. on the basis of this verse of Rājaśekhara.

It is possible to push up the lower limit of Kumāradāsa's date further. "In the *Jānāśrayī Chandoviciti*, already referred to, we have quotations from Kumāradāsa.[4] This prosodial treatise opens with a verse describing a king named Janāśraya who had performed several sacrifices. In the whole field of epigraphy there has so far been only one king known as Janāśraya, i. e. Mādhavavarman of the Viṣṇukuṇḍin Dynasty of Andhra Desa. Only five records have been known of the kings of this dynasty ; and both in their genealogical as well as chronological reconstruction, scholars have expressed divergent views[5]. Taking together the names mentioned in all the records, the following would appear to be the

1. For the verses quoted by the Alankāra writers, see below.
2. मेधाविरुद्रकुमारदासादयः जात्यन्धाः—Rājaśekhara's *Kāvyamīmāsā*, G.O.S., Vol. I, p.12.
3. जानकीहरणं कर्तुं रघुवंशे स्थिते सति ।
   कविः कुमारदासश्च रावणश्च यदि क्षमौ ॥
   See *Suktimuktāvali* of Jalhaṇa, G.O.S. edn. p. 45.
4. For actual verses quoted, see below.
5. See E. Hultzsch—"Ipur Plates of Govindavarman's son, Mādhavavarman," *Epigraphia Indica*, Vol. XVII, pp. 334 ff.
   See E. Hultzsch—"Ipur Plates of Madhavavarman II, "*Ibid* pp. 337 ff.
   K.V. Lakshmana Rao—"The Telugu Academy Plates of Viṣṇukuṇḍin Mādhavavarma III, A.D. 594", *Journal of the Dep of Letters*, University of Calcutta, Vol. XI, pp.31-64.
   R. Subba Rao—"Polamuru Plates of Viṣṇukuṇḍin Mādhava varma", *Journal of the Andhra Historical Research Society*, Vol. VI, pp. 17 ff.

proper genealogy :

```
                    Vikramendra I
                          |
                    Govindavarman
                          |
                    Mādhavavarman I, Janāśraya (Ipur I and
                                               Polamuru Plates)
          |               |                    |
   Devavarman      Vikramendravarman    Mañcyanna Baṭṭāraka
          |               |
Mādhavavarman II   Indrabhaṭṭāraka (or Varman)
   (Ipur II)
```

There is no reason for assuming more than two Mādhavavarmans. The Mādhavavarman described in identical terms as the performer of manifold sacrifices in these grants can only be the same Mādhavavarman I of the Polamuru grant. *The Jānāśrayī Chandoviciti* also specifies his performance of sacrifices ; and from the Polamuru grant, we know also that this Mādhavavarman had the title "Janāśraya." Now, the date

D.C. Sircar—"Successors of the Sātavāhanas", Ch. V, pp. 84 *Journal of tha Dept. of Letters*, University of Calcutta, Vol. XXVI.

"Genealogy of the Viṣṇukuṇḍins", *Indian Historical Quarterly*, Vol. IX, pp. 273-78.

"Chronology of the Viṣṇukuṇḍins *Ibid.*, pp. 957-66

K. Gopalachar—"Early History of the Andhra Country". Ch. XI, pp. 200-208.

B.V. Krishna Rao—"Early Dynasties of Andhra Deśa", pp. 414-421.

M. Ramakrishna Kavi—"Janāśraya School of Sanskrit Prosody *Tirumalai Sri Venkateswara*, Vol. I, No. 2, pp. 133 ff.

V. A. Ramaswami Sastri—"Jānāśrayī Chandoviciti", *Journal of Oriental Research*, Madras, Vol. XVII, Part III, pp. 138-142.

Introduction to the two editions of "Jānāśrayī" already referred to.

of the Polamuru grant is 593 A.D.[1] We may have to hold, therefore, that Kumāradāsa who is quoted in the *Jānāśrayī Chandoviciti* was earlier than this date.

But this chronological scheme would leave only very short intervals between Bhāravi, Kumārdāsa and the *Jānāśrayī*. This time is too short for Bhāravi's poem to have gained vogue in Ceylon and for a Simhala writer's poem to have gained popularity in the Andhra country. Owing to this tightness of the scheme, we may be tempted to take the patron of *Jānāśrayī* as Mādhavavarman II and gain some years. But there is no evidence to show that Mādhavavarman II was also known as Janāśraya.

From the foregoing it is clear that Kumāradāsa cannot be placed after 620 A.D. and that he was definitely later than Bhāravi.[2] We have to ignore the attempts of some scholars to place Kumāradāsa at a date later than that of Māgha. Māgha was the grandson of one Suprabhadeva, the minister to King Varmalāta who on epigraphic evidence may be placed in 625 A.D. After allowing a minimum interval of sixty years for the two generations, we can place Māgha at

1. K. Gopalachari—*Early History of the Andhra Country*, p. 208.

Note :—Ramakrishna Kavi would take the Janāśraya of the *Chandoviciti* as Mādhavavarman II, sixth in descent from Mādhavavarman I, (*T.S.V.* Vol. I, No. 2, p. 138) and the date of the Polamuru grant as 609 A.D. B.V. Krishna Rao would take Mādhavavarma Janāśraya of the Palamuru grant as Mādhavavarman III and give his time as from 546 to *Circa* 611 A.D. (*Early Dynasties of Andhra Desa*, pp. 410, 418 and 544-45.) Dr. N. Venkataramanayya, in a forth-coming study of his on the Viṣṇukuṇḍins, proposes that the donees of the Jayasimha grant and the Polamuru grant are not father and son, but ancestor and descendant separated by two generations. This would take the date of Mādhavavarman I, who is the founder of the dynasty according to him, very much earlier and this re-adjustment of the chronology is necessary, according to him, to accommodate the Durjayas, hither to not taken note of, from whom and not from the Viṣṇukuṇḍins, the Eastern Chalukyas won Veṅgi. On this view, the dates of Kumāradāsa, Bhāravi etc. would all go up very much earlier.

2. Walter as cited by Keith (*A History of Sanskrit Literature*, p. 121, Fn. 1) seems to have wrongly held (*Indica* III, 34-36) that Bhāravi borrows from Kumāradāsa.

about 685 A.D., which means definitely that he was a successor to Kumāradāsa. If we are to give due consideration to some of the striking parallel passages between these two poets, we have to accept that Māgha was influenced by Kumāradāsa. Incidentally we may also push further down the date of Māgha allowing sufficient interval for Kumāradāsa's fame to spread throughout India. It is impossible to accept the theory of some scholars[1] that Kumāradāsa was influenced by Māgha in the instances of similarity that have been pointed out between the two.[2] It is the opinion of Dr. Keith also, who notes the parallel in one case, that it is Māgha who is the borrower.

There are some traditions that have been handed down with referenee to Kumāradāsa.[3] A Sinhalese work by name *Poerakumba Śirite* (*Parākramabāhu carita*) of the 14th Century contains a record of the traditional story that links the life-history of Kumāradāsa with that of Kālidāsa. The story as it appears in this work is narrated by Prof. T.W. Rhys Davids in his article entitled 'Kālidāsa in Ceylon.'[4] Kumāradāsa, the

1. See Nandargikar's Introduction to the *Jānakīharaṇa*.
   K. Krishnamacharya, B.A., L.T., "A note on Kumāradāsa and the Jānakīharaṇa", *T.S.V.* (Dec. 1932), Vol. 1, No. 5, p. 385.
2. A.B. Keith's *A History of Sanskrit Literature*, p. 119.
   "Finally he was probably earlier than Māgha who seems to echo a verse of his".
   Also p. 121, Fn. 1—"The reverse is probable", See Kumāradāsa, III, 34 with Māgha, V, 29.
   Also p. 124.
3. The *Pūjāvali*; *Nikāya Sangraha*; *Saddharmaratnākara*; *Rājaratnākara*, *Rājāvali* and *Poerakumba Śisite*.
   See C. Bendall (*J.R.A.S.* (1888), p. 440) who cites also two other recent Sinhalese works which support the traditional story.
   (a) The historical tragedy entitled 'Kālidāsa' by Simon De Silva Seneviratna, Muhandrum (1887); and (b) 'Kālidasa Caritaya—Hevat Kālidāsa Kavinduge ha Kumāradāsa mirunduge da Jīvita-Kāvya (1887).
4. *J.R.A.S.* (1888), pp. 148-149.
   See also "Three Traditional Tales" by J. A, Ceylon Literary Register Vol. IV., pp. 227-231.
   The author of this article identifies the king with the author of the *J.H.*, but adds about Kālidāsa that he is 'not Irshi Kālidās, the Shakespeare of the East.

royal bard of Ceylon, who had a great admiration for the greatest of Indian poets, Kālidāsa, is said to have once invited the latter to his court. Kālidāsa happened to stay in the house of a courtezan which the monarch also used to frequent. One day the king wrote the first half of a verse on the wall of the bed-room with a promise of big rewards for anybody who completed that verse. Kālidāsa who visited her later happened to notice this half-verse and completed it. The greedy courtezan, eager to grab the promised reward, murdered the poet and presented the latter half of the stanza to the king, as if it were composed by herself. The monarch perceiving in it the genius of a poet, questioned her and found out the fact of his friend's murder. Much grieved at this, he ordered for the funeral of the poet in all pomp and when the friend's body was being consumed by fire, he threw himself into the flames. According to this authority the first half of the verse was :--

> "Wana tambarā mala no talā ronatā wanī
> Mala dederā pana gālawā giya sewanī"

which Rhys Davids translates thus :

> "The forest bee got to the honey without hurting the flower, but (being caught in the flower as it closed) he got away with his life to the cool shades of the jungle only when (in the morning) the lily unfolded its petals."

The latter half of it added by the poet runs as :

> "Siyaṭ ambarā sīya tambarā siya sewenī
> Siya sā purā midi no labā un sewenī"

Which is translated as :

> "The relation of the Sun (the king of the Solar race) seeking the society of the lotus-eyed (beauty) enjoyed, indeed, her company, but sleepless was caught in his toils."

H.C. Sirr—"Ceylon and the Cinghalese", Vol. II, pp. 256-25
Grierson—*Indian Antiquary*, Vol. XVI, pp.
H. Parker—"Ancient Ceylon", p. 273.

The very fact that this riddle is not in Sanskrit casts some doubt on the whole story. Granting that it would have been in Sanskrit in the original, we cannot justify the sound-effect and perfection of these lines as they are found. Because, they appear more to be originals than translations into Sinhalese. Another version of the story which is also purely traditional and which is accepted by K. Dharmarama Sthavira,[1] states that the riddle was—कुसुमे कुसुमोत्पत्तिःश्रूयते न तु दृश्यते and this was completed by Kālidāsa as बाले तव मुखांभोजे दृष्टमिन्दीवरद्वयम् ।। This stanza is quoted also in other traditions relating to Kālidāsa but not at all connected with Kumāradāsa. Mr. A.M. Hocart in one of his articles[2] refers to a place in Mātara called Hatbodhivatta, or the Garden of the seven Bo-Trees. "It is said that seven Bo-Trees were planted on the place where the poet Kumāradāsa was cremated."[3] Local tradition still current in that place associates these trees with the place where King Kumāradāsa, his five queens and his minister died in the funeral pyre of his friend Kālidāsa.

The validity of these traditions is almost nil as long as they are not corroborated by other historical evidences. Now we shall see whether history allows us to accept the contemporanity of these two poets. Literary historians have identified this poet, Kumaradasa, with King Kumāradhātusena who might have ascended the throne in about 512 A.D. According to the *Mahāvaṁśa*, the Ceylonese chronicle, Kumāradhātusena was the son of one Moggalāna.[4] He rued for nine years i.e. 512 to 521 A.D. But the *Mahāvaṁśa* makes no mention of his literary achievements, nor does it refer to any infirmity which, according to Rājaśekhara, amounted to congenital blindness. It only mentions that he caused a revision of

1. See K. Dharmarama's Introduction to his edition of the *J.H.* of Kumāradāsa, Peliyagoda (1891).

2. & 3. A.M. Hocart—"Mortuary use of the Bo-Tree"—*Cylon Journal of Science*, Sec. G., Vol. 2, p. 31.

4. *Mahāvaṃśa*—Ch. 41, verses 1 to 3.

the sacred texts and also contains some conventional words of praise about his prowess and liberality towards religion.

Another historical work called 'Pūjāvali' which is comparatively later (13th Century) identifies this King with Kumāradāsa and refers to his tragic end at the funeral pyre of his friend Kālidāsa. But this work is almost of the same period as *Poerakumba Sirite* and hence, its historical value cannot be accepted.

Recent archaeological discoveries have revealed two inscriptions[1] belonging to this period at Nagirikanda situated in the North Central Province of Ceylon. One of them with which we are concerned here covers a rock-surface of 7½″ × 2″ and contains seven lines of writing. The importance of this inscription lies in the fact that this period is the most obscure in the epigraphical history of the island, for it has left very few inscriptions which contain the name of the reigning King and can therefore be dated."[2] The contents of this record is about a gift of some tanks and paddy-fields to the ancient monastery on the site. The King who made this gift is named; but it is unfortunately not preserved intact. Dr. Muller, in the text of this record given in the "Ancient Inscriptions in Ceylon"[3] has read it differently from S. Paranavitana, and has not recognised a proper noun at all in it. But the latter reads in it the line, "Siddham Mahā-Kumāratāsa Rāja—Apaya........"[4] He identifies the king with Kumāradhātusena of *Mahāvaṁśa* but refuses to accept the theory that this king is identical with the poet. Elsewhere also[5] he says, "After a reign of eighteen years, he

1. S. Paranavitana—"Nagirikanda Rock Inscriptions of Kumāradāsa", *Epigraphica Zylanica*, Ins. No. 44-.
 Also see Paranavitana's "Epigraphical Summary"—*Ceylon Journal of Science*, Sec. G., Vol. II, pp. 103, 104.
 Also see the *Annual Report of the Archaeological Survey of Ceylon* for 1890-List of Inscriptions on page 9.
2. S. Paranavitana—*Epigraphica Zylanica*, Ins. No. 445.
3. Dr. E. Muller—"Ancient Inscriptions in Ceylon. No. 97".
4. S. Paranavitana—"Nagirikanda Rock Incriptions of Kumāradāsa", *Epigraphica Zylanica*, Ins. No. 4?5.
5. "A New History of Indian People", Vol. VI, p. 261 Gupta Age.

(Moggalāna) was succeeded by his son Kumāradāsa (515 to 524) who for several centuries, has enjoyed a reputation, to which he had no claim, as the poet who composed the *J.H.*"

Hence these epigraphical evidences do not help us much with regard to the identity and date of the poet. The inscription shows that a name contained in it can be read as 'Kumāratāsa Apaya' and that this name approximates with the only similar royal name of the period, namely King Kumāradhātusena I of the 6th century. To base the argument for establishing the identity of these two on such an obliterated record, which is interpreted with great difficulty as Kumāratāsa Apaya, is itself a risky step. Even if it is proved that the king and the donor of this grant are identical, we have nothing in the inscription to show that the poet and the donor of this grant are the same.

These are the scanty historical materials that we have to help us on the question of the date and identity of our poet. So we have to go to other evidences which may guide us in deciding the question. One thing that we can definitely say is that Kumāradāsa is later than Kālidāsa. Rājaśekhara's verse[1] refering to these two poets is very significant from a historical point of view. The use of the *sati saptamī* in रघुवंशे स्थिते सति definitely proves that Kumāradāsa while writing his poem had already before him the *Raghuvaṁśa* of Kālidāsa. It is not possible to brush aside Rājaśekhara's verse, as some attempt to do,[2] as a piece of mere rhetoric devoid of any chronological significance. A reading of all the verses of Rājaśekhara in praise of poets in this strain will convince one of the sense of chronology and historical accuracy that Rājaśekhara had when he wrote them. The employment of pun in these cases can hardly be taken as detrimental to a historical interpretation of his eulogies. Exception[3] has been taken to the doubtful meaning of Rājaśekhara's verse in this series on Kālidāsa, making an obscure reference to 'Kālidāsa-

1. Jalhaṇa's *Sūktimuktāvali*, G.O.S. Edition. Ch. IV, p. 45.
2. See M. Doraswamayya's "Kumāradāsa and Jānakīharaṇa", *T.S.V.* Vol. I, No. 3 pp. 203 to 212.
3. *Ibid.* No. 5, pp. 386 ff.

trayī.' But it should be noted that it is not impossible to explain the expression 'Kālidāsatrayī.' Not only is the priority of Kālidāsa quite clear but as can be seen from the detailed treatment in another section[1], Kumāradāsa is seen in his poem as a close imitator of Kālidāsa: in fact this happens to be the most dominant characterisitc of his work[2]. Apart from these imitations, Kumāradāsa's style also definitely proves the fact that he belonged to a period when the simplicity and the natural grace of style which is the characteristic of the Kālidāsian age, was gradually being replaced by the artificial and laborious style of the later writers. Though like Kālidāsa, he makes references to Yavanas, Kumāradāsa mentions also the Turuṣkas,[3] not to be met with in Kālidāsa and this mention of some later intruders in the Indian soil proves that Kumāradāsa was later to Kālidāsa.

It will be clear from a further section in this Thesis that in the plan and style of the Mahākāvya in Kumāradāsa, the progressive change towards an increasing artificiality mentioned above, owed much to the influence of Bhāravi. Kumāradāsa is thus to be placed, as already indicated, in an age subsequent to that of the author of the *Kirātārjunīya.*

We can now canvass the information contained in the four colophonic verses found at the end of the Madras manuscript of the *J.H.* In the Sinhalese version as edited by Dharmarama, we find only one colophonic verse dealing with the life of the poet. Even this verse is incomplete and the lacunae are filled up by Dharmarama himself. It reads as follows :—

क्रतज्ञ (इति मातुलद्वितययत्न) सानाथ्यतो
महार्थमसुरद्विपो व्यग्चयन् महार्थं (कविः) ।
(कुमारपरिचारकः) सफलहार्द (सिद्धिः सुधीः)
(श्रुतो जगति जानकीहरण) काव्यमेतन्महत् ॥

1. See Chapter on "Kumāradāsa and Kālidāsa".

2. This would form the real significance of the legend that associates the two poets, as Geiger also points out in his Singhalese Language and Literature, pp. 3-4.

3. Nandargikar's "Introduction to Raghuvaṃśa", p. 121 to p 127

The words within brackets are reconstructions made by Dharmarama.[1] Since this verse is not to be found in any other manuscript, and since the ideas contained in this are to be found distributed in four verses in the Madras manuscript, this verse may be a later composition based on a recollection of the original. It is probable that King Rājasundara composed it as a mark of his appreciation and in order to record the information that he got about the life-history of the poet. We have already stated that King Rājasundara was having a text same as or at least similar to the Madras manuscript. Hence it is probable that he did not feel it necessary to continue the Sanna after the story was over and that he condensed the ideas contained in the four verses of the Madras manuscript into one and added it as an appendix to his commentary.

In the Madras manuscript there are four colophonic verses dealing with the life of the poet. The first verse reads as follows :—

> नित्यं सद्गुणभक्तिरिन्द्रियदमश्रीसंयतः संयतः
> शस्त्रद्योतितमूर्ध्नि मुक्तहृदयोऽभीसङ्गतः सङ्गतः ।
> विद्वानस्य कवेः पितार्यहृदयं धीमानितो मानितः
> लङ्कैश्वर्यभुजः कुमारमणिरित्यासन्नयः सन्नयः ।।

This may be translated as follows :–

> "Always devoted to virtues, possessed of the beauty of sense-control, unassociated with any fear, (there was Mānita, a man of learning (*Vidvān*) and intelligence (*Dhīmān*), who was the poet's father, of sound policy (*San-nayaḥ*), a fighter in the rear-guard (*Ā-sannayah*) of Kumāramaṇi, King of Laṅkā, who engaging himself (*Saṅgataḥ*) at the head of the battle flashing with arms (*Samyataḥ Śastra-dyotita-mūrdhni*), gave up his heart (life) but entered the hearts of all noble men (*Ārya-hṛdayam*) . . . . . itaḥ)."

1. Doraswamayya—"A Reply", *T.S.V.*, Vol. I, No. 5, pp. 386-392

The second verse runs thus :—

येनारिप्रकृतिं निराकृतवता सम्मानितो मानितः
यस्य स्वाङ्गमभिघ्नतो रिपुभृशंनाशोऽभितः शोभितः ।
श्रीमेघोऽस्य कवेरसौ किल बृहद्धामातुलो मातुलः
दृष्टस्त्रासजडं द्विषामधिगतत्रासेनया सेनया ॥

This verse which has reference to one of the maternal uncles of the poet may be translated thus :

> "This incomparable (*Atulaḥ* and highly powerful (*Bṛhaddhāmā*) Megha was this poet's maternal uncle (*Mātulaḥ*), Megha who defeated the enemy people and honoured Mānita, he who striking all around himself (*Svāṅgam-abhi-ghnataḥ*), made the complete destruction of the enemies shine all around (*Ripu-bhṛśam-nāśaḥ abhitaḥ śobhitaḥ*), and who was looked upon with stupefaction of fear (*Trāsa-jadam*) by the enemy-army whose leader also was in fright (*Adhigatatrāsa-inayā*)"

The third verse dealing with another of his maternal uncles runs thus :

श्रीमानेकः शरण्यः परिभवविपदाभाजनानां जनानां
रूपेणानुप्रयातो दिवमतिसुभगं रञ्जयन्तं जयन्तम् ।
भ्राता तन्मातुरन्यः शशिधवलयशःकारणानां रणानां
कर्ता पुत्रोऽग्रबोधिर्जनशिरसि लसद्भासुराज्ञः सुराज्ञः ।

This may be translated thus :—

> "Another brother of his mother was Agrabodhi, son of the good King (*Su-Rājnaḥ*), the one refuge of the people subjected to humiliation and calamities, resembling in personality the exceedingly beautiful Jayanta who is gladdening the Heavens, he who waged wars productive of fame pure like the moon and one whose command shone on the heads of (honoured by) the people (*Jana-Śirasi-lasad-bhāsura-ājñaḥ*)."

The last verse which sums up the life of the poet himself runs as follows :—

आदायैनं दशायां स्थितमपि तदहस्स्रस्तनाभ्यां स्तनाभ्यां
तुष्टे तस्मिन् गदानामरिहतपितृके पारयन्तौ रयन्तौ ।
आत्मापत्याविशेषं पुपुषतुरहतप्रेमदान्तौ मदान्तौ
यत्सानाथ्यात् स काव्यं व्यरचयदसुरद्विण्महार्थं महार्थम्

The following is a rendering of the verse :—

> "Taking this poet in that very state when he had just been born (*tadaha-srasta-nābhyām*) and overcoming the virulence of his ailments *Gadānām-rayam pārayantau*) while yet he was being suckled (*Sthanābhyām tuṣṭe*) and his father had been killed by the enemies, those two (uncles), continuously affectionate and self-possessed (*Ahataprema-dāntau*) and devoid of intoxication (*Mada-antau*) tended him (the poet) as if he was their own son; and it was with their help that the poet composed the poem of great meaning (*Mahā-artham*) having for its subject-matter the glory of (the Lord), the enemy of the demons (*Asura-dvit-mahā-artham*)."

From these verses we come to understand that the poet's father was called Mānita who was a commander or a military official in charge of the rear-guard of the King of Ceylon named Kumāramaṇi ; that he lost his life on the battle-field ; that the poet had two powerful uncles named Megha and Agrabodhi; that he was brought up by them from his infancy ; that he had some ailments from the very birth and that he received the help of his uncles in writing the poem.

The Report[1] on the working of the Peripatetic Party of the Government Oriental Manuscript Library, Madras, in its statement about the manuscript of this work at the time of

1. The Report on the working of the Peripatetic Party of the Govt. Oriental Manuscripts, Library, during the triennium 1916-17 to 1916-19 (Madras), Enclosure I, p. 3.

its discovery gives the following interpretation of these verses :—

> "The poet gives a brief account of himself in four stanzas at the end of the poem. He was born of Kumāramani, King of Ceylon, who committed suicide in the battle-field. His two uncles Megha and Agrabodhi brought him up and this work was written when he was with them.[1]"

From the interpretation which we have given above to these colophonic verses, it would become clear that there is no justification in these verses for holding Kumāradāsa the poet as the King of Ceylon or as the son of King Kumāramani. It is also wrong to deduce from the verses that the poet's father committed suicide on the battle-field. Kumāramaṇi, according to our interpretation, becomes the maternal grandfather of the poet.

Before we conclude this discussion about the colophonic verses, we have to take note of their absence in the London manuscript. While the latter contains many more verses in addition to those in the Madras manuscript, the absence of these four verses is, indeed, conspicuous. Since we have no definite knowledge about the sources and pedigree of these manuscripts, we cannot definitely say whether these colophonic verses were written by the poet himself or by a later copyist, or commentator who was aware of the details connected with the life of the poet. The single verse that Dharmarama gives, condensing the ideas contained in these four verses, proves that he, and therefore his authority namely, King Rājasundara were familiar with them. That helps us to decide that they are not very late additions but possess sufficient antiquity.

About the nativity of the poet there are no two opinions. All manuscripts available mention in the colophons in all or some of their cantos that the poet belongs to the Simhala country. It is further proved by the eulogy of Rājaśekhara. His classification of the poet along with Rāvaṇa in the matter of attempting at Jānakīharaṇa, apart from other implication, definitely hints at the common nativity of these two,

1. Jalhaṇa's *Sūktimuktavai*, Ch. IV, 76. G.O.S. edn. p. 45.

the one who was thoughtless enough to commit the abduction of Sītā while the race of the Raghus in the person of Rāma and Lakṣhmaṇa was there, and the other whose effort was superfluous in his composing the poem, *J.H.* when the masterpiece of Kālidāsa, the *Raghuvaṅśa*, was already there.

Historians of Ceylon have not considered in detail all the names and incidents mentioned in the four Colophonic verses of the Madras manuscripts. S. Paranavitana has made a reference to the evidence of these verses when he says in his contribution in "New History of Indian people,"[1] "A manuscript of this poem discovered some years ago in Malabar contains evidence to show that Kumāradāsa, the author of the *J.H.* was a scion of the Sinhalese Royal family, but was a personage distinct from the King of that name."

Even he has not taken the trouble to discuss the names and facts contained in these verses in full in the light of the information available to a close student of Ceylonese history like him. So far as we can see, the only royal name in the annals of the island having any element of our poet's name is Kumāradhātusena invariably called in the chronicles and inscriptions by our poet's name and neither are historians like Paranavitana agreeable to identify our poet with this personage, nor do our Colophonic verses support such an identification. Our verses mention the King concerned as Kumāramaṇi. Two of this King's sons are mentioned as Megha and Agrabodhi. Like Kumāra, the name Megha also is seen in the annals of Ceylon in names like Meghavarṇa or Śīlamegha. We are not in a position to identify exactly this Megha. Near our period we have Kiṭṭiśiri Meghavarṇa II, 560 (Geiger), 595 (Cordington). But the genealogy differs with regard to the name of this king's father. Similarly we have also for the Agrabodhi of our verses, Agrabodhi I and II of the chronicles of the Island, the first placed between (564-578), or (600-634) and the II placed between 598-608 or (634-644). Aggrabodhi I is described as a "patron of the arts" and "surrounded by

1. "New History of Indian People," Vol. VI pp. 261., fn.

twelve talented poets."[1] The age of our poet arrived at on other grounds agrees with that of this Agrabodhi. Accordidg to Mallalasekhara, a new Sanskrit movement had started in Ceylon, the first fruit of which was the medical work of Buddhadāsa,[2] the Sārārthasaṅgraha of the 4th Century. The influx of the Tamils from South India who were earnest students of Sanskrit Literature gave a fillip to Sanskrit studies in the Island and it was in the spell of literary activity inspired by Sanskrit that the *J.H.* came to be composed by Kumāradāsa in that language; and later Śilameghasena (846-866) [3] produced his Sinhalese rhetorical work "Siyabaslakāra" under the influence of Daṇḍin's *Kāvyādarśa.* The pioneer to foster Sanskrit in the poetic field in Ceylon was probably our poet Kumāradāsa. As is usual with all pioneers of new types of literary art, he had before him the works of the great masters of India, namely Kālidāsa and Bhāravi and he had also acquainted himself with the up-to-date canons that govern the making of the *Mahākāvya* form, from which he assiduously copied and upon which he modelled his work. Mention has already been made of the progressive increase of artificiality and display of *Śabda-citra* when we pass from the *Kirātārjunīya* to the *J.H.* A comparative scrutiny of the *Śabda-citras,* as can be made out from a tabulation of these given elsewhere in this Thesis, discloses the fact that *J.H.* has a few more varieties not found in Daṇḍin's *Kāvyādarśa.* On the other hand there is at least one verse in which there are a number of striking effects parallel to Daṇḍin and Kumāradāsa.[4] While the date of Daṇḍin would make him later to Kumāradāsa, the features pointed out above in the *Śabda-citra* would agree for Kumāradāsa's posteriority. It would not be possible to throw Daṇḍin also into the tight chronological hole in which we have thrust already Bhāravi, Jānāśrayī and Kumāradāsa. As Kāñcīpura where Daṇḍin flourished (and which Kumāradāsa knew[5]) and

1. Mallalasekhara—"Pali Literature of Ceylon", pp. 74, 751,48, 168-231.

2. *Ibid.* pp. 162

3. *Ibid.* p. 167. Mallalasekhara would assign Kumāradāsa here to the beginning of the 6th Century.

4.,5. Ch. I, Verse 18.

the Āndhra Deśa were also centres of Budhistic activity, frequent contact with Ceylon, the island of Buddhism, would have been quite natural and it is not impossible to suppose that literary productions of South India and Ceylon were quickly transmitted to each other.

CITATIONS FROM THE JĀNAKĪHARAṆA

A. Anthologies.

It has already been mentioned, while discussing the date of Kumāradāsa, that the well-known anthologies contain verses of this poet. We shall devote here some attention to the Kumāradāsa verses in the anthologies and their value for textual criticism of the *J.H.* Most of the quotations are from the descriptive passages of the *J.H.*, particularly from cantos I and XI. They can be classified under four heads from the point of view of the source-names mentioned for them in the anthologies.

1. Those that are given over the name 'Kumāradāsa';
2. Those that are attributed to 'Kumāradatta';
3. Those that come over the name 'Nāthakumāra';
4. Those that are quoted without any mention about their authorship.

Altogether we have been able to pick out twentyfour verses belonging to Kumāradāsa's *J.H.* and some of them are repeated in more than one anthology. Eight of them are from the description of the rainy season in the 11th canto of the *J.H.*, while six are from the 1st canto of this work. Sometimes, in the same anthology, we find the author referred to by two different names. Of verses for which the author is not mentioned but which we can identify as from the *J.H.*, there are only three in the anthologies.

The earliest available anthology called the *Kavīndravacanasamuccaya*, whose complete version bearing the name *Śubhāṣitaratnakośa* has been edited by Prof. D.D. Kosambi, contains one quotation from the *J.H.* This verse is given over the name 'Kumāradāsa'. It belongs to the 11th canto of the *J.H.* The same verse is to be found qouted in the *Subhāṣitāvali*,[1] and the *Śārṅgadharapaddhati*,[2] These two anthologies give the author's name as 'Kumāradāsa'. While in the *Subḥāṣitaratnakośa* it appears under the heading 'Vāta-vrajyā',

1. *Subhāṣitāvali* edited by Peterson, p. 297 *śloka* 1757.
2. *Śārṅgadharapaddhati* edited by Peterson, p. 591, *Sl*. 3897.

in the *Subhāṣitāvalī* it comes under 'Varṣā' and in the *Śārṅgadharapaddhatī* it is given under the heading 'Pathika-kāminī'. All these three anthologies almost agree with the manuscripts and the printed editions of the *J.H.* with regard to the reading of this Verse which runs thus :

शिशिरशीकरवाहिनि मारुते चरति शीतभयादिव सत्वरः ।
मनसिजः प्रविवेश वियोगिनीहृदयमाहितशोकहुताशनम् ।।
(*J.H.*, XI, 66)

Apart from this verse, the *Subhāṣitāvali* contains eight more quotations from the *J.H.* Under the heading 'jaṅghe' he quotes an anonymous verse[1] which belongs to the 1st canto of the poem. The same quotation is given in the *Sūktimuktāvali* under the same heading, where too the author's name is not given.[2] These two anthologies slightly differ in the reading of this verse and they have some negligible differences with the reading of the verse found in the manuscripts and printed editions of the *J.H.*

Under the heading 'Vasanta', the *Subhāṣitāvali* quotes a verse from the 3rd canto of Kumāradāsa's work.[3] The name of the author is given as 'Kumāradāsa'. This verse is to be found quoted only in this anthology. While it completely agrees in its reading with that of Nandargikar's printed edition, it has some slight differences with the readings in the manuscripts and with those of Haridasa Sastri's edition. The *Subhāṣitāvali* gives another verse as belonging to 'Kumāradatta' under the heading 'Śarad'[4]. This is from the 12th canto of the *J.H.* This is also to be found quoted only in this anthology. The reading of the verse given here is almost in agreement with those of our manuscripts. The other five verses of Kumāradāsa found in this collection are given under the heading 'Varṣā'[5] and all of them are from

1. *Subh.*, p. 265, Sl. 1569.
2. *Sūktimuktāvali*, Gaekward's Oriental Series, No. 82, (1938) p. 188, Sl. 82.
3. *Subh.*, p. 281, *Sl.* 1654.
4. *Subh.*, p. 307, *Sl.* 1812.
5. *Ibid.* pp. 296-97, *Sl.* 1751, 52, 53, 54 & 55.

the 11th canto of the *J.H.* All these five verses are attributed to Kumāradatta and they are not to be found in any other anthologies. These verses bear some differences in their readings with the manuscripts of the *J.H.*, but they are not very conspicuous. We have, in this anthology, verses belonging to the same canto of the *J.H.* appearing under 'Kumāradatta' as well as 'Kumāradāsa.'

The *Sūktimuktāvali* contains the maximum number of quotations (fourteen) from the *J.H.* Out of these, there is only one verse of Kumāradāsa quoted anonymously,[1] even as in the *Subhāṣitāvali*. Out of the rest, eleven verses are to be found only in this anthology while there are only two verses of Kumāradāsa in this, which are to be found in the *Śārṅgadharapaddhati* also. Twelve verses are attributed to Kumāradāsa and one verse to Nāthakumāra.[2] The two verses that are common to this anthology[3] and the *Śārṅgadharapaddhati*[4] appear in both over the name 'Kumāradāsa'. In both these they appear under the same headings, i.e. 'Madhyam' and 'Uru' respectively. They belong to the lst canto of the *J.H.* where Kausalyā is described. The readings of these two anthologies have some negligible differences and they have some common variants with the readings of the manuscript and the printed texts of the *J.H.* In the 53rd chapter of this work, which is named 'strīṇām aṅgavarṇanapaddhati' we have six quotations from the J.H. under various subheadings like 'ūru'. Out of these, five are from the 1st canto while one verse is from the 7th canto of the *J.H.* Two verses of the 11th canto appear under 'Varṣāpaddhati'[5] and two from the 6th canto under 'Sarvapadārthasaṃstutipaddhati'[6]. The remaining four verses are distributed in four chapters which are named 'Jalakrīḍāpaddhati;[7] 'Pāna-

1. *Sūkti.*, p. 188, *Sl.* 82
2. *Sūkti.*, p. 378.
3. *Ibid.* pp.185, 188.
4. *Śārṅg*, p. 484, Sloka 3344; p. 487, Sloka 3356.
5. *Sūktt.*, p. 222.
6. *Ibid.*, p. 289.
7. *Sūkti.*, p. 245.

goṣṭhīpaddhati,'[1] 'Sarovarṇanapaddhati,'[2] and 'Nagarīvarṇanapaddhati'[3]. The verses in these chapters are from cantos III, VIII, XII, and I respectively. The importance of this anthology consists in the fact that it contains verses representative in their nature. It quotes from seven cantos of the *J.H.* representing seven different contexts. Only in the case of the verse quoted from the 1st canto under the heading 'Nagarīvarṇanapaddhati', we have the author's name given as 'Nāthakumāra'. From the same canto another verse is quoted anonymously. Barring these two, all the other citations are attributed to Kumāradāsa only.

The *Saduktikarṇāmṛita*[4] has only two verses from the *J.H.* The first one appears in the 74th section of this collection under the sub-heading 'Vacanam'.[5] This verse belongs to the 7th canto of the *J.H.* The reading given here agrees with that of the Madras manuscript and the printed editions. The next verse appears in the 16th section under the sub-heading, 'Lakṣitāsatī'[6] This verse is from the 16th canto of the *J.H.* The uniqueness of this anthology is that it is the only collection of its type that quotes a verse from the 16th canto of the *J.H.* In no other anthology have we any quotation from any part of the work beyond the 12th canto. While the first quotation from the 7th canto appears over the name of Kumāradāsa, the second one is anonymously quoted. The reading of the latter one is in complete agreement with our edition of the same given in this book.

The *Śārṅgadharapaddhati*, as already stated, contains three verses, one from the 11th and two from the 1st cantos of the *J.H.* The first one is also found in the *Subhāṣitāvali*, while the other two in the *Sūktimuktāvali*.

To indicate some of the general conclusions of textual criticism that can be deduced from the evidence of the antho-

1. *Sūkti*, p. 267.
2. *Ibid.* p. 376.
3. *Ibid.* p. 378.
4. *Saduktikarṇāmṛita*, Punjab Oriental Series No. XV (1933).
5. *Ibid.* p. 117.
6. *Ibid.* p. 78.

logy-citations :

1. The word-order found in the restorations of Nandargikar and Haridāsa Śastri is not supported; the order found in the manuscript versions stands supported.
2. Barring a single citation from the 16th canto, the latter part of the poem (beyond the 12th canto) is not utilised at all by the anthologists.
3. None of the additional verses in the London manuscript finds a place in any anthology.
4. The only verse in the anthologies mentioned as Kumāradāsa's which cannot be traced in the J.H. is,

   बाले नाथ विमुञ्ज मनिनि रुषं

   which is found in other collections like Amaruka.
5. The author-name 'Nāthakumāra' evidently refers to a different poet, as a large number of verses over that name appearing in the anthologies has nothing to do with those of our poet; and the one *J.H.* verse found over the name 'Nāthakumāra' in the *Sūktimuktāvali* is due to the confusion caused by the common part of the two names, 'Kumāra'.
6. As regards readings,
   (a) the anthologies themselves disclose differences in their readings:
   (b) there are only two verses for which there is complete agreement of readings between anthologies and manuscripts;
   (c) The anthologies have readings not found in MT. or L. or even in N. and H. and
   (d) it is impossible to establish any definite relation between any of the anthologies and any of the manuscripts here used.

A complete table of verses cited in the anthologies together with correspondences and differences with the manuscripts and printed text of the *J.H.* is given below to facilitate reference.

B. Commentaries on the Amarakośa.

As mentioned already while considering the question of Kumāradāsa's date, commentators on the *Amarakośa* show some acquaintance with him and his poem. They classify him along with great poets who have established the usage of certain word-forms. They recognise him as an authority and quote some of his lines as illustrations in their commentaries. Here, we shall consider the nature of these citations and the information that they can give us with regard to the poet and the text of his poem.

Altogether we have five quotations with the name 'Kumāradāsa' or *J.H.* in these commentaries. While all these five are found quoted in the *Padacandrikā* of Rāyamakuṭamaṇi,[1] the other commentaries cite only some of them. Out of these, only three can be traced in the available manuscripts of the poem. The other two, though they bear much similarity to the verses in the 17th canto of the *J.H.*, are not to be found in any of the available manuscripts. The first of these two runs thus:

> अथोडुबन्धुश्च भयङ्करे करे
> महोषधीनष्टकरांशुभे शुभे । इति जानकीहरणयमकात् ।[2]

This line is cited in the *Ṭīkāsarvasva* of Sarvānanda[3] also, but it gives different and better readings:

> अथो बबन्धुश्च भयंङ्करे करे महोपधीरुष्णकरांशुभे शुभे ।
> इति जानकीहरणे तालव्योंऽशु: ।।[4]

The second one not found in the manuscripts of the *J.H.* and quoted in the *Padacandrikā* of Rāyamukuṭa and in the *Kāmadhenu* of Subhūticandra,[5] runs thus, the former quoting a

1. A manuscript of Rāyamukuṭamaṇi's *Padacandirkā* preserved in the Adyar Library, MS. No. 38, I, 4.

2. *Ibid.* Vol I, p. 200.

3. *Nāmalingānuśāsana* of Amarasimha with the commentary, *Ṭīkāsarvasva* of Sarvānanda, Ed. by T. Ganapathy Sastry, T.S.S. No.

4. *Ibid.* Part I, p. 73.

5. A manuscript of Subhūticandra's *Kāmadhenu* preserved in the Madras Oriental Manuscripts Library, MS No. R. 2933.

Pāda and the latter the whole Ardha; *Padacandrikā*:

रविर्मनाग्दर्शितवासरस्सरः । इति जानकीहरणबद्धः ।[1]

Amarakośaṭīkā

विबोधयामास समन्ततस्ततो

रविं मनाग्दर्शितवासरस्सरः । इति जानकीहरणश्च ।।[2]

The third quotation which appears over the name of Kumāradāsa both in the *Padacandrikā* as well as in the *Amarakośaṭīkā* of Vidyāvinoda Nārāyaṇa[3] is found in the 9th canto of the *J.H.* These two commentaries have a small difference in the reading of this citation.

Padacandrikā reads:

रवः प्रगल्भाहतभेरिसंभवः

प्रकाशयामास समन्ततस्ततः । इति कुमारदासः ।[4]

Vidyāvinoda Nārāyaṇa gives it thus:

रवाः प्रगल्भाहतभेरीसंभवाः । इति कुमारदासः ।[5]

The reading of this line in the available manuscripts of the *J.H.* is in agreement with the reading given in the *Padacandrikā*.

The last two quotations of Kumāradāsa found in the *Padacandrikā* are from the 11th canto of the *J.H.* One of them is common to all the commentaries. The *Padacandrikā* quotes it in elucidation of the word Dhūsara', ईषत्पाडुरस्तु धूसरः and it runs thus:

महिषधूसरितस्सरितस्तट इति जानकीहरणम्[6]

The same citation is made in the same context by Subhūti-

1. *Padacandrikā*, Vol. I, pp. 207, 208.

2. *Kāmadhenu*, p. 45.

3. A manuscript of the *Amarakośaṭīkā* by Vidyāvinoda Nārāyaṇa preserved in the Govt. Oriental Manuscripts Library, Madras, MS. No. R. 3645.

4. *Padacandrikā*, Vol. I, p. 323.

5. *Amarakośaṭīkā*, Vol. I, p. 125.

6. *Padacandrikā*, Vol 1, p. 274.

candra also in the *Kāmadhenu*[1]. The only difference between these two is that the latter reads 'taṭam', neuter, while the *Padacandrikā* reads 'taṭaḥ', masculine. In the *Amarakośaṭīkā* of Vidyāvinoda Nārāyana, we have the same reading[2] as in the *Kāmadhenu*; but it has 'sarittaṭaḥ' instead of 'saritastaṭaḥ' which is most probably the mistake of the copyist. Sarvānanda's commentary also makes this quotation, but it gives the whole half, though the additional quarter quoted is corrupt.

तथा च जानकीहरणे 'महिषधूसरितस्सरितस्तटः
परिगतो विषदा विषदापितः' । इति ।[3]

The last citation that is given only in the *Padacandrikā* is also from the 11th canto of *J.H.* This citation is not complete,since the original manuscript is damaged in that portion. The citation is to illustrate the various usages of the word 'jyeṣṭha'. The line quoted from Kumāradāsa has the word 'jyeṣṭha' used in Śleṣa to mean both the elder brother and the month called 'Jyeṣṭha'. It is found in this manuscript thus:

'प्रणाशो......त्रस्य प्रसभमजनि ज्येष्ठविरहः' इति कुमार..... ।

This is the 96th verse in the 11th canto of the *J.H.* which reads thus:

प्रणाशो मित्रस्य प्रसभमजनि ज्येष्ठविरहः[4]

In the commentary on the *Amarakośa*, we find the name of the author mutilated. But it is clear that our poet is meant.

We have in these commentaries citations over the name of both Kumāradāsa and *J.H.* which can be classified under two heads, namely those that can be traced in the available manuscripts of the *J.H.* and those that are not to be found in them. In both these categories we have citations attributed to Kumāradāsa and his work. The same commentary gives lines over the name of Kumāradāsa which come under both the categories. The readings given in them are in general agreement with those in the manuscripts of the *J.H.*

1. महिषधूसरितस्सरितस्तटमिति जानकीहरणे यमकम् ।
Kāmadhenu, Vol. I p. 83.
2. *Amarakośaṭikā*, Vol I, p. 104.
3. *Ṭikāsarvasva*, Part I. p. 110.
4. *Padacandrikā*, Vol. I. p. 230.
5. *J.H.* XII-96.

C. Alaṅkāra Writers.

We have already mentioned in the chapter on the date of Kumāradāsa that he is known to the Alaṅkāra writers like Rājaśekhara and Bhoja. While Rājaśekhara does not quote any verse from the *J.H.* in his works so far available, Bhoja and Hemacandra, his two successors, cite passages from Kumāradāsa's *J.H.* in their works. In all the relevant contexts in the *Śṛṅgāraprakāśa*,[1] (*Śr. Pra*) Bhoja refers to the *J.H.* as one of the standard works illustrative of the many aspects of the *Mahākāvya* in its accepted form. In the matter of description of the hero, he mentions the *J.H.* along with the *Raghuvaṁśa*, *Rāvaṇavijaya* and *Haravijaya*; and with regard to the characterisation of the heroine, he mentions it along with *Kumārasambhava*, *Mālatīmādhava* etc.[2] Thirdly, he refers to the *J.H.* along with the Kumārasambhava as a poem where the Ratotsava is dealt with *specially*.[3]

Apart from these references, Bhoja quotes some verses from the *J.H.* both in his *Sarasvatīkaṇṭhābharaṇa*[4] (*SKĀ.*) and in his *Śr. Pra.* In the latter we have altogether six verses quoted from the *J.H.* Out of these, two are quoted in the *SKĀ.* also. The authorship is mentioned in the case of these verses. From the 1st canto of the *J.H.* we have two verses. Due to the lacuna in the manuscript, only the latter half of the first verse is preserved. It reads thus :

इतीव जङ्घायुगलं तदीयं चक्रे तुलाकोट्यधिरोहणानि ।।[5]

1. Govt. Oriental Manuscripts Library, Madras] MS. No. R. 3252, Vols. I to IV.

2. नायकवर्णनं यथा—हरविजय रावणविजय **जानकीहरण** रघुवंशादौ।···
नायिकावर्णनं यथा—कुवलयाश्वचरितकुमारसंभव **जानकीहरण**······
Ibid, Vol. II, p. 339.

3. महाप्रबन्धेषु रतोत्सवोऽपि द्विधा—सामान्यतो विशेषतश्च।······
विशेषतो यथा—कुमारसंभवे **जानकीहरणे** चेति ।
Ibid, Vol. II, p. 441.

4. *Sarasvatīkaṇṭhābharaṇa*, Kāvyamāla 95, Bombay (1925).

5. *Śr.Pra.*, Vol. I, p. 346.

This verse is quoted in the *Subhāṣitāvai*, and the *Sūkṭimuktāvali*. The reading given by Bhoja agrees, as far as it goes, with the reading of the *Subhāsitāvali* and the manuscripts of the *J.H.*[1] The second quotation is also from the 1st canto of the *J.H.* This is quoted also in the *SKĀ*. The citation is in connection with the flaw (*Doṣa*) of the sentence (*Vākya*) called *Vyākīrṇa* or disorder of words, ceasing to be a flaw in some sentences. In both the works he quotes a verse from the *J.H.* under the same *Kārikā* which reads thus :[1]

पदानां व्युत्क्रमो यत्र क्रमेण व्युत्क्रमेण वा ।
तद्व्याकीर्णं विदुस्तस्य न दोषः कोऽपि तद्यथा ॥
जुगुप्सत स्मैनमदुष्टभावं मैवं भवानक्षतसाधुवृत्तः ।
इतीव वाचो निगृहीतकण्ठैः प्राणैररुध्यन्त महर्षिसूनोः ॥

अत्र 'मा स्म जुगुप्सत' इति वक्तव्ये "जुगुप्सतस्मैनमदुष्टभावं मैवम्" इति पदव्यतिक्रमस्य 'व्यस्तेपीच्छन्ति केचित्' इति लुङ्लङोर्विशेषलक्षणत्वाद् गुणत्वम्॥

This is the 84th verse in the first canto of the *J.H.* where the hermit boy hit by the arrow of Daśaratha, after finding fault with the latter for his rash action, sinks to death. The reading given by Bhoja in both his works agree with the manuscripts of the *J.H.*, excepting for very minor differences. We have in the MT. 'Mainam' and 'Vṛttam' for 'Maivam' and 'Vṛttaḥ' in the second pāda. Bhoja's quotations have marked differences with the printed editions of the *J.H.*

The next quotation that Bhoja gives is of special significance as it is not to be found in the MT manuscript or in the printed editions of Nandargikar and Haridasa Sastri and appears as an additional verse in the London ms., just after the 86th verse in the 8th canto. This verse is quoted in the *SKĀ*. also, with whose help we can fill up a gap in the introductory remarks here in the *ŚṛPra*. It appears under the *Sāmyālaṅkāra* under the subdivision *Upamānāpakarṣa* :[3]

1, *J.H.* I. 28.
2. *ŚKĀ*. Pariccheda 1, p. 92.
   Śr.Pra. Vol II, p. 230.
3. *Śr.Pra.*, Vol. II, p. 335.
   SKĀ, Pariccheda IV, pp. 371, 372.

अन्यतो नय मुहूर्तमाननं चन्द्र एष सरले कलामयः।
मा कदाचन कपोलयोर्मलं संक्रमय्य समतां[1] नयिष्यति[2] ॥

The reading of this verse agrees with that of the London ms. As far as the quotations from the *J.H.* in other works are concerned, this is the only verse which is from among the extra verses of the London ms. of the poem. The verse is cited to show how an object of comparison is depicted as inferior to the subject compared.

The third verse which Bhoja quotes in both his works is from the 10th canto of the *J.H.*[3] In the *SKĀ* he quotes it under the heading 'अर्थगुणसंप्रयोगात् कनिष्ठो यथा'[4] and in the *Śṛpra.* it appears under 'Anugama'[5] or continuity of the bhāva called 'harṣa', The verse is in complete agreement with the readings found in the available manuscripts of the *J.H.*

Bhoja cites two verses from the 16th canto of the *J.H.* which deal with the heroine reproaching her lady-messenger for having illicit relation with the lover of her mistress. These are valuable as, according to the evidence already set forth by us in the earlier section on the anthologies, extracts from the portion beyond the 12th canto are scarcely made by later writers. The first one he quotes under the heading 'हिंसाविशेषो वैपरीत्यं यथा'[6] and the verse as given by him reads thus :

दशनपदमतिस्फुटं विभाति, स्फुरति तनुः, श्रमवारिसिक्तमास्यम्।
अवितथमभिधत्स्व कामिनि त्वां कुटिलगतिर्ननु दृष्टवान् भुजङ्गः[7] ॥

1. *ŚṛPra. Nayatām* ; evidently a corruption.
2. London ms. *Gamiṣyati.*
3. एकस्मिन् शयने मया मयसुतामालिङ्ग्य निद्रालसा-
मुन्निद्रं शयितेन मच्चरणयोः संवाहनव्यापृता
पादाग्रेण तिलोत्तमास्तनतटे सस्नेहमापीडिता
हर्षावेगसमर्पितानि पुलकान्यद्यापि नो मुञ्चति ॥

J.H. X, 86.

4. *SKĀ*. Pariccheda V, p. 590.
5. *ŚṛPra.* Vol. III, p. 35.
6. *Ibid*, Vol. IV, p. 809.
7. The last foot of this verse as re-constructed by us in the edition of this Chapter reads thus : कुटिलगतिर्ननु दष्टवान् भुजङ्गः।

J.H., XVI, 43.

The reading as given in this quotation is in agreement with the London ms. reading. The second verse from the same canto appears under the heading 'अवगमविशेषोऽपि परामर्शं यथा ।.'[1] This is also quoted from the same context. The verse as given here has got some slight differences with both MT. and the London manuscript and it reads thus :

मधुकुसुमविलेपनादि भागग्रहणविदर्शितसौहृदस्य वृत्या ।
अयमपि च सखि स्वयं वृतस्ते प्रियपरिभोगसुखस्य संविभागः ।।[2]

The next Alaṅkāra writer who quotes from the *J.H.* is Hemacandra, author of the *Kāvyānuśāsana*.[3] He too refers to the *J.H.* for its description of the hero and heroine as well as for the special treatment of the *Ratotsava*,[4] all these references being taken from the *Śr.Pra.* An additional verse of interest that Hemacandra quotes is to be found in his treatment of the indebtedness of later poets to their predecessors :

पुराणप्रतिभेद एव इतिहासः । यथा––

न स संकुचितः पन्था येन वाली हतो गतः ।
समये तिष्ठ सुग्रीव मा वालिपथमन्वगाः ।।[5]

Vāl. Kiṣk., 34-18.

तन्नैपुणं यथा––

मदं नवैश्वर्यबलेन लम्भितं विसृज्य पूर्वः समयो विमृश्यताम् ।
जगज्जिघत्सातुरकण्ठपद्धतिः न वालिनैवाहिततृप्तिरन्तकः ।।

J.H., XII, 36.

1. *ŚṛPra.* Vol. IV, p. 811.
2. The reading of this verse as re-constructed by us varies only in the second *pāda* where it gives 'सौहृदय्यवृत्त्या' (*J.H.*, XVI, 44) for 'सौहृदस्यवृत्त्या ।'
3. *Kāvyānuśāsana* of Hemacandra, *Kāvyamālā* 70 ; also ed. by Rasiklal C. Parikh, Sri Mahavira Jaina Vidyalaya, Bombay (1938).
4. *Ibid.* Ch. VIII, pp. 458, 459.
5. *Ibid.* Ch. I, p. 9.

The reading given here agrees more with the London ms. though it differs even from this.

Thus the Alaṅkāra writers Bhoja and Hemacandra, quote altogether seven verses from the *J.H.* out of which two are from the 1st canto, one each from cantos VIII, X, and XII and two from the XVIth. One verse (canto VIII) is to be found only among the extra verses in the London and Adyar mss., and generally speaking, the readings of these quotations are more in agreement with the London and Adyar mss. Here too we do not find any quotations beyond the 16th canto of the *J.H.*

D. *Jānāśrayī Chandoviciti.*

In the prosody work called *Jānāśrayī Chandoviciti*[1], the importance of which in deciding the date of Kumāradāsa has already been discussed, we have three quotations from *J.H.* In the 4th chapter of this treatise, while dealing with the particular metre called *Indramālā* which is a combination of *Indravajrā* and *Upendravajrā*, the author cites three verses from the 1st canto of the *J.H.* The first one reads thus :[2]

इयत्पृथुत्वं कृशदेहयष्टेर्नितम्बचक्रस्य परं प्रमाणम् ।
इतीव बद्धा रशनागुणेन श्रोणी पुनर्वृद्धिनिषेधतोऽस्याः ॥[3]

The reading given here bears a few differences with the readings given in the MT. and L. while it differs widely from the printed texts of Nandargikar and Haridasa Sastri.

1. *Jānāśravyī Chandoviciti* TSS. 1969.
   Jānāśrayi Chandoviciti. Also M. Ramakrishna Kavi, Sri Venkateswara Oriental Series.
2. *TSS.* Edn., Ch. IV, p. 40.
3. MT., L.- 1st pāda यष्टया for यष्टेः ।
   N., H.-1st & 2nd pada तथाहृतं तस्य तया पृथुत्वं
   यथाभवन्मध्यमतिक्षयिष्णु ।
   MT., N., H.,-3rd pāda इतीव बद्ध्वा for इतीव बद्धा
   reads इतीव नद्धा

In the same chapter under the same *sūtra* the *Jānāśrayī* quotes from *J.H.* as an illustration for another variety of Indramālā[1]. It reads thus :

विविक्षुरन्तः[2] सरसीमलङ्घयामासाद्य हंसः समुदीक्ष्य वप्रम् ।
सस्मार नूनं दृढकौञ्चकुञ्जभागच्छिदो भार्गवमार्गणस्य ।।[3]

It differs from the manuscripts and the printed editions all of which read this verse without any mutual variation.

The next verse from the *J.H.* is also to be found in the same context and it reads thus :[4]

आसीदयं चन्द्रमसो विशेषस्त्वद्वक्त्रचन्द्रस्य च भासुरस्य ।
बभार पूर्वः सकलङ्कमङ्गं तस्यैव नेत्रद्वितयं द्वितीयम् ।।

The reading here varies more with the printed editions than with the mss. available.

E. *Vyākaraṇa Works.*

1. *Gaṇaratnamahodadhi.*

In Vardhamāna's *Gaṇaratanamahodadhi* of 1140 A.D.[5], we have one quotation from the *J.H.* The name of the author is given as Kumārila[6] or Kumārala.[7] The quotation as given there reads :[8]

संपिण्डितात्मावयवा उदीयुः पद्मा नवाः कण्टकितोर्ध्वदण्डाः ।
अन्तर्जलावासविवृद्धशीतत्रस्ता वसन्तातपकाम्ययेव ।।

1. TSS. Ch. IV, p. 40.
2. The editors of the *Jānāsrayi* in the *T.S.S.* and Sri Venkateswara Oriental Series fail to identify this verse.
3. All the MSS. and the printed editions give- दिदृक्षु...मलङ्घयं यत्खात...।

MSS. alone reads in the third line क्रौञ्च for कौञ्च ।

4. 'Sakalam kuraṅgam is the correct reading.
5. S. K. Belvalkar, Systems of Sanskrit Grammar, Poona 1915, p. 54., Fn. 2.
6. Vardhamāna, *Gaṇaratnamahodadhi*, Ed. by Julius Eggeing, Sanskrit Text Society, London 1879, p. 112.
7. *Ibid.* p. 112, Fn. 8.
8. *Ibid.* p. 113.

This is the fourth verse in the 3rd canto of the *J.H.* All the available mss. of Kumāradāsa's poem give विरुद्ध for विवृद्ध in the third foot. Except for this, they agree with the readings given in the *Gaṇaratnamahodadhi*.

2. *Uṇādisūtrā Vṛtti.*

In Ujjvaladatta's *Uṇādisūtra Vṛtti* of *circa* 1250 A.D.,[1] we have two quotations from the *J.H.* The first one appears under the *Sūtra*. 'कृधूमदिभ्यः कित्' (III-73).[2] The quotation is with reference to the word 'Dhūsara' and is already noticed as being found in all the commentaries on the *Amarakośa*. Ujjvaladatta gives it thus :

धूमर ईषत्पाण्डुरः । महिषधूसरितस्सरितस्तट इति

जानकीहरणे यमकम्

The reading given here is in agreement with the mss. readings of the *J.H.* (IX. 74).

The next quotation is given under the *Sutra* वंक्रयादयच (IV. 66)[3]. The quotation is given as follows :

भेरिर्वाद्यविशेषः । रवः प्रगल्भाहतभेरिसंभव इति कुमारः ।

This word 'Kumāra' has created a confusion with regard to the authorship of this line. Strangely this line has crept into the latter part of Kālidāsa's *Kumārasambhava* XIV-32, as a variant of the first pāda; and consequently scholars have used this citation in Ujjvaladatta for discussing the antiquity and authenticity of the sequel of the *Kumārasambhava* beyond the 8th canto.[4] The authors of the *Padacandrikā* and the *Amarakoṣaṭīkā* expressly give the name of the author of this

1. S.K. Belvalkar, Systems of Sanskrit Grammar, Poona 1915, p. 54.
2. *Uṇādisūtras* with the commentary of Ujjvaladatta, Ed. by Pandit J. Vidyasagara, Calcutta (187.), p. 121.
3. Ibid. p. 159
4. See S.K., *History of Sanskrit Literature*, p. 135, fn.

line as Kumāradāsa and we find the line in all the available mss. of the *J.H.* So it is needless to assume that this line has any reference to the sequel of the *Kumārasambhava* or has any value for the discussion on the authorship or authenticity of the latter part of that poem.

KUMĀRADĀSA AND VĀLMĪKI

Vālmīki's Rāmāyaṇa, rightly designated *Ādi Kāvya*, has been the inspiration for generations of poets and dramatists not only in Sanskrit but also in all other Indian languages. Apart from being the source from which they derived their themes, it served also as the primary model for poetic embellishments and artistic technique. Their originality would have brought in a few more details, their imagination would have worked a few more fancies, but these details and fancies were only the super-structures that they built over the foundations laid by the *Ādī kavi*. Poets of varied tastes, varied outlooks and having different methods of approach have uniformly found it as an inexhaustible source of inspiration. It is rightly stated in the text of the Rāmāyaṇa itself that it is *Param Kavīnām ādhāram* (Vāl., Bāl., IV-26), the greatest reservoir from which the poets drew.

Kumāradāsa is also one among the many classical poets who received their inspiration from Vālmīki. He not only chose the story of the Epic for his theme, but throughout his poem he also exhibited a close intimacy with the ancient poet. In this chapter, it shall be our endeavour to examine the nature and degree of Vālmīki's influence on this Ceylonese poet.

Before, however, dealing with the details of this influence, it would be legitimate to examine the question of the nature and identity of the particular text of Vālmīki's Rāmāyaṇa which Kumāradāsa had before him. With regard to the main theme and some minor details, there are deviations in the different recensions of the Epic. Allowing himself the freedom that a poet always enjoys, Kumāradāsa has introduced some changes of his own and omissions in the story proper, to shape the theme for his poem and these, we shall discuss later. Here we shall consider which of the different recensions of the epic, the Southern[1], the Eastern[2], and the North-western[3], is followed by Kumāradāsa in developing the theme. There are at least two places in his poem which may be used to determine this question. Firstly, the episode of Kālanemi which is absent from the Southern recension but is found in the Eastern and the North-western, is mentioned by our poet in the opening verse of the 19th canto. In Gorresio's[4] edition as well as in the North-western, we have a long canto devoted to this episode.[5] And this episode is referred to by Kumāradāsa thus :

अथारिणा वर्त्मनि कालनेमिना रयादयश्चक्रनिभेन निर्हृतः ।
कथञ्चिदेनं विनिगृह्य मारुतिः समुद्वहन् भूधरशृङ्गमाययौ ।।

Secondly, an incident which is to be found only in the Eastern recension is that Mātali advised Rāma about the method of killing Rāvaṇa. Kumāradāsa says that Mātali informed Rāma about the mortal point of Rāvaṇa and gave him the arrow sent by Indra which could pierce through the enemy's armour.[6] Neither of these two details is found mentioned in the Southern and North-western recensions of the *Rāmāyaṇa*. But in Gorresio's edition we find the authority for the former. But none of the recensions says that the *Brahmāstra* which Rāma aimed at his enemy was sent by Indra. The person from whom Rāma got it was Agastya and not Indra or Mātali.

With regard to Mātali informing Rāma about the mortal spot of the enemy, we have the following verse in Gorresio's edition :

1. *Rāmāyana*, Ed. by T.R. Krishnacharya, Kumbhakonam.
2. *Rāmāyana*, Ed. by G. Gorresio, Parigi, 1844.
3. The Rāmāyna of Vālmiki, Ed. by Vishva Bandhu Sastri M.A., M.O.L., Lahore 1928.
4. Gorressio's *Ramāyana*, *Yudh.*, Canto 82, *Sl.*, 64 to 84, 143 to 184;
5. North-western Edition, *Yudh.*, Canto 81, *Sl.*, 51 to 102.

6. अथो हिताय प्रहितं मरुत्वता सुरद्विषो मर्म निगद्य मातलिः ।
नरेन्द्रपुत्राय तनुत्रभेदिनं विचित्रपत्त्रं वितताऱ पत्त्रिणम् ।।

(*J.H.*, XIX-7)

उत्तमाङ्गं न चैतस्य च्छेत्तव्यं राघव त्वया ।
नैष मूर्ध्नि प्रभो वध्यः वध्य एष हि मर्मसु ॥[1]

A consideration of these two contexts would suggest Kumāradāsa's acquaintance, not with the Southern recension, but with the other two, especially the Eastern. It may also be added here that the narration of the *Kākāsura*-episode is made by Kumāradāsa, even as by Kālidāsa, in its proper chronological place and this accords not with the Southern recension but with the other two. However, it is not easy to state categorically that Kumāradāsa was solely basing himself on the Eastern recension, for, as would be clear from the table of parallel passages given at a further stage in this section, there are certain expressions in Kumāradāsa which agree clearly with those in the corresponding contexts in the Southern recension. Elsewhere we have touched upon Kumāradāsa's knoweldge of South India. Because of contiguity South Indian contacts would be most natural. This means that Kumāradāsa was acquainted with all the three recensions of the Epic. Apart from the question of the recensions of the Rāmāyaṇa used by Kumāradāsa, the fact that the Rāmāyaṇa was so well known in Ceylon at the time of our poet is itself highly significant for a student of the Epic and its history.

Throughout his poem, Kumāradāsa echoes the ideas and expressions of Vālmīki. In the very first canto, while describing Daśaratha's hunting expedition and the tragic death of the sage-boy, he adopts many ideas and expressions of Vālmīki. The ancient poet has so perfectly developed the sentiment of *karuṇa* in this context, that it is inevitable that later poets should copy him. When Daśaratha who had shot down the boy under a mistake, approaches him and stands trembling in fear on seeing the crime committed by him, the unfortunate boy addresses him in Vālmīki :

एकेन खलु बाणेन मर्मण्यभिहते मयि ।
द्वावन्धौ निहतौ वृद्धौ माता जनयिता च मे ॥[2]

1. Gorresio's *Rāmāyana*, Canto 92, Sl., 41, p. 490.
2. Vālmīki, *Ayodhyā Kāṇḍa*, 63-41.

This same idea is put by Kumāradāsa in the following words :

फकं त्वया साधयतापि लक्ष्यं नीतं विनाशं त्रितयं निरागः ।
मच्चक्षुषा कल्पितदृष्टिकृत्यौ वृद्धौ वने मे पितरावहं च ।।

(*J. H.* I-78)

Almost every verse of Valmiki in this context has got a corresponding verse in Kumāradāsa. The following table pertaining to this particular episode may be useful for a fuller appreciation of the similarity here :[1]

Kumāradasa

एकं त्वया साधयतापि लक्ष्यं
नीतं विनाशं त्रितयं निरागः ।
मच्चक्षुषा कल्पितदृष्टिकृत्यौ
वृद्धौ वने मे पितरावहं च ।। I.76
वनेषु वासो मृगयूथमध्ये
क्रिया च वृद्धान्धजनस्य पोषः ।
वृत्तिश्च वन्यं फलमेषु दोषः
संभावितः को मयि घातहेतुः ।। I.77
जीर्णो जतुन्यासनिरुद्धरन्ध्रः
कुम्भश्च मौञ्जी तरुवल्कलं च ।
एतेषु यन्मां विनिहत्य गृह्यं
तद्गृह्यतामस्तु भवान् कृतार्थः ।। I.78
त्वया जरावेगजडीकृतस्य
वने विनाथस्य गुरुद्वयस्य ।
विचक्षुषोऽयं व्रतजीर्णमूर्तेः
भग्नः किमालम्बनदण्ड एकः ।। I. 75

Valmiki

एकेन खलु बाणेन मर्मण्यभिहते मयि ।
द्वावन्धौ निहतौ वृद्धौ माता जनयिता च मे ।। II. 63.40

1. Vālmiki *Rāmāyana*, Kumbhakonam Edn.

ऋषेर्हि न्यस्तदण्डस्य वने वन्येन जीवतः ।
कथं नु शस्त्रेण वधो मद्विधस्य विधीयते ॥ II, 63.28.
जटाभारधरस्यैव वल्कलाजिनवाससः ।
को वधेन ममार्थी स्यात् किं वास्यापकृतं मया ॥ II. 63.29
गतिस्त्वमगतीनां च चक्षुस्त्वं हीनचक्षुषाम् ।
समासक्तास्त्वयि प्राणाः किं त्वं नो नाभिभाषसे ॥ II. 64.10

There are some verses in Kumāradāsa which are almost the same as their counter-parts in the corresponding contexts in Vālmiki. A typical instance of this can be had in the 10th canto where he describes Bharata meeting Rāma in the forest.

भरतश्शोकसन्तप्तो राममादाय पादयोः ।
उक्त्वार्येति सकृद्दीनः पुनर्नोवाच किञ्चन ॥

(*J.H.*, X. 60)

A student who is familiar with both Vālmīki and Kumāradāsa cannot easily distinguish this from its corresponding verse in Vālmīki which runs thus :

दुःखाभितप्तो भरतो राजपुत्रो महाबलः ।
उक्त्वार्येति सकृद्दीनं पुनर्नोवाच किञ्चन ॥

(Vāl., Ayodhyā, Canto 99, Sl. 38)

The latter half of this verse, which deals with the state of Bharata, depicts so well the inexpressibility of his feelings that our poet could not improve on it nor could he avoid repeating it.

On certain other occasions Kumāradāsa borrows the ideas of Vālmīki but effects some improvements on them. For example we have Rāma's advice to Bharata to look after his mother Kaikeyī without any ill-feeling towards her, which Vālmīki expresses thus :

मातर रक्ष कैकेयीं मा रोषं कुरु तां प्रति[1]

1. Vāl., Ayodhyā, 112-27.

Later, in the end, Bharata reports to Rama that he obeyed this advice of his, when he says, "पूजिता मामिका माता".[1] Our poet wants to improve on this idea by making Rāma support his advice by a reasoning. Of course this reasoning he gets from the 14th canto of the *Raghavamśa*.[2] The skill of Kumāradāsa lies in the fact that he condenses both these ideas, one from Vālmīki and the other from Kālidāsa, into one simple statement which he too puts into the mouth of Rāma as an advice to Bharata which runs thus :

पूजनीया च सा देवी पत्युः सत्यानुपालिनी ।

(*J.H.*, X. 65)

Kaikeyī deserves the protection at the hands of Bharata not only because she is his mother but also because she was responsible for seeing that Daśaratha did not leave his path of truth.

Kumāradāsa freely uses Vālmīki's ideas and expressions not only during the narrative but even in his descriptive passages. Some aspects of Nature found expression in the *Rāmāyaṇa* are echoed in the work of our poet. While describing the closing of the rainy season, Vālmiki says :

सन्ध्यारागोत्थितैस्ताम्रैः अन्तेष्वधिकपाण्डरैः ।
स्निग्धैरभ्रपटच्छेदैः बद्धव्रणमिवाम्बरम् ।।

(Vāl., Kiṣk., 28, 5)

The following lines of Kumāradāsa will definitely remind one of the above verse of Vālmīki :

निराशस्योत्कस्य स्फुटति नवमेघस्य हृदये
रयादुद्यद्धारा असृज इव निर्भान्ति तडितः ।

(*J.H.*, XI 96)

In some other cases Vālmīki's ideas are exactly copied in the descriptions given by Kumāradāsa without being subjected to any change. The following passage in the descrip-

1. Vāl., Yuddh., 131. 2.

2. कृताञ्जलिस्तत्र यदम्ब सत्यान्नाभ्रश्यत स्वर्गफलाद्गुरुर्नः ।
तच्चिन्त्यमानं सुकृतं तवेति जहार लज्जां भरतस्य मातुः ।।

(*Raghu.*, XIV 16)

tion of the fight between Rāvaṇa and Jaṭāyus is as it is found in Vālmīki :

रणमवेक्ष्य विहङ्गपतेर्जगुः सपदि साधुवचः सुरकिन्नराः ।

(*J.H.*, XI. 17)

The corresponding verse in Vālmīki reads as :

साधु साध्विति भूतानि गृध्रराजमपूजयन् ।

(Vāl., Āraṇya., 51, 21)

In other occasions we find Kumāradāsa improving over the idea of Vālmīki. While Vālmīki describes the sky in the rainy season as crying out in agony due to its being struck by the whip in the form of lightnings, Kumāradāsa describes the clouds as huge elephants who are beaten with the fire-brand of lightning ; wild elephants when they come out of the forests and begin to roam about in the town are thus beaten with fire-brands.

अतिविमृज्य वनानि कृताटना मनुजलोकसमीपनिषेविणः ।
तडिदलातशतैरभिताडिताः वनगजा इव सस्वनुरम्बुदाः ।।

(*J.H.* XI-77)

which corresponds to the following verse in Vālmīki :

कशाभिरिव हैमीभिः विद्युद्भिरभिताडितम् ।
अन्तस्तनितनिर्घोषं सवेदनमिवाम्बरम् ।।

(Vāl., Kiṣk., 28., 11)

The fact that Kumāradāsa was a close student of Vālmīki can be further proved by his usage of some of the typical words and phrases of the latter in the same contexts in which they are used in the *Rāmāyaṇa*. When Rāma hesitates to kill Tāṭakā due to her being a woman, Viśvāmitra bids Rāma to leave off that consideration. That hesitation on the part of Rāma is termed as Ghṛṇā' by Vālmīki, when he says,

न हि ते स्त्रीवधकृते घृणा कार्या नरोत्तम ।

(Vāl., Bāla., 25. 18)

तस्मादेनां घृणां त्यक्त्वा जहि मच्छासनान्नृप ।

(Vāl., Bāla., 25-23)

अलं ते घृणया वीर पापैषा दुष्टचारिणी ।

(Vāl., Bāla., 26-24)

The same expression is used in this context in the *J.H.*

घृणिनं नृपतेरिदं वचस्तनयं वीक्ष्य जगौ कृतस्मयः।

(*J.H* IV. 64)

Some other memorable phrases of Vālmīki are also to be found used by Kumāradāsa; for example, *Puruṣasārajñaḥ* and *Anvaya*-varjitaḥ :

शूरं पुरुषसारज्ञं नीतौ पटुमलम्पटम्

(*J.H.*, X 34)

लोके पुरुषसारज्ञः साधुरेको विनिर्मितः

(Vāl., Ayodh., I-18)

नोच्चैः पदं लम्भनीयो गुण्योऽप्यन्वयवर्जितः ।

(*J.H.*; X, 35)

अमार्गेणागतां लक्ष्मीं प्राप्येवान्वयवर्जितः ।

(Vāl., Āraṇya., VIII. 8)

Thus we see that Kumāradāsa adopts Vālmtki's ideas, expressions and even individual words. The following additional parallels may also be cited to show how Kumāradāsa was often keeping himself close to Vālmiki :

Kumaradasa

1. निनाय सह यत्नेन प्रस्थितं हरिणव्रजम् ।
   स्वयं संवर्धितं रुद्ध्वा बाष्पपूरितलोचनौ । VI. 6

2. द्वयेनादौ त्रिवर्गस्य साम्यं तत् क्व गतं चिरम् ।
   सहाद्य वयसो वृद्धया कच्चिद्धर्मोऽपि वर्धते ।। VI. 43

3. इति पपात वितन्वति पौरुषं
   परुषवह्निशिखोद्गमनिष्ठुरम् ।
   रिपुदृढाङ्कविदारिणि वालिनि
   क्षितिपनन्दनबाणमहाशनिः ।। XI. 39

4. मुहुरुदग्रपयोदमतङ्गज-
   श्रवणचामरभावमुपेतयः ·

गगनसागरशङ्खवपुःश्रिया
विरचितं प्रमदेन बलाकया ।। XI. 52

4. विमलवारि निपीय नदीगतं
सलिलभारनिरन्तरितोदरः ।
क्लममिवाभिवहन्नतिपानजं
गिरितटे निषसाद पयोधरः ।। XI. 56

5. परस्पराघातनिवृत्तवृत्ति तत्
बलं च तस्थौ निहितेक्षणं तयोः ।। XIX.5

6. मुखैरसक्तं दशभिर्दशाननो
नदन् तडित्सन्निभहेमभूषणः ।
युगान्तमेघप्रतिमो महेषुभिः
ततान धाराभिरिवान्तरं दिवः ।। XIX. 9

7. उवाह रूपस्य विरूपचक्षुषः (श्रियम्) XIX. 22

Vālmiki

1. मृगपक्षिगणाश्चैव सिद्धाश्रमनिवासिनः ।
अनुजग्मुर्महात्मानं विश्वामित्रं महामुनिम् ।। Bala. 31-18

2. कच्चिदर्थं च धर्मं च कामं च जयतां वर ।
विभज्य काले कालज्ञ सर्वान् भरत सेवसे ।। Ayodhya. 100-63

3. मुक्तस्तु वज्रनिर्घोषः
प्रदीप्ताशनिसन्निभः ।
राघवेण महाबाणो
बालिवक्षसि पातितः ।। Kiskindha. 16-35

4. तडित्पताकाभिरलङ्कृतानाम्
उदीर्णगम्भीरमहारवाणाम् ।
विभान्ति रूपाणि बलाहकानां
रणोद्यतानामिव वारणानाम् ।। Kiṣkindhā. 24-31
समुद्वहन्तः सलिलातिभारं
बलाकिनो वारिधरा नदन्तः ।
महत्सु शृङ्गेषु महीधराणां
विश्रम्य विश्रम्य पुनः प्रयान्ति । Kiṣkindhā 28-22

5. तस्थुः प्रेक्ष्य च संग्रामं नाभिजघ्नुः परस्परम् । Yuddha 109.4
पश्यतां विस्मिताक्षाणां सैन्यं चित्रमिवाबभौ । Yuddha 109.5

6. तान् दृष्ट्वा रावणश्चक्रे स्वशरैः खं निरन्तरम् ।
ततस्ताभ्यां प्रयुक्तेन शरवर्षेण भास्वता ।

7. शरबद्धमिवाभाति द्वितीयं भास्वदम्बरम् ॥ Yuddha 109.22-23
बभूव रूपं रामस्य रुद्रस्येव पिनाकिनः Āraṇya 24.25

Deviations fram Vālmīkı

Generally speaking, Kumāradāsa closely follows Vālmīki in the matter of the story. Occasionally he deviates from his source. These deviations are either on the lines of his favourite predecessor Kālidāsa in his *Raghuvaṁśa* or in his original way. Some of them are due to poetic necessities or his eagerness to display some originality. Such differences in the story with Vālmīki's *Rāmāyaṇa* can be broadly classified under two heads: One, deviations that alter to some extent the details of the narrative and the other, those that affect the fundamental skeleton of the story. The following are some of the striking differences between Kumāradāsa and Vālmīki.

According to Vālmīki, in the *Putrakāmeṣṭi* sacrifice, the Devas assemble to receive their oblations and then, they report to Brahmā their miseries at the hands of Rāvaṇa. Viṣṇu appears there itself and promises to incarnate as Rāma.[1] But in the *JH.* the Devas go to the Milky Ocean with Brahmā and pray to Viṣṇu to relieve them of their miseries which Viṣṇu undertakes to do. This deviation has a precedent in Kālidāsa.[2]

In Vālmīki's *Rāmāyaṇa* Daśaratha is much perturbed on hearing the request of Viśvāmitra to send Rāma along

1. Vālmīki, Bāla 15 :
ततः समेत्य यथान्यायं तस्मिन् सदसि देवताः ।
अब्रुवन् लोककर्तारं ब्रह्माणं ववनं महत् ॥

2. तस्मिन्नवसरे देवाः पौलस्त्योपप्लुता हरिम् ।
अभिजग्मुर्निदाघार्ताः च्छायावृक्षमिवाध्वगाः ॥
(*Raghu.*, X 5)

with him. Vālmīki puts him in a most unenviable position when his duty to oblige a sage is depicted as in direct conflict with his paternal love.[1] Daśaratha offers many alternative suggestions to appease Viśvāmitra. Lastly Vasiṣṭha had to interfere and induce the king to part with his son. Kumāradāsa, on the other hand, says that Daśaratha immediately agrees to the wishes of the sage without any hesitation and calls for his son. This is followed by a long advice by the father on the duties of a *kṣatriya* and on the importance of fame for a king. The weak and indecisive Daśaratha of Vālmīki is transformed into a courageous monarch who is an inspirer to his young son. The meek and timid behaviour of Vālmīki's Daśaratha later justifies his helplessness before his hard-hearted Queen who is obstinate in her demand for the pound of flesh. We do not find these aspects in Kumāradāsa's characterisation of Daśaratha; but we see in the *JH.* the courage and chivalry which our poet has imparted to this king. While even Kālidāsa, in this context, has a word[2] referring to the great difficulty with which Daśaratha had begotten the children, Kumāradāsa boldly eschews all suggestions of weakness on the part of the King.

The narration of the episode of his killing the *Munikumāra* by mistake in the course of his hunt, which, Daśaratha gives to Kausalyā in a reminiscent mood, on the eve of his death in the original epic,[3] is given here by Kumāradāsa in its natural chronological order[4] and here he has followed his illustrious predecessor, Kālidāsa.[5]

Another major deviation in the story is that Kumāradāsa never mentions the golden deer that is coveted by Sītā. According to Vālmīki, Subāhu and other Rākṣasas excepting Mārīca are killed by Rāma during Viśvāmitra's sacrifice, and later this Mārīca, on the threat of Rāvaṇa, assumes the form of a golden deer and takes away Rāma into the forest. In

1. Vālmīki, Bāla., Canto 20.
2. कृच्छ्रलब्धमपि लब्धवर्णभाक्

—Kālidāsa, *Raghu.*, XI.2

3. Vāl., Ayodhyā, Cantos, 63-64.
4. *JH.* I. 74 to 90.
5. Kālidāsa, *Raghu.*, IX. 72-82.

the same form he dies and while dying he cries out in such a way that Lakṣmaṇa also is separated from Sītā and thus enables Rāvaṇa to achieve his purpose. But Kumāradāsa, even in the beginning, says that Mārīca and Subāhu were both killed during the sacrifice of Viśvāmitra :

ततो मरुत्पावकशस्त्रनिर्धुतप्रदग्धमारीचसुबाहुविग्रहम् ।

(*JH*. V. 54)

Later in the context of Rāvaṇa abducting Sītā, we have the following verse reading in a slightly different manner in the two Mss. (*JH*, X. 77).

N.&H. : मृगयाहृतराजन्यो वर्णलिङ्गी निशाचरः ।
उग्ररूपो निजं घोरं रूपं प्रादुरबीभरत् ॥

MT. : मृगव्येण हृते रामे वर्णी लिङ्गी निशाचरः ।
उग्ररूपो निजं रूपं घोरं प्रादुरबीभरत् ॥

L. : मृगव्याहृतराजन्ये वर्णिलिङ्गी निशाचरः ।
उग्ररूपो निजं रूपं घोरं प्रादुरबीभरत् ॥

Interpreting this verse in the light of the earlier statement of Mārīca also having been finished off at the time of Viśvāmitra's sacrifice, we have to assume that Kumāradāsa eschews completely the episode of the golden deer, which at one stroke helps the poet to save the character of Mārīca on the one hand and removes the provocation for the unseemly outburst of Sītā against Lakṣmaṇa on the other. It should be particularly noted that in this canto the poet rushes over the whole story; and the very needs of the extreme brevity that he adopts here, are mainly responsible for this deviation from the original in this context.

Apart from these major differences, Kumāradāsa deviates from Vālmīki on many other minor details. An imaginative poet like him does not naturally care to follow all the details in the original. An example of such a deviation can be seen when the poet describes Bharata's meeting with Rāma in the Citrakūṭa forest. Vālmīki says that Bharata saw his elder brother from a distance, ran up to him in great haste and prostrated before him even before reaching his feet.[1] But Kumāradāsa depicts Bharata as going to the hermitage of Rāma and announcing about his arrival thus :[2]

निर्घृणो राजघः कश्चित् संप्राप्त इति साघवे ।
उच्यतामिति तद्वाक्यं द्वारि शुश्राव राघवः ॥

JH. X. 58.

Since the poet is particularly aiming at great brevity in this canto, he could not elaborately deal with the intense feeling on either side in this context; but in a few lines he manages to depict the agony and self-reproach of Bharata where Bharata announces himself as the ungrateful, heartless murderer of the king. The line gives a brief but effective idea of Bharata's character.

Another such minor deviation is the creation of a new scene before Rāma's marriage wherein Rāma is depicted as meeting Sītā as soon as the bow was broken.[3] Vālmīki could not think of Janaka bringing about this meeting of the would-be couple before Daśaratha, the guardian of the boy, is intimated. This unofficial meeting is introduced by our poet just to introduce the idea of the two loving each other before marriage. In this the poet has evidently grafted to Mahākāvya the Pūrvānurāga technique followed in the dramas. It is important to note this, as later we find the author of the Tamil Rāmāyaṇa, Kambar, and the author of the Hindi Rāmāyaṇa, Tulsidas, adopting this feature.

Other minor differences that can be noticed between Kumāradāsa and Vālmīki are negligible, either because they do not considerably affect the narrative proper and hence are

1. निरीक्ष्य स मुहूर्तं तु ददर्श भरतो गुरुम् ।
उटजे राममासीनं जटामण्डलधारिणम् ॥

(Vāl., Ayodhyā., 99.25)

2. A similar announcement with some verbal similarities is to be found in the same context in the *Pratimānāṭaka* of Bhāsa (IV.5) :

निर्घृणश्च कृतघ्नश्च प्राकृतः प्रियसाहसः ।
भक्तिमानागतः कश्चित् कथं तिष्ठतु यात्विति ॥

3. *JH*. VII. 1 to 30

casual in their nature, or because they are necessary to cut short the story and hence relevant. For example, Vālmīki says that the bow that was broken by Rāma before his marriage was used by Śiva during Dakṣa's sacrifice.[1] But Kumāradāsa says that it was used by Śiva to destory the Tripuras.[2] In either case it is not an important matter as far as our narrative is concerned.

In Vālmīki's *Rāmāyaṇa*, Viśvāmitra quotes two instances where ladies had been killed to uphold *Dharma*. One is Indra killing the daughter of Virocana and the other is Paraśurāma killing his mother.[3] But Kumāradāsa quotes only the former.[4]

While entering into an alliance with Rāma, Sugrīva gives him two tests to re-assure himself with regard to Rāma's capacity to kill Vālin. One is to pierce the seven Sāla trees with a single arrow and the other to throw off the skeleton of Dundubhi.[5] But Kumāradāsa mentions only the *Sālabheda*.[6]

The story contained in the *Ayodhyākāṇḍa* and half of the *Āraṇya-kāṇḍa* in Vālmīki's *Rāmāyaṇa* is condensed to one chapter where Kumāradāsa makes a rapid survey of the whole portion. Naturally he leaves off many details in the middle. In the story contained in the latter half of the *Āraṇya-kāṇḍa*, he elaborately deals with the fight between Jaṭāyus and Rāvaṇa at the beginning of the eleventh canto. He makes a brief mention about the slaying of Kabandha while he totally omits the episode of Śabarī. With regard to the story contained in the *Sundara-kāṇḍa* of the original Epic, Kumāradāsa effects a major deviation. The whole narration of Hanumān's adventures is condensed in twenty verses and put

1. दक्षयज्ञवधे पूर्वं धनुरायम्य वीर्यवान् ।
रुद्रस्तु त्रिदशान् रोषात् सलीलमिदमब्रवीत् ।

(Vāl., Bāla., 66.9)

2. अदायि चैकं त्रिदशाधिपेन तत्
त्रिलोचनाय त्रिपुरं दिधक्षते ।

(*JH.*, IX. 36)

3. Vāl., Bāla., 25. 21, 22.
4. *JH.*, IV. 66.
5. Vāl., Kis., II. 74. 85.
6. *JH.*, XI. 26.

through the mouth of Hanumān himself towards the end of the thirteenth Canto.[1] Rāma going along with the monkey-army to the sea-shore, his anger towards the God of the seas and Vibhīṣaṇa's Śaraṇāgati are all compressed in the last verse of the thirteenth canto.[2]

It is in the narration of the story of the *Yuddhakāṇḍa* that we have the maximum cut in the events and episodes. Kumāradāsa omits many details connected with the battle, like Rāvaṇa sending Śuka and Sāraṇa as spies, the chopping of the head of a counterfeit Rāma by Vidyujjihva to frighten Sītā and the brief fight between Rāvaṇa and Sugrīva even before the actual battle. Mālyavān, according to Vālmīki, advises Rāvaṇa to make peace with Rāma as soon as the latter arrives in Laṅkā with his army.[3] But Kumāradāsa takes it to a later context just after Aṅgada's mission.[4] While in the Vālmīki *Rāmāyaṇa* Dhūmrākṣa, Vajradamṣṭra, Akampana and Prahasta are killed before Kumbhakarṇa's death, in the *JH* all these persons are taken together with those disposed off after Kumbhakarṇa's death, Prajaṅgha, Devāntaka, Narāntaka, Vidyujjihva, Mahāpārśva and Mahodara.[5] In the *Rāmāyaṇa* of Vālmīki, we have the killing of the Māyā Sītā which causes dejection even to Rāma. But Kumāradāsa does not mention this incident at all, nor does he make any mention of the Nikumbhilā sacrifice by Indrajit. The imparting of the *Āditya-hṛdaya mantra* to Rāma by Agastya is not mentioned by Kumāradāsa.

On the other hand Kumāradāsa has introduced some additions in accordance with the *Mahākāvya*-practice in the form of a long description of the evening and the sports of Rākṣasa couples on the eve of the battle (*JH.* XVI).

1. *JH.* XIII. 25 to 43.
2. *Ibid*, 45.
3. Vāl., Yuddha. 35, 6 to 38.
4. *JH.*, XV. 42 to 55.
5. *Ibid*, XVIII. 64, 65.

KUMĀRADĀSA AND KĀLIDĀSA

The historical value of the Sinhalese tradition on the contemporaneity of a Kālidāsa and a Kumāradāsa has already been discussed. In the same place it has also been pointed out that the author of the *JH.* came after the time of the great poet. Here it is proposed to set forth at some length the influence of Kālidāsa on our poet. In fact it will be clear as one examines this question of the influence of the other poets on Kumāradāsa, that Kumāradāsa stood in a peculiarly significant relation to Kālidāsa, and derived more from him than from anybody else.

In the *Sūktimuktāvali* of Jalhaṇa, it is well-known that a number of eulogies on earlier poets by Rajaśekhara are found extracted.[1] One of these, as already mentioned, gives the following verse with reference to Kumāradāsa's *JH.* and Kālidāsā's *Raghuvaṁśa*:—

जानकीहरणं कर्तुं रघुवंशे स्थिते सति ।
कविः कुमारदासश्च रावणश्च यदि क्षमः ।।

The significance of this verse for the question of the date and nativity of Kumāradāsa and his chronology with reference to Kālidāsa have already been discussed. The verse, however, being an appreciation and assessment of Kumāradāsā's poetry has a literary significance which may be pointed out here. When Kumāradāsa attempted to compose his poem on the theme of the *Rāmāyaṇa*, he had before him the masterpiece of Kālidāsa. It was indeed foolhardy on the part of the Ceylonese poet to have attempted a poem on this theme and Rājaśekhara adopting the device of paranomasia opines definitely that the eventual outcome was hardly praiseworthy. This, Rājaśekhara suggests by comparing the poet to Rāvaṇa and his disastrous abduction of Sītā (*Jānakīharaṇa*), when there was the powerful Raghu race (*Raghuvaṁśe sthite*) (in the

1. *Gaekwad's Oriental Series* LXXXII, p. 45.

person Rāma) to rescue Sītā and destroy Rāvaṇa. There is no doubt that Rājaśekhara's judgment is correct and the effort of Kumāradāsa in *Mahākāvya* is nowhere before that of the great poet. But the verse underlines also the fact that Kumāradāsa stood in a specific relation to Kālidāsa, namely that he had Kālidāsā's *Rāghuvaṁśa* before him as the ideal and assiduously imitated the eminent performance of the great poet and derived from him much material in the form of ideas, expressions and fancies. This can be seen from the following comparative study of the two poets.

The very theme and its execution in the *JH.* are almost in line with those of Kālidāsā's *Raghuvamśa.* The *Rāmāyaṇa*-part of the *Raghuvaṁśa* is almost imitated by Kumāradāsa. In the *JH.* we find a separate treatment of Daśaratha's life ending in his hunting expedition as in the *Raghuvaṁśa.* The description of Daśaratha's old age is also introduced as a prelude to the story of Rāma. But in this case Kumāradāsa is more elaborate than the author of the *Raghuvaṁśa.* The description of Rāma's marriage and his encounter with Paraśurāma are dealt with in the same way as in *Raghuvaṃśa.* The story contained in Vālmīki's *Āraṇya kāṇḍa* and *Ayodhyā kāṇḍa* is narrated very briefly by both alike. Even in this process of abbreviation, our poet closely follows the method of Kālidāsa. The elaborate treatment by Kumāradāsa of the story contained in Vālmīki's *Kiṣkindhā, Sundara* and *Yuddha kāṇḍas* is due to the needs of a poem, which unlike the *Raghuvaṁśa,* is wholly devoted to the story of the *Rāmāyaṇa.* As literary practice also required descriptive elaborations and the display of poetic skill in the form of *Śabda-citras,* Kumāradāsa had to lengthen out certain portions of the poem.

Even on such occasions when he becomes more elaborate than Kālidāsa, the descriptions that he introduces are mostly based on similar ones of Kālidāsa in different contexts, not only in the *Raghuvaṁśa* but in the *Kumārasambhava* also. For example the second and eighth cantos in the *JH.* dealing respectively with the plight of the Gods under the tyranny of the demons and the descriptions of *Sambhoga Śṛṅgāra* are based on their respective counterparts in *Kumārasambhava* ; that portion of the ninteenth canto in the *JH.* which describes

Maṇḍodarī's lamentation is mostly based on the *Rati-vilāpa* in the fourth canto of the *Kumārasambhava*. The tenth canto dealing with the *Rāmāyaṇa*-story upto the abduction of Sītā and the twentieth describing the return of Rāma on the *Puṣpaka-vimāna* are based by Kumāradāsa on the twelfth and thirteenth cantos of the *Raghuvaṁśa* respectively.

The theme of the Gods suffering under the reign of terror of Rāvaṇa is an echo of the sufferings of the same under Rāvaṇa in *Raghuvaṁśa* X, and under Tāraka in the second canto of the *Kumārasambhava*. The description of the Lord in the milky ocean has its counterpart in the tenth canto of *Raghuvaṁśa*. The prayer-portion of it in which the Gods propitiate Viṣṇu is a mixture of Kālidāsa's ideas contained in both *Raghuvaṁśa* and *Kumārasambhava*. The rest of the canto in which the Lord enquires of them about the cause of their coming and the Gods narrate their woes is completely in agreement with the corresponding portion in the *Kumārasambhava*.

The most striking similarity between the two poets is seen in the 8th canto of Kumāradāsa wherein he describes the love-sports of Rāma and Sītā. This canto has got many points in common with the eighth canto of the *Kumārasambhava* where the love-sports of Śiva and Pārvatī are described. The last verse of the seventh canto (VII. 61) in the *JH.* in which the subject-matter of the succeeding canto is introduced is definitely an imitation of the similar verse in *Kumārasambhava* (VII. 54). The whole idea of this verse shows deliberate imitation of Kālidāsa, and the poet too has not concealed this fact. As if desirous of recording his indebtedness to Kālidāsa and as if to draw the attention of the critical reader to a predecessor who has described the conjugal pleasures of a divine couple, he deliberately compares his hero and heroine with Śiva and Pārvatī (*Bhavaprabhāvo bhavanam viveśa*) and describe their amorous sports in canto VIII on the same lines as those in *Kumārasambhava* VIII. That the *Kumārasambhava* was throughout in the mind of the poet while he was writing this canto, is evident from the fact that he gives numerous allusions to Śiva and Pārvatī. Many words and ideas of Kālidāsa are to be found in this canto. Even the sequence of the phrases and ideas of the description here is the same as in *Kumārasambhava*. The bashfulness on the part of the lady, her overcoming it gradually, *rata*, *viparīta-rata*, fatigue, drinking, garden-sport and description of the sun-set-all these are dealt with in the same order as in *Kumārasambhava*. Throughout this canto one would feel as if he was reading just a re-cast of Kālidāsa's own poem. The example afforded by the 57th verse in the *JH.* and the 30th verse in the *Kumārasambhava* will do to illustrate this fact.[1]

In the tenth canto of the *JH.* the author imitates the twelfth canto of the *Raghuvaṁśa* to some extent. Just as Kālidāsa, our poet too tries to condense a major portion of the *Rāmāyaṇa*-story in this canto. But unlike Kālidāsa, he has to end this canto with the abuction of Sītā. Except for this fact he has adopted the methods and means of Kālidāsa in condensing a long story within the confines of a single canto. The very first verse of this canto is modelled on the first verse of the tenth canto of the *Raghuvaṁśa* (*JH.* X. 1. *Cf R. V.* X. 1). After this verse Kumaradāsa gives an elaborate description of old age and introduces a lengthy advice by Daśaratha to Rāma. These ideas are not to be found in Kālidāsa. The latter part of this canto is an exact imitation of the twelfth canto of *Raghuvaṁśa*. The most striking similarity between these two cantos is the brevity of expression adopted by both the poets in their condensation in a few short suggestive expressions of the story contained in the long chapters of Vālmīki's *Rāmāyaṇa*. In this canto we find Kumāradāsa using a good number of the actual words and phrases of Kālidāsa. For instance, expressions like *palitacchadmanā* and *vṛṣasyantī* are typical of Kālidāsa in the twelfth Canto of *Raghuvaṁśa* which Kumāradāsa uses. When the story reaches the stage of Sītā's abduction by Rāvaṇa, our poet ends this canto and in the further portions allows himself free deviation from the plan of the *Raghuvaṁśa*. This deviation affords Kumāradāsa the means to introduce the description of the rainy season in the next canto.

The next instance in which our poet imitates Kālidāsa

1. See Table of parallel passages below.

is in the nineteenth canto where he deals with the lamentations of Maṇḍodarī over the death of Rāvaṇa. This portion has got much in common with the *Rati-vilāpa* in the fourth canto of the *Kumārasambhava.* Here too we find Kumāradāsa freely taking over many ideas and expressions of Kālidāsa from the corresponding portion of the *Kumārasambhava.*

The last canto of the *JH.* is based on the thirteenth canto of the *Raghuvaṁśa.* Both deal with the same part of the story namely, Rāma's journey to Ayodhyā by the aerial chariot. The very first verse of the thirteenth canto of the *Raghuvaṁśa*[1] is echoed in the third verse of the twentieth canto in the *JH.*[2] The descriptions of the ocean, forests, hermitages, mountains and rivers are similar to those in the *Raghuvaṁśa*, the only difference being that Kumāradāsa adds a description of Himavān. Though this is absent in the thirteenth canto of the *Raghuvaṁśa*, it is clear that our poet had his inspiration from the description of Himavān in the opening canto of the *Kumārasambhava.*

While the above account would give us an adequate idea of the indebtedness of Kumāradāsa to Kālidāsa and the closeness of the corresponding portions of the works of the two poets, a more intensive examination of the large amount of parallel passages and identical expressions between the two poets would enable one to appreciate the extent to which Kumāradāsa's mind was saturated with Kālidāsa and his works. It may be seen that these parallels do not confine themselves to the two longer poems of Kālidāsa but extend to *Meghadūta* and even to his play *Śākuntala.* Irrespective of the theme or parts thereof and their corresponding contexts in Kālidāsa's works, there are numerous ideas and expressions taken from Kālidāsa that are strewn all over Kumāradāsa's work. Only a regular tabular statement, given in corresponding columns, can bring out fully the quantitative and qualitative significance of these parallels in ideas and expressions.

1. रत्नाकरं वीक्ष्य मिथः स जायां रामाभिधानो हरिरित्युवाच ।
2. मिथः प्रियामेवमुवाच राघवः

KUMĀRADĀSA		KĀLIDĀSA	
अत्रान्वयः पङ्क्तिरथाभिधानः	I.12	कृतवान् पङ्क्तिरथो विलङ्घ्य यत्	*Raghu* X.7
पूर्वं पडन्तर्द्विषतां त्रिजिग्ये	I.14	अतः सोऽभ्यन्तरान् नित्यान् षड्पूर्वमजयद्रिपून्	*Raghu* XVII.45
स्तनद्वयस्योद्वहनश्रमेण	I.32	आपीनभारोद्वहनश्रमेण	*Raghu* II.18
अरालकेश्या अलके विधात्रा	I.33	भित्वा निराक्रामदरालकेश्याः	*Raghu* VI.81
अदृष्टपुत्राननवन्ध्यदृष्टिः	I.44	शापोऽप्यदृष्टतनयाननपद्मशोभे	*Raghu* IX.80
स्वं रक्षितव्यं श्वगणिप्रचारैः	I.45	श्वगणिवागुरिकैः प्रथमास्थितम्	*Raghu* IX.53
मृगेन्द्रगामी मृगयां बभूव	I.46	ततो मृगेन्द्रस्य मृगेन्द्रगामी	*Raghu* II.30
पुत्रीकृतानीश्वरया शिशुत्वे	I.47	पुत्रीकृतोऽसौ वृषभध्वजेन	*Raghu* II.36
अधिज्यधन्वा धनदप्रभावः	I.52	अधिज्यधन्वा विचचार दावं	*Raghu* II.8
विश्रामहेतोः स विहाय वाहं	I.63	तत्र विश्रामहेतोः	*Megh* I.25
प्रभुः प्रजानामथ स प्रभाते	I.70	अथ प्रजानामधिपः प्रभाते	*Raghu* II.1
शरं शरण्योऽपि मुमोच बाले	I.74	वधाय वध्यस्य शरं शरण्यः	*Raghu* II.30
रावणेन रणे भग्ना देवा दावाग्नितेजसा । जग्मुर्जगत्पतिं द्रष्टुं पुरस्कृतपुरन्दराः ॥	II.1	तस्मिन् विप्रकृताः काले तारकेण दिवौकसः । तुरासाहं पुरोधाय धाम स्वायंभुवं ययुः ॥	*K.S.* II.1
निवृत्ततत्सरःपद्मतापकारणतेजसा । बोधनीयं किलाशेषं वनं कौमुदमिन्दुना ॥	II.61	पुरे तावन्तमेवास्य तनोति रविरातपम् । दीर्घिकाकमलोन्मेषो यावन्मात्रेण साध्यते ॥	*K.S.* II.3

KUMĀRADĀSA		KĀLIDĀSA	
पातालहृदयान्तस्थं पद्मरागं पयोनिधिः ।		तस्योपायनयोग्यानि रत्नानि सरितां पतिः ।	
अग्रमांसमिवोद्धृत्य ददाति पिशिताशिने ।।	II.61	कथमप्यम्भसामन्तरानिक्षिप्तैः प्रतीक्षते ।।	*K. S.* II. 37
पुनरुक्तैरिव पाद्यवारिभिः	VI.16	मीनपङ्क्ति पुनरुक्तमेखलाः	*K. S.* VIII.26
त्वदणुप्रियमाश्रयामहे न परस्मादतिविस्तराण्यपि	VI.26	याच्ञा मोघा वरमधिगुणे नाधमे लब्धकामा	*Megha* I.6
सन्ध्यामकालघटितां गगने वितेनुः	V.58	अकालसन्ध्यामिव धातुमत्तां	*K. S.* I.4
आदाय करमाढ्येभ्यः कीकटेष्वभिवर्षसि ।		प्रजानामेव भूत्यर्थं स ताभ्यो बलिमग्रहीत् ।	
प्रपीय वारि सिन्धुभ्यः स्थलेष्विव घनाघनः ।।	VI.39	सहस्रगुणमुत्स्रष्टुमादत्ते हि रसं रविः ।।	*Raghu* I.18
सतल्पभूभागमनल्पशोभं		कनककलशयुक्तं भक्तिशोभासनाथं	
भवप्रभावो भवनं विवेश ।	VII.56	क्षितिविरचितशाट्यं कौतुकागारमागात्	*K. S.* VII.94
मेखलागुणसमीपसङ्गिनं		मेखलाप्रणयलोलतां गतं	
तस्य हस्तमबला व्यपोहितुम्,	VIII.8	हस्तमस्य शिथिलं रुरोध सा ।	*K. S.* VIII.14
स्वामिसम्मदफलं हि मण्डनम्	VIII.42	प्रियेषु सौभाग्यफला हि चारुता ।।	*K. S.* V.1
भूय एव रविमण्डले रुचिर्लीयते जलधिमध्यवर्तिनि ।		संक्षये जगदिव प्रजेश्वरः	
अन्तराणि तमसः प्रयच्छती स्रष्टरीव जगती युगक्षये ।।		संहरत्यहरसावहर्पतिः ।।	*K. S.* III.30
	VIII.57	कुले प्रसूतिः प्रथमस्य वेधसस्त्रिलोकसौन्दर्यमिवोदितं वपुः ।	
परःप्रकर्षो वपुषः समुन्नतिः कुलस्य तातो नृपतिर्नवं वयः	IX.4	अमृग्यमैश्वर्यसुखं नवं वयः	*K. S.* V.41
स्त्रियो न पुंसामुदयस्य कारणं त एव तद्धामविभूतिहेतवः ।		शशिना सह याति कौमुदी सह मेघेन तडित्प्रलीयते ।	

KUMĀRADĀSA		KĀLIDĀSA	
तडिद्वियुक्तोऽपि घनः प्रजृम्भते			
विना न मेघं विलसन्ति विद्युतः ।।	IX.5	प्रमदाः पतिवर्त्मगा इति प्रतिपन्नं हि विचेतनैरपि ।।	*K. S.* IV.31
गताऽपि भर्त्रे परिकोपमायतं			
गिरं कृथा मा परुषार्थदीपिनीम् ।	IX.6	भर्तुर्विप्रकृताऽपि रोषणतया मा स्म प्रतीपं गमः।	*Śākuntala* IV.18
नयेन नयतस्तस्य राज्यं राजीवचक्षुषः ।		पृथिवीं शासतस्तस्य पाकशासनतेजसः ।	
ततः शक्रसमानस्य समानामयुतं ययौ ।।	X.1	किञ्चिदूनमनूनर्द्धेः शरदामयुतं ययौ ।।	*Raghu* X.1
पलितच्छद्मना दोषा	X.3	पलितच्छद्मना जरा	*Raghu* XII
इत्थं वादिनि राजेन्द्रे रामो मौनमधिश्रितः	X.42	एवं वादिनि देवर्षौ पार्श्वे पितुरधोमुखी	*K. S.* IV . 8
दूषयिष्यति पूज्येषु पूजा वैमुख्यमायतिम्	X.65	प्रतिबध्नाति हि श्रेयः पूज्यपूजाव्यतिक्रमः	*Raghu* I. 79
अथ रामं वृषस्यन्ती	X.72	इति रामो वृषस्यन्तीं	*Raghu* XII. 34
क्लममिवाभिवहन्नतिपानजं		खिन्नः खिन्नः शिखरिषु पदं न्यस्य गन्तासि यत्र	*Megha* I.13
गिरितटे निषसाद पयोधरः ।			
स्मराहतं राजसुताविनाकृतं	XI.14	लब्धप्रशमनस्वस्थमथैनं समुपस्थिता ।	
वनेऽथ लब्धावसरेऽत्रसेवितुम् ।		पार्थिवश्रीर्द्वितीयेव शरत्पङ्कजलक्षणा ।।	*Raghu* IV.14
अफुल्लपङ्केरुहकर्कशस्तनी			
शरत्प्रपेदे नृपवासमात्मजम् ।।	XII.1		
जनस्य चेतो दधतः समुन्नतिं		उष्णत्वमन्त्यातपसंप्रयोगा-	
रुषः प्रणीपातविधिः प्रतिक्रिया ।	XII.25	च्छैत्यं हि यत्सा प्रकृतिर्जलस्य ।	*Raghu* V.54

KUMĀRADĀSA		KĀLIDĀSA	
सुरपतिरिपवः प्रियानिरस्त-		नीवीबन्धोच्छ्वसितशिथिलं यत्र बिंबाधराणां	
श्रवणसरोरुहनिर्वृतेऽपि दीपे ।	XIX.48	क्षौमं रागादनिभृतकरेष्वाक्षिपत्सु प्रियेषु ।	
रतिषु, ददृशुरेव काञ्चिरत्न-		अर्चिस्तुङ्गानभिमुखमपि प्राप्य रत्नप्रदीपान्	
द्युतिपरिभिन्नतमिस्रमूरुमूलम् ॥		ह्रीमूढानां भवति विफलप्रेरणा चूर्णमुष्टिः ॥	*Megha* II.5
तथातिदीनैः परिदेविताक्षरैः		अथ तैः परिदेविताक्षरैः	*K. S.* IV.25
मियः प्रियामेवमुवाच राघवः ॥	XX.3	रत्नाकरं वीक्ष्य मिथः स जायां रामाभिधानो हरिरित्युवाच ॥	
हरौ हृतेऽश्वौ हरितुल्यतेजसा			*Raghu* XIII.1
क्रतुप्रसङ्गे सगरस्य सागरः ।		गुरोर्यियक्षोः कपिलेन मेध्ये रसातलं संक्रमिते तुरङ्गे ।	
विभिद्य तत्संभववीरबाहुभिः		तदर्थमुर्वीमवदारयद्भिः पूर्वैः किलायं परिवर्धितो नः ॥	
गभीरभावं किल भूरि लम्भितः ॥	XX.15		*Raghu* XIII.3
लतावितानावरणे शिलातले			
गिरावमुष्मिन् सुरसिद्धयोषिताम् ।		यः पण्यस्त्रीरतिपरिमलोद्गारिभिर्नागराणाम्	
सुवृत्तकाञ्चीगुणघृष्टरेखया		उद्दामानि प्रथयति शिलावेश्मभिर्यौवनानि ॥	*Megha* I.25
विदन्ति वृत्तं सुरतं वनेचराः ॥	XX.49		
रक्षस्सैन्यनगो रामबाणाक्षिप्तजलोऽपि सन् ।		तस्यानीकैर्विसर्पद्भिरपरान्तजयोद्यतैः ।	
अचलश्शत्रुसेनायाः प्रपेदे नैव सह्यताम् ॥		रामास्त्रोत्सारितोऽप्यासीत् सह्यलग्न इवार्णवः ॥	*Raghu* IV.53

An analysis of the parallel instances would show three categories into which they can be classified:

1. Where the ideas alone are copied and presented in different expressions.

2. Where the words alone are copied for use with reference to different ideas and contexts.

3. Where both words and ideas are borrowed and are used more or less in the same contexts.

Apart from these categories we have another type of passages which, though not coming under any of these, definitely echo Kālidāsa's ideas. On reading these passages one can definitely say that the poet was inspired to write them by similar ideas in Kālidāsa. A typical example of this is to be had in the following verse (III. 2):

> अथ त्यक्त्वा विवस्वानथ दक्षिणाशामालक्ष्य सर्वत्र करप्रसारी ।
> ऋत्विक्ततो निःस्व इव प्रतस्थे स्वरूपलब्ध्यै धनदस्य वासम् ॥

In this the poet has dealt with the northward movement of the Sun during the *Uttarāyaṇa* and has compared him to a Priest who goes to the abode of Kubera to get money. This picture definitely reminds us of the fifth canto of the *Raghuvaṁśa* wherein Kālidāsa deals with Raghu who is penniless after the Viśvajit sacrifice and who proceeds to the city of Kubera to fetch money for Kautsa to enable the latter to pay his *Guru-dakṣiṇā*. Though this whole idea is not exactly copied by Kumāradāsa, in the above verse we can clearly perceive the source of his inspiration in the conceiving of the Sun as a Priest going to Kubera to get money for the sacrifice.

In the majority of the cases of imitation, Kumāradāsa has proved to be successful. We have to say to his credit that he never tried to conceal his indebtedness to Kālidāsa. It is but natural that any poet-critic should get absorbed in Kālidāsian works and find it difficult or feel it necessary to get rid of the latter's influence on his creative mind. It can be legitimately suggested that it is this high degree of saturation with Kālidāsa's ideas and expression that had given rise to legends associating the lives of these two poets.

KUMĀRADĀSA AND BHĀRAVI

We have already noticed, while discussing the date of Kumāradāsa, that Bhāravi was his immediate predecessor among the followers of Kālidāsa in the *Mahākāvya*-tradition. As is natural to one who suceeeded a poet of Bhāravi's eminence, Kumāradāsa exhibits in his work much influence of the former. Moreover, the *Kirātārjunīya* is a landmark in the development of the *Mahākāvya* in Sanskrit for more than one reason It not only inaugurates the adoption of an ornate and comparatively difficult style in the *Mahākāvya*-form, substituting the simple and easy flow of Kālidāsian poetry, but it also marks the beginning of the introduction of Śāstraic and academic ideas into the body of the poem. The exhibition of the all-round knowledge of the poet in matters of science and philosophy was gradually begun to be recognised as an essential trait of poetry. Marking, as it does, such an important landmark in the history and development of the *Mahākāvya*-literature, it is but natural that the *Kirātārjunīya* should influence the works of later writers like Kumāradāsa.

Such identity of ideas and copy of expressions as seen between Kālidāsa and Kumāradāsa may not be demonstrable in the case of Bhāravi and Kumāradāsa. Nevertheless the general influence of Bhāravi on the *JH.* is undoubtedly present there. While he borrows ideas and words from Kālidāsa and bases his theme on the lines of the latter's *Raghuvamśa*, Kumāradāsa resorts to Bhāravi for the form and descriptions in his poem. We have in the *JH.* many fancies akin to those of Bhāravi and many descriptive methods more or less based on the lines of the latter. We cannot miss the fact that both of them proceed on a common trend of thought and adopt the same poetic technique and exhibit a similar working of the imagination. We shall in this chapter endeavour to describe Bhāravi's influence on Kumāradāsa.

In the planning and introduction of the descriptive passages, we find Kumāradāsa closely following Bhāravi. The description of the water-sports in the third canto of the

JH. has a close resemblance with the corresponding passages in the eighth canto of the *Kirātārjunīya*. Both Bhāravi as well as Kumāradāsa devote 30 verses each for this description. When we read this portion in the *JH.* we feel that the poet had before his mind's eye the fancies and ideas of Bhāravi which he has tried to modify with the help of his own originality. Though we have only a few passages in the whole of this description, which can be said to bear similarity with those in Bhāravi's description, we have many more ideas of the latter hidden in the verses of *JH.* in an imperceptible manner. One of these definitely similar passages is where the poets describe how a lady under the pretext of plucking a bunch of flowers at a height lifted up her arms, a sight which kindled her lover's passion. Kumāradāsa says :

दूरस्थपुष्पस्तबकावभङ्गव्याजेन सन्दर्शितबाहुमूला ।

(*JH.* III. 17)

More or less the same idea is found in Bhāravi who says:

कयाचिदाविष्कृतबाहुमूलया तरुप्रसूनान्यपदिश्य सादरम् ।

(*Kirāta* VIII. 18)

Before describing the water-sports, Bhāravi deals with some love-quarrels and jealousies of the heavenly ladies and these passages are echoed in the sixteenth canto of the *JH.* wherein Kumāradāsa deals with such love-quarrels of the Rākṣasa couples. While the general trend of thought in Kumāradāsa's passages leaves no doubt with regard to the source of his inspiration, we have at least one passage where the ideas of the former are entirely copied and even some words and a grammatical usage of Bhāravi in that context are also utilised by Kumāradāsa. The pacifying maid-friend asks her companion to leave off the adamant attitude towards her lover and addresses her thus in the *JH.*

सखि जहिहि रुषं हिनस्ति पश्चात्तव तरलं हृदयं पुराऽनुतापः ।
इति निपुणसखीगिरा निरासे मनसि निशाचरयोषितोऽभिमानः ॥

(*JH.* XVI. 40)

The same idea we find in Bhāravi thus :

जहीहि कोपं दयितोऽनुगम्यतां पुराऽनुशेते तव चञ्चलं मनः ।
इति प्रियं काञ्चिदुपैतुमिच्छतीं पुरोऽनुनिन्ये निपुणः सखीजनः ॥

(*Kirāta* VIII. 8)

A continuous and parallel trend of thought in the two works can be had in the descriptions of natural sceneries like sun-set. The ninth canto in the *Kirātārjunīya* wherein the sun-set is described, has much in common with the latter half of the eighth canto and the first half of the sixteenth canto of the *JH.* Kumāradāsa has brought about some slight changes over the ideas of Bhāravi. Still, they do remind us of the corresponding verses in the *Kirātārjunīya.* The conception of the Moon as a golden pot is presented by Bhāravi thus :

हेमकुम्भ इव पूर्वपयोधेरुन्ममज्ज शनकैस्तुहिनांशुः ॥

(*Kirāta.* IX. 23)

Kumāradāsa, on the other hand, compares the Moon to a silvery pot and says that the night drops it in the lake of the sky :

गगनसरसि चन्द्ररूप्यकुम्भे
व्यपसरति स्म निपातिते रजन्या ।

(*JH.* XVI. 21)

In some other cases Kumāradāsa draws his similes from the same sources as those of Bhāravi. For example; while describing the *Śarad* season, Kumāradāsa compares the row of parrots to the lightning thus :

प्रभाभिराम्रेडितशक्रकार्मुका तनोति तोषं जगतश्शुकावली ।

(*JH.* XII. 15)

Bhāravi had already attempted this very same comparison in a more detailed manner when he said :

मुखैरसौ विद्रुमभङ्गलोहितैः शिखा पिशङ्गीः कलमस्य बिभ्रती ।
शुकावलिर्व्यक्तशिरीषकोमला धनुःश्रियं गोत्रभिदोऽनुगच्छति ॥

(*Kirāta.* IV. 36)

While describing the *Śarad*-season both of them draw the picture of the *Kalama-gopikā*, the rustic lass that guards the fields, in more or less the same simple and beautiful lines. Both are struck by the lotus or lily that she is wearing either on the tresses or at the ear and the similarity of the flower to her eyes :

निजेक्षणस्पर्धि निकृत्य पङ्कजं दधुश्शिरोभिः कलमस्य पालिकाः ।

(*JH*. XII. 6)

कपोलसंश्लेषिविलोचनत्विषा विभूषयन्तीमवतंसकोत्पलम् ।
सुतेन पाण्डोः कलमस्य गोपिकां निरीक्ष्य मेने शरदः कृतार्थता ।।

(*Kirāta*. IV. 9)

While describing the sun-set, Kumāradāsa says that the Sun, while setting, deposits his heat in the hearts of the lovers travelling abroad. Bhāravi says that it is deposited in the hearts of the *Cakravāka* birds which are separated during nights.

निधाय तापं तपनः पतत्यसौ प्रवासिनां चेतसि चिन्तयातुरे ।

(*JH*. III. 64)

आससाद विरहय्य धरित्रीं चक्रवाकमिथुनान्यभितापः ।

(*Kirāta*. IX. 4)

Apart from the descriptions, we have other incidents in the *JH*. and the *Kirātārjunīya* which look very much similar. For example, the hand-to-hand fight between Kirāta and Arjuna in the eighteenth canto of the *Kirātārjunīya* will definitely remind one of the similar fight between Jaṭāyus and Rāvaṇa, and Vālin and Sugrīva depicted in the eleventh canto of the *JH*. Both of them adopt the same metre and have even some words and phrases common to both. Kumāradāsa says, while describing the huge war-cries of the monkey-heroes:[1] प्रतिनिनादितभीमदरीमुखः Almost the same expression can be found in the *Kirātārjunīya* in the same context [2]: प्रतिनिनाद दरीषु दरीभृतः

1. *JH*. XI, 30.
2. *Kirāta*. XVIII, 2.

In these contexts even some sound-effects are produced by both in the same way.

Kumāradāsa : प्रववृते धृतिसंहरणो रणः (*JH.* XI. 6)
Bhāravi : अचलसञ्चलनाहरणो रणः (*Kirāta.* XVII. 8)

From the following table it will be clear that Kumāradāsa adopts some of the phrases and words of Bhāravi :

	Kumāradāsa	*Bhāravi*
1.	सकुङ्कुमस्त्रीकुचमण्डलद्युतिः III.64	कुङ्कुमारुणपयोधरगौरः । IX.23
2.	वर्णिलिङ्गी निशाचरः X.77	स वर्णिलिङ्गी विदितः समाययौ । I.1
3.	परिक्वणत्सारसपङ्क्तिभूषणाः XII.4	परिक्वणत्सारसपङ्क्तिमेखलैः VIII.9
4.	जगज्जिघत्सातुरकण्ठपद्धतिः XII.36	जगज्जिघत्सन्तमिवान्तवह्निम् III.20
5.	श्वसितहृतरुचिर्वराधरोष्ठः XVI. 46	श्वसितचलितपल्लवाधरोष्ठः X.34
6.	समीयते नाकृतपुण्यकर्मणा XX.5	प्रवर्तते नाकृतपुण्यकर्मणाम् XIV.3

As we have already remarked, Kumāradasa had Bhāravi before him for the general plan of the composition and particularly in the matter of making the work a more learned type of composition and a medium for the display of the poet's dexterity in the execution of *Śabdacitra*-varieties. The setting apart of a separate canto for the last-mentioned, the *Śabdacitras* and the allotting this for the identical context of the fight, is a practice which we can now trace only to Bhāravi as the earliest. The influence of Bhāravi on Kumāradāsa in this respect is patent. As a separate section has been devoted in this thesis for a consideration of the *Śabdacitras* in Kumāradāsa, the parallels between these two poets in this respect may be seen in that section.

KUMĀRADĀSA'S DESCRIPTIONS

Besides the description of Nature which we have dealt with in detail in another section, there are many other themes on which Kumāradāsa exhibits his descriptive powers. As a close follower of Bhāravi in observing the conventions of the *Mahākāvya,* he depicts the various themes of description like the city, the hero and heroine, the garden-sports, the water-sports, the *Ratotsava,* the drinking parties, the ministerial consultations of kings, the despatching of messengers and battles. He creates suitable opportunities to introduce such descriptions; but what is significant is that he is very careful to see that these are not made unduly long. On certain occasions, when he has got more ideas to be expressed on a particular topic, instead of prolonging the description in the same context, he cuts it short there and avails himself of the opportunity to deal with that topic for a second time in another context and introduce the remaining ideas. The description of the heroine is divided between Kausalyā in canto I and Sītā in canto VII; while the depiction of the drinking scene is spread over three different contexts, i. e. cantos III, VIII and XVI. The device not only avoids boredom but adds to the interest of the different sections of the poem. Just as he attributes human behaviour and reactions to natural objects while describing Nature, while describing humanity he equates the human action and reactions with natural phenomena. In his descriptions he uses mostly *Śleṣa* and *Utprekṣā,* though other figures of speech are not rare in them. The main characteristic of his descriptive passages is the simplicity of his style and the usage of fancies which are not much involved and laborious.

In the beginning of the first canto, he devotes eleven verses to describe the city of Ayodhyā. In the very first verse, he says that the city of Ayodhyā has all the splendour and wealth of the celestial city and that if it has come down to earth, it is only because of its weight due to excess of prosperity (I. 1). The moon when it appears over the city puts on a reddish pale colour due to the reflection of the rubies set on the golden pitchers placed on the terraces of the mansions. The poet attributes this change of colour in the moon to its jealousy and shame caused by its being overpowered by the beautiful faces of the ladies (I. 2). With its abundance of wealth and prosperity it gives joy to all its inhabitants except the Abhisārikās. Because they, who pray for darkness so that they could go to meet their lovers unnoticed by anybody, are inconvenienced by the splendour of the gems that are set on the arches (I. 3). The silken banners fluttering on the top of the sky-scraping mansions are fancied as the slough cast off by the moon as he pulls himself across the pointed ends of the dove-cots. The walls of the city are so glossy that the elephants mistake their own images on them for their rivals and dash in vain against the walls and have only the smell of ichor to distinguish themselves from their image-enemies (I. 6). The white rumbling clouds of Autumn resting on the mansions appear to the poet as depositing their rumbling sounds in the drums in those mansions and seeking in return a share in the white splendour of the latter (I. 9).[1]

In the sixth canto we have a description of the city of Mithilā when Viśvāmitra enters it along with the two princes. The round disc of the moon at the centre of the sky is fancied as the lid on the high circular parapet wall of the city (VI. 20). The parapet of the city is imagined in another verse (VI. 22) as encircling the city and crushing it as it were, like a huge python. By the red glow of the rubies flashing from the tops of mansions, the Sun even at noon appears red as in the morning (VI. 25). The serpent-chord that ties together the horses of the Sun get loosened due to the fear caused by the peacocks on the terraces of the houses (VI. 28). The row of houses in the city of Mithilā is compared to Paraśurāma and Śukra simultaneously by using some words with double meanings.

1. Nandargikar's observations on this verse are too wide of the mark.

विटङ्कभुजसंप्राप्तसहस्रकरमूर्तिना।
विग्रहेण यदावाससन्तानो भार्गवायते ॥

The houses touching the thousand-rayed sun with their hands in the form of the dove-cots resemble Paraśurāma who killed the thousand-armed Kārtavīrya with his hand that held the Paraśu. It also resembles the planet Venus (Bhārgava) which touches the orbit of the thousand-rayed Sun.

The beauty of the feminine form called forth the exercise of Kumāradāsa's imagination more than once; first, while describing Kausalyā in the opening canto and again for a second time, while depicting Sītā when she appears after Rāma breaks the bow in the seventh canto. Within these two descriptions the poet has completed a full portrait of a lady of ideal beauty. Particularly in the first canto his fancies are so charming that anthologists have quoted many verses from this context. Kausalyā's gait resembles so much the movement of the swan or the intoxicated elephant that she may be mistaken for stealing it from either of them. To disprove this doubt, she looks as if balancing the beauty of those two with her own gait by the movement of her knees and show that it is natural to her since she surpasses the other two (I. 28). While describing her thighs, the poet leaves the reader to understand for himself their beauty by just casting a doubt on the skill of Brahmā thus :

दृष्टौ हतो मन्मथबाणपातैः शक्यं विधातुं न निमील्य चक्षुः।
ऊरू विधात्रा नु कथं कृतौ तावित्यास तस्यां सुमतेर्वितर्कः॥

(I. 29)

One will be tempted to doubt as to how Brahmā created her thighs. Because, if he had done it with his eyes open he would have been struck by the arrows of Cupid and could not have completed the work; if he had done it by closing his eyes he could not have attained such a perfection. The three folds of skin on her abdomen are fancied as the three lines drawn by the creator to record the fact that there is no one in all the three worlds who has so beautiful an abdomen (I. 31). The thinness of her waist is attributed to its being worn out by carrying for a long time her pair of breasts that grows in size as she advances in age (I. 32). Her two breasts with their tips upturned looked like a pair of *cakravāka*-birds who mistake her face for the moon, but are convinced that it is not the moon since they are not separated from each other (I. 34). Even though they are unintelligent beasts, a sense of shame weighs down the peacocks whose plumes are put to shame by her locks of hair and who have consequently taken their abode in the forests (I. 41).

In the seventh canto, the poet describes Sītā who comes to bow before Viśvāmitra and Rāma. She bends down to bow before Viśvāmitra with obvious ease, as she is helped by her bosom; but the same circumstance renders her getting up difficult (VII. 2). The stars seem to fall at her feet in the guise of the shining nails, as if to pray to her thus : 'Be kind. Let not the splendour of your face bring so much disgrace to our Lord, the moon."

> प्रसीद मैवं परिभूदखण्डं ताराधिपं ते वदनामृतांशुः ।
> इति प्रियायाः पतितेव पादे तारावतिर्दीप्तनखच्छलेन ॥ (VII. 7)

Having made her waist slender, the creator thought that he was endangering the position of the heavy loins and therefore, gave the latter, the support of two pillars in the form of her thighs (VII.8). Her hands are so powerful in kindling the passion in others, that by contacting them even the *Aṅgada* (bangle) turns to be *Anaṅgada* (producer of love) (VII.9). Her long curved eye-brows resembled the two pieces of Cupid's bow that was broken in the middle by Śiva in his anger (VII.12). The *Kauṭilya* or crookedness is the common characteristic of both her eyes and her brows and both extended upto her ears. The poet fancies that it cannot be ascertained as to whether the brow goes to the root of her ears to inform her of the crookedness of her eyes or *vice-versa* (VII. 13). The blackness of the cuckoo is due to its sorrow on the discomfiture that it suffers from the pleasing sweet voice of Sītā (VII. 14). Rāma's reaction on seeing this beauty is effectively expressed in the following verse :

चित्रीयते तन्न यदात्मयोनेः तीव्रा मयि व्याहतिरायुधानाम् ।
कुर्वीत सीताकृति वीक्ष्य रत्नं पुष्पायुधः स्वात्मनि शस्त्रपातान् ॥

'It is no wonder that I am hurt by the arrows of the God of Love; because, after seeing this gem in the form of Sītā, the God of Love will direct his arrows against himself'. Thus we have in these contexts taken together a complete picture of ideal beauty and it is no wonder that the anthologists and Alaṅkāra-writers have quoted some of these verses in their collections.

After describing the *Vipralambha* which we have dealt with in the section on the *Rasas,* the poet gives in the seventh canto a graphic description of the marriage of Rāma and Sītā with the manifold preparations associated with it. The usual fuss that precedes the marriage-hour is set forth in six verses which are remarkable for their striking realism. Brahmins, after finishing their ablutions, mount the intoxicated elephants and sprinkle all over the places inside the palace the holy water contained in the golden jars (VII. 34). Following the panegyrists, people give forth loud cries of victory for the prince, and trumpets and conches befitting the auspicious occasion are being sounded (VII. 36). Servants employed to note the correct time by looking into the water-clock are going about in great haste (VIII. 38). The elders in both the families, eager to perform the marriage function at the auspicious moment, hasten Rāma to have his sacramental bath (VII. 39). Attenders with canes in their hands are regulating the rushing crowd and with threatening words and gestures, clear the place.

The poet also sets forth in detail the marriage rituals. First the *Pāṇigrahaṇa* or holding of the bride's hand by the bridegroom, then offerings into the fire and going round the fire which is made a witness for the marriage are described (VII.47ff). In the midst of these religious rites, the poet also dwells on the personal charm of the couple and fancies that the drops of perspiration produced by the fire might have been due to the inner warmth of love. The poet then refers to the *Lāja-homa* or offering of fried rice into the fire by the bridegroom. According to the traditional practice the couple then bow before the elders.

Drinking party or *Pānagoṣṭhī* which is one of the favourite topics of description with poets receives due attention at the hands of Kumāradāsa. At the end of the third canto, after describing the garden-sports, the poet depicts a drinking scene in seven verses. To Daśaratha who takes the wine from off his own beloved's mouth, her very mouth and lip formed the cup and the condiment (III.70). The intoxicated lover offering a cup of wine to his beloved addresses her by the name of a rival lady. Enraged at this, the lady, though she refuses to drink the wine, gets the red hue in her eyes and the drops of perspiration on her cheeks, as if she had drunk (III.71). When the natural lotus closed either due to the splendour of her moon-like face or the rays of the actual moon itself, the face of the damsel reflected in the wine-cup became as it were the lotus. The reflection in the wine of her face inside the wine looks as if eager to kiss her own face and this eagerness is shown when the image inside is throbbing due to the shaking of the wine (III. 73). Having rendered them less bashful, the wine deposited love in their hearts, the red colour in their eyes and the sweet odour in their mouths. This same idea is more elaborately given in the sixteenth canto :

> हृदयवदनलोचनेषु तासां मधु मदगन्धवपुःश्रियं निधाय ।
> श्रमसलिलकणच्छलेन शुद्धं बहिरभवच्छरपाण्डु गण्डबिम्बात् ॥

Here the poet says that the wine underwent a course of purification in the body of the ladies and re-appeared as fresh water. It deposited its intoxication or passion in the hearts of the ladies; its smell in their faces and its colour in their eyes. Having got rid of all the three Guṇas, it re-appeared as fresh water in the form of drops of perspiration on their cheeks.

At the end of the eighth canto too, we have five verses dealing with drinking. While drinking wine, the lady is being profusely kissed by her beloved and due to repeated kissing the red colour on the lips gradually faded. This process is described by the poet thus :

नियतमिह पतन्ति दन्तधारा मदमदनोद्धतयोरितीव भीत्या ।
अधरकिसलयं विहाय यूनोर्मधु पिबतोर्नयनान्युपास्त रागः ॥

Due to the intoxicated and passionate nature of the lover, his violent kisses are sure to make some marks with the teeth on the lips. As if to escape from this the red colour left that place and took refuge in her eyes. In the sixteenth canto we have a longer description of drinking. The wine that they drink from the jars made of *Padmarāga* stone gives them the impression that it is only the *Padmarāga* that is oozing out in the form of the liquid. When the wine is being consumed, the last remnants of that feminine bashfulness also disappeared, unable to keep its stand between intoxication and passion, the wine and the Cupid (XVI. 58).

When Rāvaṇa, after consuming the wine contained in the mouth of a lady, begins to cause pain to her lips, the lady asks whether any man in his senses will stoop to eat the glass after drinking the wine contained in it.

Descriptions of the themes of *Sambhoga*, *Vipralambha* and *Saṅgrāma* may also be similarly analysed here. But, as they are closely linked up with the Rasas of *Śṛṅgāra*, *Vīra*, *Raudra* and *Bībhatsa* they have been kept over to the section on *Rasas*.

DESCRIPTION OF NATURE

The manifold beauties of Nature are Subjects which the poets are never tired of describing and they find in Nature an inexhaustible scope for the exercise of their imagination. Since Nature serves as the main source of inspiration for poets, it became the practice of the authors of *Mahākāvyas* to devote ample and repeated attention to the depiction of Nature in all her aspects and her influence over the characters. We find that descriptions of Nature, though covering the same ground again and again, have something original in the treatment by each poet. Daṇḍin has included in his description of the *Mahākāvya*, pictures of sun-set and sun-rise, of darkness and moon-light and of the changing effects of the different seasons and of forests, rivers, hills and seas.[1]

Kumāradāsa has given in his *JH.* no negligible account of his powers at drawing scenic miniatures from Nature, some of which are indeed memorable. It is significant to note in this connection that a large part of Kumāradāsa-citations in the anthologies are concerned with the poet's descriptions of the various aspects of Nature. No doubt, his descriptions are not marked with such simplicity of style as is associated with Kālidāsa but they are definitely simpler than those of Māgha. Situated as he was in an era which was in between the two landmarks in the development of Sanskrit poetic composition, the former predominated by Kālidāsa and the latter by Māgha, we can find in his descriptions a combination of the features of both. One of the favourite methods of the poets in their descriptions of Nature is to invest it with life and deal with aspects of Nature in terms of human feelings giving rise to fine examples of Samādhi and Samāsokti; here even inanimate objects are made to react and express their feelings like human beings by the touch of the magic-wand of the poet's imagination.

1. नगरार्णवशैलर्तुचन्द्रार्कोदयवर्णनैः ।

Kāvyādarśa I. 16.

In such descriptions too, Kumāradāsa has some notable achievements. He, however, is not solely devoted to the softer and the pleasanter aspects of Nature, but evinces equally keen delight in the forceful, wild and boisterous phenomena also, so that his portrayal of Nature is endowed with beauty and power.

After depicting the love-sports between Rāma and Sītā in the eighth canto, Kumāradāsa introduces long descriptions of the evening and the Sun-set. This description is given in the words of Rāma addressed to his beloved. Again, in the sixteenth canto, before dealing with the noctural sports of the Rākṣasas, the poet describes the evening twilight in all its glory. In the former instance he devotes about forty verses while in the latter, twenty-seven verses to the description of the evening. On these two occasions together, the poet has covered indeed a very wide field and his powers of observation of men and things in a variety of situations is very conspicuous in these contexts.

The Sun, lingering for a while on the top of the setting mountain, appears to be like one who had gathered up his things and has decided to go away from a place; but then feels a little nostalgic, turns and looks back upon his place with a sigh of yearning.

> सन्निगृह्य करसन्ततिं क्वचित् प्रस्थितोऽपि रविरेष रागवान् ।
> अस्तमस्तकमधिश्रितः क्षण पश्यतीव भुवन समुत्सुकः ॥
>
> *JH.* VIII. 56

Just as the whole of the manifested world gets absorbed in God, its creator, at the time of the deluge, leaving the universe in darkness, the rays of the Sun go back to their source and the whole world is immersed in darkness (VIII.58). The fact that the Sun sinks into the ocean is explained by the poet as due to the increase in its bodily weight caused by its rays getting back into it (VIII.61). The stars that appear on the western horizon are fancied as the sparks of fire produced by the wheels of the Sun's chariot, when they dash against the rocky surface of the setting mountain (VIII.68). The rays of the moon are compared to the milky ocean which rises up in level on his sight and the phenomenon of the gradual rise of the moon is fancied as due to its being tossed on the surface by the surging waves of the ocean (VIII.72). The whole darkness which appears like a collection of bees is said to have been drunk up by the moon and this explains the presence of a deer-like black spot in his transparent disc (VIII.76). The stars that have risen look like *lājas* (fried rice) strewn by the ladies in the form of the Quarters to celebrate the voyage of the moon who had started from the rising mount (VIII.83).

In the sixteeth canto, the poet presents another set of pictures associated with the evening time. The sun who runs down on the slopes of the setting mountain is depicted as being chased by a host of bees in the form of darkness. Eager to get rid of them, lest they should sting him, the sun disappears into the waters of the ocean (XVI.3). The poet notices a single bee that goes about humming round the lotus-pond and he is out to find out the reason for the same. Numerous bees have got into the lotuses to drink honey. In their eagerness to consume more of it or in their intoxication due to too much of drinking, they would have failed to notice the setting of the sun which means they will be soon imprisoned inside the flowers, since the petals will be closing very soon. To inform them of this impending disaster, the solitary bee goes about giving a note of warning that it is time for them to come out since the lotuses will be closing due to sun-set :

द्रुतमपसरतेति भानुरस्तं सरसिरुहेषु दलार्गला: पतन्ति ।
भ्रमरकुलमिव ब्रुवन्निवालिः क्वणितकलं विचचार दीर्घिकायाम् ।।
(*JH.* XI. 6)

It shows the imaginative skill of the poet which enables him in interpreting this, otherwise insignificant, humming of a bee as a warning to its friends.

The moon who leaves the rising mountain is gradually rid of its red colour and this is compared to the process of drinking wine. The eastern quarer, which is fancied as a lady, is drinking wine from the crystalline cup in the form of the moon. As the wine is being consumed gradually, the disappearance of the red hue owing to the emptying of the cup is visible due to its trasparent nature leaving back the original colour of the jar (XVI.12). The moon that has newly risen and with its brilliant rays bestows happiness on the earth, is greeted with *Arghya* by the arch of moon-stones that are oozing out water (XVI.17). The most effective simile that is presented in this context is when the poet compares the whole sky to a big lake wherein the lady in the form of the night drops a silvery pot to draw water. The pot is the moon. Due to its fall, ripples are created on the surface of the water. These concentric circles of ripples dash off the stretch of moss that is spread over the water and push it towards the banks. This collection of moss is the darkness that is dispelled by the moon.

गगनसरसि चन्द्ररूप्यकुम्भे प्रविसरति स्म निपातिते रजन्या ।
तदुपहिततरङ्गधूतनीलीनिकर इवातिघनस्तमःप्रवाहः ॥

(*JH* XVI. 21)

Unlike the sun-set, the sun-rise receives a briefer treatment at the hands of the poet. At the end of the third canto, we have five verses devoted to describe the sun-rise and similarly at the end of the 16th canto another five verses. In both these occasions the poet describes the rise of the sun through the mouths of the court-ladies in attendance and bards who have to wake up their matiers. Daśaratha and Rāvaṇa are awakened respectively in the two cantos.

The sun's rays that sweep over the lotuses are fancied as the hands of a husband waking his beloved in the form of the lotus-pond. It looks as if he is saying that the night has ended and the moon has gone to the setting mountain (III.78). The elephants of the king rise up with their heads held high, dragging the noisy chains behind them and warding off the bees that have settled down on their temples (III.79).

The peacocks get up and with increasing cheerfulness begin to dance after spreading their heavy feathers from which particles of snow trickle down (III.80).

The morning breeze blows tossing the bees that cling to the lilies and the chirping water-birds that stand on the waves of the water (XVI.70). In a short compass of about ten verses the poet has succeeded in capturing the salient features of the rising sun.

Kumāradāsa proves equally effective in the description of the seasons. *Vasanta*, *Śarad* and *Varṣā* are the three seasons that are mainly dealt with by our poet. Of these, he devotes the maximum number of verses for the description of the rainy season. In the third canto of the *JH.* we have a description of the Spring season in thirteen verses, followed by the description of the water-sports of Daśaratha with his damsels. The Spring season happens to be the precursor of the Lord of *Lakṣmī*. Knowing as if that the latter is going to incarnate as man, the Spring set the stage for Him by spreading the surface of the earth profusely with flowers (III. 1). The *Campaka*-trees put forth blossoms all over and they gave the forest the appearance of lamp-stands with thousands of lamps lit over them (III.3). Lotuses which had long been under the water and therefore appear to have been suffering from the chill, rise above the water as if to warm themselves in the vernal sun-shine (III.4). On the top of a mountain there is a *Karṇikāra*-tree which glitters all the more in the morning sun of the Spring season. On it there are numerous bees and peacocks. The poet fancies the whole tree as a crown on the head of the mountain, set with blue stones in the form of the necks of peacocks and saphires in the form of bees (III.8). During mid-days the glittering sprouts of the trees agitated by the breeze resemble their tongues thrown out due to the fatigue caused by the hot sun (III.12).

Kumāradāsa's descriptive capacity and his keen observation are best revealed in his depicting the rainy season in the elevnth canto of his work. He devotes 58 long verses to describe the rains. Many a verse from this portion of his work is found quoted in the anthologies. That itself shows that the poet is at his best in this canto. The *Drutavilambita* metre adopted in this description together with the simple *Yamaka*-effects employed here add to the general appeal of this canto.

First the poet deals with the clouds blown by the wind which have covered the skies. With the streaks of lightning on them, they resembled the cage in which the lion in the form of the Sun is imprisoned (XI.44). The clouds that have widely spread themselves over the post-like peaks of the mountains of *Malaya*, *Mandara* and *Vindhya*, with their dripping water, appear in the sky like a canopy with hanging pearl-decorations (XI-45). The advent of the clouds is such a happy event that the poet says that the end of the heat of the world is being celebrated; lightning like a golden stick is striking the drum of the cloud and to its rumbling, the peacocks are called upon to dance (XI.46). Swept across in great speed by winds, the elephants in the form of clouds let out continuously drops of their sweat caused by exhaustion, in the form of showers (XI.50). The incessant showers resembled the sacrificial oblation poured down by Indra on the earth bearing the fire of the Sun's heat and the *Lāṅgalī* (plant or tree) shone like flames of fire that shot up therefrom. It is believed that the sacrifice and the rains have an intimate relation, the former being held to be the cause of the latter. Evidently this belief is in the mind of the poet who appears to suggest here that even before the sacrifice, Indra came down with his showers and that the very rain is a counter-sacrificial oblation performed by Indra (XI.75). Clouds are compared to a host of wild elephants that have come out of the forests and roam about in the urban areas. When these elephants transgress the boundaries of the forests and cause havoc to the habitable regions, they are driven back to their homes by using fire-brands. The lightnings are compared to such fire-brands and being struck by them the elephants of the clouds roar in the form of thunders (XI.77). In another verse the long streaks of shining showers are imagined as long ropes of silver and hundreds of crystal-like pillars supporting the mass of the clouds from falling down on earth (XI.81).

In the twefth canto of the *JH.* we have a description of the *Śarad* season, immediately following the description of the rainy season. The poet devotes 32 verses to a description of the *Śarad*. He introduces the *Śarad* as a lady who has come to attend upon Rāma in his forlorn condition in that forest. The Sun becomes brighter, the quarters get clearer and the hosts of birds return to their aquatic abodes. Gradually the lotus-petals begin to open. This phenomenon is fancied by the poet as a part of a grand music performance. When the white swans sing beautifully with melody, the lotus-pond with its lotus-petals moving one after the other appears to keep time with count of fingers (XII. 7). The waters in the lake become clear and due to the absence of wind they are still. Inside them the stars and the planets get reflected and are clearly visible. The poet fancies that it looks as if a part of the sky had fallen down on earth along with the rains (XII. 8). The long rows of flying parrots resemble the wave-lines of the sky (XII. 15). Swans attracted by the smell of lotus, carried far and wide by the wind, fly back to their homes; and they look like pieces of white clouds tossed about by the wind (XII. 16). There is a solitary lotus that has sprung up in a lotus-pond. Seeking for a reason for its solitary appearance, the poet's imagination conceives of a group of lotuses inside the lake, meeting together and discussing about their springing up above the water-level. To know whether the clouds that destroy them have gone or not, they might have deputed this scout of theirs to go up first and see (XII. 19). The cowherd lass having made marks with her nails resembling the crescent moon and having decorated her cheeks with the petals of *Bandhūka*-flower, wants to stimulate the suspicion in her lover that she has had the company of somebody else (XII. 30).

The uniqueness of Kumāradāsa's descriptions is that he gives equal importance to the tumultuous and the soft aspects of Nature. While we have many pictures of the lotus-ponds, birds and other beauties of Nature, his descriptions are not lacking in thunderous clouds, and intoxicated elephants and bulls. For example, the poet fancies the streaks of lightning on the cloud as the rays of the sun who is imprisoned behind those clouds and is tearing open their bellies with his hands in his effort to come out (XI. 55). The cloud has darkened the whole universe by spreading all over the sky. Against its will the lightning appears and dispels the darkness frequently. As if enraged at this the cloud roads aloud in the form of thunder (XI. 62). The huge clouds resembling mountains collide with each other by the force of the wind, as a result of which fire in the form of lightning flashes forth. Scratching the earth with his hooves and crying out in rage, the wild bull is fancied by the poet as either marking the number of victories it has won or challenging its rival bulls for a fight (XII. 31).

Often our poet takes to the device of Śleṣa or paranomasia to render his fancies pointed. In such cases he is able to draw some effective similes for natural phenomena from human beings. For example, the Sun in the Spring season in his northward journey is compared to a sacrificial priest, with the help of a few words with double meaning.

भ्रान्त्वा विवस्वानथ दक्षिणशामालम्ब्य सर्वत्र करप्रसारी।
ऋत्विक्ततो निस्स्व इव प्रतस्थे वसूपलब्ध्यै धनदस्य वासम् ॥

(III. 2).

The sun like a penniless sacrificer, having attached himself to the southern direction (throughout *Dakṣiṇāyana*) being motivated by the desire to get *Dakṣiṇā* or money and spreading his rays everywhere (stretching his begging hand before everybody), started his journey to the north (started towards Kubera's abode), to get some wealth. With the help of words like दक्षिणाशा, करप्रसारी and धनदस्य वास, the poet has succeeded in drawing out a complete similarity between the two. Such pictures reinforced by Śleṣa are not rare in Kumāradāsa's poem. Similarly in the 11th canto, we have the following verse where words with doublemeanings are used to depict a human feeling and reaction in an inanimate object of Nature.

स्निग्धद्विजालीरुचिरं प्रियङ्गुश्यामद्युतिश्चारुतमालकान्तम् ।
बिभर्ति गन्धाहृतभृङ्गचक्रं तन्माधवीमण्डपमेतदास्यम् ॥

(III. 21).

Here a comparision is drawn between the face of a damsel

and the bower of Mādhavī creepers by using words with doublemeanings like 'tamālakānta' which can be split in two ways to give the two senses.

We have any number of instances where human behaviour, feelings and reactions are imported into the realm of Nature. Only gifted poets can infuse life into inanimate objects and interpret the natural phenomena from a human angle and equate them with human experiences. It is an usual feature that during the Spring season the nights are of lesser duration and the days become longer. Kumāradāsa explains this by comparing the night to a lady who has been separated from her lover, the winter, and consequently in a shrunken condition. The day is compared to a wayfarer who walks in the hot Sun of the Spring and naturally gets exhausted and takes a longer time to proceed (III. 13). The clouds that have consumed water from many rivers have their bellies full and hence are not able to move due to fatigue. So they are fancied as taking rest on the peaks of mountains (XI. 56). Similarly their thunder is humorously fancied as their belching due to a heavy meal (XI. 94). In the dripping of water from the moon-stones on the rise of the moon the poet sees the image of a friend sorrowing at a friend's misfortune; the moon having been vanquished by the face of Sītā and consequently besmirched with a black mark, the moon-stone, its friend, appears to be moved to tears (VIII. 92). While the cold blast of wintry breeze is blowing, Cupid, as if afraid of its chillness, takes refuge in the hearts of the separated lovers to warm himself in the fire of grief raging in their hearts.

शिशिरशीकरवाहिनि मारुते चरति शीतभयादिव सत्वरः ।
मनसिजः प्रविवेश वियोगिनीहृदयमाहितशोकहुताशनम् ॥

(XI. 66)

Equally skilled is the poet in depicting the influences of Nature on human beings. The hearts of the separated ladies shudder on seeing the clouds rising; dark with the water and flashing with showers (with the sharp edge—dhārā), the cloud appears before them verily like the sword of Cupid threatening them. The wives of the travellers shed streams of tears along with the clouds that shed water (XI. 63). They begin to muse over the possible sufferings of their lovers on hearing the peacocks sounding, and on smelling the fragrance of the *Ketakī* (XI. 64). The eyes of the wives of travellers resembled ruby-gems only in their lustre. But when the moon was up their similarity with the moon-stone was complete since they began to drip with water (tears) (XVI. 24).

The *Lāngalī* in blossom with bees hovering and humming around, makes the young lover travelling abroad think of the young wife he left behind at home and hurry back; in a fancy worked on this, the poet says that the *Lāngalī* seems to lift up its hands in the form of its blossom and through the voice of the hum of the bees tell the wandering youth, forgetful of his home, that in the long interval of his absence his young wife at home had shot up into a picture of youth and beauty.

निरस्तगृहसंगतिभ्रंमत एव तन्व्यास्तव
स्तनद्वयमियद्वपुः पथिक जातमुद्यौवनम् ।
इतीव वदति स्फुटं कुसुमहस्तमुद्यम्य सा
भ्रमद्भ्रमरमण्डलक्वणितपेशला लाङ्गली ।।

In some other pictures the poet's depiction of sentiments through scenes of Nature is more complete. Sentiments like *Śṛṅgāra*, *Bhayānaka*, *Bībhatsa*, *Hāsya*, *Śoka* and *Karuṇa* are depicted in objects of Nature.

While describing the Rainy season, the poet finds the opportunity to depict Śṛngāra in the case of a bee-couple. In spite of the thunderous rains accompanied by lightning and in spite of the general agitation caused to the whole world, a pair of bees is having its quiet enjoyment in a secure corner undisturbed by the tumultuous season. It is indeed a remarkable flight of imagination that takes tne poet to the interior of the newly-blossomed *Ketakī* flower, wherein, on the soft couch of its pollen dust, rest in peace the romantic bee-couple who have not even known that the rains have set in.

नवविबोधमनोहरकेतकीकुसुमगर्भगतः सह कान्तया ।
अविदितानिलवृष्टिसमागमो सुखमशेत चिराय शिलीमुखः ॥

While describing the *Śarad*, the poet gives another instance of *Śṛṅgāra* in Natural objects. The *Sārasa* bird approaching the lotus-bud makes it blossom by poking his beak into it. The lotus-bud with its fragrance concealed inside and with its closed petals being thus opened by the *Sārasa*, resembles the face of a newly wedded girl. The feminine shyness associated with the initial inexperience and delicacy on the part of the girl and the impatient nature of the youth in the lover are fully depicted in the case of the lotus-bud and the *Sārasa* bird respectively.

निपीड्य चञ्च्वा कमलस्य कुड्मलं विबोधयामास बलेन सारसः ।
सुगन्धिगर्भं मुकुलीकृत ह्रिया पतिः प्रयत्नोदितकन्यकामुखम् ॥

In the same way he depicts in natural objects the sentiment of fear or *Bhayānaka*. The timid female-deer are not yet out of the grip of fear of the forest-conflagrations, though the latter had been put down by the timely down-pour, for the flaming *Kandalīs* with bees hovering around them gave them the same fright of the fire and smoke.

We have also glimpses of the *Bībhatsa* sentiment in some verses of the poet. For example, in one verse, he says that the stomachs of the clouds have burst open due to over-eating, as a result of which their entrails in the form of lightning are exposed.

In another verse, the poet has a graphic picture of the cloud conceived as a mad man. In this the poet has brought out the sentiment of *Hāsya* most effectively with reference to the cloud by using a few words bearing double meanings. The cloud like a mad man is making sudden noises (thunder), giving up his clothes (*ambara*-sky), doing his antics in the proximity of the world of people and hitting them with stone (hail-stones) and drenching with water.

धावन्नकाण्डविहितध्वनिरम्बरस्य
त्यागं विधाय विलसन्निकटे जनस्य ।

निघ्नन् शिलाभिरुदकेन जगन्निषिञ्चन्
उन्मत्तवद्भ्रमति वायुवशात् पयोदः ॥

The capacity to depict human sentiments in Natural objects is best revealed in the case of attributing *Śoka* or pathos to the objects of Nature. An example of the depiction of *Śoka* in a natural object can be had in the following verse in the fourth canto :

श्लथभित्तिविरूढभूरुहक्षतमूलाग्रविनिर्गमक्षतम् ।
स्फुटतीव भृशं शुचातुरं हृदयं तद्गृहचित्रयोषितः ॥

While describing a ruined city, he conceives of a broken wall which is unprotected from rain and sun. Over that wall, trees and plants have grown in abundance. On the side of the wall a figure of a lady is painted which, though looking pale and gloomy, has withstood the ravages of time. Roots of plants grown on the wall have come down penetrating through the wall and just protruded through the heart of the portrait. This, the poet says, appears like the heart of the lady breaking at the tragedy that had overtaken that city.

In the eighth canto, while describing the sun-set, the poet attributes the sentiment of pathos to the lotus-ponds :

सुप्तपद्मविनिमीलितेक्षणाः पश्य शातकलहंसकूजिताः ।
मित्रनाशपरिरोदिताश्चिरं मूर्च्छिता इव विभान्ति दीर्घिकाः ॥ (84)

Here by using the word 'mitra' which means both a friend and the sun, the poet says that the lotus-ponds with the swans crying, looked as if weeping aloud at the loss of their friend, the sun. After crying for a while their grief becomes boundless and they swoon, their lotus-eyes closing.

FLORA AND FAUNA IN THE JĀNAKĪHARAṆA

A wide acquaintance with flora and fauna forms a true index of a poet's love of Nature and close observation. In Kumāradāsa's description of Nature, the plant kingdom figures prominently and shows that he is not one who is satisfied merely with the more common vegetation that one ordinarily knows in his surroundings. Even while describing human behaviour, he draws his comparisons from plant-life. His acquaintance with the botanical world is naturally confined to those plants that are common in the Deccan plateau and on the sea-shores of the peninsula. Unlike Kālidāsa, he does not make any reference to trees Devadāru etc. which grow on very high altitude like that of the Himālayas. Except for such trees, he shows a familiarity with a wide variety of plants, creepers and shrubs. His knowledge of the agricultural plants is also revealed in many places. A review of Kumāradāsa's Botany affords an interesting study and we shall here, for the sake of convenience, notice the various tress, plants and creepers that attracted his attention, in an alphabetical order. The following enumeration does not contain the very common ones like the lotus and the lily which are the conventional favourites of all poets.

AGARU—This tree is referred to in I.53, while describing the hunting expedition of Daśaratha. *Agaru* is said to have grown on the slopes of the Himālayas where Daśaratha went for hunting. It is referred to as a *Pādapa* (tree) by the poet himself: *Vātair vikṛṣṭa-agarupādapānte.* There are two varieties of *Agaru* mentioned by the poet, white and black. He speaks of *Kālāgaru* or black variety in IX. 43, as used to burn incense. In VII. 35, he refers to it also as *Kṛṣṇāgaru. Agaru* is the fragrant aloe tree botanically known as *Aquilaria gallocha.*

AŚOKA—There are numerous references to this tree in the poem, as is only natural in a work based on the story of the *Rāmāyaṇa* (III. 5, 7, 10, 22, 24; VIII. 40; XII. 29. etc.)

The tender foliage of the *Aśoka* on the ears of the dark-eyed ladies attain the colour of full-grown leaves by coming into contact with the rays of their eyes (II. I5).

बालो ह्यशोकप्रभव. प्रवालः कान्ति प्रपेदे परिणामरम्याम् ।

Its *dohada* is referred to in III-7. Its flowers are described as fire-like in their appearance.

The botanical identity of *Aśoka* is still uncertain. The plant in question has been identified with three distinct trees which belong to three unrelated families. The respective identities appear to conform to certain geographical regions in India and Ceylon. Thus in the eastern part of the peninsula and in certain parts of Bengal, *Aśoka* is identified with a species of *Polyalthia*. In the western part of the peninsula and in North India, it is equated with *Saraca Indica*. This opinion appears to have found general favour.[1] The third identity is the one that is prevalent in Ceylon. It is a common experience of botanical explorers or students of Botany, who visit the island, to be shown a species of *Rhododendron* as *Aśoka*.[2] It may be noted here that *Rhododendron* in Ceylon (as elsewhere) grows at altitudes of five to seven thousand feet.

We shall now analyse as to which one of these three comes nearest to the description given by Kumāradāsa. There is documentary evidence to show that species of *Polyalthia* have been introduced into South India from Ceylon in recent years and thus the identity of this plant with the classical *Aśoka* is negatived. On the other hand *Saraca Indica* is exclusively an Indian plant and not indigenous to Ceylon, though it is common in Ceylon during recent years due to horticultural introduction. Thus this identity too is untenable.

1. M.S. Randhawa, 'Progressive desiccation of Northern India in Historical Times', *Journal of Bombay Natural History Society* Vol. 45, pp. 555-565.

2. I am thankful to Dr. B.G.L. Swamy, Professor of Botany, Presidency College, Madras who kindly supplied me with the above information.

Because Kumāradāsa happens to be a Ceylonese poet and that too of about the 7th century, it remains to be seen how far *Rhododendron* would fit in with the identity of *Aśoka* according to the poet's description. The tender leaves of *Rhododendron* are reddish in colour and it fits with the description of the tree in the Spring season as comparable to the fire that burnt Cupid. A foliage of such colour, when placed on the ears of the dark-eyed ladies, attain a new effect which gives it a novel appearance (a curious blend of the dark and the red), the change being in conformity with the colour of the mature foliage.

Incidentally it may be pointed out that the local name prevalent near about Anurādhapura (where *Rhododendron* is showed to be the *Aśoka*), is Asak or some variant which sounds almost similar.

BAKULA—In XII. 28, while describing the rustic lass who guards the farm, the poet compares the lower lip of these girls to a fully ripened *Bakula*: अनुव्रजन्त्या बकुलं विपाकवत्समस्त-बद्धारुणिमाधरश्रिया । Here by the comparison with the ripened *Bakula*, we have to suppose that the poet was having in mind the brown-complexioned country-folk. whose lips are not likely to be as red as those of the fair-complexioned ones. *Bakula* which is well-known is identical with *Kesara* and is botanically known as *Mimusops Elengi*. The poet uses the name *Kesara* also in III. 52 and XIV. 36. It bears a strong-smelling flower and is very ornamental in pleasure-gardens.

BANDHŪKA—In the same context as above, Kumāradāsa says that the rustic lasses decorated their cheeks with the petals of the *Bandhūka* flower. This is also called *Bandhujīva* and is identical with *Pentapetes Phoenicea*.[1] It yields red flowers of excellent hue but with out smell. They blossom in the afternoon and fade away in the evening.

CAMPAKA—In III. 27, the poet refers to the *Campaka* trees which are well-known. In II. 3, the whole *Campaka* tree, fully blossomed is compared to a lamp-stand with thousands of lights in the form of flowers lit over it. It is known as *Michelia Champaka*. It flowers during rainy season and bears white and yellow fragrant flowers.

1. Other identifications of this are also made.

CANDANA—The poet mentions the *Candana* tree on many occasions. It is the abode of serpents during the hot Summer (IV. 24). While describing the *Hemakūṭa* mountains in the twentieth canto, the poet says that it abounds in *Candana* trees (XX. 12). This is the common sandal tree, botanically known as *Santalam Album*. It is of two varieties, white and red.

CŪTA—This is also known as *Sahakāra* and is the common mango tree. Kumāradāsa refers to it only on three occasions though earlier poets like Kālidāsa have frequently referred to it. It is described as the abode of bees (III. 10).

DARBHA—In VI. 12, the poet describes the elephant in Janaka's palace eating the heaps of *Darbha* put before them. In VII. 37, it is referred to as a requirement for the religious ceremonies associated with the marriage. *Darbha* is the grass, otherwise known as *Kuśa* which the botanists call *Imperata Arundinacea*. It is also identified with *Imperata Cylindrica*. Though both *Darbha* and *Kuśa* stand for the same variety, they seem to mean two types of grass; one, with a tapering end and the other cut into pieces with cut ends. Because, usually the word *Kuśa* is associated only with the long tapering grass, as Kumāradāsa himself has said in V. 7. This ordinary grass is not a popular fodder for elephants. But a particular variety of it called the Elephant-grass is relished by the elephants. Perhaps the word *Darbha* is commonly used to indicate both the varieties.

IKṢU—While describing the route taken by Rāma, Lakṣmaṇa and Sītā when they started on their Vanavāsa, the poet says in X. 52, that they reached the *Gaṅgā* after passing through the *Uttara Kosala* country abounding in sugar-cane crops (*Saccharum Officinarum*). The fields in which *Ikṣu*-plants are grown are called *Śākaṭa*.

INGUDĪ—A reference to the fruits of *Iṅgudī* being dried up in the Sun is made by the poet in V. 9, while describing the hermitage of Viśvāmitra. This is a wild tree identified with *Ximeria Aegyptiaca*. A kind of oil can be extracted from its fruits. This oil was used by ascetics to burn their lights and also as an ointment and considered as having some medicinal properties. *Iṅgudī Piṇyāka* or the oil-cake of this is referred to in other works as edible. The tree is otherwise known as *Tāpasataru*.

KADALĪ—This is the common plantain tree known as *Musa Sapientum*, whose inner sheaths or coverings are referred to by the poet as being used in the course of the *Śaityopacāra* for the love-sick (VII. 28).

KALAMA—This is a variety of *dhānya* or rice. The poet refers to it as being cultivated in forest-regions and the fields in which they are grown, are protected by the farm-girls (XII. 6, 10, 11, 27).

KANDALĪ—According to the lexicon *Medinī*, *Kadalī* and *Kandalī* refer to the same plant. In the *Apadāna* (I. 16) *Kadalī* is found as a different reading of *Kandalī*. But Kumāradāsa refers to it as *Kandala* in XI. 43, 47. His pointed reference to its blossomed state runs thus:

इति यथा विजहास वनस्थली प्रविकसद्दलकन्दलशोभिनी ।

The forest-regions during the rainy season, with *Kandala* plants bearing flowers fully blossomed, appeared as if laughing. B.S. Upadhyaya identifies *Kandalī* with a plant whose leaves are green and which dries up in the hot season and all at once makes its appearance at the beginning of the rain. B.C. Law dercribes it as an underground creeper with blue flowers. But these identifications do not conform to the description given by Kumāradāsa. So we have to infer that the poet meant only *Kadalī* when he said *Kandala*, in line with the lexicographers. By saying that it looks like laughing he would have meant that the red outer sheaths are just separating from the bud and about to fall down, and it is thereby exposing the white flowers inside, which resemble the row of teeth.

KARAVĪRA—In III. 6, Kumāradāsa compares the blood-red fresh buds of the *Karavīra* flowers that appear in the Spring to the blades of the arrows of the God of love, besmeared with the blood of lovers. The second reference in III. 14 is also to the brightness of the flowers beaming forth with redddish lustre. This is botanically known as *Nerium Odorum* or *Nerium Odoratum*.

KARṆIKĀRA—This tree is described in III. 8 as putting forth blossoms during the Spring season. With peacocks and bees sitting on it, it is compared to a crown worn by the mountain on which it has grown. B.S. Upadhyaya identifies it as *Hibiscus Mutabilis* which flowers in the Spring and 'bears red flowers of excellent hue but without smell'. B.C. Law opines on the other hand that it is a small tree with large bright yellow flowers with fragrance and identifies it with *Cassia Fistula*. C.A. Rhylands discussing in detail its identity, states that is has bright-coloured yellow flowers and it grows on hill-sides. On the authority of the *Dhanvantarīya Nighaṇṭu*, which gives *Karṇīkāra* as a variety of *Āragvadha* or *Cassia Fistula*, he says that it must bust belong to the *Cassia*-family. Since Kumāradāsa also mentions it as growing on the top of a mountain and fancies it as a golden crown with gems and rubies in the form of bees and necks of peacocks, we can safely conclude that the tree in question is one that grows on hillocks and bears yellow or gold-coloured flowers. This agrees more with the conclusion of Rhylands, which means we can only say that *Karṇikāra* belongs to the *Cassia*-family.

KETAKĪ—This plant which is well-known, is mentioned by Kumāradāsa on two occasions (XI. 64, 76). He refers to it as having a rich stock of pollen dust and thickly grown petals. He also makes mention of a *Vana-ketakī* which is a variety of it found in forests. This plant is botanically known as *Pandanus Odorattissimus*, a green plant with needle-pointed blades for leaves and bears a strong-smelling flower. It flowers chiefly during the rainy season. There are two kinds of them, male and female. Only the flowers of the male plant are sweet-scented.

KIMŚUKA—This is same as the *Palāśa*. Kumārdāsa refers to it by both the names (III. 11; IV. 20, etc.). *Palāśa* is supposed to be the red species. It is botanically known as *Butea Frondosa*. It bears beautiful red flowers without smell. Kumāradāsa fancies the *Palāśa* fully blossomed, as the fire that burnt Cupid. When the flowers of the *Kimśuka* drop down due to wind, they drip with red juice from their stems. Hence the poet compares it to the dropping of blood by the

Rākṣasas on the sacrificial altars of Viśvāmitra (IV. 20).

KUMKUMA—This is the saffron. The poet refers to it in this description of women, who smear their breasts with its paste.

KUNDA—This is a shrub of the jasmine species and its flowers are white and delicate.

LĀṄGALĪ—Kumāradāsa refers to this plant in five or six places in his poem. He describes its foliage as resembling rising flames of fire. It puts forth leaves at the advent of the rainy season. With bees hovering around it, it looks like a forest conflagration emitting volumes of flame and smoke. Its flowers resemble the palms spread to receive the water. On another occasion he compares the flower of this plant to the budding breasts of a young girl.

The *Śabdakalpadruma* mentions one *Lāngalikī* which is also known as *Agnijvālā*. The *Amarakośa* mentions it as *Agniśikhā* and the *Ratnāvalī* as *Agnijihvā*. Kumāradāsa himself mentions it in one place as *Vanhiśikhā* thus : *Vitata-vahniśikhākusumaśriyah* (XI. 83). The association of the flame of fire in the above names given to it, is very significant. In the *Bhāvaprakāśa*, *Lāṅgalī* is given as a synonym for *Nārikela* or coconut. But this does not bear any common feature with the one described by the poet. So it is more probable that our poet has meant the *Lāngalikī*, which is called *Agniśikhā*. This is a shrub botanically know as *Gloriossa Superba*. Each flower has five or six petals which exactly resemble the figures of the palm held in the shape of a cup and they are red in colour. This exactly fits in with the description given by the poet who says :

निरस्तगृहसंगतिर्भ्रमत एव तन्व्यास्तत्र
स्तनद्वयमियद्वपुः पथिक जातमुद्यौवनम् ।
इतीव वदति स्फुटं कुसुमहस्तमुद्यम्य सा
भ्रमद्भ्रमरमण्डलक्वणितपेशला लाङ्गली ॥ XI. 95

The plant is said to lift up its hand in the form of the cup-shaped flower and inform the traveller, who had left his young wife at home, that in his absence she has grown up to maturity. The idea that the plant is fancied as conveying to the traveller, needs a cup-shaped hand to represent the budding breasts, which is well served by the shape of its flower. This fits in very well with the flowers of *Lāṅgalikī* or *Gloriossa Superba*, which have petals resembling the fingers of the hand.

This plant is a climbing herb with leafy stems and possesses leaves with elongated and spiral tips functioning as tendrils. It is known in the Sinhalese as *Niyangala* and in Tamil as *Ventoṇṭi* or *Kārtlikai Kiḷangu.* It is common in bushy places of low-country area. It flowers during the rainy season. The flowers are 'at first greenish passing through yellow, orange and scarlet to crimson from base to apex.'[2] The Sinhalese name *Hiyangala* and the Sanskrit name *Lāngalikī* have some phonetic similarty and perhaps *Lāṅgalī,* as used by Kumāradāsa, was its name at an intermediate stage when the old Sanskrit *Lāṅgalikī* was undergoing a colloquialisation to *Niyangala.*

MĀDHAVĪ:—It is described as used to form a resting bower in a garden (III. 21) It is identified with the *Vāsantī* creeper (*Hiptage Madablota*).

MALLIKĀ—This belongs to the jasmine group and is classified by Suśruta as a *Gulma* (shrub). It has several kinds, both shrubs and creepers.

MUÑJA—Kumāradāsa refers to the *Mauñjī* which is the girdle worn by ascetics made of the *Muñja* grass (*Saccharium Arundinaceum*).

NĪVĀRA—It is a variety of *Dhānya* and is used as food by the forest-dwellers.

NĪPA—(XI. 85) This is the same as *Kadamba*. It is a large tree breaking into blossom in the rains. It is botanically known as *Anthocephalus Cadamba*.

NĪLĪ—There is a reference to this in XVI. 21. This is other-

1. *Flora of the Presidency of Madras*, C.E.C. Fischer, London (1928), p. 1519.

2. *A Hand-book to the Flora of Ceylon*, Henry Trimen, London (1898), p. 294.

wise known as *Jalanīlī*. It is the moss that collects on the surface of the lakes.

PRIYAṄGU—In III. 12 there is a reference to the *Priyaṅgu*. This is usually identified with a dark-coloured creeper called *Setaria Italica* or Panic seed. The black *Priyaṅgu* is mentioned in the *Jātaka Nidānakathā* and is very delicate. It is also mentioned in Aśvaghoṣa's *Saundarananda* (VII. 6). But according to Varāhamihira it is a tree. He mentions it thus: 'Let us first of all talk of trees that should be planted in a garden, or in the house itself, *Ariṣṭa*, *Aśoka*, *Punnāga*, *Śirīṣa*, *Priyaṅgu*,[1] etc. Girija Prasanna Majumdar, in the list of plants that he gives at the end of his edition of *Upavanavinoda*, identifies it with *Aglaia Roxburghiana*[2].

TAMĀLA—This is referred to by Kumāradāsa in XX. 12 where he describes the Hemakūṭa mountain thus: *Parisphurattamālakānanām*. It is botanically known as *Cinnamomum Ceylanicum* and is found on high altitudes of three to five thousand feet in rain forests. Older leaves are thick and leathery in texture and dark olive green in colour. Young leaves are somewhat pinkish and relatively thin. The dried matured leaves are used as spices.

TĀLA—Kumāradāsa refers to *Tāla* in XX. 17 while describing the ocean: *Upāntabhāgasthita-tālabhūṣaṇaḥ*. It is very common in the island of Ceylon and on the Tamil and Kerala coast. It is a species of *Pandaus*.

1. *Upavanavinoda* ed. by G.P. Majumdar, Calcutta, 1935, p. 7.
2. *Ibid*, p. 124.

B. FAUNA

Kumāradāsa is equally familiar with the world of animals and birds. He refers to numerous animals that are familiar to the island of Ceylon and also a few which are not so common there.

Throughout his poem he makes frequent references to elephants which are so evident in the Kandyan forests of Ceylon. He also alludes to a prevalent method of catching wild elephants with the help of tamed female ones. By attracting the wild elephants towards the female one, people used to catch the wild ones (XVI.52). The wild forest-grass and the sugarcane are referred to as the fodder for them.

Animals like lion (I. 88, XII. 45), leopard or *Dvīpin* (V. 23, IX. 27), *Ṛkṣa* or bear, *Varāha* or boar, the bison or *Mahiṣa* (XI. 74), the wild ox called *Gavaya* (XIV. 10), and the wolf or *Vṛka* (XII. 45) are also mentioned. Among the forest-animals we have the wild bull referred to as *Gavāmpati* (XII.31), and *Vṛṣa* (XII. 31). Monkeys are also mentioned in numerous places with various names like *Valīmukha*, *Kapi*, *Plavaṅga*, *Plavaṅgama*, etc.; *Śarabha*, the eight-legged animal is referred to in I. 71.

Among the aquatic beings, the fish of many varieties is mentioned. The poet often refers to the *Makara*, a kind of sea-monster. Of this he particularly refers to one *Mātaṅgama-kara*, which may be identified with the *Mātaṅganakra* mentioned by Kālidāsa (XIII. 11). Whales are referred to as *Timiṅgila* (XIV. 59), or *Timi* (XIV. 49), and crocodiles as *Nakra* (XV. 73). Tortoise or *Kūrma* comes in XIV. 60.

Nakula or the mongoose is mentioned in VI. 11. Reptiles of various kinds are referred to. Apart from the common snakes which he calls *Sarīsṛpa*, *Ahi*, *Uraga*, etc., we have the more fearful types like *Ajagara* or the python, which is of a huge size (XIV. 15, 66, VI. 22) and the *Kṛṣṇasarpa* or the dark poisonous serpent (VIII. 65, 67).

Among the domestic animals we have the elephants, that are trained and utilised in the battles (XVII. 40), cows deer and its varieties. Horses used for battles are referred to as *Vājins* (V. 39, 42), *Turaṅgama* (V. 28) etc.

Birds of almost all kinds are described. The white swans are most often referred to as *Hamsa*, *Sitavihaṅgama* (XI. 42), *Sitacchada* (XII. 7), etc. *Balākas* or cranes are also described as inseparable companions of clouds (XI. 52). The peacocks are mentioned by various names like the *Barhin* (XI. 46), *Śikhin* (I. 41), *Śikhaṇḍin* (XII. 13) and *Śitikaṇṭha* (XII. 26). The famous *Cakravāka* bird is also referred to as *Rathāṅga* (XI. 68), *Cakranāman* (XI 11) etc. Birds like the cuckoo or *Kokila* (IV. 74), *Cātaka* (IV. 26), *Śuka* or parrot (XII. 17, 25) and the *Sārasa* or a kind of crane (I. 64) are also mentioned, The ordinary crow is referred to as *Vāyasa* (V. 60) and *Balipuṣṭa* (X. 56).

Insects like the *Lūtikā* or spider (IV. 56) and the worms or *Kīṭa* (V. 7) are also mentioned.

DEPICTION OF RASAS IN THE JĀNAKĪHARAṆA

As a poet of no mean capacity, Kumāradāsa has revealed throughout his work his power to depict and evoke the various sentiments. Of course *Śṛṅgāra* and *Vīra* form the major Rasas depicted by him in the poem. In *Śṛṅgāra*, the *Sambhoga*-phase is dealt with more elaborately. Among other *Rasas*, *Karuṇa* and *Bībhatsa* figure with some prominence.

Śṛṅgāra occupies the major portions of cantos III, VIII and XVI. In each of these cantos the poet deals with different situations of love and thus avoids repetition. In the eighth canto of the poem the poet describes elaborately the amorous sports of Rāma and Sītā, particularly on their nuptial night, in 53 verses. This whole canto is, as we have already stated, entirely based on the eighth canto of the *Kumārasambhava* and the poet never tries to conceal his indebtedness to Kālidāsa who is the source of his inspiration. The whole description can be divided broadly into three sections according to the nature and progress of the pleasures depicted here. The first section deals with the bashfulness and fear on the part of Sītā who was just initiated into the art of love. The psychological and physical reactions to the first expressions of love are well brought out in the following verse :

सप्रयत्नमुपवेशिताप्यसौ कामिना समुपगूह्य बालिका ।
साध्वसेन चपला मुहुर्मुहुः वाञ्छति स्म समुदेतुमङ्कतः ॥

Though seated on his lap with great effort and closely embraced by the husband, she out of bashfulness tried again and again to get up from his lap. This state of mind where love and delicacy prevailed with equal strength until the former completely overcame the latter, put her in a dilemma and the poet describes it thus :

विप्रयोगसमये मनोभुवा सन्निधौ नृपसुतस्य लज्जया ।
इच्छति स्म भृशमाकुलीकृता कामिनी न विरहं न सङ्गमम् ॥

Agonised by love during the time of separation and afflicted by bashfulness during the time of union, Sītā suffered in both ways and so she wished for neither separation nor union with her lover. The usual physical reactions in a lady when she feels the first shafts of the God of Love namely *Sāttvika-bhāvas* like perspiration, horripilation and shivering, are also depicted by the poet in the case of Sītā. Her lower lip quivered as if due to the fear of being wounded by the lover's teeth. When she lifted her hands to tie her dishevelled tresses, her arms invited the ardent gaze of her lover (VIII. 22). When she, out of bashfulness, pushed aside her lover's hand which tried to untie her girdle, he pretended to be offended and immediately she embraced him with an appealing look that implied apology (VIII. 10). Like a *Rājahaṁsa* endeavouring to enjoy the unblown lotus, Rāma had great difficulty in having access to the face of Sītā (VIII. 14).

In the second stage of the description the poet depicts the gradual disappearance of this delicacy in the heroine and her resistance becoming less and less. Slowly her skill in the art of enjoyment unfolded itself and the poet draws many a fine picture in this context which can best be enjoyed in the original. Though Sītā could not speak due to her feminine bashfulness, her tears and horripilation proclaimed her sports and joy :

अश्रुणा रतिषु खेदमात्मनः सम्मदं च पुलकेन कामिनी ।
भावनृत्तकुशलेव नर्त्तकी व्याजहार न तु लज्जया गिरा ।।

By the complete disappearance of all delicacy, the heroine became an adept or *Prauḍhā*. In this third stage again, the poet shows his mastery in depicting the free initiative that the beloved took.

चोदयत्यवनिपालनन्दने शिक्षितं युवतिकृत्यनैपुणम् ।
देहजन्मशरखण्डितत्रपा सा ययौ रहसि कर्मकर्तृताम् ।।
प्रार्थितानि न चकार कानिचित् कानिचित् स्वयमपि व्यधत्त सा ।
अन्वभूद्धृदयरत्नविक्रयक्रीतमेनमबला यथेप्सितम् ।।

(VIII. 29, 44)

In the earlier context of the third canto the poet presents another set of pictures in connection with the *Śṛṅgāra* of Daśaratha. Here he depicts the garden-sports and water-sports of Daśaratha with his damsels. If in the 8th canto he has followed Kālidāsa, here he has drawn upon the similar description in Bhāravi's *Kirātārjunīya.* The various devices that are adopted by the lover to avoid creating jealousy in the minds of other ladies when he is over-attached to one, are described there. A typical example of this is found in the following verse :

पातुं सुदत्या वदनारविन्दमादाय दृष्टो ललनाभिरीशः ।
अपुष्परेणुव्यथितेऽपि तस्याश्चिक्षेप नेत्रे मुखगन्धवाहम् ।।

(III. 19)

When the king was about to kiss a particular lady, he was noticed by others and just to save himself from the situation he blew his breath into the eyes of that lady and thus pretended to remove the dust that was supposed to have fallen into her eyes. When the king dived into the waters and wanted to embrace a lady inside the water without being noticed by others, the transparent water betrayed him (III. 38). The guilt of the lover closetted within a bower with his beloved would have been proclaimed by the noise of the girdle, but for the fact that the music of the swans drowned it (III. 42). The naughty looks of the lover were set at naught by a lady by directing a jet of water at his eyes.

In the sixteenth canto, we have the description of another variety of lovers. While depicting the love of the *Rākṣasa*-damsels at Laṅkā, the poet elaborately deals with the love-quarrels (*Praṇayakalaha*) among the couples, the usual jealousy of ladies and the plight of a *Khaṇḍitā Nāyikā.* When the lover was delaying to come, one lady removed the floral decoration on her breasts by the flow of tears from her eyes (XVI. 28). A *Nāyikā* being duped by her own lady messenger whom she had sent to fetch her lover, is very elaborately pictured in this canto. The lady messenger, after having taken her own mistress's place, came back with some excuse for her delay to return. The intelligent *Nāyikā* easily detected the treacherous behaviour of her lady messenger and addressed her in caustic and pointed words. The poet ekes out this theme of *Nāyikā*-type called *dūtī-sambhoga-vañcitā*, in a number of fine ideas. Another picture that is presented is the *Nāyikā* herself detecting her husband's faithlessness and chastising him for the same in very sarcastic language. Being bit at the lip by the other lady, the lover held his palm against his mouth when he approached the *Nāyikā* and the latter asked him whether it was to hide the wound on his lip or was a mark of respect for her. The sparsely-grown moustache on his upper lip could not completely explain the thick dark colour there, because it was due to the collyrium that had been transferred there from the eyes of the beloved when he kissed the latter. The description of the love-sports of Rāvaṇa with his numerous faces and arms affords much scope to Kumāradāsa to show his ingenuity in improvising many interesting fancies.

The *Vipralambha* phase of *Śṛṅgāra* is depicted here and there in cantos XI, XII, and XIII. In the first two, while describing the seasons, Kumāradāsa devotes a few verses to depict the influence of these seasonal changes in the minds of separated lovers. A typical example is found in the eleventh canto where a lady is described as weeping on thinking of the torments that her lover who had gone abroad would be suffering from :

विततपावनके वनकेतकीसुरभिगन्धवहे धव हे पथि ।
शिखिगिरं सहसे सहसे भवान् इति रवैरुदिता रुदितास्त्रियः ।।

When the cool breeze carrying the sweet-smelling pollen dust of the *Ketakī* flowers is blowing, how can a separated lover on his travels brook the heart-rending cry of the peacocks? But a regular attempt at depicting *Vipralambha* is made by the poet in the seventh canto, where he describes the mental state of Rāma and Sītā during their separation after their first meeting. As if to prepare the ground for this, Kumāradāsa introduces a *Pūrvānurāga*-scene at the beginning of the canto and makes his hero and heroine completely understand each other and respond to each other's love. The special significance of this *Pūrvānurāga*-description has already been noted under the heading 'Kumāradāsa and Vālmīki' (p. 63 above). The poet makes use of this opportunity to describe *Vipralambha Śṛṅgāra* in eleven verses. As if to protect Sītā from the fire of separation that had increased her mental agony, Rāma did not leave the heart even though he was physically separated (VII. 20). The eyes of Sītā were filled with tears. This is fancied by the poet as due to her unwillingness to see the space before her from where Rāma had disappeared (VII. 21). Then the poet refers to the conventional *Śaityopacāras* and says that they proved to be fruitless in the case of Sītā:

मृदुप्रवालास्तरणेऽपि तन्वी शिलातले नैव धृतिं सिषेवे ।
असृक्स्रवार्द्रे शरतल्पमध्ये सा पुष्पकेतोरिव वर्तमाना ।।

(VII. 26)

She failed to have comfort even on a slab of stone spread with soft leaves; she felt as if she was lying on a bed of Cupid's arrows besmeared with blood. The lotus of her eyes did not close even after the rise of the moon (VII. 27). The tender interior leaves of the plantain tree with dripping water placed on her heart by her friends, resembled a bandage tied over the wound caused by the arrows of Cupid (VII. 28). Thus the daughter of Janaka passed through those few days of separation during which even in the midst of maid-friends, she was not happy and even the cool rays of the moon were a torture to her.

At the end of the thirteenth canto where he narrates the miserable state of Sītā through the mouth of Hanumān, we have another description of *Vipralambha*. Within the short compass of four verses he gives a fine pen-picture of Sītā suffering in her separation :

मुखेन्दुमरुणत्विषं सततचिन्तया बिभ्रतीं
कपोललुलितालकं विगलदश्रुणी लोचने ।
तदीयमवलोकयन् व्रजति मार्दवं चेतसि
क्षपाचरगणश्रुतं सपदि शूकमुत्प्रेक्षते ।।

Equally skilled is the poet in the depiction of the sentiment of *Karuṇa* or pathos. Even in the first canto, while describing the tragic end of the sage-boy at the hands of Daśaratha, he devotes about ten verses to the depiction of pathos. When the king approached the target of his arrow, he found, contrary to his expectation, a young sage with his chest pierced by the arrow and the poet fancies that Daśaratha was hit at heart by a terrible shaft in the form of the boy's cry of agony rendered more unbearable by the tears :

नेत्राम्बुदिग्धेन विलापनाम्ना
बाणेन भूयो हृदि तं जघान ।।

Every word that the sage-boy addressed to Daśaratha adds intensity to the tragic event and moves more and more the heart of the reader. Comparing himself to a supporting stick for his old parents, the young sage describes the condition of his parents and the poet leaves it to the reader to imagine the consequences for them, now that they are bereft of the supporting staff, namely, their only son:

त्वया जरावेशजडीकृतस्य वने विनाथस्य गुरुद्वयस्य ।
विचक्षुषोऽयं व्रतजीर्णमूर्तेः भग्नः किमालम्बनदण्ड एकः ।।

The poet intensifies the pathos of the situation not only by emphasising the old age of the parents but also by drawing a graphic picture of the extreme poverty of the family :

जीर्णो जतुन्यासनिरुद्धरन्ध्रः कुम्भश्च मौञ्जी तरुवल्कलं च ।

The boy's possession comprises an old water-pot with its holes sealed by wax.

The next occasion where the poet develops the sentiment of *Karuṇa* is while describing Mandodarī's lamentation over the death of Rāvaṇa. This theme which is more or less developed on the same lines as the *Rati-vilāpa* in the 4th canto of the *Kumārasambhava* has been effectively handled by the poet. Her heart was about to burst due to the grief of her husband's death and as if to put down the heat and prevent it from breaking, the eyes shed showers of tears on it (XIX. 35). The intensity of grief overpowered her so much that she could not even realise the difference between the dead and the living. Just like Aja (*Raghu.* VII) who felt that the corpse of his wife would feel uneasy if placed on the rough funeral pyre, Mandodarī, while removing the dust that had collected at the arrow-wound on Rāvaṇa's body, did so with maximum care, lest it should give him pain. This was the stage when she forgot that, dead as he was, he could not feel any pain.

> प्रियस्य बाणव्रणरन्ध्ररोधिनं महीरजस्सञ्चयमश्रुवर्षिणी ।
> प्रिया परासोरपि खेदशङ्कया सकम्पहस्ता शनकैरपाहरत् ॥

The limbs of her beloved lord, moving, though only due to being pulled by the wolves desirous of flesh, rouse in her the joy and hope that her husband was alive and she took them up in her hands. But soon she realised that they were lifeless and put them down. Here we find a little of the *Bibhatsa* sentiment enhancing the effect of *Karuṇa.*

> प्रियस्य सोऽयं पिशिताभिकाङ्क्षिभिः वृकैर्विकृष्यावयवोऽपि कम्पितः ।
> प्रहर्षमाशाविषयं विधाय मे पुनर्यथार्थविगमे निरस्यते ॥
>
> (XIX. 41)

The description of her pleading for mercy to each one of the Gods and her disappointment at their silence are effectively portrayed.

The sentiment of *Vīra* is depicted in more than one place—in the 5th canto, while describing the fight between Rāma and the Rākṣasas, in the 9th canto where Rāma encounters Paraśurāma, in the 11th canto where Jaṭāyus and Rāvaṇa, and Vālin and Sugrīva fight with each other and in the 19th canto where the battle between Rāma and Rāvaṇa is described. On each of these occasions, the poet makes use of other *Rasas* to add to the effect of *Vīra.* For example, in the 5th canto, we have the *Bibhatsa* employed to heighten the effect of the *Vīra.* Here the poet devotes about 35 verses for the description of the battle between

Rāma and the Rākṣasas at the sacrifice of Viśvāmitra. The dexterity and speed with which Rāma discharged his arrows is well brought out in the following verse:

शरासने वर्त्मनि लक्ष्यभेदने परैरुपालक्ष्यत नेषुसन्ततिः।
ऋतेऽपि हेतोरिव दीर्णवक्षसो निपेतुरस्य प्रथने सुरद्विषः ॥ V. 30

The placing of the arrows on the bow, the course that they took when they were discharged and their hitting at the desired object were hardly perceived by the onlookers; so quickly did the torn Rākṣasas fall, as if of themselves. In the great wind that was produced by the feathered arrows of Rāma, those discharged by the enemies were turned back against themselves and made to hit their own bodies (V. 33). A Rākṣasa rushing on towards Rāma was beheaded by an arrow and there was the spectacle of his trunk still advancing in its original momentum.

A cavalier was cut at his head by an arrow of Rāma but the lower portion did not drop down, because it was firmly bound to the horse by the thighs and the fist that held the reins tight was just dangling above the head of the horse automatically:

कृपाणकृत्तस्य दृढोरुयन्त्रितं न पश्चिमार्धं निपपात सादिनः ।
तुरङ्गवल्गादृढसक्तमुष्टिना परेण भागेन च लम्बितं पुरः ॥ V. 48

The headless trunks of the enemies struck terror, because they looked at if the enemies themselves had risen up again for fighting.

While describing the encounter of Rāma with Paraśurāma, the poet employs the *Bhayānaka* and the *Raudra* also. The very entrance of Paraśurāma was preceded by a series of fearful omens. The four quarters put on a monstrous appearance with enveloping darkness. With contrary winds that foretold misfortune, they acquired gloom like persons on the verge of destruction. The very form of Paraśurāma is described in such a way as to strike terror in anybody. The leopard's skin that he wore on his shoulders with its variegated spots looked like bearing the sparks of the fire of penance with which he was glowing.

In the beginning of the 11th canto, Kumāradāsa gives a description of another type of battle in which Rāvaṇa with his bow, arrows and sword had a very tough fight with Jaṭāyus, whose weapons were only his beak and claws. In the same canto he depicts the hand-to-hand duel between Sugrīva and Vālin. With his nails and beak, Jaṭāyus struck at the row of crowns on the heads of Rāvaṇa from which sparks of fire were produced due to friction with the gems on those crowns. With the edge of Rāvaṇa's spear thrust into his chest, the lord of the birds with his stretched wings appeared like an umbrella held open.

The very description of Vālin and Sugrīva getting ready to fight with each other is a picture of valour and rage that thrills the reader. With their hands removing with ease the trees that were thrown on their heads by each other, with blood flowing from their lips by biting them in rage with their own teeth, with fists held ready to hit, they approached each other with caution (XI. 32). Due to the crushing effect of the hands tied around each other, they vomitted blood (XI. 34). Vālin, holding Sugrīva by his head, whirled him in the air and the two feet of the latter hitting against the trees around, made them fall down with a huge noise (XI. 38).

The sentiment of *Vīra* coupled with *Raudra* and *Bībhatsa* is powerfully depicted in the 19th canto while describing the fight between Rāma and Rāvaṇa. Roaring with his ten mouths, and bedecked with shining ornaments flashing like lightning, Rāvaṇa resembling verily the cloud that appeared at the time of deluge, filled the whole space between the earth and the skies with his shower of arrows (XIX. 9). The process of discharging the arrow and then the fall of the enemy being hit by that arrow, were so quickly effected by Rāma that the sequence of cause and effect in that process had to be inferred. The arrows that were discharged from the bow of Rāma appeared as if they started on their own accord towards the enemies (XIX. 16). When the heads of Rāvaṇa were felled down by the arrows of Rāma, new ones immediately substituted them. Thus Rāvaṇa himself could see his own heads rolling on the earth with their crowns tossed away and with blood flowing from the lips that were crushed between the rows of teeth.

ददर्श भल्लाभिनिपातपातितप्रकीर्णमौलीनि समुद्गताननः ।
मुखानि दन्तक्रकचक्षताधरप्रवर्तितासृञ्जि निजानि राक्षसः ॥

As we have already stated, Kumāradāsa is equally at home in depicting the quiet sentiment of *Śānta.* In the 5th canto, while describing the hermitage of Viśvāmitra, he depicts the spiritual atmosphere there, surcharged with the feeling of compassion and love. The old hermit sitting underneath the tree with a young antelope sleeping on his lap was not willing to get up though his body was paining due to continuous sitting in the same posture, because he did not want to disturb the sleep of the deer (V. 4). The young ones of the doves which had fallen from the trees were taken care of by the young hermit-boys who prepared a soft nest of feathers for their comfortable stay.

महीरुहभ्रष्टविहङ्गपोतिकासुखोपवेशाय महर्षिसूनुभिः ।
इषीकतूलेन विधाय मार्दवं क्वचित्समासज्जितनीडपञ्जरम् ॥

METRES IN THE JĀNAKĪHARAṆA[1]

Kumāradāsa employs as many as twenty-three metres in his work. He has exhibited his skill in handling the most popular metres like the Vaṁśastha as well as the rare ones like the Nardaṭaka. Like any other great poet, he handles these metres with ease. Following the poetic convention, he generally employs a single metre throughout a canto, with larger ones to mark the end of each canto. In the matter of choosing metres appropriate enough to the sentiment or theme depicted, he has generally followed Kālidāsa. For example, while describing the Sambhoga Śṛṅgāra of Rāma and Sītā in the eighth canto, he has adopted the Rathoddhatā metre which has been effectively used by Kālidāsa in the eighth canto of the *Kumārasambhava* for a similar purpose. Both in the *Kumārasambhava* and the *Raghuvaṁśa*, Kālidāsa uses the Viyoginī effectively for depicting separation and sorrow. Though no such situation of pathos is handled in the *JH*, the use of the Viyoginī in the latter in canto IV (1 to 70), describing the scene of Viśvāmitra taking away the two sons from Daśaratha may be said to have some connection with the meaning of the metre-name. Some appropriateness may also be seen in the poet's employment of the Drutavilambita in cantos XI and XIV, describing Rāvaṇa's fight with Jaṭāyus, and Sugrīva's fight with Vālin in the former canto and the building of the causeway in the latter. A similar purposefulness of metre is seen also in the sixteenth canto, where the evening sports of Rākṣasa-couples are described in the Puṣpitāgrā.

The most favourite metre of our poet seems to be the Vaṁśastha in which he has composed the maximum number of verses. Twelve verses towards the end of the third canto and the major portions of cantos V, IX, XII, XVII, XIX, and XX are composed in this metre. Cantos I, III and VII are predominated by the Upajāti metre in which the total number of verses composed comes to 211; and as the Upajāti

1. For purposes of this metrical analysis, the text of the Madras ms. is followed.

is most closely related to the Vaṁśastha, we may say that the poet finds himself most at home in this measure. A total number of 281 verses in the Śloka metre is distributed among cantos II, VI, X, and XVIII. Next in numerical importance comes the Drutavilambita, which predominates the eleventh and fourteenth cantos, with a total number of 173 verses for its share. While Puṣpitāgrā figures in the major portion of the sixteenth canto, it also appears in limited numbers in seven other cantos. The prominence given to this Ardhasama metre itself shows the metrical skill of the poet. Another metre of the Ardhasama category is Viyoginī which is mainly used in the fourth canto.

Other rare metres like the Toṭaka (2), Praharṣiṇī (4) and Rucirā (2) are also found sparingly at the end of the cantos. Vasantatilaka is employed for the concluding verses of seven cantos, while Mālinī which has one more syllable than the former appears only in two verses.

Other longer metres that are used, containing seventeen syllables, are Śikhariṇī, Mandākrāntā, Pṛthvī, Nardaṭaka and Hariṇī. Of these, Mandākrāntā and Pṛthvī get eleven and ten verses respectively, while the number of verses in other metres of this group ranges from one to five. The two longest metres that are employed are Śārdūlavikrīḍita (nineteen syllables) and Sragdharā (twenty-one syllables). The Śārdūlavikrīḍita metre appears in the concluding verses of eight cantos while Sragdharā is used in four.

Except in the case of the third canto in which from the 63rd verse onwards the poet changes from the Upajāti to the Vaṁśastha, he never changes the metre in the middle of the canto. In some other cantos as in the case of V and XV, he gives some seven or eight concluding verses each in a different metre.

Thus, the even flow is generally maintained with care, except on some rare occasions. The poet is not in the habit of disturbing the metrical form too frequently within a canto. In this also, he closely follows Kālidāsa. Comparing the incidence of the metres used for variations in the latter parts of the cantos in Kumāradāsa's work with those of earlier poets, we may observe that he resorts to a larger number of the longer metres. A fuller idea of his handling of these metres can be had from the following tables.

TABLE I.

Canto No.	*Number of verses*	*Metres employed*
I	1 to 87	Upajāti
	88,89, & 90	Puṣpitāgrā
II	1 to 77	Anuṣṭubh
	78	Puṣpitāgrā
	79	Śārdūlavikrīḍita
III	1 to 63	Upajāti
	64 to 76	Vaṁśastha
	77	Puṣpitāgrā
	78,79	Śikhariṇī
	80,81	Sragdharā
IV	1 to 70	Viyoginī
	71,72 & 73	Nardaṭaka
	74	Śārdūlavikrīḍita
V	1 to 52	Vaṁśastha
	53	Vasantatilaka
	54,55	Vaṁśastha
	56	Vasantatilaka
	57	Mālinī
	58	Vasantatilaka
	59	Praharṣiṇī
	60,61	Vasantatilaka
VI	1 to 55	Anuṣṭubh
	56,57 & 58	Praharṣiṇī
	59,60	Vasantatilaka
VII	1 to 58	Upajāti
	59	Mālinī
VIII	1 to 92	Rathoddhatā
	93 to 99	Puṣpitāgrā
	100, 101	Nardaṭaka

Canto No.	*Number of verses*	*Metresemployed*
IX	1 to 66	Vaṁśastha
	67	Vasantatilaka
	68	Nardaṭaka
X	1 to 81	Anuṣṭubh
	82,83	Vasantatilaka
	84 to 89	Śārdūlavikrīḍita
	90	Sragdharā
XI	1 to 90	Drutavilambita
	91 to 94	Vasantatilaka
	95	Pṛthvī
	96,97	Śikhariṇī
	98	Śārdūlavikrīḍita
	99	Śikhariṇī
	100	Śārdūlavikrīḍita
XII	1 to 52	Vaṁśastha
	53,54, & 55	Puṣpitāgrā
	56	Pṛthvī
XIII	1 to 36	Pramitākṣarā
	37 to 44	Pṛthvī
	45	Hariṇī
XIV	1 to 83	Drutavilambita
	84	Mandākrāntā
XV	1 to 55	Svāgatā
	55 to 60	Upendravajrā
	61	Śārdūlavikrīḍita
	62,63, & 64	Sragdharā
XVI	1 to 69	Puṣpitāgrā
	70,71, & 72	Mandākrāntā
	73	Śārdūlavikrīḍita
	74	Sragdharā
XVII	1 to 42	Vaṁśastha
	43	Mandākrāntā
XVIII	1 to 68	Anuṣṭubh
	69,70	Indravajrā
	71,72	Toṭaka

Canto No.	*Number of verses*	*Metres employed*
	73	Pṛthvī
	74,75	Śārdūlavikrīḍita
XIX	1 to 59	Vaṁśastha
	60,61 & 62	Vasantatilaka
	63	Mandākrāntā
	64	Sragdharā
XX	1 to 51	Vaṁśastha
	52	Puṣpitāgrā
	53,54	Rucirā
	55,56	Vasantatilaka
	57 to 60	Mandākrāntā
	61,62	Śārdūlavikrīḍita
	63,64	Sragdharā

TABLE II.

Metres employed	*Canto*	*Number of verses in each canto*	*Total*
Anuṣṭubh	II	1 to 77	
	VI	1 to 55	
	X	1 to 81	
	XVIII	1 to 68	281
Indravajrā	XVIII	69,70	2
Upajāti	I	1 to 87	
	III	1 to 63	
	VII	1 to 58	208
Upendravajrā	XV	56 to 60	5
Toṭaka	XVIII	71,72	2
Drutavilambita	XI	1 to 90	
	XIV	1 to 83	173
Nardaṭaka	IV	71,72 & 73	
	IX	68	4

Metres employed	*Canto*	*Number of verses in each canto*	*Total*
Puṣpitāgrā	I	88,89 & 90	
	II	78	
	III	77	
	VIII	93 to 99	
	XII	53,54 & 55	
	XVI	1 to 89	
	XX	52	85
Pṛthvī	XI	95	
	XII	56	
	XIII	37 to 44	
	XVIII	73	11
Pramitākṣarā	XIII	1 to 36	36
Praharṣiṇī	V	59	
	VI	56,57 & 58	4
Mandākrāntā	XIV	84	
	XVI	70,71 & 72	
	XVII	43	
	XIX	63	
	XX	57 to 60	10
Mālinī	V	57	
	VII	59	2
Rathoddhatā	VIII	1 to 92	92
Rucirā	XX	53,54	2
Vaṁśastha	III	64 to 76	
	V	1 to 52,54,55	
	IX	1 to 66	
	XII	1 to 62	
	XVII	1 to 42	
	XIX	1 to 59	
	XX	1 to 51	337
Vasantatilaka	V	53,56,58,60 & 61	
	VI	59,60	

	IX	67	
	X	82,83	
	XI	91 to 94	
	XIX	60,61 & 62	
	XX	55,56	19
Viyoginī	IV	1 to 70	70
Śārdūlavikrīḍita	II	79	
	IV	74	
	X	84 to 89	
	XI	98,99. & 100	
	XV	61	
	XVI	73	
	XVIII	74,75	
	XX	61,62	16
Śikhariṇī	III	78,79	
	XI	96,97 & 99	5
Sragdharā	III	80,81	
	X	90	
	XV	62,63 & 64	
	XVI	74	
	XIX	64	
	XXX	63,64	10
Svāgatā	XV	1 to 55	55
Hariṇī	XIII	45	1

ŚABDA-CITRAS

According to the convention seen for the first time in the poem of Bhāravi, who set apart one full canto to difficult forms of śabda-citras, Kumāradāsa devotes almost the whole of canto XVIII for exhibiting his skill in this form of composition. Though he generally covers the same types of Śabda-citras as handled by Bhāravi and as defined by Daṇḍin, he at times goes into further ramifications based on those employed by them. Thus the following Śabda-citras are common to Bhāravi, Daṇḍin and Kumāradāsa:

Kumāradāsa- XVIII.	*Bhāravi- XV.*	*Daṇḍin- III.*
Gūḍhacaturtha 2.	Gūḍhacaturtha-pāda 43.	
Dvyakṣara 6.	Dvyakṣara 38.	Dvi-varṇa 94
Caturakṣari 13.	Ekākṣarapāda 5.	Caturvarṇa 92.
Gomūtrikā 18.	Gomūtrikā-bandha 12.	Ardhagomū-trikā 79.
Ardhabhramaka 21.	Ardhabhramaka 27.	Ardhabhrama 81.
Sarvatobhadra 30.	Sarvatobhadra 25.	Sarvatobhadra 82.
Samudga-yamaka 16.	Samudgaka 16.	Samudga 54.
Anuloma-pratiloma 34	Pratiloma-anuloma 22, 23	Pratiloma 76, 77.
Niroṣṭhya 36.	Niroṣṭhya 7.	
Ardhaprati-loma 49.	Pratiloma-anulomapāda 18.	Pāda-viṣaya-pratiloma 74.
Ādyāmreḍita 56.	Pādādi-yamaka 10	

We may note here a few instances in which there are some differences in nomenclature and also some novel designs worked out by Kumāradāsa.

In XVIII. 47, we have the Śabda-citra called the Nirantarānuprāsa, which is named by Bhāravi and Daṇḍin as Ekākṣara. This is a single letter forming the whole verse. Letter 'ta' alone is used by Kumāradāsa in this verse.

In the ninth verse of the same canto, we have a Śabda-citra which is named Pāda-yamaka. Here the second and the fourth pādas are similar. Daṇḍin calls it a variety of Samudga (III. 61), whereas Bhāravi names it as Dvi-caturtha-yamaka (XV. 35). Māgha adopts it in 19 verses, without giving any name.

Another variety of Yamaka used by Kumāradāsa is called Ādi-yamaka, which, though not used by Bhāravi or Māgha, is given by Daṇḍin. The latter calls it Ādibhāga-yamaka (III. 30). In this the first halves of the first and second pādas are the same and the first halves of the third and fourth pādas are also similar. Kumāradāsa gives it thus:

विराजन्तमिदं दीप्त्या विराजं तं स्मृतिक्षणे ।
सह्सन्नासितो भ्रात्रा सह्सन्नाख्यदागतम् ॥ XVIII. 10.

Pratiloma is a Śabda-citra wherein the first half of the verse, if read in the reverse order, gives the second half. This is not found in Bhāravi but is found in Daṇḍin under the name Ślokārdhaviṣaya-pratiloma. In Māgha (XIX. 88) it is termed Gatapratyāgata.

XVIII. 23 in the *JH* is given as Gomūtrikā-Murajabandha. But in Murajabandha, if we do as we do in the case of Gomūtrikā, we do not get the same verse but a different one with a different meaning. In the verse in question we have only the requirements of a Gomūtrikā. In 'L' the verses to be deduced from the designs have also been written down; but under this verse no new verse has been noted as yielded by any Murajabandha-design here. Therefore there is some mistake in the name or in the copying in the manuscripts.

Reading more than one meaning in the same verse, without changing the order, is presented by Bhāravi and Māgha. But they reach only a record of three meanings or Arthatrayavācī (Bhāravi, XV. 45; Māgha XIX. 116). But Kumāradāsa goes a step beyond by presenting a verse with four meanings or Arthacatuṣṭayavācī in XVIII.35.

Another variety of Yamaka though commonly called Ādyanta-yamaka, is not the same in the case of all poets. Daṇḍin gives as an example of this a verse where all the four lines begin and end in the same pair of syllables (III. 47,48). Bhāravi gives the same syllables in the second and fourth pādas (XV.37). But what Kumāradāsa names as Ādyanta-yamaka is also given by Bhāravi over the name Pādādyantayamaka (XV.31), which is more significant.

In XVIII. 51 we have a specimen of three different

verses drawn out of a single one, by removing or adding some mātrās in the original letters. The verse in question, as it is, gives one meaning; by removing the existing suffixes, a second sense; and by adding new suffixes a third one.

Sandaṣṭaka is another variety of Yamaka where the last part of the preceding pāda is repeated to form the beginning of the succeeding one. This is also called Śṛṅkhalā-yamaka by Bhāravi (XV.42). The latter uses the same principle in the case of the first and second pādas in XV.8 and names it as Pādānta-yamaka. Daṇḍin calls it Sandaṣṭa-yamaka in III. 52.

Ardha-yamaka is another variety where the first pāda is repeated to form the second pāda and the third one is repeated for the fourth. This is given as a variety of Samudga by Daṇḍin (III. 55) and as Samudga by Māgha (XIX. 18). But Bhāravi gives in XV. 16 and 50, a Samudgaka which is slightly different from those of others. In Bhāravi, the first foot repeated forms the third instead of the second and the fourth foot is formed by repeating the second and not the third.

The last Śabda-citra exhibited by Kumāradāsa is called Cakra-vṛtta, XVIII. 75. This is found in Māgha as Cakra-bandha, XIX. 20. The following diagram may be helpful to understand it:

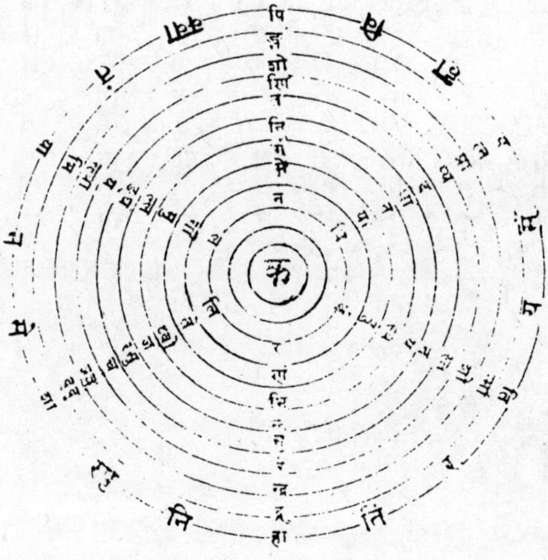

The construction of Jāla Ślokas is another unique feature of Kumāradāsa. In XVIII.37, we have the following verse:

न या चा र यु तो रा मः
प्र या स र हि तो श्र मः।
न या ति र ण तो भी मः
श्रि या सा र श्च्यु तो प मः॥

In this the second, fourth, sixth, and eighth letters of each pāda are the same. This is an improvement over the simple Gomūtrikā but Bhāravi does not give this. But this name Jāla seems to be a common name used for further verbal feats of various kinds. Thus we have in XVIII. 32, a Muraja-bandha verse named as Jālena Ślokadvayam. Two other verses given under the headings Jālena Ślokadvayam and Jālena Śloka-Catuṣṭayam respectively are illustrated in the following charts:

I	II	III	IV	V	VI	VII	VIII
य	सि	स	त्त	त	म	स्वा	शं
1	2	3	4	5	6	7	8
शं	सि	ता	त्रा	स	मा	न्य	सः
A	B	C	D	E	F	G	H
स	द	ग्धा	ध	म	सा	मा	सः
a	b	c	d	e	f	g	h
स	स्म	या	ग	म	नु	द्धि	या

II	g	IV	e	VI	c	VIII	a
सि	द्धि	त्त	म	म	या	शं	स
1	B	3	D	5	F	7	H
शं	द	ता	ध	स	सा	न्य	सः
VII	2	V	4	III	6	I	8
स्वा	सि	त	त्रा	स	मा	या	स
h	A	f	e	d	E	b	G
या	स	नु	ग्धा	ग	म	स्म	मा

I	II	III	IV	V	VI	VII	VIII
सा	रा	ह्व	स	क	र	स्र	स्त
1	2	3	4	5	6	7	8
र	मा	पा	त्र	स्व	सा	ध्व	ना
A	B	C	D	E	F	G	H
सा	रा	सा	पा	न	या	गा	या
a	b	c	d	e	f	g	h
ह	सा	व	न	ध	र	स्व	ना

VII	7	G	h	g	H	8	VIII
स्र	ध्व	गा	स्व	न	या	ना	स्त
II	2	B	b	a	A	1	I
रा	मा	श	सा	ह	सा	र	सा
III	3	C	e	f	F	6	VI
ह्व	पा	सा	व	र	या	सा	र
IV	4	D	d	e	E	5	V
स	त्र	पा	न	ध	न	स्व	कः

VII	8	G	h	g	H	7	VIII
स्र	ना	गा	न	स्व	या	ध्व	स्त
V	6	E	f	e	f	5	VI
क	सा	न	र	ध	या	स्व	र
III	4	c	d	C	D	3	IV
ह्व	त्र	सा	न	व	पा	पा	स
I	2	A	b	a	B	1	II
सा	मा	सा	सा	ह	रा	र	रा

8	F	7	VI	VII	6	G	f
स्व	या	ध्व	र	स्र	सा	गा	र
IV	5	D	e	d	E	4	V
स	स्व	पा	ध	न	न	त्र	क
C	B	3	II	III	२	c	b
व	रा	पा	रा	ह्व	मा	सा	सा
VIII	8	H	h	a	A	1	I
स्त	ना	या	न	ह	सा	र	सा

KUMĀRADĀSA'S LEARNING

The Indian ideal of the poet tended very early to become a combination of learning and artistic gift, Vyutpatti and Śakti. The greatest of the poets was also a profound scholar but one like Kālidāsa carried his learning lightly, and the instances where his erudition protruded were few and far between. The ideal of Mahākāvya as the medium of presenting a noble heroic character for the edification of the reader, engendered the bringing into the writing the essential elements of Indian culture as enunciated in the various branches of mental and moral discipline. Poetry thus gradually assumed in a pronounced manner, an educative role; it was thought of as a legitimate medium for expounding scholarly matter. On the part of the author an increasing anxiety to show off his varied erudition was evident; and from the point of view of the reader, the Kāvya, one of whose avowed objects was Vyutpatti, served as a means of introducing the student to scholarly ideas pertaining to the different Śāstras. This tendency to render writing weighty with learned material is seen in progressive increase right from Bhāravi onwards. The exhibition of learning is certainly more conspicuous in Māgha. Kumārdāsa who preceded Māgha, naturally, does not show this tendency to such an extent as the latter. But at the same time it is definitely more conspicuous than in Kālidasa. While Kālidāsa introduced such learned ideas but rarely and mostly through similes, Kumāradāsa presses into service Śleṣa also for this purpose. A survey of the instances where Kumāradāsa shows his skill in enriching his work with learned concepts proves his acquaintance with the whole field of Sanskrit learning.

Philosophical schools:

His knowledge of the Sāṅkhya philosophy is confirmed by a verse where he describes the armies of Rākṣasas who come to spoil the sacrifice of Viśvāmitra. The whole verse with the help of Śleṣa presents one of the fundamental doctrines of the Sāṅkhya school, namely that of three Guṇas:

पिशाचरक्षस्ततिभिर्निरन्तरं कृतान्धकारं रथचक्ररेणुभिः ।
असांख्यगृह्या अपि तत्र सैनिका जगज्जगुस्सत्त्वरजस्तमोमयम् ।

JH. V. 27

The verse literally means: "The innumerable hordes of Piśācas and Rākṣasas, creating darkness by the dust raised by the wheels of their chariots, though they were not Sāṅkhyas, proclaimed the world as constituted of Sattva, Rajas and Tamas." According to the Sāṅkhya philosophy, the universe is constituted of twenty-five Tattvas, the chief of which are the Puruṣa (the soul) and the Prakṛti (Matter). Prakṛti which is the cause of all further evolutes is made up of the three Guṇas—Sattva, Rajas and Tamas. In fact, it is the state of equilibrium of these three Guṇas that is Prakṛti and the evolution starts when, by the proximity of the Puruṣa, the equilibrium of the three constituents of Prakṛti is disturbed. According to the Sāṅkhya system, these three constituents of Prakṛti have each its own characteristic nature—Sattva being light, enlightening and blissful; Rajas being responsible for activity, passion and misery; and Tamas being heavy and leading to delusion and stupor. Accordingly it is usual to describe the pure Sattva as white, Rajas as red and Tamas as dark in colour. In utilising these ideas for his description, Kumāradāsa adopts the medium of śleṣa alaṅkāra. The expression 'asāṅkhyagṛhyā' means by śleṣa both 'innumerable' and 'those who are not influenced by Sāṅkhya system'. The word 'Sattva' is used in śleṣa again to mean Sattva guṇa on one side and spirits and ghosts on the other who abound in the battle-field. The word Rajas means both Rajoguṇa and dust. The battle-field is full of the dust raised by the wheels of the chariot and the dense dust is itself responsible for the eclipse of the light and darkness (Tamas). Large numbers of Rākṣasas, obviously of very dark complexion, contribute to the darkness of the place and the poet conceives this as the Tamoguṇa of the Sāṅkhyas.

His reference to the Śākyas or Buddhist monks clearly

shows his familiarity with the religion of the Buddha. Here also he adopts the use of puns which refer to some of the characteristics of these monks:

स्थित्वा गुणे महति तत्क्षणलब्धमोक्षाः
सुश्लिष्टयुक्तिसफलाननसम्पदस्ते ।
शाक्या इवास्य विशिखा रिपुसैनिकेभ्यः
चक्रुस्त्रिविष्टपसभागमनोपदेशम् ॥

(*JH*. V. 56)

"The arrows of Rāma which were well-shaped so as to bring forth the desired results, having stayed on the bow-string for a while, and being released immediately from them, taught to the soldiers of the enemies the way to enter the other world, like the shaven monks." The Śākyas are the Bhikṣus who are expected to conquer the two other Guṇas, Rajas and Tamas, and take their stand on Sattva alone. This idea is based on the two meanings of the word 'Guṇa', namely, the bow-string, and one of the three Guṇas. The expression may also refer to the moral qualities which the monks should cultivate and more especially the greatest of all qualities, Karuṇā or compassion. They will have the wonderful tactics of putting forth effective argumentation in support of their line of thought. They are also Viśikhas, bereft of their tufts. They too act as the torch-bearers for the common man on the path of wisdom, leading to ultimate salvation. In this verse, Nandargikar[1] traces a reference to the *Buddhacarita* of Aśvaghoṣa. He interprets the word 'Ripu-sainikebhyaḥ' as meaning 'the soldiers of Māra'. It is stated in the *Buddhacarita* that Māra called for his army to his aid while fighting with Buddha. While the relevancy of this statement in the present context is not clear, we can take that word to denote that Buddhist monks went to and worked for the emancipation of even those persons who were hostile to them.

The poet shows some familiarity with Buddhistic literature as well. In the context of sending the princes for the assistance of Viśvāmitra, our poet emphasises the importance

1. *JH*. ed. by Nandargikar, p. 181.

of Paropakāra or service to others[1] which is almost in line with the Buddhistic teachings. The ethical exhortation here calling upon Rāma to value righteousness over material happiness may again be said to bear the impress of certain Buddhistic writings. Particularly the emphasis laid on the uncertainty of mortal life and the transient nature of worldly pleasures, as revealed in verses like 'विरते शवतामभिव्रजति' etc. (IV. 44), has its inspiration from works like Aśvaghoṣa's *Saundarananda.*

Some words and expressions which have peculiar usages in the Buddhistic literature are found used in the same way by Kumāradāsa. For example, the word 'Dhātu' is well-known in classical usage to refer to minerals and elements of the body. But in Buddhistic texts it is common to find it as referring to the ashes or relics of the body such as are enshrined in Buddhistic Stūpas and are worshipped. In the following verse (*JH.* XVI. 68) the poet uses the word 'Dhātu' in the sense of 'ash' which indicates his acquaintance in his Ceylonese surroundings with Buddhism.[2]

अथ कटकनिवासदृप्तनागप्रविततधातुविभूषणस्सुमेरुः ।
द्युतिमभृत पुरत्रयस्य भेत्तुः शिरसि मुहुः स्थितशीतरश्मिबिम्बे ।।

Religious Sects :

Apart from these technical references, we have some passages in the *JH.* which echo the sense contained in some passages of very familiar philosophic works like the *Gītā.* For example, in the 4th canto we have the following verse (No. 19):

द्विषतो भवबन्धभेदिना दहतश्चेतसि योगवह्निना ।
न जहाति विपत्तिरद्य नः परसंपत्तिषु निःस्पृहानपि ।।

In the above Viśvāmitra tells Daśaratha that even persons like

1. *JH.* IV. 33 to 43.
2. See also : सधातुकूटं धृतविश्वसंपदः शिवोपभोगप्रणयस्य भाजनम् ।
(*JH.* XX. 36.)

him who lead yogic lives are not free from the worldly danger. Even after developing the fire of knowledge due to yoga, which destroys the inner enemies of passion, hate etc. and having no desire to acquire another's riches, one has to seek other's help for the removal of difficulties that befall one. Here the practice of yoga, the destruction of the six internal enemies, and yogic realisation as the destroyer of the cycle of birth and death and the bondage caused by it are referred to.

There are some expressions in Kumāradāsa's poem which remind us of their significance dealt with elsewhere. For example, phrases like 'मायामनुज',[1]'पुमान् पुरातनः' and 'रामच्छलमादिपूरुषं'[2] though they can be understood in a very general manner according to the context, from the way in which the poet couches the ideas definitely reminds us of some lines in the *Gītā* like:

अजोऽपि सन्नव्ययात्मा भूतानामीश्वरोऽपि सन् ।
प्रकृतिं स्वामधिष्ठाय संभवाम्यात्ममायया ॥
(IV. 6)

embodying the doctrine of Avatāra.

There are many references to the theory of Karman and re-birth. The poet utilises the Karman doctrine to explain the downward course of Rāvaṇa's arrows after hitting Rāma:

विभिद्य रामच्छलमादिपूरुषं हृता यथा दुष्प्रसहेन पाप्मना ।
प्रपद्य तिर्यग्गतिमस्य सायकाः क्रमेण पातालमपि प्रपेदिरे ॥
(*JH*. XIX. 8)

For the sin of hitting at Rāma who is God incarnate, the arrows of Rāvaṇa driven by their bad Karman enter into the lives of insects, beasts and other Tiryak-beings and even go down to the Pātāla (nether regions) for eternal damnation.

Kumāradāsa refers to Śaivism also in his poem. In the

1. पुमानमित्रस्य पुरं पुरातनः प्रविश्य मायामनुजो विभीषणे. . . .
(*JH*. XIX. 53)
2. *JH*. XIX 8.

following verse there is a definite reference to some technical details of Śaivism:

> प्रथमगमितमन्धकारिभावं पुनरतिपिङ्गलतारकं विधाय ।
> भुवनमथ कलात्मना समस्य त्रिनयनरूपमलम्भयत् प्रदोषः ॥
> (*JH*. XVI. 10)

Kalā is a technical term used in different schools of Śaivism in more than one sense. Kalā is one of the five Śaktis by which the unlimited Śiva manifests Himself in the world with limitations.[1] It is also used as the name of one of the six Adhvans—Mantra, Pada, Varṇa, Bhuvana, Tattva and Kalā. In the former sense Kalā, along with three other Śaktis, is also referred to as Dhāraṇa, in so far as they become the sustaining media of creation. In either sense it signifies God in His external aspect as the created Universe, and a reference to this by Kumāradāsa in the above verse would show his acquaintance with the tenets of Śaivism.

Ājīvikas:

In canto X in the description of Rāvaṇa when he enters in the disguise of a recluse to carry off Sītā, the following verse is found in Nandargikar's edition:

> दाम्भाजीविकमुत्तुङ्गजटामण्डितमस्तकम् ।
> कञ्चिन्मस्करिणं सीता ददर्शाश्रममागतम् ॥

Nandargikar notes both under the text as well as in his notes at the end,[2] that the expression 'dāmbhājivikam' has the variant 'dāṇḍājivikam'. He however selects the former and writes in the notes that the old sect of Ājīvikas is referred to here. Obviously following Nandargikar Dr. Barua also sees a reference to the Ājīvikas in this verse and writes as follows in his contribution on the Ājīvikas. ".... there are a few other Brahminical works, e.g., the *Jānakīharaṇa* and the

1. Śl. 13, *Paryantapañcāśikā* ed. by Dr. V. Raghavan, Annals of oriental Res., University of Madras, 1951.
2. *JH*. ed. by Nandargikar, *V. infra*, pp. 160 ff.

Bhaṭṭikāvya, where Ājīvika is found to be a synonym of Maskarin and Ekadaṇḍin. But these usages do not go unquestioned, for in some of the Jaina and Buddhist works the Ājīvikas have been clearly distinguished from the Parivrājakas or Paramahaṁsas of whom the ekadaṇḍins and tridaṇḍins were two main divisions."[1] Adverting to the same topic and reference in Kumāradāsa, Dr. A.L. Basham[2] also understands Kumāradāsa as not only referring to the Ājīvikas but also implying the possible identity of the Ājīvikas with the Maskarins and adds that Ājīvikas might have included any mendicant bearing a staff.[3] The reference had also been relied upon by Dr. D. R. Bhandarkar[3] and as this passage in Kumāradāsa has been used by more than one scholar for arguing about the identity and tenets of the Ājīvikas, it is necessary to point out here the baselessness of the reference in question. According to our manuscripts the verse reads:

सीता मस्करिणं कञ्चित् ददर्शाश्रममागतम् ।
दाण्डाजिनिकमुत्तुङ्गजटामण्डितमस्तकम् ॥

The reading 'dāmbhājīvikas' is not found in any of our manuscripts. Nandargikar also notes in passing, that the expression 'dāṇḍājinika' is after Pāṇini (V. 2. 76); there is no reason why this classic idiom should be ignored and the reading 'dāmbhājīvika' preferred and a non-existent reference seen here to the Ājīvikas. Earlier than Nandargikar, Thomas discussed this verse for lexicographical peculiarities in his article on the *JH*. in *J.R.A.S.* for 1901 (pp. 261-2). He shows how 'dāṇḍājinika' was likely to be the word actually used by Kumāradāsa, though he would not preclude the possibility of Kumāradāsa, having changed the Pāṇinian idiom on the basis of the Kāśikā. The evidence of our manuscripts is clear on the point that 'dāṇḍājinika' is the correct reading

1. 'Ājīvika, what it means', *ABORI*. Vol. VIII, p. 183.
2. Dr. A.L. Basham, 'History and Doctrine of the Ājīvikas', London 1951. pp. 97, 99, 106, 165, 166 and 167.
3. *I.A.* XLI, p. 290; Basham *Ibid.* p. 167.

here. The meaning of the verse also and the presence of the other expression 'maskarin', preclude the Ājīvika definitely. Neither Dr. Barua nor Dr. Basham has failed to point out also the difficulty in assuming the identity of the Ājīvika and the Maskarin; in any case there is no support for such a supposition in the *JH*.

Cosmogony:

With regard to cosmogony, he makes two references. While describing the Sun-set in the 8th canto, Kumāradāsa says that the rays go back and get absorbed in the orbit of the Sun itself leaving the world in darkness. He compares the process to the time of deluge when the manifested world gets back into its source, namely God and the whole Universe is in darkness:

भूय एव रविमण्डले रुचिर्लीयते जलधिमध्यवर्तिनि ।
अन्तराणि तमसः प्रयच्छति स्रष्टरीव जगती युगक्षये ॥
(VIII. 58)

It is one of the beliefs of Hindu cosmogony that God who manifests a portion of Himself as the world, withdraws this manifestation by a mere wish of His when the whole Universe ceases to exist. Another reference is while describing the shower of arrows discharged by Rāvaṇa, where he says that Rāvaṇa looked like Kāla, the destroyer of the whole Universe at the time of the deluge. Just as the latter will flood the whole world with an incessant downpour of rains with the clouds like Puṣkara and Āvartaka, Rāvaṇa flooded the battle-field with his arrows. Hindu Purāṇas agree that at the deluge twelve Suns will scorch the world and clouds like Puṣkara and Āvartaka will shower huge downpour of rain.

Mythology:

Throughout his poem, Kumāradāsa exhibits his close acquaintance with the *Purāṇas* and the *Itihāsas*. Many stories and anecdotes contained in Hindu mythological literature are referred to by the poet on various occasions. Among the Hindu Trinity, apart from Viṣṇu, the story of one of whose incarnations he deals with in his poem, he gives maximum importance to Śiva. Though in canto II he refers to the omniscience and the omnipotence of Viṣṇu, just as Kālidāsa has done in canto X of the *Raghuvaṁśa*, the numerous references of Kumāradāsa to Śiva would tempt one to feel that he is attached to Śiva also. Śiva's marriage with Pārvatī is referred to in many places. His vehicle, the bull (III. 62), the third eye on His forehead (XVI. 10), the serpent ornaments that He wears (II. 44), the burning of Cupid (VI. 55, III. 11), Paraśurāma as His pupil (IX.34), the cresent moon on His head (VIII. 54), the Meru mountain as His bow (IX. 34), the burning of the three Demon-cities by Him (IX. 37), the Gaṅgā on His head (X. 88) etc. are referred to by the poet.

Śiva is also referred to as birthless (Aja) and the ultimate unchanging basis (Kūṭastha), possessing terrible power (Ugratejāḥ), the destroyer of the demon Andhaka etc. Special reference is made to His evening dances along with Pārvatī and the latter getting frightened by the serpents on his arms. There is a reference to Rāvaṇa worshipping him by offering his heads in the fire and also the former lifting up the Kailāsa mountain.

With regard to Viṣṇu, we have numerous references in the *JH*. His serpent-couch during the rainy season (II. 5, XII. 85), His vehicle, Garuḍa (II. 5), His discus, Sudarśana (I. 15), His brother-hood with Indra (II. 77), His incarnation as Vāmana and subjugation of Bali (V. 21), His killing Madhu and Kaiṭabha (II. 14), the churning of the milky ocean (II. 10), and His incarnation as a boar (XIII. 13).

Apart from these, His function of protecting the Universe (II. 16), the predominance of Sattva Guṇa in Him (II. 16), His teaching Brahman the art of creation (II .18), and His omnipotence and eternality (II. 8, 77) are also referred to.

The next deity that is referred to frequently in the course of the poem is Indra. Indra washing away the sin due to his killing Vṛttra (IV. 52), his killing the daughter of Virocana with his thunderbolt (IV. 65), and cutting into pieces the embryo in the womb of Diti and the birth of seven Maruts therefrom (VI. 16), are all referred to.

There is a reference to the story relating to the origin of the Śaiva and Vaiṣṇava bows. Viśvakarman presents Indra with two bows which the latter gives to Śiva and Viṣṇu. Eager to see their comparative prowess, Indra makes them fight with each other. There ensued a battle for one thousand years between these two, after which Viṣṇu gave his bow to Ṛcīka and which ultimately reached the hands of Paraśurāma. The bow of Śiva came to the possession of Janaka and was broken by Rāma (IX. 35 to 39). This story is narrated by Paraśurāma when he challenges Rāma on his way back after his marriage with Sītā.

The basic oneness of the Trinity is also recognised by Kumāradāsa. While praying to Viṣṇu to incarnate as man, Devas address Him as the One who manifests in three different forms with one of the three Guṇas predominating in each of the forms to perform the duties of creation, protection and destruction respectively:

त्रिधा ते समभूद्योगः स्पृष्टसत्त्वरजस्तमाः ।
स्थितिनिर्माणसंहारभेदयोगेन भेदिताः ॥

(*JH.* II. 17)

Here the poet takes care to say that the Viṣṇu-aspect which is entrusted with protection is predominantly Sāttvika.

Apart from these, there are references to other mythological stories and episodes. The encounter of Kārtavīryārjuna the thousand-armed enemy by Paraśurāma, is alluded to in the following verse while describing the city of Mithilā:

विटङ्कभुजसंप्राप्त-सहस्रकरमूर्तिना ।
विग्रहेण यदावाससन्तानो भार्गवायते ॥

(*JH.* VI. 23)

The story of Viśvāmitra sending Triśaṅku to the heavens by the might of his penance even after he was cursed to become a Caṇḍāla by the sons of Vasiṣṭha is referred to in the following line:

स वसिष्ठतनूजपातितक्षितिपस्वर्वसतिप्रदो मुनिः ।

(*JH.* IV. 64)

The episode relating to Agastya putting down the growth of the Vindhya mountain is alluded to in the following verse:

हृतः पदा पातितगर्वखर्वतामगादगस्त्येन स्यादगाधिपः ।

(*JH.* XX. 27)

Agastya consuming the waters of the ocean is also mentioned while describing the army, coming along with Rāma after the marriage, entering the city-gates of Ayodhyā. The army that entered through the small city-gate with huge noise resembled the body of Agastya drinking the whole of the waters of the ocean.

व्यपावृतद्वारमुखेन सन्ततं बलेन भूम्ना विशता कृतध्वनिम् ।
पुरीमुदन्वन्तमुदग्रनिःस्वनं तनुं पिबन्तीमिव कुम्भजन्मनः ॥

(*JH.* IX. 47)

While referring to Tāṭakā, the poet says that her Yakṣa-form was destroyed by the Brahminical lustre of the sage who drank the ocean.[1]

मकराकरपायिधामभिः क्षतयक्षाकृतिविग्रहा

(*JH.* IV. 59).

Alaṅkāra Śāstra :

In the *JH.* we have some references to Alaṅkāra Śāstra also. In the first canto itself, while describing Daśaratha's hunt, the poet works through śleṣa a comparison between the mountain and a defective specimen of poetry. Sarcastically referring to the poetasters who, without enough

1. See also Vālmīki *Rāmāyaṇa*, Bāla. XXVI, XXVII.

learning, vocabulary and poetic talents, start writing poetry, the poet says :

अथ स विषमपादगोपितार्थं जगदुपयोगवियुक्तभूरिधातुम् ।
बहुतुहिननिपातदोषदुष्टं गिरिमसृजत्कुकवेरिव प्रबन्धम् ॥

(*JH.* I. 89)

The verse composed by a poetaster will have uneven metrical construction; will lack the quality of clarity (Prasāda Guṇa) and hence its meaning will be obscure; will abound in obsolete roots and will be dumped with indeclinables tu, hi, etc., just to fill up the number of required syllables in each line.

In canto XX also, he has a similar verse referring to the tricks that are adopted by the poetasters to complete the required number of syllables in a pāda by using letters like ha, vi, pra and hi.

न न विदधति पादपूरणानि प्रथितयता[1]वचले किरातदेशाः ।
विशदमतिभिरीर्ष्यया प्रबन्धे रचित इवार्थवतीहविप्रहीनाम् ॥

(*JH.* XX.52)

These verses clearly show Kumāradāsa's acquaintance with the Doṣas or literary flaws dealt with in Alaṅkāra works; namely, Viṣama which is defined by Bharata as a metrical flaws Gūḍhārtha or obscure meanings Aprayukta or the use of words devoid of poetic vogue; and Vyartha or useless words which merely fill space.

In Canto XVIII in the description of the battle, Kumāradāsa works in by śleṣa some technical ideas pertaining to drama. In verse 56, according to MT., there is a śleṣa between the elephants and the Nāṭaka thus :

नागास्सरसगण्डास्ते बिन्दुचित्रमुखान्विताः ।
सपताकावृतिभृशं चक्रुस्सन्नाटकोपमाः ॥

Both of them are 'Sarasagaṇḍa', 'Binducitramukhānvita' and 'Sapatāka'. So far as the elephants are concerned, their temples

1. *Yati* means 'recluse' and 'metrical caesura'.

are wet with ichor and their faces variegated by (white and pink) dots and they are bearing standards. In the same terms Kumāradāsa shows his knowledge of dramaturgy : Rasa is the well known eight or nine Rasas which the drama is to evoke. *Gaṇḍa* according to the *Nāṭyaśāstra* is the third of the thirteen Aṅgas of the *Vīthī* ; the obvious ślesa with technical terms of the *Nāṭyaśāstra* precludes the MT. reading here—*Gandha* instead of the correct Gaṇḍa of L. In the expression 'Binducitramukha', Mukha is the Mukhasandhi or the opening juncture of the play. Bindu is the second Arthaprakṛti which figures in the *Pratimukhasandhi*; by reason of the development of various subsidiary issues, the course of action which had a simple beginning in the *Mukhasandhi* becomes variegated (*citra*) in the next *Sandhi*. Patākā is well known as the major episode. In the further portion of the verse, MT. reads Vṛtibhṛśam cakruḥ sannāṭakopamāḥ' ; L. reads here 'Dhṛtibhṛśam cakruḥ sannāṭakopamāḥ' ; the requirements of the sense of the verse drive us to adopt a composite re-construction following L in the former part and MT in the latter part of this expression ; for 'Vṛtibhṛśaṁ in MT. is obviously meaningless. On the other hand, the L reading 'Dhṛtibhraṁśam cakruḥ' may mean that while elephants shook the fortitude of the combatants on the opposite side, the drama by its display would shake the man off his mundane pre-occupation or even his firmness and cause a melting of the heart as it were, by the manifestation of *Rasa, Cittadruti*. In the last expression introducing the comparison, it should certainly be Nāṭaka of MT., and not Nāṭaka of L. If we take the L reading, the meaning 'actor' becomes very tame and the significance of the other epithets in ślesa would merely refer to the actor and in respect of the expression Sapatākā, it would even become meaningless.

Music and Dance :

There are four contexts in which Kumāradāsa shows his acquaintance with the arts of music and dance and uses technical expressions belonging to these two branches of knowledge. First, in VIII. 100, there is a description of dawn and the women in waiting, waking up the hero and the heroine with music appropriate to the morning time.

अथ हृदयङ्गमध्वनितवंशमृदङ्गकृतानुगमै-
रनुगतवल्लकीमृदुतरक्वणितैर्ललनाः ।
तमुषसि भिन्नषड्जविषयीकृतमन्दरवैः
शयितमबोधयन् विविधमङ्गलगीतिपदैः ॥

The orchestra in attendance comprises flute (Vaṁśa), drum (Mṛdaṅga) and lute (Vallakī), to the accompaniment of which ladies sing auspicious songs (Maṅgala-gīti-padas). Here the poet mentions that the accompanying instruments were played softly (Mṛdutara) and in a pleasing style (Hṛdayaṅgama), and the voice was also suitably, to the occasion, kept soft (Mandarava). If we adopt the more appropriate and in all likelihood the correct reading here 'mandrarava' found in the London manuscript and adopted by Nandargikar, we have one more technical term of music used by Kumāradāsa: Mandra means the third of the three registers (Sthāyins), the low, and it is the Sthāyin suited for the occasion. What is most noteworthy in this verse is that the poet mentions that the rāga in which they sang the songs was Bhinnaṣaḍja. As pointed out in another section, this verse has a clear echo in Māgha (XI. I).

In XII. 7, the poet in the midst of his description of Autumn has the following verse:

सितच्छदे गायति तत्त्ववृत्तिना लयेन कालस्य कुशेशयाकरः ।
सरोजपाणावनुपूर्वमुल्लसद्दलाङ्गुलीभिः कलनामिवाददे ॥

The verse presents a graphic picture of a responsive concert-audience or an appreciative listener reacting characteristically to the music that is going on. The white swan is said to sing and the lotus-pond like the understanding connoisseur is said to keep time through the pretext of the lotus-petals that are throbbing in the breeze. The movement of the petals in succession is described by the poet as the indication of the count of the particular measure in which the song is set, by the action of the fingers. Here the poet uses not only the general musical terms Laya and Kāla but also two other terms Tattva and Vṛtti, which refer to aspects of playing on the instruments.[1]

1. Bharata's *Nāṭyaśāstra*, XXIX. 72, 73, 78, 79.

In his description of the causeway built in the waters of the sea in XIV. 38, Kumāradāsa is again struck by the picture of one keeping time for music. The rows of waves of the sea are described as moving about like the arms keeping rhythm. With the help of śleṣa the poet re-inforces the comparison. The sound created by the waves dashing on the Setu is described as the music (Svaracita) and the regular movement and dashing on the Setu as the sound of the rhythmic measure (tāla-kṛta-dhvaniḥ). In I. 9, the poet refers to Puṣkara-drums played in mansions and their sounds resembling those of clouds; and in VI. 30 he refers to Vīṇā music played in the mansions of Mithilā.

In the description of Rāvaṇa's revelry in Canto XVI, we have reference to all the instruments, music and the conduct of dance:

ततविततघनाद्यवाद्यजातैर्निजकरसन्ततिवादितैस्स एकः ।
त्रिविधलयपरिग्रहेण वक्त्रैर्युवतिमनर्तयताष्टभिश्च गायन् ॥
(XVI. 63)

Here 'tata' means stringed instruments like Vīṇā. Drums are usually referred to by the term 'Avanaddha' because they are tied over with stretched skin; but sometimes they are referred to as ātata or vitata also; for obvious reasons of metre, our poet has used the word 'vitata' in the sense of drum, signifying of course the same meaning of leather spread over the surface. Ghana is metal, like bronze, which is used to mark rhythm (Tāla). The other class of instruments included by the term Ādya (etc.), is Suṣira or bored ones like flutes or pipes which are to be played both by the hands and by the mouth. One mouth the Rāvaṇa should have been preoccupied with the flute. Of the remaining nine faces, only eight are mentioned as singing. And we are told that he is also conducting the dance. So his main central face might have been left out for speaking or for giving instructions. Perhaps the eight faces are mentioned so as to correspond with the eight Rasas which are to be portrayed in dance. It will, then, be significant from the point of view of the history of poetics as also the early date of Kumāradāsa, that at his time we did not yet have the ninth Rasa, Śānta.[1] The three layas mentioned in this verse are the three kinds of tempo, fast, middling and slow (Druta, Madhya and Vilambita).

In XVII. 8, there is a reference to Śiva, the Divine Dancer and the poet mentions here the Tāṇḍava mode of dance of which he was the promulgator and the expression Lāsaka which means dance-master:

बले रणस्थेऽयुगलोचनश्च नः पिशाचिकाताण्डवलासकस्सकः ।

In VIII. 20, there is a more specific reference to the lady proficient in dancing and the depiction of feeling:

अश्रुणा रतिषु खेदमात्मनः सम्मदं च पुलकेन कामिनी ।
भावनृत्ताकुशलेव नर्त्तकी व्याजहार न तु लज्जया गिरा ॥

The poet here refers to the Abhinaya of the Sāttvikabhāvas, namely tears (aśru) and horripilation (pulaka).

Painting :

Only a couple of stray references are made to the art of painting. In IV. 58 the poet refers to frescoes painted in the palaces, and the female figures drawn therein:

श्लथभित्तिविरूढभूरुहक्षतमूलाग्रविनिर्गमक्षतम् ।
स्फुटतीव भृशं शुचातुरं हृदयं तद्गृहचित्रयोषितः ॥

In I. 33 working a conceit on the Romarāji as a trickle of dark paint, the poet refers to the brush (tūlikā) and the line (rekhā):

अरालकेश्या अलके विधात्रा विधीयमाने चलतूलिकाग्रात् ।
च्युतस्य बिन्दोरसितस्य मार्गरेखेव रेजे नवरोमराजिः ॥

1. See Dr. V. Raghavan, *The Number of Rasas*, Adyar, 1940, 1967.

POLITY

The ideal of benevolent autocracy, firmly based on the principles of Dharma as laid down in the great Smṛtis of Manu and other sages, and on principles of polity as set forth in the treatises of Artha-śāstra, and guided by able and sincere ministers, extending its patronage and help to all branches of art and science, was indeed an inspiration for poets like Kālidāsa to write poems like the *Raghuvaṁśa*, in which, under the guise of characterising epic-heroes, they held forth the ideals of kingship. The poets played the role of public opinion at its best which could direct the destinies of their contemporary society by reminding the ruling authority of its duties and obligations. Kumāradāsa too, on various occasions, refers to the essential qualities of an ideal king. He deals with the responsibilities of kingship, the dangers to a king, the diplomacy to be adopted by him and even some part of the daily routine of monarchs. He creates opportunities to introduce such ideas in the course of his poem. While describing Daśaratha (I.12 to 25), during Viśvāmitra's visit to Daśaratha and the latter's advice to Rāma (IV.17 to 48), during Viśvāmitra's visit to Janaka (VI. 35 to 42), during Daśaratha's advice to Rāma (X.19 to 36) and duringAṅ gada's misson to Rāvaṇa, and Mālyavān's advice to the latter (XV. 4 to 27, 39 to 55).

In his description of Daśaratha, he stresses the need on the part of a king to practise self-control. This is emphasised even by early writers on polity like Kauṭalya and Kāmandaka. For example, the latter says:

प्रकीर्णे विषयारण्ये धावन्तं विप्रमाथिनम् ।
ज्ञानाङ्कुशेन कुर्वीत वश्यमिन्द्रियदन्तिनम् ॥[1]

On the same subject, we have the following of Kauṭalya:

1. *Nītisāra* of Kāmandaka, T.S.S., XIV. I. 27.

विद्याविनयहेतुरिन्द्रियजयः कामक्रोधलोभमानमदहर्षत्यागात् कार्यः ।[1]
तस्मादरिषड्वर्गत्यागेन इन्द्रियजयं कुर्वीत ।[2]

Following this principle, our poet says that Daśaratha, as a preliminary to his conquest of the whole world, brought under his control the speed of the horses in the form of his senses with the help of his scriptural knowledge and thus conquered the six internal enemies like Kāma.

आजावजय्यावजनन्दनोऽसौ पूर्वं षडन्तर्द्विषतो विजिग्ये ।
जिगीषुरभ्यस्तसमस्तशास्त्रज्ञानोपरुद्धेन्द्रियवाजिवेगः ॥
(*JH*. I. 14)

This Indriyajaya is emphasised again in Aṅgada's address to Rāvaṇa, इन्द्रियाणि etc. (XV. 18)

Secondly the king should be guarded against three sources of danger which undermine his position in no time. They are enumerated in the following verse which is addressed by Viśvāmitra to Daśaratha:

स्वजनादपि लब्धवैशसे नृपतित्वे शठभृत्यसंपदि ।
प्रियवादिरिपावपि स्थितो नृप दिष्ट्या कुशलेन वर्तसे ॥
(*JH*. IV. 18)

"Being placed as you are in kingship which may be undermined by one's own kith and kin, do you get on well in the midst of untrustworthy servants and enemies who speak agreeably ?"

The very first threat to a king's position comes from the disappointed or jealous kinsmen. According to Kauṭalya, a relative is the first enemy for anybody and more so for a king. Friends and relatives who would have supported a man in attaining kingship on the hope of getting many things done through him for themselves, are likely to feel disappointed

1. *Arthaśāstra* of Kauṭalya, T.S.S. No. LXXIX, I. 6, p. 37.
2. *Ibid*, I. 7, p. 38.

and they will be the first to think of some device to overthrow him. The second danger is from the insincere servants who will divulge out all the secrets of the palace and who can be easily utilised as instruments to do harm to the king by interested outsiders. The third source of danger is the enemy who speaks pleasantly and makes the king confide in him and is only waiting for an opportunity to do away with the king.

The poet says that a king should be able to win over anybody to his side by his amiable talks. He should speak in such a vein that even an avowed enemy leaves off his offensive attitude and turns to be neutral; a person who is neutral is made a friend and one who is already a friend is induced to have more intimate attachment to the king:

औदासीन्यं यतश्शत्रुः उदासीनश्च मित्रताम् ।
मित्रं भक्तिदृढत्वं च याति तद्वक्तुमर्हसि ॥

(*JH*. X.22)

The context in the 4th canto where Daśaratha gladly sends his sons along with Viśvāmitra is full of exhortations to the princes to hold fast to the noblest ideals of service to others[1]; of affording security to those in trouble[2]; of observing righteousness even at the cost of one's life[3] and of not swerving from the right path.[4] A king should have a highly humanitarian outlook. He should always feel compassion for a man who has fallen at his feet and give him all protection. At the same time he can never afford to see the rise of his enemies. Kumāradāsa condemns in strongest terms a king who fails to protect a person who has sought his protection and who tolerates the rising of enemies.

शरणोपगतं न पाति यो न भिनत्ति द्विषतां समुन्नतिम् ।
न स बाहुरसाधनक्षमो नरवृक्षप्रभवः प्ररोहकः ॥

(*JH*. IV. 37)

1. *JH*. IV. 35.
2. *JH*. IV, 37.
3. & 4. *Ibid*. 43, 44, 46.

There are references even to some details of administration in the *JH*. The king has to extract taxes from the wealthier classes and utilise them for the benefit of the poorer section of the community (VI. 39). He should always try to consolidate the goodwill of all and should never incur the enmity of any one. He has to encourage even those members of society who may do something beneficial with the sole purpose of attaining fame; the policy of looking down upon such a person is not conducive to social welfare :

लोकसंग्रहकामेन शत्रुभावमनिच्छता ।
निन्दनीयं न तत्तस्य ख्यातिं यो येन वाञ्छति ॥
(*JH*. X. 23)

In the course of Viśvāmitra's enquiry about the way in which Janaka is administering his kingdom (VI. 35 to 43), the poet introduces a number of Rājadharmas. For example:

त्वद्विक्रमेण वैधव्यं प्रापिता रिपुयोषितः ।
बालत्राणार्थिनीः कच्चित् सम्यग्रक्षसि बन्धुवत् ॥
(*JH*., VI. 41)

Here the sage asks the king whether he is giving protection to the queens of the enemy-kings killed by him, who are eager to save the lives of their children. We do not have any special mention about this in Kauṭalya's *Arthaśāstra* or in the *Kāmandakīya*, Our poet clearly states that the protection of the lives of queens and babies of the enemies is a sacred duty cast on the king.

The system of paying pension to the Govenment servants in their old age is also found in a unique reference made to it by the poet. This is an interesting subject on which, however, earlier writers on polity are silent, from which one may be led to imagine that ancient India did not think of this as an important duty. The early texts refer in general to the protection of the old and the orphans as a king's duty. But no special mention is made about the Government's duty to their servants in their old age. Kauṭalya refers to the gratuity that is to be paid to the families of soldiers who die in the battle-field, and incidentally includes the children, the disabled and the sick who are dependents on such soldiers, as recipients of such gratuity.

कर्मसु मृतानां पुत्रदाराः भक्तवेतनं लभेरन् ।
वालवृद्धव्याधिताश्चैषामनुग्राह्याः ।
प्रेतव्याधितसूतिकाकृत्येषु चैषामर्थमानकर्म कुर्यात् ॥[1]

Mr. N. C. Bandyopadhyaya, in his book entitled *Kauṭilya*, interprets these statements in the *Arthaśāstra* thus:

> "The grant of *pensions to retired officials* was also another source of expenditure. *Not only those who retired after meritorious service*, but those dying in harness, had their wives and children provided for."[2]

There is no justification for the former half of this interpretation, since we do not find in Kauṭalya's work any mention about remuneration after retirement, nor is there any reference to pension in the *Kāmandakīya Nītisāra* and in the sections bearing on Rājadharma in the *Rāmāyaṇa* and the *Mahābhārata*.

Therefore, the reference to pension in Kumāradāsa is of utmost value. In the course of Viśvāmitra's enquiry of king Janaka, in the manner of Rāma's enquiry of Bharata in the *Rāmāyaṇa*[3] and Nārada's enquiry of Yudhiṣṭhira in the *Mahābhārata*,[4] our poet introduces this idea thus:

नवे वयसि राज्यार्थं प्रविधाय जरां गतान् ।
अक्षमत्वेऽपि तान् भृत्यान् कच्चित्पुष्णासि सादरम् ।

(*JH*. VI. 40)

1. *Arthaśāstra* of Kauṭalya, T.S.S., V. 3. *Cf*. also *Mahābhārata*, Nārada to Yudhiṣṭhira, Sabhā, V.

2. Narayana Chandra Bandyopadhyaya, M.A., B.L., *Kauṭilya or An Exposition of His Social Ideal and Political Theory*, Calcutta, 1927, p. 173. (Italics ours)

3. Ayodhyā, 100.

4. *Mahābhārata*, Sabhā, V.

Here it is categorically stated that those who have served the king and the country during their youth and have grown old are not to be neglected by the king, though they may not be any more in active service. Sometimes Kumāradāsa conceives of the king from the general point of view of an ideal man and from this view-point we have dealt with some of the passages on kingly duty under moral and ethical teaching of Kumāradāsa in another part of this Thesis.

We shall now deal with the other ideas of Kumāradāsa on the subject of polity. References to these are to be found mainly in canto X of the *JH.* where Daśaratha advises his son Rāma on how he should conduct himself as the head of the State.

Advocating the method of conciliation as the best expedient, he says that it is always crowned with good results and will give pleasure to oneself and the opposite party. Adepts in sound polity uphold it, since it does not involve violence or torture:

सुभगंकरणी वृत्तिः साम्नः स्वपररञ्जनी ।
नायश्शूलिकतेत्याहुः नये निष्णातबुद्धयः ॥

(*JH.* X. 24)

In this connection he uses the word Āyaśśūlikatā[1] which means 'one in which threat and violence are employed' the importance of Sāman is stressed in other texts also like the *Kāmandakiya* and the *Pañcatantra*. For example, the latter says[2]:

आदौ साम प्रयोक्तव्यं पुरुषेण विपश्चिता ।
सामसाध्यानि कार्याणि विक्रियां यान्ति न क्वचित् ॥

1. Kauṭalya uses this word in some other contexts, but in the same sense thus :

कुशीलवैः चारणादिभिक्षुकाश्च व्याख्याताः । तेषामयश्शूलेन यावतः पणानभिधेयुः तावन्तः शिफाप्रहाराः दण्डाः ।

(*Arthaśāstra*, IV. 1)

2. *Pañcatantra*, I. 379.

He then refers to two kinds of Sāman, one associated with the giving of material presents or bribes and the other without it. The poet says that the former type of Sāman is approved by Uśanas or Śukra.

साम शाठ्यं जनो वेत्ति दानादत्यन्तवर्जितम् ।
तत्सामौशनसं साधु युक्तं दानस्य मात्रया ।

(*JH.* X. 26)

This may be compared with the following verse from the *Kāmandakīya*[1] where, however, there is no mention of Uśanas as the authority advocating this view:

दानरिक्तेन सर्वत्र साम्ना कृत्यं तृणेन वा ।
निर्दानं साम नायाति कलत्रेष्वपि संस्थितिम् ॥

Similarly, with regard to the second expedient of winning over by gifts, the poet says that the most fruitful way of employing this is to couple gift with both honour and conciliation (Satkāra and Sāman).

मा दा रहितसम्मानं त्यक्त्वा सत्कारसामनी ।

JH. X. 58.

The idea that this expedient should be employed with the show of due honour is also present in the *Kāmandakīya*.[2]

Coming to the third Upāya, Bheda he stresses that the hereditary and experienced minister should be guarded against being won over by disaffection practised by the enemy. He says that the enemies by whispering into his ears may win him over to their side and use him to destroy the king:

उपजापहृतस्वामिस्नेहसीम्नि पराश्रयम् ।
मौले वाञ्छति मेदिन्याः पत्युः पातो न संशयः ॥

(*JH.* X. 26)

1. *Kāmandakīya Nītisāra*, XXVII, 64.
2. सामभेदौ तु कर्तव्यौ दानमानपुरस्सरौ *Ibid*. 63.

Winning over the chief minister of the enemy to one's side is recommended as a type of Bhedopāya by ancient writers. For example, *Kāmandakīya* says[1] :

भेदं कुर्वीत यत्नेन मन्त्र्यमात्यपुरोधसाम् ।

Preventing one's officials being misled by outsiders is emphasised by Kauṭalya also, who it may be noted, uses the expressions Upajāpa and Maula in this context.

परोपजापात् संरक्षेत् प्रधानान् क्षुद्रकानपि ।[2]

अवमानितं विकुर्वीत मौलमननुरक्तं वा यदस्य व्यसने अपकुर्यात् ।[3]

Lastly, he prescribes Daṇḍa when all the other Upāyas fail; when other means are not useful, Daṇḍa alone will make a king enjoy the full fruits of his polity.[4] Daṇḍa is said to be as much essential and useful as the collection of taxes for a stable Government.[5]

The poet also gives some clues with regard to the appointment of Ministers and other high officials. He says that a person who is not having high family tradition should not be appointed as a high official, though he may be having other qualifications like merit.

नोच्चैः पदं लम्भनीयो गुण्योऽप्यन्वयवर्जितः ।
रत्नाढ्यमपि कुर्वीत मूर्ध्नि कः पादमण्डनम् ।। *JH*.X.35.

At the same time, a person who has claim for a high lineage but has no other merits, does not deserve to be appointed in office. The same idea is contained in the following verse of Kāmandaka:[6]

कुलीनाः शुचयश्शूराः श्रुतवन्तोऽनुरागिणः ।
दण्डनीतेः प्रयोक्तारः सचिवाः स्युर्महीपतेः ।।

1. *Kāmandakīya Nītisāra*, XXVII. 27.
2. Kauṭalya's *Arthaśāstra*, I. 13.
3. *Ibid*, XII. 1.
4. *JH*. X. 30
5. *Ibid*, X. 32.
6. *Kāmandakīya Nītisāra*, VII. 24.

Summing up the enumeration of the qualities of a Minister, the poet says that a king never swerves from his path of righteousness only if he gets persons with the following qualities as his Ministers :

तद्युक्तमुपधाशुद्धमन्वयेन गुणेन च ।
साचिव्यं लम्भयन्मौलं न प्रमाद्यति भूमिपः ॥
(*JH*. X. 37)

A person of good character and lineage should be put to further tests by the king before he is appointed as a Minister. These tests are called Upadhā which is defined in the *Kāmandakīya* thus[1] :

उपेत्य धीयते यस्माद् उपधेति ततः स्मृता ।
उपाय उपधा ज्ञेया तयामात्यान् परीक्षयेत् ॥

Kauṭalya also advocates this testing of Ministers when he says:

...अमात्यान् उपधाभिश्शौचयेत्[2] ।

He further gives four kinds of Upadhās by which the person to be appointed can be tested. They are, Dharmopadhā, Arthopadhā, Kāmopadhā, and Bhayopadhā. He also enumerates particular portfolios to be assigned to those who come out successful in each one of these tests. These tests comprise placing the person concerned in such circumstances where he will be tempted to make complaints about the king or will divulge his reactions to trusted men of the king. If one is able to come out pure and untempted in these tests, then he will be called Upadhāśuddha.

The poet has also something to say with regard to winning over friends. Daśaratha warns Rāma not to trust those who come and court his friendship suddenly, just to get some obligation done for themselves. Such pretenders will not care for him when once their object is achieved, just

1. *Ibid*, VII. 26.
2. *Arthaśāstra*, I. 10.

like a person who has crossed a ferry will have nothing to do with the boat that helped him to cross. Those who court the friendship of a person without any personal motive will be selfless and intimate throughout their life.

यस्मिन् कृत्यानुरोधेन सौहृदं प्रतनोति यः ।
स तं त्यजति कृत्यान्ते तीर्णतोय इव प्लवम् ॥

(*JH.* X. 38)

KUMĀRADĀSA'S CONCEPTION OF IDEAL WOMANHOOD

The ideal of Indian womanhood viewed woman always as inseparable from her husband and as accessory to him either in domestic life or in the practice of those religious injunctions which gradually lead to the higher and higher spiritual evolution of the couple. The ideals of chastity of the virtuous wife have been inculcated through the ages by the exposition to the people of the character and life of the exemplary heroines of the epics. The service which Vālmīki did in this respect by presenting Sītā as the great ideal of Indian womanhood is unique; and our poet who is working on a theme as Vālmīki's own poem, has a proper realisation of Vālmīki's teachings in this respect being an essential part of the epic and its message. He, accordingly, sets forth at some length the essential characteristics than constitute the pativratā ideal.

In the various references throughout his poem, he has given a more or less complete picture of an ideal woman, according to his conception. He bases his ideas on the ground that the life of a wife is complementary to that of her husband. Apart from the sexual life which he deals with elaborately in a separate chapter, a lady in her normal household life should always devote herself to the promotion of the happiness of her husband. A lady rises in stature and esteem to the degree to which she is able to please her husband.

पतिप्रसादोन्नतयो हि योषितः ।

A lady should always be conscious of this fact and behave in such a way as to please her husband at all costs, an ideal which as Milton says, "He for God only; and she for God in him." Obedience and adjustment to the mind of the husband are methods through which she can achieve this end. A lady born of a high family, with a father placed in high status and blessed with abundant riches may get intoxicated with the pride of birth and status and the poet points out the undesirability of this through the words of Janaka addressed to Sītā :

परः प्रकर्षो वपुषः समुन्नतिः कुलस्य तातो नृपतिर्नवं वयः ।
इति स्म मा मानिनि मानमागमः पतिप्रसादोन्नतयो हि योषितः ।। IX.4

Pride may be due to four causes, beauty, nobility, wealth and youth. All these four are present in Sītā. Hence her father particularly warns her. Beauty is the foremost thing that makes a lady proud and boastful. Second comes high birth, i.e. pride due to blood. Third wealth, and lastly her youth which she considers as the supreme period to command the allegiance of her husband. The poet rightly reminds that these four are not intended to heighten her false prestige, but are the instruments in her hand to make her husband more and more happy.

To avoid the setting in of such a complex, it is enough if she realises that even with all this equipment a lady can shine forth at her best only through the medium of her husband. She cannot stand independent of her husband.

नारीमाश्रयसम्पदेव नयति श्रेयस्करीमुन्नतिम् ।

This fact is also put forth by the poet through the mouth of Janaka as part of his advice to his daughter. He also illustrates it with an apt simile.

स्त्रियो न पुंसामुदयस्य कारणं त एव तद्धामविभूतिहेतवः ।
तडिद्वियुक्तोऽपि घनः प्रजृम्भते विना न मेघं विलसन्ति विद्युतः ।। IX.5

Even without lightning, a cloud can rise up in the sky and make its existence felt on the world. But, without a cloud, a lightning cannot shine nor can it make the world feel its splendour.

The next characteristic of an ideal wife is that she should never utter harsh words. If her husband is angry, she should convert him by her silence. The very silence will cool him down and make him see or sympathise with her view-point.

गतापि भर्त्रा परिकोपमायतं गिरं कृथा मा परुषार्थदीपनीम् । IX.6

In fact, the wife's behaviour can be so excellent that it can change the very mind of a man and replace aversion by love. On the other hand, she who does not take her stand on character and proper behaviour brings only irremediable insult to her husband and shame to herself.

करोति शीलेन पतिं पतिव्रता गुणस्पृहं वश्यमवश्यमङ्गना ।
पराभवं भर्तुरुपैति दुस्तरं विनष्टचारित्रगुणा गुणैषिणः ।। IX.7

The poet concludes this discourse of Janaka by saying that the greatest satisfaction for a parent is to hear that his daughter with her excellent character, leads a happy life with her husband. The severest blow that can hurt his heart is the news that his daughter is drifting away from the path of chastity. Janaka says that if he hears anything unpleasant about her, his heart which is already weak due to old age will burst into thousand pieces.

कृतं त्वयि व्याहृतिविस्तरेण तत्कुरुष्व यन्मे चरितं त्वदाश्रयम् ।
श्रुतिप्रयातं जरसैव जर्जरं हस्रधेदं हृदयं न दारयेत् ।। IX.8

Thus the conclusion echoes Kālidāsa's statement in a similar context where he says, "वामाः कुलस्याधयः ।"

This trend of thought need not make us think that the poet is always eager to place ladies in a subordinate position and he makes them mere instruments of enjoyment at the hands of men. He, on the other hand, is equally conscious of the greatness of a lady and the important part she plays in moulding the life of her husband. He is always aware of the potent strength of a chaste woman to do and undo things. He is sure of the fact that the husband of a chaste lady wins all glories, only by virtue of her chastity. This he puts through the mouth of his hero, Rāma, who confesses :

पतिव्रतायास्तव देवि तेजसा हृतप्रभावो निहतो निशाचरः ।
मनुष्यमुक्तः कथमन्यथा शरः क्रमेत लोकत्रितयस्य जेतरि ।।

Rāma says to Sītā that he could destroy the most powerful Rāvaṇa only with the help of her *Pātivratya-agni* (fire of chastity). But for that moral force supplied by her, he who is after all a human being, could not have destroyed with his arrows a person who had conquered all the three worlds. This verse reminds us of the famous verse of Vālmīki spoken by Maṇḍodarī namely:

पतिव्रतायास्तपसा नूनं दग्धोऽसि मे प्रभो (Yuddha. 114.24)

The poet puts through the mouth of Rāma the fact that blessed are those who get a wife of unquestionable character. He says that he and the sage Vasiṣṭha can legitimately feel proud of their wives, great in the virtue of chastity.

जगद्द्वयं द्वावधितिष्ठतः प्रिये पतिव्रतालाभविभूतिगर्वितौ ।
अहं भवत्या भूतको महीतलं महामुनिः स्वर्गमरुन्धतीपतिः ।।

Such an obedient and modest lady can also rise to a lofty stature when called for. After the battle is over, when Rāma hesitates to accept her due to his fear of criticism, our poet does not hesitate to infuse Sītā with a heroic spirit which condemns the fear-complex in her husband and she is made to announce to the whole world that she values her life only as long as she can have the honour that is due to a lady of character and dignity. When it comes to the question of challenging her character, she would prove to the world at large that she would court death, if she could not live as one of character and nobility.

श्रीकुमारदासकृते जानकीहरणे

षोडशः सर्गः

अथ दिवसविधेयमिन्द्रशत्रो-
निरवसितं प्रतिहारतो विदित्वा ।
अनुमतिमधिगम्य तस्य भानुः
गिरिमपरान्तमहार्णवस्थमीये ॥ १ ॥

अरुणकरदृढावकृष्ट[1]रश्मि-
प्रणमित[2]कन्धरभुग्न[3]चारुघोणाः ।
दिवसकरहया गिरीन्द्रभित्ते[4]-
र्जघनपतद्रथनेमयोऽवतेरुः ॥ २ ॥

सरभसनिपतद्घनान्धकार-
भ्रमरकुलैरवलुप्यमान[5]मूर्तिः ।
अपसरणविधानमीहमानः[6]
पयसि भयादिव मज्जति स्म भानुः ॥ ३ ॥

अरुणितमथ सन्ध्यया मुहूर्तं
तदनु तमोभिरुपात्तकोशरन्ध्रम् ।
कुमुदमलिगणो ददर्श दूरा-
दरुणसितेतरवारिजाभिशङ्की ॥ ४ ॥

सरसिजमणिवेदिकासुभिन्न-
प्रचुरतरङ्गकणावकीर्णवाते[7] ।
उपवनसरसीरुहं दिनान्ते
हृतमिव शीतरयेण संचुकोच ॥ ५ ॥

द्रुतमपसरतैति भानुरस्तं
सरसिरुहेषु दलार्गलाः[8] पतन्ति ।

---

१. MT. अरुकरं; L. अरुणदृढकरावकृष्ट । २. L. व्रणमिव । ३. MT, R. भग्न । ४. MT. भि.........gap ....जंघन; R. भित्तीर्जघन । ५. L. अनुलिप्यमान । ६. L. विधौसमीहमानः; MT. उदीहमानः; R. उदीहमानं । ७. MT, L. पाते । ८. MT. दलार्गला ।

भ्रमरकुलमिति ब्रुवन्निवालिः[१]
क्वणितलयं विचचार दीर्घिकायाम् ॥ ६ ॥
सति दिवसपरिक्षयस्य योगे
निपतितसद्वयसस्तमोऽभिभूताः ।
विनमितचल[२]मस्तका बभूवुः
समुपहृ[३]ता जरसेव[४] वृक्षगुल्माः ॥ ७ ॥
विगलितवति[५] तिग्मभासि सन्ध्या-
परिगतलोहिततारकं नभस्तत्[६] ।
त्रिदशशरशतव्रणावकीर्णं
हृदयमनुव्रजति स्म रावणस्य ॥ ८ ॥
दिवसकरभयादिवोपलीनो[७]
जलधिजलान्तरितस्तुषाररश्मिः ।
रविरपचलितो[८] न वेति बोद्धुं
नभसि करानिव चारयांबभूव ॥ ९ ॥
प्रथमगमितमन्धकारिभावं
पुनरतिपिङ्गलतारकं विधाय ।
भुवनमथ कलात्मना समस्य[९]
त्रिनयनरूपमलम्भयत्प्रदोषः ॥ १० ॥
दिवसविगमलङ्घितस्य[१०] भानो-
रवनतिरुन्नतिरिन्दुमण्डलस्य ।
अविकलवपुषः समानकालं
नभसि तुलामधिरूढयोरिवास्ताम् ॥ ११ ॥
उदयमरुणिमा परित्यजन्तं
प्रविसृजति स्म शशाङ्कमच्छबिम्बम् ।
चषकममलमिन्द्रदिङ्मुखेन[११]
स्फटिकमयं मधुनीव पीयमाने[१२] ॥ १२ ॥

---

१. MT. ब्रुवन्निवालि—; R. ब्रुवन्निवाली २. MT, R. नमितचपल । ३. L. समुपगता । ४. MT. जरसैव । ५. MT. विगलितपति । ६. MT. नभस्तः । ७. L. इवावलीनो । ८. L. रविरथचलितो । ९. L. समस्यं । १०. L. लम्भितस्य । ११. MT. इन्दुदिङ्मुखेन; R. अमलबिन्दु... gap ..। १२. R. नीयमाने ।

शठमिव दयितं दिशः प्रदोषं
मुहुरधिगम्य रुषेव भिन्नवर्णाः[1] ।
स्थितमुपरि पयोधरस्य सन्ध्या-
विलसितकुङ्कुममण्डनं ममार्जुः[2] ॥ १३ ॥

क्षिपति निशि[3] पयोधरे[4] निशान्ते
रहयति किं तिमिरोत्तरीयमाशा ।
इति रचितविपर्ययस्य साक्षि[5]
स्फुटमिव कौमुदमाततान हासम्[6] ॥ १४ ॥

परभृतरुचितामसं हिमांशो-
रुदयगिरेरुदितस्य मण्डलेन ।
अतिपटु पटलं विपाटच विश्वं[7]
विवरगते[8] विहितं नु संहृतं नु[9] ॥ १५ ॥

इह हरिणकलङ्ककान्तिलेशैः
सह पतिता मृगलक्षणस्य कान्तिः ।
अलिभिरवततैर्न्यधत्त[10] वापी-
कुमुदवनैरिति शङ्कितं जनेषु ॥ १६ ॥

अचिरसमुदिताय हारगौरैः
हिमशिशिरैरनुगृह्यते करौघैः ।
उदकलवपरम्पराभि[11]रर्घ्यं
शशिमणितोरणमिन्दवे ततान ॥ १७ ॥

द्युतिभिरवजितो निशाचरीणा-
महमतुलस्य न केवलं मुखस्य ।
अयमपि हरिणो जितः[12] कटाक्षै-
रिति जगतामिव दर्शयन् मृगाङ्कम्[13] ॥ १८ ॥

घृणिभि[14]रधिपुरं पुरस्सुवेल[15]-

---

१. MT, R. वर्णा । २. MT, R. ममार्ज । ३. MT, L. दिशि । ४. L. पयोधरं । ५. L. साक्षी; R. साक्ष । ६. MT, R. हासा । ७. L. gap । ८. L. gap upto ते । ९. MT. संहृतन्नु । १०. L. अवततैर्न्वथैव । ११. MT. चरंपराभिः । १२. MT, R. हृतः । १३. MT. मृगोङ्कः; R, L. मृगाङ्कः । १४. MT. ग्रणिभिः । १५. MT. पुरस्यवेल; R. पुरस्सवेल ।

क्षितिधरमस्तकजर्जरैः पतद्भिः ।
प्रमदमधि[1]मनो नितम्बिनीनां[2]
अभिनवनिर्झरशङ्कया वितन्वन् ॥ १९ ॥

मनसि मनसिजं मनस्विनीना[3]-
मविरलमुन्नमयन्निजेन धाम्ना ।
द्विपदशनरुचिः पदं कलाना-
मुदयगिरेरुदियाय दिक्प्रदीपः ॥ २० ॥

गगनसरसि चन्द्ररूप्यकुम्भे
व्यपसरति स्म निपातिते रजन्या[4] ।
तदुपहिततरङ्गधूतनीली[5]-
निकर इवातिघनस्तमःप्रवाहः[6] ॥ २१ ॥

सुरकरिण इवाहतः[7] करेण
प्रविततसन्तमसाम्बुराशिरिन्दोः[8] ।
अनुपहतगतिर्दिगन्तवेला-
वलयवनानि विलङ्घयन् प्रतस्थे ॥ २२ ॥

प्रियविरहसमागमाश्रयाणां
मुखकमलानि निशा[9] नितम्बिनीनाम् ।
उदितवति मृगाङ्क[10] चन्द्रबिम्ब-
द्युतिभिरिवोडुपतावलञ्चकार[11] ॥ २३ ॥

पथिकयुवतिदृष्टयोऽनुजग्मुः
सरसिजरागमणिश्रियं रुचैव[12] ।
शशिनि समुदिते शशाङ्ककान्तं[13]
किरणवृतं क्रियया निदर्शयन्त्यः[14] ॥ २४ ॥

---

१. MT. प्रमदमथ; L. प्रमदमध । २. MT, R. मनस्विनीनां । ३. MT, R. नितम्बिनीनां । ४. L. missing । ५. L. missing । ६. L. प्रहारः । ७. R. हतं । ८. R. रश्मिमिन्दोः । ९. R. नरा । १०. L. शशाङ्क । ११. R. उडुपलंघनं चकार । १२. MT. रुचैवं । १३. R. कान्त । १४. L. क्रिययापि दर्शयन्त्यः; MT. gap upto विदर्शयन्त्यः; R...gap...विदर्शय...gap ।

[1]अपिहितसलिलेन निष्प्रदेशं
कुमुदवनेन कुमुद्वती विरेजे ।
घननिपतितभृङ्गचित्रभासा
मृगरिपुचर्मकृतावकुण्ठनेव[2] ॥ २५ ॥
निशि पयसि पदानि कुर्वतीषु
ग्रहनिकरप्रतिमासु मल्लिकाक्षः ।
इतरमपि जलाशयं निकूजन्
समुपससार कुमुद्वतीति हृष्टः ॥ २६ ॥
इति तुहिनरुचौ[3] विकीर्णधाम्नि
प्रचुरतमोभिदुरस्व[4]रश्मिजाले ।
मनसि मकरकेतनस्य यूनां
विलसितमात्मनि विक्रिया[5] विवव्रुः ॥ २७ ॥
स्वयमपि विरचय्य पत्रभङ्गी[6]-
र्वदनहिमद्युतिलक्षणं कया[7]चित् ।
चिरयति हृदयेश्वरे रमण्या
नयनजलेन फल[8]च्युता निरासे ॥ २८ ॥
म भवति दयितस्य सन्निकर्षे
फलरहितो विरहेषु तस्य रागः[9] ।
इति मनसि निधाय[10] यावकेन
व्यरचयदन्यतरा न दन्तवासः ॥ २९ ॥
इतरयुवतिपादघातचिह्नं
सरससमर्पितयावकं पदं यत् ।
उरसि न दयितस्य तद्विवेद
स्फुटमणिकुण्डलरागरुद्धमन्या ॥ ३० ॥
प्रियवचनविधायिनी न भर्तुः
चलदलकच्युतचूर्ण[11]लेशमक्ष्णोः ।

---

१. MT. अविहित । २. MT, R. अवकुण्ठनेन । ३. MT. तिमिरकचौ । ४. MT. भिदुरस्य; R. भि... gap । ५. MT, R. विक्रियां । ६. L. भक्तिं; R. भक्ती । ७. MT, R. कदाचित् ८. R. gap between न and ल । ९. L. विरहे किमस्य रागः । १०. MT, R. विधाय । ११. MT. पूर्णं ।

मदन[1]समुचिताङ्ग[2]सङ्गिदृष्टे-
व्र्यपनयति स्म मुखानिलेन काचित् ॥ ३१ ॥

सुरपतिरिपवः प्रियानिरस्त[3]-
श्रवणसरोरुहनिर्वृतेऽपि दीपे ।
रतिषु[4] ददृशुरेव काञ्चिरत्न-
द्युतिपरिभिन्नतमिस्रमूरुमूलम् ॥ ३२ ॥

विवसनविहितोपगूहनानां
घनजघनस्तनकुम्भकुङ्कुमेषु ।
अपि परिगलितेषु कामिनीनां
न विगलितानि तनूदराश्रयाणि ॥ ३३ ॥

चरणतलसरोरुहेण यत्त्वां
प्रहृतवती शिरसि प्रियाति[5]कोपे ।
स किल परमनुग्रहः[6] प्रसादे
हृदि रचिते तव कीदृशो नु लाभः ॥ ३४ ॥

अधरपुटमिदं मदार्तरामा-
रभससमर्पितदन्तखण्डितं ते ।
अयि शठ परिशान्तय रुजायाः
नयनजलेन निषिञ्चसि[7] प्रसक्तम् ॥ ३५ ॥

करकिसलयगोपितं मुखं खं
किमिह विधाय वदस्ययं[8] ममाग्रे ।
तिरयसि[9] दशनक्षतं प्रियायाः
वयमुत गौरवभाजनं किमेवम्[10] ॥ ३६ ॥

इति वचसि रुषा परिस्खलन्त्यः
प्रणयिषु राक्षसयोषितो विपक्षैः ।
परिमिलित[11]विसर्जितेषु रूक्षं
नयनजलग्रथितं वचो वितेनुः ॥ ३७ ॥

---

१. MT. वसन; R. वचन । २. MT. समुदित । ३. L. निरस्य । ४. R. नतिषु । ५. MT, R. प्रिया हि । ६. L. परमनिग्रहः; MT. परमनिग्रह । ७. L. निषिञ्चति । ८. L. अलं । ९. L. तिरयति । १०. MT, R. एतत् । ११. L. परिमलित ।

अपि तव दयिते समीपभाजि
श्वसितरयग्लपिताधरस्य कान्तिः ।
चरणनिपतिते निपातितस्ते
न च करुणापरिमन्थरः[1] कटाक्षः ॥ ३८ ॥

स्तनतटनिहितः करोऽवधूतः
परिगदिते[2] समधिश्रितं च मौनम् ।
विहसितमपि सान्त्वने सरोषं
प्रणयिजने युवतेरयं हि दण्डः ॥ ३९ ॥

सखि जहिहि रुषं हिनस्ति पश्चात्
तव तरलं हृदयं पुरानुतापः ।
इति निपुणसखीगिरा निरासे[3]
मनसि निशाचरयोषितोऽभिमानः[4] ॥ ४० ॥

यदि चिरयति दूति वल्लभो मे
भृशमजनि त्वयि किं रुषोऽवकाशः ।
निजमतिरभसं यतो विदश्य[5]
क्षतिभिरिमं समयूयुजस्त्वमोष्ठम् ॥ ४१ ॥

मधुकुसुमविलेपनादिभाग[6]-
ग्रहणविदर्शितसौहृदस्य[7] वृत्त्या ।
अयमपि च[8] सखि स्वयं वृतस्ते[9]
प्रियपरिभोगसुखस्य[10] संविभागः ॥ ४२ ॥

दशनपदमतिस्फुटं विभाति
स्फुरति तनुः[11] श्रमवारिसिक्तमास्यम् ।
अवितथ[12]मविधत्स्व कामिनीं[13] त्वां
कुटिलगतिर्ननु दष्टवान्[14] भुजङ्गः[15] ॥ ४३ ॥

---

१. MT. परिमन्थरं; L. परिपन्थिकः । २. MT, R. परिगलिते । ३. L. सखीभिरा निरासे ४. MT. अभिमानम् । ५. MT. विदश्यं । ६. L. भाव । ७. R. सौहृदश्च । ८. MT. 'च' missing । ९. R. हृतस्ते; L. प्रतस्ते । १०. MT. सखस्य । ११. MT, L, R. तनु । १२. MT, R. अपि कथं । १३. MT, R. कामिनी; L. कामिनि १४. MT. दष्ट्वा; L. दृष्टवान् । १५. MT. भुजङ्गम् ।

अवितथ[1]मिदमात्मनि[2]विशेषा[3]
सखि भवसीति वचः पुरा यदुक्तम् ।
अभिदयितमनुष्ठितं त्वया हि[4]
स्वयमखिलं मम[5] यत्नतो विधेयम् ॥ ४४ ॥

इति रचितरुषः सहासगर्वं[6]
श्रमजलबिन्दुचितं मुखं दधत्याः ।
श्रवणकटु निशाचरस्य वध्वा-
श्चलितधृतेरुपदूति वागजृम्भे ॥ ४५ ॥

श्वसितहतरुचिर्वराधरोष्ठः
करतलसंक्रमितश्च[7] पत्रलेखः ।
निजगदतुरुपागते चिरेण
प्रणयिनि राक्षसयोषितः प्रचिन्ताम् ॥ ४६ ॥

विफलपरिकरा विधाय दूती[8]-
स्तदनु समेत्य च पृष्ठतो निलीनैः[9] ।
युवतिनिगदितं सरोषगर्वं
परिहृषितैरुपशुश्रुवे तदीशैः ॥ ४७ ॥

क्षतिरियमधरस्य यत्सुरासु
स्रुतसहकाररसाहिता तदस्तु ।
अतरलहृदयस्य गण्डबिम्बे
तव कतरोऽद्य नखक्षतस्य[10] हेतुः ॥ ४८ ॥

युवतिनयनचुम्बितेषु[11] पक्ष्म-
प्रविरचिता पटुरञ्जनस्य राजिः[12] ।
तव चपल निरूपिता नवोद्य[13]-
त्प्रविरलरोम्णि[14] कथंचिदुत्तरोष्ठे[15] ॥ ४९ ॥

---

१. MT, R. अपिकथं । २. MT. आत्मनी । ३. MT, R. विशेषाः । ४. R. gap after त्वया । ५. L. gap upto यत्नतो । ६. R. हर्षं । ७. MT, R. सञ्चरित । ८. R. मूर्त्ती । ९. R. नि. . . . नैः । १०. MT, R. नखरक्षतस्य । ११. L. चुम्बितेषु । १२. MT, L. राशिः । १३. R. अनवद्य; L. अतिसूक्ष्मा । १४. L. बकुलफलाकण । १५. MT. कथं निदुत्तरोष्ठे; L. रोचिरुत्तरोष्ठे; R. कथं. . . . gap. . रुत्तरोष्ठे ।

युवतिमुखगतेन लोचनेन
स्फुटमपि मे न श्रृणोषि[1] जल्पतानि।
मुखमधुर[2] भुजङ्ग येन[3] सत्यं
कुटिलगते नयन वोऽपि[4] जातः ॥ ५० ॥

इति मनसिजचञ्चलं[5] युवानं
रजनिचरप्रमदा निरूपयन्ती।
अनिमिषनयना सहासगर्वं
प्रणयरुषः[6] प्रथनं[7] वचो बभाषे ॥ ५१ ॥

स्वतनु[8]वितरणेन तं प्रलोभ्य[9]
द्विपमिव वन्यमिहोपनेतुकामा।
सखि गजगणिकेव चेष्टितासि
स्मरति[10] हि सज्जन एव[11] मित्रकृत्यम्[12] ॥ ५२ ॥

अकरुणमधिगम्य तं मदर्थे
विशसनमेवमसह्यमास्थितायाः[13]।
क्षतमिदम[14]धरस्य केवलं ते
मम हृदयस्य सखि व्यथा तु तीव्रा ॥ ५३ ॥

इति सखिहसितां[15] कृतव्यलीका-
मरुणित[16]लोचनरम्यवक्त्रबिम्बा[17]।
सुररिपुवनिताऽपदिश्य दूती-
मकृत गिरः[18] परुषा रुषा[19] परीताः[20] ॥ ५४ ॥

सरसिजमणिकुन्तलोपमुक्तं[21]
मधु पपु[22]रङ्गजमन्थरा युवत्यः।
कथमपि[23] परिनिस्सृत[24]स्तदीयो
रस इति मुग्धतया विशङ्कमानाः[25] ॥ ५५ ॥

---

१. MT, R. श्रृणोति। २. L. मुखमधर। ३. R. भुजानयेन। ४. MT, R. श्रवोसि। ५. MT. चञ्चला। ६. MT. रुषं; L. रुषा। ७. L. चतुरं। ८. MT, R. सुतनु। ९. L. विलोभ्य। १०. L, R. स्फुरति। ११. L. एव missing। १२. MT, R. मित्रकृत्ये; L. साधुकृत्ये। १३. R. आस्थितायाम्। १४. L. कृतमिदं। १५. MT, L, R. हसिता। १६. L. लोचनवक्त्रचन्द्रबिंबा। १७. MT. बिंबां। १८. MT, R. शिरः। १९. MT. रुहा। २०. R. परीताम्। २१. L. युक्तं। २२. L. वपुर्। २३. L. कथमिव। २४. R. परि. . . gap . . . त।। २५. MT. विशङ्कयमानान्; R. विशङ्कयमानाः।

हृदयवदन[१]लोचनेषु तासां
मधु मदगन्धवपुःश्रियं निधाय[२] ।
श्रमसलिलकणच्छलेन शुभ्रं[३]
बहिरभवच्छरपाण्डुगण्डबिम्बात् ॥ ५६ ॥

मुकुलयति सितेतरं सरोजं
शशिनि समग्रकलास्पदे तदीयः[४] ।
असितकुवलयद्युतिः[५] कुरङ्ग-
प्रतिनिधिरत्र ततान सीधु[६]पात्रे ॥ ५७ ॥

प्रियगुणशतजर्जरैव[७] पूर्वं[८]
मधुषु चिरं परिभोगवस्तु[९] लज्जा ।
न युवतिहृदये पदं विधातुं
मदमदनस्थितिसङ्कटे विषेहे ॥ ५८ ॥

अभिनवरविबिम्बलोहिनीभि-[१०]
र्द्युतिभिरभिन्नतया मनोहराभिः ।
सरसिजमणिशुक्तिषु प्रणष्टं
युवतिजनैर्मधु गौरवेण जज्ञे ॥ ५९ ॥

स्वयमथ पवनेन सौधपृष्ठे
हृतरजसि प्रतिहारचोदितेन ।
किरणमनुपहत्य[११] शीतभासः[१२]
क्षणमधिगम्य पयोधरैः निषिक्ते ॥ ६० ॥

सुरयुवतिकदम्बकस्य गीतै-
रनुगत[१३]तुम्बुरुवल्लकीनिनादे ।
सपदि परिवृतस्समन्मथेन
त्रिदशरिपुः प्रमदाजनेन रेमे ॥ ६१ ॥

---

१. MT. वचन । २. L. निनाय । ३. MT, R. शुद्धं । ४. MT, R. तदीयं । ५. L, R. द्युतिं । ६. MT. शीथु । ७. MT. जर्झरे च; R. जर्जरे च । ८. R. वधूयं । ९. L. परिपीतवत्सु; R. परिभोगवत्स । १०. L. वाहिनीभिः । ११. L. अनुवहति । १२. MT. शीतभासं; R. गीतभासं । १३. MT, R. परिकृत ।

मधु विनमितशातकुम्भकुम्भ-
स्रुतमखिलाननसक्तहेमशुक्तिः[1][2] ।
सपदि दशमुखः पिबन् विजिग्ये
सलिलनिधिं दशदिङ्नदीः[3] पिबन्तम् ॥ ६२ ॥

ततविततघनाद्यवाद्यजातैः
निजकरसन्ततिवादितैः स (ए)कः ।
त्रिविधलयपरिग्रहेण वक्त्रै-
र्युवतिमनर्तयताष्ट[4]भिश्च गायन् ॥ ६३ ॥

प्रतियुवति विषक्तबाहुपङ्क्त-
र्दशवदनागततन्मुखारविन्दः[5] ।
सममथ परितः प्रिया निषण्णाः[6]
परिरमयन् न ददौ रुषोऽवकाशम् ॥ ६४ ॥

इतरयुवतिदष्टदन्तवासाः
वदनततिस्थितसीत्कृतिः प्रियाभिः[7] ।
नवसु मनसिजन्मना शिरस्सु
क्षतधृतिभिर्दयितो रुषा[8]ऽभिजघ्ने ॥ ६५ ॥

शठ यदि चषकीकृतं मुखं मे
किमधरमद्य विखण्डयस्यकाण्डे ।
भवति मधु निपीय भाजनाग्र-
ग्रसनरतिर्न हि कश्चना[9][10]प्रमत्तः ॥ ६६ ॥

पिबति कथमिवापरा युवत्या
दशनपदः परिमुद्रितं तवोष्ठम् ।
इति युवतिजनेन राक्षसेन्द्रः
स्फुटरचितभ्रुकुटीपताकमूचे ॥ ६७ ॥

अथ कटकनिवासदृप्तनागः[11]
प्रविततधातुविभूषितः[12] सुमेरुः ।

---

१. MT. श्रुत; R. श्रित । २. MT. शुक्तिम्; R. शुक्ति । ३. R. दीर्नदीः । ४. L. अहर्षयदष्टभिश्च; A. अहन्नियदष्टभिश्च । ५. MT, R. मुखारविन्दम् । ६. A. निषण्णः । ७. L, A. सीत्कृतस्समाभिः; R. सीत्कृत-प्रियाभिः । ८. L,A. क्रुधा । ९. A. रिपु । १०. MT, L, R, A. कश्चन प्रमत्तः । ११. MT. नाग । २१. MT, R. विभूषणः ।

द्युतिमभृत पुरत्रयस्य भेत्तुः
शिरसि मुहुः स्थितशीतरश्मिबिम्बः[1] ॥ ६८ ॥

त्रिभुवनभयरोगदानवन्तं
द्विपमिव निर्भयमेत्य दानवन्तम् ।
नवशशधरकोटिधामदन्तं[2]
दधतमगुः सुरमागधा[3] मदन्तम् ॥ ६९ ॥

मेरोः[4] शृङ्गं तुहिननिकरस्पर्शशीतः शशीतः
पृथ्वीभागोऽ[5]प्यरुणकिरणैर्व्यक्तमस्तस्समस्तः[6] ।
धुन्वन्[7] पङ्क्ति वहति कुमुद[8]प्रेमलीनामलीना-
मस्य[9]न्वीचीनिलयमनिलस्सारसन्तं रसन्तम् ॥ ७० ॥

लब्ध्वा मुञ्चत्युदधिरुदकह्रासवेलां[10] स वेलां
याता निद्राविगमविरुतीश्चा[11]विरामा[12] विरामाः[13] ।
पाण्डुच्छायामुपयति दिशामानने तन् ननेतं[14]
ताराचक्रं विगत[15]किरणोल्लासमस्तं समस्तम् ॥७१॥

ऋक्षश्रेण्यां[16]विहितपरिघोल्लङ्घनायां घनायां
[17]सौमित्रे चागतवति रिपुत्रासहेतौ सहेतौ ।
को रामे च घ्नति पर[18]भटस्तत्सहस्ते स हस्ते
किं तत्सैन्ये[19] प्रहरति रिपुच्छिद्यशेषेऽद्य शेषे ॥ ७२ ॥

रक्षोलोकविनाशनेषु रहितच्छेदं[20]सितो दंसितो
दृप्तः पाणियुगेन दुस्तरतरस्स्वर्हेतिना हेतिना ।
युद्धायोपगतः करोति मनसा कम्पं स नः पंसनः[21]

---

१. MT. बिम्बे; R. बिम्बम् । २. MT. धामवन्तं । ३. R.मा. . . धा । ४. MT. सुमेरोः । ५. MT, R. भोगो । ६. L,A. व्यस्तमस्तस्तमस्त । ७. R. धुन्वन् । ८. MT, R. कुमुदे । ९. R. अन्यन् । १०. MT, R. ग्रासवेलां; L, A. ह्लासचेलां । ११. MT, R. विगमयति रुतीः । १२. R. चापि । १३. R.रामापि । १४. L, A. नेतन्; MT. नेकं । १५. L, A. चरणोल्लासं; MT. किरणोद्भासं; R. किरणाभासं । १६. L, A. पिहित । १७. MT. सौमित्राया; R. सौमित्रावा । १८. MT, R. परभटं । १९. MT,R. सैन्यैः । २०. MT. च्छेदां । २१. MT. वासनंवासनः; R. पासनं पासनः ।

सेयं मानद तावदश्रुतपुराक्रोशायिता शायिता[1] ॥७३॥

नक्तं नक्रा[2]धिवासं कुसुमशरशतत्रासितानां सितानां
क्रीडायामङ्गनानां[3] घनकुच[4]कलशैः कातरन्तं तरन्तम्।
उत्थाप्यैनं ततस्ते सततरति[5]सुखव्यासकामं सकामं
तूष्णीमासन् सशङ्खध्वनिपटहरवज्यानिशान्ते निशान्ते॥॥७४॥

इति जानकीहरणे षोडशः सर्गः[6]

१. MT. वराकोशायिका शायिका; R. वराक्रोशायिका शायिका। २. R. नक्ता। ३. R. अङ्गनायां। ४. A. रुच। ५. L, A. रत। ६. MT. इति श्रीमत्सिंहलकवेः कुमारदासस्य कृतौ जानकीहरणे महाकाव्ये षोडशस्सर्गः समाप्तः।

अथ सप्तदशः सर्गः

प्रणम्य भक्त्याथ पितामहं महं
विधाय बद्धादरमग्नये नये।
स्थितः सुवेलादचिरादगादगा-
दजस्य बन्धुः[1] समरक्षमां क्षमाम् ॥ १ ॥

द्विषो हि[2] तस्यारिनिवारणे रणे
विधित्सवः पौरुषदर्पवं पदम्।
हुताशनाम्नि[3] द्युति[4]भासुरे सुरे
विधिं वितेनु[5]र्बलिसंहितं हितम् ॥ २ ॥

अथाञ्जनक्ष्माधरपीवरो वरो
गतः सुहृद्वक्त्रविकासदस्सदः।
इमानि वाक्यानि दशाननो न नो
जगाद वह्निप्रविकासभां सभाम् ॥ ३ ॥

यथा भवन्तो मयि[6] धीरतारताः
हिताह्वयं[7] प्रेम सुशीभरं[8] भरम्।
वहन्ति नैवं जननी सती सती
प्रियात्मजो[9] नाप्यनुकम्पिता पिता ॥ ४ ॥

तदेतदस्मिंस्तु कथं भवे भवे-
दनेकशो यन्मयि नाहितं हितम्।
असौ च कीर्तिर्भुवि सान[10]यानया
गुणेन[11] वो मामभिरक्षताक्षता ॥ ५ ॥

प्रसह्य कर्तुं[12] हृतवैभवं भवं
भयं विधातुं च विवस्वतः स्वतः।
भवत्सु नित्यं ननु शक्तता तता[13]

---

१. L, A. पौत्रः । २. L, A. द्विषोपि । ३. MT, L, R. मानि । ४. L, A. अशक्नुवन्तोजय । ५. L. यथावदूचुर्नुति । A. यथावदूचुनुति । ६. L,A. युधि । ७. L,A. तथामाय । ८. R. सुगीमरं । ९. L,A. प्रियात्मजे । १०. R. नानया । ११. L,A.R. गणेन । १२. A. शक्त्या । १३. L, A. निशाचराः खण्डितरावणे रणेः ।

तथापि मानेन न साधुता धुता[1] ॥ ६ ॥

बलेन वस्तेन भयानके न के
रणस्य भीमस्य बभञ्जिरेऽजिरे ।
प्रकम्पते येन कृते रवे रवे-
रनूनभा मातलिसारथी रथी ॥ ७ ॥

पुरेव यूयं युधि कातरेतरे[2]
जनादितस्तीव्रमसुन्दरं दरम् ।
बले रणस्थेऽयुगलोचनश्च नः
पिशाचिकाताण्डवलासकस्स कः ॥ ८ ॥

युधि प्रचेता विषवाहिनाहिना
जनस्य कण्ठे कृतशृङ्खलः खलः ।
सलीलवीक्षाविधितर्जितो जितो
भवद्भिराक्रोशहुताशनैः शनैः ॥ ९ ॥

प्रकाशितक्रोध[3]समुद्भवो भवो
गण[4]ध्वजिन्या च समन्ततस्ततः ।
प्रयाति यो[5] भीतिमजय्यतो यतो
न कोऽपरस्त्रस्यति हस्ततस्ततः ॥ १० ॥

परद्विपासृक्स्रव[6]लोहितोऽहितो
निकृत्तविद्याधरचारणे रणे[7] ।
उमासुतश्शक्ति[8]वियोजितो जितो
भवद्भिरभ्रध्वनि[9]भैरवै रवैः ॥ ११ ॥

जयन्त्यमित्रा युधि सन्नयं न यं[10]
समुन्नता[11] यत्र च शूरता रता[12] ।
तमप्यपश्यं[13] मदवर्जितं जितं

---

१. L,A. दृता निपेतुर्जयभाजनैर्जनैः । २. L,A. प्रयाति भूप्या खलु माधवो धवो । ३. MT. क्रोड । ४. MT,L. गुण । ५. L,A. प्रयात्यसौ; R. प्रयाति वो । ६. L,A. परिस्रवच्छोणित । ७. L,A. रक्षोगणचारणै रणैः । ८. L,A. त्रिभिश्शिरोभिस्स । ९. L, A. मुमोच जीवं सह । १०. L, A. सन्नयन्नयन् । ११. MT,R. समुन्नतो । १२. L. धीरता रता । १३. L,A. बलं तदेको ।

गुरुं भवद्भिः[१] क्षतविग्रहे ग्रहे[२] ॥ १२ ॥
धनाधिपः संयति[३] धामतो[४] मतो
जहाति नित्योन्नतशासनः स नः[५] ।
प्रपद्य सन्नीति[६]महाबलं बलं
[७]रणार्थिदीक्षाविधिसंवरं वरम् ॥ १३ ॥
बलद्विषः प्रोच्छ्रितगोपुरं पुरं
जयद्भि[८]रुन्मूलित[९]तोरणे रणे ।
स्थितैर्भवद्भिः[१०] बलधामदे मदे
न संगृहीता[११] रिपुभङ्गदा गदा ॥ १४ ॥
रणे हृताखण्डलपौरुषो रुषो
रयेण तन्वन् महति स्वरं स्वरम् ।
सुरेषु को [१२]नारिभयङ्करं करं
न्यपातयद्यो [१३]जयभागुरुं गुरुम् ॥ १५ ॥
जिता न शक्त्या युधि भीमया मया
सवि[१४]ष्फुलिङ्गायुधसंचया च या ।
असौ भवद्भिः[१५] कृतयाचिता चिता
मरुच्चमू[१६]रङ्घ्रिषु नामितामिता ॥ १६ ॥
× × × × ॥ १७ ॥
रणस्य युक्ता फणबन्धुरा[१७] धुरा
वितन्वती दर्शितरंहसं हसम् ।
भुजङ्गसेनाप्रियसंयता यता
बलेन वो[१८] वासुकिचोदिता दिता ॥ १८ ॥
अनन्तनाम्नश्च फणावतोऽ[१९]वतो

---

१. A. चकार वीरः । २. MT, R. ग्रहं ग्रहम् । ३. L. पलायितान्यो युधि । ४. MT. धामभो । ५. L. जयोन्मुखो निर्जितविक्रमः क्रमः । ६. L. तन्नीति । ७. L. रणार्थं । ८. R. जयाभि । ९. MT, R. उन्मीलित । १०. L,A. गतं कपीन्द्र । ११. MT, L. ग्रहीता । १२. L. प्लवङ्गमे कोपि । १३. L. न्यपातयन्निर्जय । १४. A. विष्णु । १५. L, A. प्लवङ्गैः । १६. L, A. द्विषच्चमू । १७. MT,R. युक्ताथ बवन्धुरा । १८. MT. चो; L,A.क्षणेन यै । १९. L. वलस्य दूरादभिध. . . . .तोवतो

विषैरमित्रा[1]नभिहिंसतस्सतः ।
स्थितस्य तेजस्यविखण्डितेडिते[2]
सुरारिभिः [3]प्रस्फुरदीहता हता ॥ १९ ॥
इति प्रतापैररितापदं पदं
श्रितैर्भवद्भिः सह सेनयाऽन्यया ।
स जीयतां संयति मानवो नवो
गृहीतमौञ्जीकृतमेखलः खलः ॥ २० ॥
यमेत्य नष्टः कुलशेखरः खरः
कृतं च मे[4] वैरसमाधुनाऽधुना ।
अनेन दर्पादभिभाविना[5] विना
विनाशनीयो भुवि कोऽपरः परः ॥ २१ ॥
यशोविनाशेन विर्वाजितोर्जितो[6]
रिपु[7]प्रवीराङ्गविदारणे[8] रणे ।
न संमुखं तिष्ठति वासवस्स वः
कथैव का संभृतवानरे नरे ॥ २२ ॥
यशस्युपेते मम तानवं नवं
सहे न[9] दैन्यं बलहानिजं निजम् ।
करोमि यद्यङ्घ्रियुगानतं नतं
जुहोमि हस्तौ कटकोचितौ चितौ ॥ २३ ॥
मुखं यदीयं[10] मद[11]षट्पदापदा
विहन्यते फुल्लकुशेशयाशया ।
असौ दहन्ती स्मरधाम नो मनो
हतं निरीक्षेत[12] सदेवरं[13] वरम् ॥ २४ ॥
सुता नरेन्द्रस्य सबान्धवं धवं
निरीक्ष्य युद्धे महतीह तं हतम् ।

---

१. L. नखैर..... नभि २. R. अविकम्पितेपिते । ३. MT, R. रणेभवद्भिः स्फुर । ४. L,A. ते । ५. MT,R. अविभाविना । ६. L, MT, R. जितो; A. विलज्जितोजितो । ७. L,R. रिपुः । ८. L,A. प्रवीराङ्गदवारणे । ९. R. सहेत । १०. L, A. मदीयं । ११. MT,R. मम । १२. MT, R. निरीक्षेतु । १३. MT, R. सदैवरं ।

छलानुरक्ते मयि तद्विधा द्विधा[1]
प्रयातु शोषं व्रजतोरसारसा ॥ २५ ॥
सभैवमुक्ताऽवनिकम्पदं पदं
वितन्वती शात्रवमाकुलं कुलम् ।
विधातुकामा स्फुरदङ्गदागदा
शुभाथ हारेण वि[2]वलगता गता ॥ २६ ॥
जगाम कश्चिन्निजवेश्मनो मनो
विधाय तन्व्या[3] मृदुवालकेऽलके ।
भृशं किरन्त्याश्रुपयोधरेऽधरे
निरीक्ष्य[4]माणो बहुचिन्तया तया ॥ २७ ॥
विलासिनीपायितसत्सुरो[5]ऽसुरो
वहन्नुरः कुङ्कुमर्चचितं चितम् ।
ययौ विमानादति[6]पानतो नतो
विगृह्य भूचुम्बनलम्पटं पटम ॥ २८ ॥
तथाऽपरः कङ्कटशोभितोऽभितो
धृतं विसर्पन् मदवासितं[7] सितम् ।
रणाय बद्धांशुकसुन्दरोदरो
गजं जगामासुरयोनिजं निजम् ॥ २९ ॥
द्रुतं दृढैर्वर्मभिराततस्ततः
समारुरोहाहवतत्परः परः[8] ।
सृजन्तमाधोरणकामदं मदं
बलं दधानं मदवेगजं गजम् ॥ ३० ॥
कृता[9] बलौघेन[10] तथायतायता[11]
रजस्ततिः[12] प्रावृतदिग्घना घना ।
यथा रवेरश्वपरम्परा परा
ययौ निमज्जत्खुरमालयालया ॥ ३१ ॥

---

१. L. दिधा । २. MT. विपद्गता । ३. R. तस्यां । ४. R. काणो । ५. R. तत्सुरो । ६. MT,R. अतिवानतो । ७. A. पासितं । ८. R. तत्परं परं । ९. MT, L. कृतं । १०. A. वलौधन । ११. R. कृतावला. . . . नः. . . . तयातया । १२. R. ततिं ।

ततो विनिर्गम्य बलं पुरः पुरः
स्थितं[1] ययौ विग्रह[2]वद्विषं द्विषम् ।
कपीन्द्रमाजौ विहितत्वरं वरं
वहन्तमन्तःस्थितपन्नगं नगम् ॥ ३२ ॥

उपेत्य गत्या मदमन्दयाऽदया
वनौकसः स्वीकृतशोभयाऽभया[3] ।
प्रवालशोभाजितविद्रुमैर्द्रुमै-
र्दृढं निजघ्नुर्गिरिसन्निभानिभान् ॥ ३३ ॥

असृक्स्रवैराहव[4]दारुणाऽरुणा
चचार दीप्ता निजवर्चसा च सा ।
पताकिनी वीतभयामयो मयो[5]
विनिर्जितस्संयति मायया[6] यया ॥ ३४ ॥

द्विषद्भिरन्तःस्थमहोरगैरगै-
र्हतस्य कस्यापि समन्ततस्ततः ।
सचर्ममांसे हि विदारितेरिते
गतायुषः प्रस्फुरदस्थिता स्थिता ॥ ३५ ॥

विपाट्य[7] कश्चिद्द्विज[8]खर्वटं[9] वटं[10]
शिखाभिरम्भोदवितानगं[11] नगम् ।
मुमोच सैन्यस्य भयं दिशन्[12] दिश-[13]
स्निनादयन्[14] संयति[15] तारवै रवैः ॥ ३६ ॥

विपाट्य[16] वेगादितरो नदन्नदं[17]
निपात्य शैलं जितभूभुजै[18]र्भुजैः ।
रुरोज कस्यापि गदाकृती कृती
ययौ स भूमिं रथपक्षतः[19]क्षतः ॥ ३७ ॥

---

१. L. स्थि ....ययौ । २. विद्विषं । ३. A. भया । ४. R. आहत । ५. A. मयामया । ६. MT. ययौ ययौ । ७. MT, R. विभिद्य । ८. R,A. निज । ९. MT, R. कर्पटं । L,A. खर्पटं । १०. MT, L,A,R. पटं ११. MT, R. विभागगं । १२. MT, R. भवन्दिशं । L A. भयं दिशं । १३. L,A,MT,R. दिशं । १४. MT. निनादयत् । १५. R. संयदि । १६. MT. विपद्य । १७. MT, L. नदन् । १८. L, A. भुजौ भुजौ । १९. MT,L, R,A. क्षतक्षतः ।

पतद्भिरस्त्रैरभिदारितोऽरितो
भुवोऽपरः शोणितशीतले तले ।
अशेत सर्पद्द्विशनांशुना शुना
हतो विलुप्तः परिराविभिर्विभिः ॥ ३८ ॥

तथा परो भूरुहधारिणारिणा
हतो दृढं कुङ्कुमपिङ्गले गले ।
विवृत्तदृष्टिर्युधि मोहितोऽहितो
महीतलं शोणितमिश्रितः[1] श्रितः ॥ ३९ ॥

बहून्[2]निहत्य द्युतिभासिनाऽसिना
पपात पश्चादसु[3]हारिणाऽरिणा ।
नगेन कुञ्जस्थितभोगिनागिना
हतस्फुरन्मस्तक[4]कर्परः परः ॥ ४० ॥

निर्जैर्बलैरेव सुरक्षितौ क्षितौ
वितत्य तेजोजितभास्करौ करौ ।
अशेत कश्चिज्जितवैरिणाऽरिणा
हतो रणे विक्रमवस्तुतः स्तुतः ॥ ४१ ॥

इति क्षता फेनवसासृजोऽसृजो
रुचिप्रतानेन सुचारुणारुणा ।
सुरारि[5]सेना पुरमुद्रुतं[6] द्रुतं
ययौ समेऽपि स्खलितापदा पदा ॥ ४२ ॥

एवं सैन्यं निजमधिगत[7]त्रासमस्तं समस्तं
श्रुत्वा रोष[8]ज्वलितवदनो भासमानस्समानः ।
लङ्कानाथो नृपसुतमुपानीतदारं सदारं[9]
हन्तुं युद्धे तनुजमवदद्भीमहासं[10]महासम् ॥ ४३ ॥

इति जानकीहरणे सप्तदशः सर्गः

---

१. R. मिश्रितं । २. MT. बहू निहत्य । R. बहूनि हत्वा । ३. A. असि । ४. L, A. मत्तक । ५. MT, R. पिशाच । ६. R. पुरमद्रुतं । ७. R. अपिगत । ८. MT, R. रोषात् । ९. A. दारन्तदारं । १०. R. सहासम् ।

अथ अष्टादशः सर्ग

संग्रामं [1]शक्रजिद्यास्यन् प्रादक्षिणयदीश्वरम्[2] ।
स्निग्धमालोकितः पङक्त्या तस्यैव परितो दृशाम् ॥ १ ॥
प्रणम्य च ततो भक्त्या विज्ञाय समयं[3] मयम् ।
निर्जगाम पुरः[4] कर्षन् केतुभिः शबलं बलम् ॥ २ ॥

गूढचतुर्थम्—

क्वणन्त[5]श्चक्रितैः[6]चापैरसृग्गन्ध[7]कृतौजसः ।
घोरेषुवितर्ति तत्र सृजन्तश्चक्रिरे रणम् ॥ ३ ॥
नगनिर्भिन्नमातङ्गघटाघटमुखोज्झितैः ।
युद्धमासीद्दुरालोकं स्नातयौध[8]मसृग्जलैः ॥ ४ ॥
रजस्सन्त[9]मस[10]च्छित्त्यै वितताार परिज्वलन् ।
ग्रावप्रहत[11]मातङ्गदन्तकोशोद्भवो[12]ऽनलः ॥ ५ ॥
सारासिरुरु[13]सूरूराः[14] सारासारासु सूरसः[15] ।
ससार सारसारासः[16] सुरासारिः ससार सः[17] ॥ ६ ॥
एत्य शोणितसंसिक्तरज[18]श्छेदेन दर्शितौ ।
बबन्ध रावणिर्वीरौ राघवौ भोगिपाश्यया[19] ॥ ७ ॥
विवेश पुरमेवाऽथ नद्धे तत्र विशारदः ।
गत्या निर्जित[20]मातङ्गमन्थर[21]क्रमहेलया ॥ ८ ॥

पाद[22]यमकम्—

दधानौ[23] नृपती खिन्ने शतधा मनसी तया ।
दृष्टौ विवशयाऽनार्ति[24]शतधाम न सीतया ॥ ९ ॥

---

१. MT. शङ्कजित् । २. L,A. अप्रदक्षणयद्गुरुम् । ३. MT. सुमय । ४. MT. पुरं । ५. L,A. क्वणद्भिः । ६. MT. चकितैः । ७. A. दिग्ध । ८. L,A. योधं । ९. A. समन्त । १०. MT,R. तमसा । ११. L. प्रहृतः । A. नवप्रहत । १२. L,A. दावोद्भव । १३. MT. सारासिसू; L,A. सारासरु । १४. MT. रूसाः । १५. L,A. सरसारासुसूरसी । १६. MT. राससुरा । १७. MT. सारिसार. . . . . gap. १८. MT, L,A. रजच्छेदेन । १९. MT. पात्ययात् । २०. L,A. विजित । २१. A. मन्घर । २२. L,A. missing । २३. A. दधाने । २४. L,A. नानार्ति ।

[1]आदियमकम्—

विराजं तमिदं दीप्त्या विराजन्तं स्मृतिक्षणे।
सह सन्नासितो भ्रात्रा स हसन्नाल्यदागतम् ॥ १० ॥

[2]प्रतिलोमम्—

पक्षिराजतयामेय हिंसारागहितान्तक।
कन्तताहिगरासाहिं यमेयातजराक्षिप ॥ ११ ॥ (?)
इत्युक्तगरुडग्रस्तपन्नगाहितविस्मयैः ।
आस्फोट[3]स्फोटितानीकश्रुति रेसे कपीश्वरैः ॥ १२ ॥

[4]चतुरक्षरी—

रुरोरारैररीरोरि[5] [6]हीहोहाहाहिहीहहि[7] ।
ततेतात्तुत्तितो तोतौ[8] विववावववावव[9] ॥ १३ ॥ (?)
कुम्भकर्णोऽथ रक्षोभिरबोधि हृदि ताडितः ।
स्वयंकृतखरक्राथवात[10]धूतैः कथञ्चन ॥ १४ ॥
चमूपतिर्बहिस्तस्थौ सेनया सह सासुरः।
कुम्भकर्णं प्रतीक्ष्याथो सेनया सहसा सुरः ॥ १५ ॥

समुद्गयमकम्—

अभिरामाशुगासन्ना सा सेना विभया सती।
अभिरामाशुगासन्ना सा सेना विभया सती॥ १६ ॥
उपविष्टः[11] पुरोवप्रभूधरस्य शिरस्तटात्।
संख्ये[12] दृष्टिं समासज्य[13] क्रोधेन विकृताननः॥ १७ ॥

गोमूत्रिका—

आसादितवसास्वादक्षत[14]स्रुतिरगोत्किरः[15] ।
ससार तरसा पादघातपातितगोपुरः॥ १८ ॥
शिरांसि कृतटङ्कारं चर्वतोऽस्य वनौकसाम्।

---

१. L, A. missing। २. L,A. अर्धप्रतिलोमम्। ३. A. अस्फोट। ४. M T. प्रासानुप्रासः। ५. L,A. रुरूरोरारररीरारि। ६. L, A. हे। ७. L,A. हिहि। ८. L,A. तीतो। ९. L,A. वः। १०. MT. पात। ११. L,A. उपाविशत्; MT. उपविष्ट। १२. MT. संघे; L. संखे १३. L,A. समासाद्य। १४. L, A. क्षत्र। १५. L. A. रगोद्धुरः।

सिषेच शोणितं वक्षः[1] सद्यः सन्त्यज्य सृक्कणी[2] ॥ १९ ॥
तच्छूलपात[3]निर्भिन्नपिष्टशिष्टा महाचमूः ।
अङ्गदेन पितुर्धीरं जगदे[4] विद्रुता दिशः ॥ २० ॥

अर्धभ्रमकम्—

सुभासा सातियातार्ति[5]भासुरा दर्पभाविता ।
सारा धीरा सशोभा या सादरा युधि सर्पति ॥ २१ ॥
इयं[6] वः शात्रवी सेना रणे वैमुख्यमायताम्[7] ।
छेत्तुमिच्छति पुच्छाग्रं[8] कुम्भकर्णपुरस्सरी ॥ २२ ॥
हनुमन्ना[9]तुरो भूत्वा मा[10] गा युध्यस्व निर्भयम् ।
ननु स्कन्नादरोऽसौ त्वा वेगाद्विध्यति निर्दयम् ॥ २३ ॥

गोमूत्रिका मुरजबन्धश्च—

सुते संयति वैमुख्यं याति क्षीरोदजन्मनः ।
सुषेणे लम्भयेदन्यः कस्तं त्रासरसं ज्ञताम्[11] ॥ २४ ॥

गूढसंबन्धः—

दोषपात्रपराधीनखलम् एष वद[12] क्षमः ।
त्वं सशैलेन हस्तेन ही न[13] किं हंसि[14] राक्षसम् ॥ २५ ॥

आद्यन्तयमकम्—

ततं दर्पेण सततं परस्संग्रामतत्परः[15] ।
सत्त्वाढ्यो बाधते स त्वामरं तेजोजितामरम्[16] ॥ २६ ॥
भुनक्ति भवति त्रासत्रस्तहस्तेऽद्य केसरी ।
[17]नैर्ऋतग्राहदन्ताग्रग्रासात्कोऽन्यो वनौकसः ॥ २७ ॥

[18]प्रतिलोमः—

तेनते सुरसाराशसामा[19]भीतर्जिताहिनः ।
नहिताजितभीमा सा[20] शरासारसुतेनते ॥ २८ ॥ (?)

---

१. MT, L,A. पक्षः । २. L. सृक्वणिम्; A. सृक्वणिः । ३. A. पाद । ४. A. जगतो । ५. MT. यातात्ति । ६. MT. अयं । ७. L,A. आगता; MT. आयतम् । ८. A. पुच्छाग्रे । ९. L, A. हनुमान् । १०. MT. माग । ११. MT. त्रासरसज्ञताम् । १२. MT. पद । १३. MT,L. हीनः । १४. MT. हसि । १५. MT. परं । १६. A. अरस्तेजोजितामरः । १७. L. वनैदृत; A. वनेदृत; MT. वनैरुत । १८. L,A. अर्धप्रतिलोमम् । १९. MT, L,A. समा । २०. MT. भीमास ।

नैकसेयकसन्त्रस्तः[१] संपदः खलु हीयसे।
राज्यं तव जयेनास्तु[२] तदेव[३] गहनं गिरेः॥ २९॥

सर्वतोभद्रम्—

सासाराससरासासा साहसाप्यप्यसाहसा।
रासापाततपासारा[४] सव्यतक्ष[५]क्षतव्यसः॥ ३०॥ (?)

गृहेऽपि सुलभो मृत्युः शिवं[६] युद्धेऽपि कस्यचित्।
प्रभुं त्रासेन ते जन्ये यतस्त्यक्तुमसांप्रतम्॥ ३१॥

मुरजबन्धेन श्लोकद्वयम्—

किं यासि[७] कपिहास्यार[८]हामी तत्राहमाकुकः[९]।
[१०]हसानिरमयाकाशं स वीक्ष्य रणमार्गलम्[११]॥ ३२॥ (?)

पतत्सु राघवे वैरिविशिखेष्व[१२]विशङ्कितम्।
पौरुषस्यापरं कालं किं सौमित्रिरुदीक्षते[१३]॥ ३३॥

हेयहासर[१४]वस्था मा न सेनाविहितार्दनः।
सातचेतनपाता सा लव्या[१५] किं बहुना[१६]सिना॥ ३४॥ (?)

अर्थचतुष्टयवाची[१७]—

बृहत्फल[१८]करः श्रीमां[१९]स्तुङ्गको वर[२०]वारणः।
किन्न गोपतिरेष त्वं प्रथते परमोदयम्[२१]॥ ३५॥

निरोष्ठ्यम्—

रणं सद्यशसः क्षेत्रं स्थिततेजस्यखण्डिते।
सन्त्यजन् सह सैन्येन हरिराज न राजसे॥ ३६॥

नयाचारयुतो[२२] रामः प्रयासरहितो[२३]ऽश्रमः।
न याति रणतो भीमश्रिया सारश्च्युतोपमः[२४]॥ ३७॥

---

१. L, A. सुंतंत्रस्तः। २. MT. नस्तु। ३. L,A. तदेवं। ४. L, A. हसारासापाततपा। ५. L, A. सारासव्य। ६. L, A. शपा। ७. MT. क्रियासि। ८. L, A. हास्यारं। ९. L. हातित्रत्रासमाकुतः। १०. L,A. भसा। ११. L,A. मार्गलः। १२. L,A. विशङ्कितं। १३. MT. उदीयसे। १४. A. हासार। १५. MT. लक्ष्या; L, A. लप्या। १६. MT. विभु। १७. L,A. अर्धचतुष्टयी। १८. L, A. करः। १९. L, A. श्रीमत्। २०. A. पर। २१. L,A. परमोदयः। २२. L,A. रतो। २३. L,A. हरितो। २४. MT. च्युतोपमा।

संख्ये[१] संख्यमिहासंख्य[२]शस्त्रसंपातभैरवे ।
विधत्स्व तस्य लोकोऽन्यः[३] सर्वस्मिन्न(?)सुखे सुखे[४] ॥ ३८ ॥

यासि स क्षतमस्वाशं शंसितात्रास[५]मान्य सा[६] ।
सदद्धा[७] धमयामास सस्ययागमबुद्धिया[८] ॥ ३९ ॥ (?)

त्रासेन[९] जहतो जन्ये जनेशं तं गुणाधिकम्[१०] ।
किन्न भ्रश्यति[११] शुभ्राभ्रविभ्रमं भवतो यशः ॥ ४० ॥

तरसा न धमासारा सातायासवरा[१२]स्थिता ।
नरता न समाधीरा मता[१३] हासस्वरानता[१४] ॥ ४१ ॥ (?)

जालकद्वयम्—
भ्रमद्भिर्भूरिभिर्भेरीरवैर्गम्भीर[१५]भैरवैः ।
भ्राम्यन्मन्दरमन्थान[१६]क्षुभ्यत्क्षीरार्णवोपमा ॥ ४२ ॥

जालेन श्लोकत्रयम्—
कृपाणज्योति[१७]रालोकस्फारदुर्दर्शना तता[१८] ।
प्रक्वणच्छर[१९]संघातसंरावपिहित[२०]श्रुतिः ॥ ४३ ॥
सा राक्षसकरत्रस्त[२१]रामापात्रस्वधा[२२]ध्वना ।
सारासा[२३]पानयागाय[२४] हसा[२५]वनधरस्वनम्[२६] ॥ ४४ ॥

जालेन श्लोकचतुष्टयम्—
द्विषतामायुधैरेवं[२७] अस्मदीया पताकिनी ।
विह्वला[२८] चलितादित्यद्युतिभिः प्रतने कृता[२९] ॥ ४५ ॥

---

१. L,A. संखे । २. L,A. संख्यमिहः संख्य । ३. L,A. अन्य । ४. MT. सर्प एव सुखे... gap । ५. MT. missing upto समा । ६. MT. समान्यत स । ७. A. सदग्धा । ८. L, A. नुद्धिया । ९. A. तत्रासेन । १०. MT. तद्गुणाधिकः । ११. MT. भ्रश्रुत । १२. MT. परा । १३. MT. तमा । १४. L नताः; A. हासन्धरानताः । १५. A. भेरी...... gap; MT, L. रवैगम्भीर । १६. MT, L, A. मन्थास्य । १७. L, A. द्योतितालोक । १८. L,A. नना । १९. MT. पति । २०. MT. विहित । २१. L. न्यस्त । २२. L. स्वसा । २३. L. साराशा । २४. L. गाया । २५. L. भसा । २६. L. स्वनः । २७. MT. संहतिद्विविधैरेवं । २८. L,A. विबला । २९. L. कृताः ।

निरन्तरानुप्रासम्[१]—

ततातीति ततोतीता[२] तातततात्ततत्ततौ ।
ततो तोतिततैतेतौ ताते तुत्तितते ततिः ॥ ४६ ॥

इति श्रुत्वा निववृते तां गिरं कपिभिर्दिशः ।
अपथत्याजने साधोर्निन्दा हि निशितोऽङ्कुशः ॥ ४७ ॥

अर्ध[३]प्रतिलोमः—

तेहिकासुकसन्त्रास[४] सत्रसंकसुकाहिते ।
तेनुरा[५]पदमत्यागगत्यामदपरानुते ॥ ४८ ॥

आयतामायतां वृष्टिं श्रृङ्गि[६]श्रृङ्गमहीरुहैः[७] ।
कुम्भकर्णं[८] किरन्तं तं नलनीलौ रणस्पृहौ[९] ॥ ४९ ॥

मात्रापहारयथेष्टमात्रादानाभ्यां श्लोकत्रयम्—

अपि तु द्युतिमत्यस्य[१०] नीलस्सेहे न वै व्यथाम् ।
सहेति[११] क्षितिजच्छिन्न[१२]प्रवीरस्स क्षितिस्तुतः ॥ ५० ॥

ततो हत[१३]हुताशात्मसम्भवे[१४] पतिते नले ।
प्रार्थयन्त[१५] बलं शत्रोः क्रव्यमत्तुं निशाचराः[१६] ॥ ५१ ॥

द्व्यक्षरानुप्रासः—

ततारीति रतीताती[१७] तन्तितारुते[१८]रिताः ।
ततारारिततीरेता रततारारतौ रतः[१९] ॥ ५२ ॥

प्रत्यागत्य ततः क्रुद्धः कुम्भकाहतिमूर्च्छितः ।
विदश्य दशनैर्नासां नीयमानश्चकर्त सः ॥ ५३ ॥

---

१. L. missing. २. L,A. ततात्तिति तते ताती. ३. L,A. पाद । ४. MT, L,A. सत्रास. ५. MT. वद । ६. MT. श्रृङ्गी । ७. MT. महीरुहाम् । ८. MT. कर्णं । ९. MT. स्पृशौ । १०. L, A. अपीतिद्रुतमेन्यस्य । ११. L, A. सुहेति । १२. L,A. छिन्नः । १३. L,A. हतं । १४. MT, L,A. संभवं । १५. MT, प्रार्थयन्तं; L,A. प्रार्थयत्तत् । १६. L. निशाचरम् । १७. L. ततारति-रतीरात्ति । १८. L. रतितं रुरुते । १९. MT. रतोरतम् ।

क्रोधादविहितस्वान्य[१]मश्नत[२]श्शस्त्रमालिनीम्[३] ।
राघवायुधघातेन[४] पेते तस्याङ्गभूधरैः[५] ॥ ५४ ॥

सन्नयोऽसन्नयो रुद्धो[६] दाना[७]दानाकुलालिभिः ।
नागैर्नागैरिवो[८]च्छ्रायैः सन्नासन्नारिविक्रमः ॥ ५५ ॥

आद्याम्रेडितम्[९]–
नागास्सरसगण्डास्ते[१०] बिन्दुचित्रमुखान्विताः[११] ।
सपताकावृति भृशं[१२] चक्रुस्सन्नाट[१३]कोपमाः ॥ ५६ ॥

शिलीमुखमुखक्षुण्णकुमुदं[१४] सप्लवङ्गमम् ।
सशरारि[१५] रणं रामो ग्रीष्मे ह्रदमिवाविशत् ॥ ५७ ॥

तन्मन्त्र[१६]साधनादीनि व्यर्थयन्तो[१७] रिपुद्विपाः ।
तेन लुप्तैक[१८]रदनाः कृताः केचिद्विनायकाः ॥ ५८ ॥

मुक्तासारा द्विजैश्शुभ्रैः भूषिता मेचकत्विषः ।
तेन केचित्क्षयं नीताः शरदेव पयोमुचः ॥ ५९ ॥

[१९]शरैरुत्सारिता दूरं हत्वा रामस्य वेगिभिः ।
बभ्रमुर्जर्झरैर्वंशैः मातङ्गा निर्मदीकृताः ॥ ६० ॥

रक्षस्सैन्यनगो रामबाणाक्षिप्तजडो[२०]ऽपि सः[२१] ।
अचलश्शत्रुसेनायाः प्रपेदे नैव सह्यताम् ॥ ६१ ॥

प्रहस्तशुकधूम्राक्षप्रजङ्घ[२२]नृसुरान्तकान् ।
विद्युज्जिह्वमहापार्श्वमकराक्षमहोदरान् ॥ ६२ ॥

---

१. L,A. स्वाङ्ग । २. MT. L,A. मग्नतः । ३. L,A. मालिनी । ४. L,A. पातेन । ५. MT. भूधरे । ६. L,A. राशि । ७. MT, L, A. दान । ८. L, A. नगोच्छ्रायैः । ९. L,A. missing. १०. MT. गन्धास्ते । ११. MT. मुखान्विता, १२. L,A. धृतिभ्रंशं। १३. L,A. नटको । १४. A. रुमुदं । १५. L,A. शरारिं । १६. L, A. सुमन्त्र । १७. L. व्यक्षयन्तो । १८. A. लुप्तेक । १९. L, A. missing. २०. MT. L,A जलो । २१. MT. सन् । २२. MT. प्रजङ्घान् ।

हत्वा भूयः स्वलाङ्गूलैः वेष्टयित्वा दृढं कटीम् ।
स्थितेष्वङ्घ्रिपहस्तेषु यूथपेषु[1] वनौकसाम् ॥ ६३ ॥

नाशमिन्द्रजितः श्रुत्वा निर्जगाम दशाननः ।
कृती सेनाकृतेनाथ रुन्धन् रासेन[2] रोदसी[3] ॥ ६४ ॥

रावणस्याभवत्तत्र रण[4]स्सौमित्रितापनः ।
व्याप्तसर्वदिगाभोगज्याघोषजयघोषणः ॥ ६५ ॥

सौमित्रिपत्रिणामित्रः[5] क्रुद्धे धनुषि खण्डिते ।
वधाय विद्विषो भीमशक्तिश्शक्तिं समाददे ॥ ६६ ॥

[6]सन्दष्टकम्—

ततः क्रोधहतं चक्रे चक्रे[7] शत्रुभयङ्करम्[8] ।
करं युद्धे पतन्नागे[9] पतन्नागेन्द्रगौरवः ॥ ६७ ॥

महायमकम्—

चक्रे रणं[10] वानर-काऽन्तकारी, चक्रे [11]रणन्वा नरका-न्तकारी ।
चक्रे रणं[12] वा नरका-न्तकारी, चक्रे रण[13]न्वानर-कान्त-कारी ॥ ६८ ॥

अर्धयमकम्[14]—

युद्धेतिजेये तरसा रसन्तं युद्धेऽतिजेयेतर-सार-सन्तम् ।
परं ससाराहतशक्तिहेत्या परं ससार-आहतशक्तिहेत्या ॥ ६९ ॥

सवितारमिवापरमस्त[15]मितं
स निरीक्ष्य भुवं परमस्तमितम् ।
चरितुं कवचैश्शबलं स्वबलं
निजगौ मनुजेशबलं स्वबलम् ॥ ७० ॥

---

१. L,A. यूथपेष्वथ । २. MT. रोघेन । ३. MT. L,A. रोधसी । ४. MT. रणे । ५. MT. पत्रिणां मित्रः । ६. L,A. missing; MT. शत्रुंदष्टकम् । ७. L, A. हतश्चक्रे । ८. MT. भयङ्करः । ९. L. तन्नागे । १०.MT रणन् । ११. L,A. रणं । १२. MT. रणन् । १३. रणं । १४. L,A. समुद्गयमकम् । १५. MT. परस्तमितं ।

यमकावलिः[१]—

महता महता समरे समरे
विभया विभया सहिता सहिता ।
विशदा विशदा शुभया शुभया
जनता जनता न हिता नहिता ॥ ७१ ॥

व्युदस्तधरणीरुह[२]क्षितिधरा[३]युधं विद्रुत-
प्रधानकपि[४]सर्वतः[५] चपलदृष्टितद्विह्वलम् ।
न कश्चिदपि रक्षितुं युधि शशाक शाखामृगः
सुरारिकबलं बलं[६] हृत[७]बलं प्रया[८]दात्मनः ॥ ७२ ॥

चक्रवृत्तम्—

पिङ्गं[९] शोणितनिर्गमेन करणं[१०] भिन्नं सुरेन्द्रद्रुहा
यत्नं प्राप्य दधानया विकलितेष्वोजस्सु चञ्चद्दृशा[११] ।
तिग्मांशोस्तनयस्य पूर्वकलनामुल्लङ्घयन्त्या[१२] भिया
यान्तं क्वापि विहाय संयतिरतिं हानिस्पृशा[१३]सेनया ॥७३॥

बिभ्राणं वदनं सरोरुहमणिक्षोदारुणं दारुणं
देहैर्भीषणमुग्रवक्त्र[१४]दशनैरासन्नखैस्सन्नखैः ।
रामोऽथ स्वबलं प्रसह्य समरे[१५]सन्त्रस्यतो त्रस्यतो
बाणेनोपरुरोध वर्त्मनि करच्छन्नादिना नादिना ॥ ७४॥

इति श्रीमत्सिंहलकवेः कुमारदासस्य कृतौ जानकीहरणे महाकाव्ये
अष्टादशस्सर्गः समाप्तः

---

१. MT. यमकालिः । २. L. धर । ३. L, A. रुह । ४. MT. कवि । ५. MT. L,A. सर्पतः । ६. L,A. कबलीकृतं । ७. L. क्षत । ८. L,A. प्रियात् । ९. MT, L. पिङ्गा । १०. MT. तरणं । ११. A. चञ्च्वा । १२. L,A. उल्लङ्घ्य यान्त्या । १३. MT. स्पृशा । १४. L,A. वक्र । १५. L,A. हन्त्रस्य ।

एकोनविंशः सर्ग

अथारिणा वर्त्मनि[1] कालनेमिना
रयादयश्चक्र[2]निभेन निर्हतः[3]।
कथंचिदेनं विनिगृह्य मारुतिः
समुद्वहन् भूधरश्रृङ्गमाययौ ॥ १ ॥

हरिर्भिषग्भूधरसानुतो नुतो
महौषधिं प्राप्य मुदाततस्ततः।
चकार रामावरजं हृतक्लमं
पुनः समुन्मीलितवीक्षणं क्षणात् ॥ २ ॥

रथस्ततः[4] सारथिना मरुत्वतो
मरुन्नदीमारुतकम्पितध्वजः।
अरान्तरासक्तपयोदखण्डकः
प्रभोरुपानीयत सूनवे भुवः ॥ ३ ॥

सुरेश्वर[5]प्राजितृ[6]हस्तसङ्गिना
करेण सव्येन स वासवोपमः।
तदन्यहस्तस्थशरासनः शनैः
समारुरोह प्रधृतं[7] वरूथिनम् ॥ ४ ॥

रणं दिदृक्षुः सुरसंहतिर्घनं
समाक्षिपत्संमुखमागतं रुषा।
परस्पराघातनिवृत्त[8]वृत्ति तत्
बलं च तस्थौ निहितेक्षणं तयोः ॥ ५ ॥

---

१. L,A. मर्मणि। २. L,A. अयं चक्र। ३. L. निर्हतम्। ४. MT,R. अथस्ततः (but original palm-leaf of MT. reads रथस्ततः) ५. L,A. प्रजेश्वर। ६. MT. व्राजितृ। ७. R,L,A. प्रसृतं। ८. L,A. निवृत्ति।

पुरन्दरारातिमरातिसूदनः
शरं सलीलं शरधेस्समुद्धरन् ।
उपाययौ सायकदष्टकार्मुकं[1]
रणे रणस्थं[2] रथिको महारथम्[3] ॥ ६ ॥

[4]शरं सृज त्वं प्रथमं प्रतीच्छ वे-
त्युदीरणानन्तरमिन्द्रविद्विषः[5] ।
विपाटयन्तः श्रुतिमस्य निःस्वनैः
निपेतुरुग्रैरभिराममाशुगाः ॥ ७ ॥

विभिद्य[6] रामच्छलमादिपूरुषं
हृता यथा दुष्प्रसहेन[7] पाप्मना[8] ।
प्रपद्य[9] तिर्यग्गतिमस्य सायकाः
क्षणेन[10] पातालमपि प्रपेदिरे ॥ ८ ॥

मुखैरसक्तं दशभिर्दशाननो
नदन्[11] तटित्सन्निभहेमभूषणः ।
युगान्तमेघप्रतिमो महेषुभिः
ततान ताराभिरिवान्तरं दिवः[12] ॥ ९ ॥

वनं ततस्तत्र शरप्रभञ्जन-
क्षतावनम्रीकृतभूरुहौषधी[13] ।
महापगापात[14]परास्तनामित-
स्फुटत्तटी[15]काननकान्तिमाददे ॥ १० ॥

---

१. R. कार्मुकः । २. MT,R. रथस्थं । ३. MT, R,L,A. महारथः । ४. L,A. missing । ५. R. विद्विषं । ६. L,A. प्रपद्य । ७. A. दुष्प्रसहोन । ८. A. पार्वना । ९. L,A. अवाप्य । १०. MT,R. चिरेण । ११. MT. नदत्तटित्; नदंस्तटित् । १२. MT. दिवं (original palm-leaf reads दिवः)। १३. L,A. वृक्षमस्तकम् । १४. R. वात । १५. L,A. स्फुटत्तटित्कानन; R. स्फुटं तटिकानन ।

न केवलं वारिणि वारिधेरगै-[१]
नरेन्द्रसूनुर्विजयाय विद्विषः[२] ।
बबन्ध भानोरपि सेतुमायतं[३]
पथि प्रतानेन[४] घनेन पत्रिणाम् । ११ ॥

ससर्ज पूगं वि ×
× × ॥ १२ ॥

निरन्तराकर्षणसृष्ट[५]सम्पदः
प्रसक्तसंचाल[६]विधिर्धनुर्गुणः[७] ।
ररक्ष वक्षो[८] नृवरस्य रक्षसः
कृत[९]प्रणादं पततोऽस्य पत्रिणः ॥ १३ ॥

शरस्य मोक्षः[१०] प्रथमं महीभुजः
ततश्च तद्वैरिशरीरविक्षतिः[११] ।
इति क्रमोऽगादनुमानगम्यतां
अलक्ष्यवेगेषु शरेषु धन्विनः[१२] ॥ १४ ॥

असौ शराताऩमयं मरुन्नदी[१३]
विधाय रूपं पतिता नु सस्वना ।
जयश्रियः[१४] संक्रमणाय भास्वतः
पथि प्रयुक्तो नु महेषुसंक्रमः ॥ १५ ॥

कटु क्वणन्तः[१५] तपनस्य दीधितिं
तिरोदधाना निकरेण पत्रिणः[१६] ।
विहाय बाणासन[१७]मस्य विद्विषः
स्वयं प्रहर्तुं[१८] नु नभः समुद्गताः[१९] ॥ १६ ॥

---

१. L. अयं । A. इयं । २. L,A. विद्विषाम् । ३. MT. आयतः । ४. L. प्रथि प्रधानेन । ५. L,A. सृष्टि । ६. MT. सञ्चार । ७. R. गुणान् । ८. MT. R. रक्षो । ९. MT. कृतः । १०. MT. R. मोक्षं । ११. MT. वीक्षतिः (original palm-leaf reads विक्षतिः); L,A. पक्षतिः । १२. MT. शरेष्वधन्विनः । १३. MT. मरूर्नदी । १४. R. श्रियं । १५. R. कटु क्षणं तत् । कटुक्वणन्तं । १६. A. नितरेण मार्गणाः; L,R. निकरेण पत्रिणा । १७. L,A. बाणाशयं । १८. MT. विहन्तुं । १९. MT. समं समुद्यताम् ।

बृहत्पृषत्कग्रथिता मरुत्पथे
मृगं ग्रहीतु[1] मृग[2]राजशायिनम्[3] ।
प्रसारिता नु प्रसरं निरुन्धती
रविप्रभाया गुरुवागुराततिः[4] ॥ १७ ॥

विधाय नाराचमयं समन्ततः
सृजन्ति धारानिकरं नु[5] वारिदाः[6] ।
इति क्षणं क्षीणबलेन[7] तत्र तत्
बलेन तीव्रं मुमुहे महाहवे ॥ १८ ॥

अशेषमन्तःकृतसैनिकं तयो-
र्बृहद्भुजस्तम्भनिबद्धमायतम् ।
निरस्ततिग्मद्युतिरश्मि भूयसा
रुरोध तद्बाणवितान[8]मम्बरम् ॥ १९ ॥

चकर्त शत्रोरधिजत्रु[9] राघवः
शरेण बाहुं शरसन्ततिच्युतः[10] ।
बभार तच्छेदविनिर्गतो[11] मुहुः
दृढं करोऽन्यो निपतच्छरासनम्[12] ॥ २० ॥

ततस्ततं घर्मजलस्य रेखया
रिपुर्महेन्द्रस्य सुतस्य भूभृतः[13] ।
लुठज्जटासन्ततिवेल्लितं ज्वल-[14]
त्तटं[15] ललाटस्य बिभेद पत्रिणा[16] ॥ २१ ॥

अथ भ्रुवोरन्तरलक्ष्य[17]हाटक-
प्रदीप्तपुङ्खेन शरेण राघवः ।
श्रियं ज्वलत्पिङ्गललाटतारका-
मुवाह रूपस्य विरूपचक्षुषः ॥ २२ ॥

---

१. L.A. गृहीतुं। २. L,A. द्विज। ३. R. शयिनः। ४. R. तती। ५. R. न। ६. MT. वारिदः। ७. L,A. मुखेन। ८. L,A. तत्सायक-वृन्दं। ९. L,A. असि जत्र। १०. R. शरसन्ततिच्युता; L,A. विशिखौघ-वर्जितं। ११. A. विनिर्जितो। १२. A. शरासनः। १३. L,A. नृपन्द्रसूनोरमरारिरुज्ज्वलं।। १४. R. वेल्लितज्ज्वलत्; L,A. वेष्टितं तटं। १५. R. कटं; L,A. हृढं। १६. MT. पत्रिणां। १७. L,A. दृष्ट।

शरैरुपक्रोशपदे[1] नृपात्मजः
शिरो रिपोरच्छिनदर्धभाषिते[2] ।
प्रणादतः[3] शेषमुदीरयन्मुहुः
शिरोऽपरं प्रादुर[4]भूदविक्षतम् ॥ २३ ॥

ददर्श भल्लाभि[5]निपातपातित-
[6]प्रकीर्णमौलीनि समुद्गताननः ।
मुखानि दन्त[7]क्रकचक्षताधर-
प्रवर्तितासृञ्जि निजानि राक्षसः[8] ॥ २४ ॥

[9]बृहद्द्विषत्सक्तपृषत्कपातित-
स्वमस्तकप्रस्तरणे रणे[10] स्थितः ।
स युध्यमानो महिमानमाहवे
विदर्शयामास नृलोकदुर्लभम् ॥ २५ ॥

तयोरयोबाणरयोपबृंहित-
स्फुटद्ध्वनि[11]स्फोटितकर्णमाहवम्[12] ।
गरुत्मदाशीविषपातदुस्सहं
निरीक्षितं तं वितितार तत्समम्[13] ॥ २६ ॥
अथो हिताय प्रहितं[14] मरुत्वता
सुरद्विषो मर्म निगद्य मातलिः[15] ।
नरेन्द्रपुत्राय तनुत्रभेदिनं
विचित्रपत्रं वितितार पत्रिणम् ॥ २७ ॥
विकर्षणादस्य मरुन्मरुत्सख-[16]
प्रसन्नसत्पुङ्ख[17]फलेन[18] वेगिना ।
स्वयं च तन्मर्म विवक्षुणा यथा
शरेण मूलं श्रवणस्य शिश्रिये ॥ २८ ॥

१. MT. उपाक्रोश; A. उपक्रोश । २. A. भाषितैः । ३. A प्रणानतः । ४. A. प्रापुरभूत् । ५. L,A. भल्लाट । ६. L,A. प्रशीर्ण । ७. A. दन्तं । ८. L,A. रावणः । ९. A, L. missing । १०. MT. रथे । ११. MT. स्फुटद्ध्वनि ।१२. R. आहवः । १३. L,A. निरिक्षितु कोऽपि शशाक तत्समः । १४. MT. प्रथितं । १५. L,A. तामलिः । १६. MT. सखः । १७. R. संपुंख । १८. A. बलेन ।

स तेन भीमं रसता भुजान्तरे
गिरीन्द्रसारेण शरेण मर्मणि ।
हतः सुराणामहितो[1] महीयसा
पपात भीमेन रवेण[2] रावणः ॥ २९ ॥

निकृत्य[3] रक्षोधिपमर्म मार्गणः[4]
पपात पातालतले महीयसः[5] ।
कृतापराधो भुवनत्रयाधिपं
निहत्य भीत्येव तिरोबुभूषया[6] ॥ ३० ॥

अथ क्षितिस्तत्क्षणबद्धनिस्स्वना[7]
चचाल भीतेव शरेण ताडिता ।
पपात वृष्टिः कुसुमस्य राघवे
दिवो निवृत्तेव रिपोर्यशस्ततिः ॥ ३१ ॥

सुता नरेन्द्रस्य परासुरीश्वर-
स्त्वया विपक्ष[8]क्षतवृत्तिरीक्षिता ।
इतीव काञ्च्या विनिपत्य पादयो-
र्निरुध्यमानाऽपि ययौ रणाजिरम् ॥ ३२ ॥

द्विधा न यातं निजमिन्द्रजिद्गुरौ
सुता मयस्योपगतेऽपि वैशसम्[9] ।
शुचा नु रोषेण[10] नु मुक्तनिस्स्वनं
रुरोज पाणिद्वयपातनै[11]रुरः ॥ ३३ ॥

नृपात्मजा संग्रहविग्रहेण[12] यत्[13]
बभूव यत्नादपि तस्य[14] दुर्लभम्[15] ।

---

१. MT. सुराणां महिती (original palm-leaf reads as above) L,A. सुरारिर्महितो । २. MT. रणेन । L. रयेण ३. L,A. विभिद्य; MT. निकृत्य। ४. R. मार्गणं ५. L,A. महीयसि। ६. MT. बभूषया। ७. MT. R,A. निस्स्वनं । ८. A. विपक्षे । ९. MT. गते विवेश सा; R. गतेपि वेशसम् । १०. L,A. कोपेन । ११. L,A. पीडनैः । १२. L,A. विग्रहेषु । १३. R. यो । १४. MT,R. तेन । १५. R. दुर्लभः ।

तमिन्द्रशत्रुश्चिरवाञ्छितं क्षणा[१]-
दवाप देव्या मृदुबाहुबन्धनम् ॥ ३४ ॥

हृदि प्रियाभावकृशानुदीपिता
भिदामुपैतीति यथा विशङ्किनी[२]।
विलोचने तामनुतापविह्वलां
असिञ्चतामश्रुजलेन सन्ततम् ॥ ३५ ॥

प्रियस्य बाण[३]व्रणरन्ध्ररोधिनं[४]
महीरजस्संचयमश्रुवर्षिणी ।
प्रिया परासोरपि खेदशङ्कया
सकम्पहस्ता शनकैरपाहरत्[५] ॥ ३६ ॥

मयात्मजाया नयने मुहुर्मुहुः
प्रियेण पूर्वं परिचुम्ब्य लालिते।
तदाश्रुभिश्चक्षु[६]पुटान्तनिस्सृतै-
र्हतस्य[७] तोयाञ्जलिमस्य तेनतुः[८] ॥ ३७ ॥
[९]पुरानुरक्तो रतिदायिनि प्रियः
प्रियामुखस्यावयवेषु यत्र सः।
तदा तदापत्कृतशोकशोषितः
स एव सावेगमकम्पताधरः[१०] ॥ ३८ ॥

कृशोदरी काञ्चनकुम्भसन्निभं
कुचद्वयं रावणमित्रमात्मनः ।
गते दिवं तत्र विलोचनच्युतै-
र्जलैरपस्नानविधावयोजयत् ॥ ३९ ॥
शुचा[११] मुखेन व्यपनीतरोचिषा[१२]
सुता मयस्य व्यथिता तपस्विनी[१३] ।

१. MT,R. चिरात् । २. A. यथाभिशङ्किनी । ३. A. वार । ४. R. बाण-व्रणरोधि. . .gap । ५. MT. उपाहरत् । ६. A. पक्षपुट । ७. L.A. गतस्य । ८. MT. तेनभः original palm-leaf reads as तेनतुः । ९. L,A. missing. १०. MT. अधरम् । ११. MT, R. शुचं । १२.A.शोचिषा । १३. MT. अनुबन्धिनी original palm-leaf reads as न पण्डिनी; R. न पण्डिनी ।

विलापमेवं करुणं समाददे
दिशि क्षिपन्ती कृपणे[1] विलोचने ॥ ४० ॥

[2]प्रियस्य सोऽयं पिशिता[3]भिकाङ्क्षिभिः
वृकैर्विकृष्यावयवोऽपि कम्पितः[4] ।
प्रहर्षमाशाविषयं विधाय मे
पुनर्यथार्थावगमे निरस्यते ॥ ४१ ॥

त्रिलोकभर्तुर्वनितासु तादृशी
न काचिदासीदनवद्यलक्षणा ।
अलक्षणायामपि यत्प्रसादतः
चिरं[5] ध्रियेताविधवा[6]यशो मयि ॥ ४२ ॥

इयानलं निग्रह[7] एव मानिनं[8]
धुरि[9] व्यवस्थापयितुं सुमेधसाम्[10] ।
प्रियं सुरा रक्षत[11] विग्रहेऽपि यत्
यशो हरन्ति श्वसितं न साधवः ॥ ४३ ॥

पुरन्दरानेन पुरा पराभवं[12]
कृतं कृथाश्चेतसि मातिमानिना ।
मुखादिमं दण्ड[13]धरस्य तेजसः
च्युतं नमन्तं तव पाहि पादयोः ॥ ४४ ॥

प्रवेपमानाधरपत्र[14]सन्तातिं[15]
विलोलदृष्टिभ्रमरं[16] त्वदिष्टये ।

---

१. R. करुणे । २. L,A. missing. ३. MT. विशिता (original palm-leaf reads as पिशिता) । ४. R. अविकम्पितः । ५. L,A. स्थितिं । ६. L,A. लभेताविधवा; MT. ध्रियेतापि धवा (original palm-leaf reads as above) । ७. L,A. विग्रह । ८. R. मानिनः । ९. R. च्युति । १०. MT,R. विचेतसां । ११ L,A. सुरारिक्षत । १२. L,A. पराभवः । १३. MT,R. मुखादि-मद्दण्ड । १४. MT. अधरमत्र । १५. L,A. सञ्चयं; R.सन्ततिः । १६. A.भ्रमरः ।

स्मरासिना[1] देव निकृत्तमुज्ज्वलं[2]
त्रिलोकभर्तुः मुखपद्मसंचयम् ॥ ४५ ॥
विधाय वित्तस्य[3] कृते कृती जनः
कुबेर ! वैरं सह बन्धुभिर्बुधः[4] ।
सति प्रवृत्ते परतः[5] पराभवे[6]
कुलस्य[7] कुल्यैः[8] कुरुते सहार्थताम् ॥ ४६ ॥

गुरो[9] गुरोरस्य गुरुप्रसादने
चतुर्मुख त्वं चतुरस्य नेक्षसे ।
विकीर्यमाणं भुवि विष्किरैरिमं[10]
शिखासमूहं[11] मणिवन्मनस्विनः[12] ॥ ४७ ॥

तथातिदीनैः परिदेविताक्षरैः
न लोकपालेषु गतेषु विक्रियाम् ।
[13]असत्प्रमाणेन च शब्दमात्रमि-
त्युदीरितं तत्र जनेन देवताः[14] ॥ ४८ ॥

विपाण्डुगण्डाधरबिम्बसंश्रया
विशेषकालक्तकमण्डनश्रियः[15] ।
सखीव[16] तत्कालविधेयवेदिनी
ममार्ज तस्या नयनाम्बुसन्ततिः ॥ ४९ ॥
जने विधिज्ञे विधिमौर्ध्वदैहिकं
सुरद्विषः कुर्वति वैदिकाग्निभिः[17] ।
प्रिया ततः स्नानविधौ जलाशयं
बलेन नीता परिगृह्य बन्धुभिः ॥ ५० ॥

---

१. MT. स्मरासिने । २. L. देवानि. . . ज्वलम् । ३. L,A. चित्तस्य । ४. L,A. धृतम् । ५. R. पतितं; MT. परितः । ६. L. पराभ. . . . . । ७. MT. कलस्य । ८. L. gap. upto ल्यैं; A. कुल्यः । ९. MT, R. गुरोः । १०. L,A. शैखरैरिमं; MT. विष्णिरेरिमं । ११. L,A. शिरस्समूहं । १२. R. मनस्थितं । १३. L,A. अतः प्रमाणेन । १४. MT. देवताम्; R. देवता । १५. R. श्रियं । १६. A. सखीय । १७. MT.R.तन्वति तस्य वह्निना ।

असौ विभिन्ने चरमे च[1] कर्मणी[2]
कृशानुप(द्मा)कर[3]दाहगाहने ।
अभिन्नवृत्त्योरिह युक्त[4]मावयो-
र्भृशं भजेते इति नादमाददे ॥ ५१ ॥

[5]शिखापरिस्पृष्टसिरा[6]वकुञ्चना-
त्करेषु[7] मुष्टिं वलयत्सु[8] मानिनः ।
हतेऽपि [9]सम्यग्ज्वलितं नभस्वता
न भीतभीतेन हिरण्यरेतसा[10] ॥ ५२ ॥

पुमानमित्रस्य पुरं पुरातनः[11]
प्रविश्य मायामनुजो विभीषणे ।
निसृष्टराज्यो रजनीचरैः चिरं[12]
सभां स भेजे[13] परितः सभाजितः ॥ ५३ ॥

निधिं[14] कलानामथ लक्ष्मणान्वितं[15]
हितं वहन्तं[16] कुमुदस्य सैनिकाः ।
प्रणेमुरिन्द्रद्विषदास्यनिर्गतं[17]
शिवेन रामाह्वयमिन्दुमादृतम्[18] ॥ ५४ ॥

कृतास्पदं धामनि कौशिकद्विषो[19]
जयेन दीप्तं दशकण्ठसूदनम् ।
हृतानुरागेण[20] जगाम वीक्षितुं
सुता नृपस्य[21] त्रिजटादिभिर्वृता ॥ ५५ ॥

---

१. MT. चरमेण; R. चरमेन । २. MT,R,L,A. कर्मणि । ३.MT. कृशानुपकर; R. कृशानुप... रदाह; L,A. कृशावतामाकर । ४. MT, R. युक्ति । ५. L,A. missing. ६. MT. शिरा । ७. R. कुशेषु । ८. MT, R,L,A. वलयन्, सुमानिनः । ९. R. सद्यः । १०. R. तेजसा । ११. MT. पुरातनं । १२. L,A. असौ । १३. A. समेदे । १४. MT, R. निधिः । १५. MT, R, अन्वितः । १६. MT. हितावहन्तं; R. हिताय हन्तुं । १७. L. निःस्पृहं; A. निस्सृतं; MT. प्रणेमुरिन्द्र.... दास्य निर्गतं; R. प्रणेमुरिन्द्र... स्य निर्गतः । १८. L,A. आहताः; MT. शिवे नराणां वयमिन्दुमादृताः; R. शिवेनरा.... ह्वयमिन्दुमादृताः । १९. R. द्विजे । २०. L,A. अथाञ्जनेयेन । २१. L, A. सहैव देवी ।

विपाण्डुनो धूसरवेणिरोचिषः
पदं दधत्या वपुरीक्षितुर्मनः[1] ।
तया शुचः स्थानमुपाहिता रतिः[2]
प्रियस्य चक्रे गलदश्रुधारया ॥ ५६ ॥

भयं विमृश्य प्रतिसंहृतेक्षणे
जनापवादादथ रावणद्विषि ।
मनस्विनी मन्युनिरन्तरा गिरः
परिस्खलन्तीरिति दीनमाददे[3] ॥ ५७ ॥

अयं सरोजस्य परं पराभवन्[4]
वपुर्विनिद्रस्य कटाक्षषट्पदः[5] ।
निपातितस्ते यशसो विपर्ययं[6]
मयि स्वयं पुष्यति वीर कीदृशम् ॥ ५८ ॥

अविच्छिदामस्य विवृद्धि[7]मेयुषः[8]
तवाननादर्शनजन्मनस्त्वया[9] ।
चिरप्रवृत्तस्य कृतं[10] कृतात्मना
कथं न विच्छेदनमात्रमश्रुणः ॥ ५९ ॥

दुःखासिकाम[11]सुतरां सुतरां प्रपद्य[12]
वैवर्ण्यसंपद[13]मिता दमिता तपोभिः[14] ।
[15]तस्थौ गुणैरविकलं विकलङ्कमेव
मुक्त्वा वचः क्षतमदान्तमदान्तमृत्युम्[16] ॥ ६० ॥

---

१. MT,R,L,A ईक्षितुं । २. MT,L,A. रति । ३. L,A. अतिदीनमाददे । ४. R. परंपराभवः । L,A. परंपराभवन् । ५. L,A. कटाक्षषड्पदो; R. कटाक्षसंपदा । ६. R. विपर्ययः । ७. A. विवृद्धं । ८. R. ईयुषः । ९. R. स्वयं । १०. A. वृतः । ११. MT. दुःखासितां (original palm-leaf reads as सिकां) । १२. MT, R. प्रपश्य । १३. MT,L. सत्पद । १४. MT,R. अमितान्तमृत्युः । १५. MT. ततोभितस्थौ । १६. R. मदान्धमदान्ध मृत्युः ।

शोकं तयानुपरमं परमं प्रपद्य
प्रोक्तं कृपारसहितं सहितं सबाष्पैः ।
श्रुत्वा विशुद्धिजननं जननन्दनार्थं
चक्रेऽनलं तरुचितं रुचितं प्रियायै ॥ ६१ ॥

आत्मप्रभा[१]वरमितैरमितैरुदस्त्रं[२]
दृष्टाऽथ[३] वानरबलैरबलैर्नमग्निम् ।
क्षत्रौजसा [४]कृतरसा तरसा विविक्षुः[५]
सा [६]सत्यवा[७]ग्रसमयं समयं चकार ॥ ६२ ॥

क्रोधाकृष्टत्रिदशवनितोत्तंसमच्छेदशास्यं[८]
चेतस्यस्मिन् विनिहितपदं तं समच्छे दशास्यम्[९] ।
नाथाऽकार्षं[१०] यदि [११]हतमहासत्त्व सा राम दाहं
गच्छेयं[१२] तद्रिपुहतमहाऽसत्त्वसाराऽमदाऽहम् ॥ ६३ ॥

स्वप्नेनापीन्द्रशत्रु[१३]स्स यदि सह मया[१४] जातु वै श्वा न रेमे
दाहः स्वल्पोऽपि मा भूत्तत इह सुमहत्यद्य वैश्वानरे मे ।
वाक्यं स्मैवं सुवीना बहुविगलितदृग्वारि सत्याह तेन
क्रूरं धाम स्वकीयं सपदि हुतभुजावारि सत्याहतेन ॥६४॥

॥ इति (श्रीमत्सिंहलकवेः कुमारदासस्य कृतौ)
जानकीहरणे (महाकाव्ये) एकोनविंशः सर्गः ॥

---

१. A. पर । २. R. उदस्तु । ३. MT, R, L, A, दृष्ट्वा । ४. R. तु तरसा । ५. A. विवक्षुः । ६. MT. तत्र । ७. R. gap upto ग्रस । ८, ९. R. शास्य । १०. MT, R, L, A. कर्षं । ११. R. गत । १२. MT, R. गच्छेयस्तद्रिपु । १३. MT, R. शत्रो । १४. L, A. यदि सह न मया ।

विंशतिस्सर्गः

अथ स्फुरत्काञ्चनभित्ति पुष्पकं
सजानिरारुह्य विभीषणान्वितः ।
समं सुमित्रात्मजवानरेश्वरैः
खमुत्पपात स्वपुरीयियासया ॥ १ ॥

ललाटविन्यस्तकराग्रवारित-
प्रभाकरांशुस्रवजिह्मितेक्षणैः[1] ।
निशाचरैरस्य विमानमीक्षितं
विवेश भृङ्गोदरसन्निभं नभः ॥ २ ॥

चिरप्रवासानलधूमसन्निभां[2]
करेण वेणीमवमोचयन्[3] स्वयम् ।
उदस्र[4]चक्षुः परिरभ्य वक्षसा
मिथः प्रियामेवमुवाच राघवः ॥ ३ ॥

जनेन रामाकृति रत्नमीदृशं
समीयते नाकृतपुण्यकर्मणा ।
इति स्वयं चिन्तयतः पदे पदे
मम स्फुरत्यात्मनि भूरि गौरवम् ॥ ४ ॥

जगद्द्वयं द्वावधितिष्ठतः प्रिये
पतिव्रतालाभविभूतिगर्वितौ ।
अहं भवत्या भृतको महीतलं
महामुनिः स्वर्गमरुन्धतीपतिः ॥ ५ ॥

---

१. L,A. जिह्मलोचनैः । २. MT. सन्निभं; A. सन्तर्ति । ३. MT. मोचयत् । ४. L,A.उदश्रु ।

पतिव्रतायास्तव देवि तेजसा
हृत[1]प्रभावो निहतो[2] निशाचरः ।
मनुष्यमुक्तः[3] कथमन्यथा शरः[4]
क्रमेत लोकत्रितयस्य जेतरि ॥ ६ ॥

इदं विधायोचितमङ्कमासनं
भुजेन मत्कण्ठतटावलम्बिनी ।
समीरणाकम्पितपक्ष्मसन्तती
दृशौ मुहुः पातय[5] देवि दिङ्मुखे ॥ ७ ॥

दिगङ्गना हारि बृहत्पयोधरा
दृशौ दहन्ती[6] बडबामुखेन[7] नः ।
शुभाशुभैरश्वमुखीव सेविता
गुणै[8]रियं दण्डधरेण रक्ष्यते[9] ॥ ८ ॥

अमूमधः[10] पश्य जवेन[11] पुष्पके
[12]नभस्समाक्रामति ते वियोगतः[13] ।
समुद्भवच्छोकरयेण ताविना
कृशीभवन्तीमिव रक्षसः[14] पुरीम् ॥ ९ ॥

पयोधिरत्नालयमीक्ष्यते[15] समं
समुन्नमद्वीचि[16]विभिन्न[17]मप्यदः ।
निमज्जतीवाम्बुनिधौ समन्ततः
क्रमेण लङ्का सहशैलकानना[18] ॥ १० ॥

विशालभृङ्गः शिखरै[19]रधिष्ठितो[20]
विभाति वल्मीक[21] इवैष भूधरः ।

---

१. MT, L. गृह; R. ग्रह; A. हत । २. MT. निहितो । ३. R. मुक्ताः । ४. R. शराः । ५. A. दिशौ मुहुः क्रीडय । ६. A. दहन्ति; R. हरन्ती । ७. L,A. बडवानलेन । ८. A. गणैः । ९. L,A. लक्ष्यते । १०. MT. मथः । ११. MT. जयेन । १२. MT. नभस्यं । १३. L,A. देवि दूरतः । १४. MT. राक्षसः; L,A. विद्विषः । १५. L. ईक्षते । १६. A. तद्वीचि । १७. MT,R. विसादं । १८. MT. काननम् । १९. L,A. शृङ्गच्छिखरैः । २०. MT. अधिष्ठितं । २१. MT. वल्मीकं ।

यतस्स्रवन्त्यः सरितः समन्ततः
परिस्फुरन्त्यः कुटिला इवोरगाः ॥ ११ ॥

सचन्दनेयं मणिचित्रमेखला
परिस्फुरन्नीलतमालकानना ।
हृदि प्रियेव प्रमदं तनोति नः
सुवर्ण[1]कूटानुगशैलसन्ततिः[2] ॥ १२ ॥

क्रमादतिक्रामति पुष्पके घनं
स्वविग्रहोल्लङ्घनशङ्कया यथा ।
तिरोदधानं गगनं समन्ततः
प्रवर्धते मण्डलमुष्णदीधितेः ॥ १३ ॥

विधाय[3] पादौ दृढमक्षपाटके
विसृज्य देहं गगने[4] सकौतुकाः[5] ।
अमी समीपागतमेघभित्तिषु
स्पृशन्ति विद्युद्वलयं[6] वलीमुखाः ॥ १४ ॥

इदं क्वणत्काञ्चनकिङ्किणीगुणं
विमानमग्रे दशनस्य पुष्करम् ।
निधाय[7] कर्णौ विनियम्य निश्चलं[8]
सकौतुकं दिग्गज एष वीक्षते[9] ॥ १५ ॥

इदं समासन्नरविप्रदीपितं
दधानमुष्णद्युतिकान्ति[10]मण्डनम् ।
भ्रमत्युपाहत्य[11] करोति निस्वनं
विमानमम्भस्स्रुति[12]मन्तरम्बुदम्[13] ॥ १६ ॥

---

१. MT. सुपर्ण । २. L,A. ननु नाद्रिसन्ततिः । ३. निधाय । ४. A. गमने । ५. MT. कौतुकाम् । ६. R. विद्युद्भ्रमयं ७. L. पिधाय; A. विधाय । ८. L,A. निश्चलः । ९. L,A. एवमीक्षते । १०. MT, R L,A. कान्त । ११. L, A. शमत्युपाहत्य । १२. R. अन्तःस्रुति । १३. MT, L, R, A. स्रुतिमन्तमम्बुदम् ।

सदैव पूर्णो बहुरत्नसंपदा[1]-
प्युपान्तभाग[2]स्थिततालभूषणः[3] ।
अयं समुद्रः[4] परिकर्षति श्रियं
प्रचेतसो रत्नसमुद्गसंभवाम्[5] ॥ १७ ॥

हरौ[6] हृतेऽसौ हरितुल्यतेजसः[7]
क्रतुप्रसङ्गे सगरस्य सागरः ।
विभिद्य तत्संभववीरबाहुभिः
गभीरभावं किल भूरि लम्भितः ॥ १८ ॥

अयं त्वदर्थे गिरिसेतुराहितः
प्रमित्सुनेव प्रथिमा[8]नमम्बुधेः ।
सकौतुकेनावनि[9]मण्डलेन यः
प्रसारितो बाहुरिवावभासते ॥ १९ ॥

समुत्प्लुतस्यो[10]दधि[11]दन्तिनो मुखे
शरीरभागे च[12] विभिन्नसंहतिः ।
[13]विभाति सा[14] भक्तिवितानभासुरा
सितेव भूतिर्नवफेनसन्ततिः ॥ २० ॥

[15]शिखिप्रभाभासुरविद्रुमद्रुम-
प्रताननिर्भिन्नतरङ्गसंहतिः[16] ।
स्वयं पयश्शोषविशेषनिस्पृहं[17]
द्वितीयमौर्वं वहतीव वारिधिः ॥ २१ ॥

---

१. MT. संपदां । २. R. उपात्ततल । ३. MT. भूषणम् । ४. R. समुद्गः । ५. R. संभवः । ६. A. हते । ७. R. तेजसा; A. तेजसं । ८. A. प्रथमानं । ९. MT. कौतुकेनावलि । १०. MT. समुत्प्लृतस्य । ११. L,A. उदक । १२. MT. भागेव; R. भोगेव । १३. R. Second half missing. १४. MT,R. विभासिता । १५. R. First half missing १६. L,A. मण्डलम् । १७. MT. अयं पयश्शोषविशेषनिस्पृहन्; L.A. अयं पयश्शेषविशेषनिस्पृहं ।

बिभर्ति[1] शङ्खप्रकरावतंसकः[2]
प्रवाल[3]रत्नाकर एष वारिधिः[4] ।
परिभ्रमन्मन्दरकोटिघट्टित[5]-
व्रणश्रियं[6] प्रस्फुरदस्थिदन्तुरा[7] ॥ २२ ॥
अपूर्वसोमार्ध[8]विभावनस्फुरत्[9]-
फणालपाशाङ्ककपालभूषणः ।
ककुत्प्रदेशो[10]ऽयमुपैति पश्चिमः
सरूपभावं[11] वपुषः[12] पिनाकिनः ॥ २३ ॥
असौ निजोत्सङ्गलुठत्पयोधरा
पतद्द्विजासन्नतर[13]त्रिविष्टपा ।
विदूरतो[14] वृद्धतरेव कामिनी
विवर्जिता मेखलयाद्रिसन्ततिः ॥ २४ ॥
हृतांबरोऽसावुपकण्ठनीलतां
समुद्वहन्निन्दुविषक्तमस्तकः[15] ।
बिभर्ति कान्तावृतभागसुन्दरः[16]
श्रियं गिरिर्देवसह[17]स्त्रिशूलिनः ॥ २५ ॥
परिभ्रमन्तो मनुजा महीतले
विदूरभावादतिसूक्ष्मदर्शनाः ।
विभान्त्यमी वर्त्मनि[18] शुक्लवाससो
मुखाहितान्ना[19] इव कीटपङ्क्तयः ॥ २६ ॥
विवर्धमानः किल सोऽयमायतं[20]
निरन्तरत्वं प्रसभं[21] दिशन्[22] दिशाम् ।
हतः पदा[23] पातितगर्वखर्वताम्[24]
अगादगस्त्येन रयादगाधिपः ॥ २७ ॥

---

१. MT· विभक्ति । २. L. प्रकरावतंसकाः; A. प्रतरावतंसकाः । ३. A. प्रवाण । ४. MT· वारिधेः । ५. MT. खण्डितं । ६. L,A· श्रियः । ७. L,A· दन्तुरम्; R. दन्तुराम् । ८. A· सोमाग्ध । ९. L A. विभाघन । १०. A·क्षरुप्रदेश । ११. A· स तु प्रभावं । १२. MT· R. वपुषा । १३. L MT. तनु । १४. MT. विदूरको । १५. MT. मस्तकम् । १६. L, A. सुन्दर । १७. R. गिरिदेव...स्त्रिशूलिनः; L,A. प्रिये देवि गिरिस्त्रिशूलिनः । १८. A. वर्मनि । १९. MT, L,A. मुखाहिताण्डाः । २०. L, A. आनतं । २१. L, A. प्रसभन् । २२. MT, L, A. दिशं । २३. A. पदां । २४. R. पर्वतः ।

[1]अयं नगस्सङ्गतनन्दकः सदा
मनोज्ञपद्माकरसक्तपादकः ।
अनन्तनागासनबद्धसंगति[2]-
र्हिरण्यगर्भो मधुसूदनायते ॥ २८ ॥

मनोज्ञसौगन्धिकजातिरञ्जितः
सपद्मरागारुणतोयसन्ततिः[3] ।
अयं कुणालो[4] बहुसागरप्रिये
विराजतेऽनेक[5]विजाति[6]मण्डनः[7] ॥ २९ ॥

परिस्फुरत्काञ्चनकान्तिरन्तिक[8]-
प्रयाततारो हरिसैन्यसेवितः ।
दिवाकराचुम्बिततुङ्गमस्तको
विभाति सुग्रीव इवैष[9] मन्दरः[10] ॥ ३० ॥

[11]सदप्सरोभिः परितोऽभिवेष्टितः[12]
समीपवर्तिद्विजराजमण्डनः ।
बिभर्ति पीताम्बर एष भूधरः
श्रियं मुरारेरपि रूपसंश्रयाम् ॥ ३१ ॥

इहानुगोदं[13] निशि चन्द्ररश्मिभिः
निषेव्यमाणौ सुरतश्रमान्तरे ।
प्रियेऽभिजा[14]नासि मनोज्ञसंकथौ
तटे[15] चरिष्याव उपान्त[16]सैकते ॥ ३२ ॥

पयःप्रवाह[17]स्सरितस्सरित्पतिं
गिरिञ्च विन्ध्यं प्रथतेऽयमन्तरा ।
भुवं[18] समालम्बितुमद्रिमस्तके
पयोधिना बाहुरिव प्रसारितः ॥ ३३ ॥

---

१. L, A. missing. २. R. संहतिः । ३. MT, R. संहतिः । ४. R. अयं....लो; L. अयं कुलो... । ५. MT. नैक । ६. L,A. विराजि । ७. R. मण्डना । ८. L. रन्तित । ९. MT,R. इवेह । १०. A. मन्दिरः । ११. L,A. missing. १२. MT. चेष्टितः । १३. MT, R, गेहं । १४. A. प्रिये विजानासि । १५. A. तटौ । १६. L, A. चरिष्यावपरान्त । १७. L. प्रवाहे; A. प्रवाहैः । १८. A. इवं ।

अनेकपुष्पप्रकराधिवासिता
भुजङ्गविक्षोभितलोलमानसा ।
स्पृहावता वेशविलासिनी यथा
दिगुत्तरासौ धनदेन सेव्यते ॥ ३४ ॥

निषेव्यमाणो हरिभिर्मतङ्गज-
क्षतक्षरद्रक्त[1]निषिक्तबाहुभिः ।
हिमालयस्सानुजरत्नभूषणो
गुणश्रियाऽसावनुगच्छतीव माम् ॥ ३५ ॥

सधातुकूटं धृतविश्वसंपदः[2]
शिवो[3]पभोगप्रणयस्य भाजनम् ।
इमं तपस्सिद्धिगुणाय[4] वृण्वते
श्मशानकल्पं व्रतिनो विरागिणः ॥ ३६ ॥

[5]हत[6]स्समुद्र[7]द्वितयेन वेगतः
तटोरसि[8] प्रस्फुरदूर्मिबाहुभिः ।
बृहद्दरीनिस्सृतधातुनिर्झरो
मुखादयं प्रोद्गिरतीव शोणितम् ॥ ३७ ॥

[9]इह प्रवृत्तं रविरश्मिसङ्गमे[10]
पतङ्गकान्तप्रभवं दवानलम् ।
निशासु निर्वापयति क्षपाकरः
प्रवाहिना चन्द्रमणिस्रवाम्बुना ॥ ३८ ॥

---

१. MT. क्षरद्ध्रूमि । २. A. संपदं । ३. L. विशो; A. विशो. . . . भोग । ४. MT. सुखाय । ५. L,A missing. ६. MT, R. ततः । ७. MT. समुद्रे । ८. R. तदोरसि । ९. L, A. missing. १०. R. नु चिदश्विसंगमे ।

[1]अनेन शैलेन सुरालयस्पृशा
तिरोभवन्नैशतमिस्रसञ्चयः ।
विवस्वतो भीत इवोग्रतेजसः[2]
परिभ्रमत्य[3]ञ्जनखण्डकर्बुरः[4] ॥ ३९ ॥

[5]निशि प्रवृत्तोदयया दवानले
तुषारवृष्टया शमितेऽपि सर्वतः ।
इहौषधिज्योतिषि दत्तदृष्टयः
सृजन्ति[6] भीतिं न[7] कुरङ्गयोषितः ॥ ४० ॥

अमुष्य शृङ्गे दुहितुर्महीभृतः
तपश्चरन्त्यास्सविता समीपगः[8] ।
शशाङ्कशोभामवह[9]द्विलोचन[10]-
प्रभाततिश्यामितमध्यमण्डलः ॥ ४१ ॥

पतिप्रसादादरमण्डितालका
गुहाननासक्तगल[11]त्पयोधरा[12] ।
अधित्यकासौ हिमशैलसंभवा[13]
बिभर्ति गौरीव मनोहरं वपुः ॥ ४२ ॥

असौ गुहा धातुपरिस्रवारुणा
विलुप्तपक्षस्य तटे महीभृतः ।
स्रवन्मुखस्य त्रिदशाधिपायुध-
व्रणस्य नालीव[14] विभाति रागिणी[15] ॥४३ ॥

[16]स एष शीतद्युतिहासिनिर्झरे
विकीर्णवारिः स्फटिकोपलोच्छ्रयः ।
गुहानिबद्धप्रतिशब्दभैरवैः
अलक्षितोऽपि ध्वनिभिर्विभाव्यते[17] ॥ ४४ ॥

---

१. L, A. missing. २. R. तेजसा । ३. MT, R. भ्रमन्त्यञ्जन । ४. MT. कर्बुरम् । ५. L, A. missing. ६. MT. स्रजन्ति; R. त्यजन्ति । ७. MT. भीतिर्न । ८. MT, L, R. समीपगे । ९. MT, L. अपहत् । १०. R. विलोचने ११. L, A. बृहत् । १२. MT. धराः । १३. MT. संभवात् । १४. L, A. नीलीव । १५. L, A. रावणी । १६. L, A. missing. । १७. MT. विदाव्यते ।

[1]शिखासु पुष्पप्रकरो महीरुहां

मुहुः किलाधोऽञ्जनशैलभित्तिषु ।

क्षणं विनष्टः[2] स्फटिकोपले घनः

सितप्रभोऽयं मरुता विधूयते ॥ ४५ ॥

[3]विमुच्यमानः सितवारिदैरसौ

विभाति धातूपलराशिरुच्छ्रितः ।

समन्ततो भस्मनि भासुरप्रभः

प्रयाति वातैरिव वह्निसञ्चयः ॥ ४६ ॥

[4]घनस्य तिष्ठन्ति ततो धृताम्भसः

तटे पतन्तश्शिरसो महीभृतः ।

अमी रवे[5]रूर्ध्वमुखांशुवह्निना

पराहताः पाद[6]तलेषु किन्नराः ॥ ४७ ॥

[7]विकृष्यमाणे[8] सितमेघमण्डले

नभस्वता यो बिस[9]खण्डपाण्डुरः ।

विभाति निर्मोकमिव त्यजन्नितः

स एष कैलासतटो विलोक्यताम् ॥ ॥ ४८ ॥

[10]कुतः कुरङ्गं[11] किरणस्य चन्द्रमाः

सदा शिरस्स्पर्शकृतं बिभर्ति सः । (?)

स्वयं च तद्धर्षणजातनिष्पत-

द्धिमांशुधूलीकृतशुक्लिमाचलः ॥ ४९ ॥

[12]लतावितानावरणे शिलातले

गिरावमुष्मिन् सुरसिद्धयोषिताम् ।

---

१. L,A. missing. २. MT, R. विनप्ट । ३ & ४. L,A. missing. ५. MT. रवैः । ६. MT. पार । ७. L,A. missing. ८. MT, R. विकृष्यमाणो । ९. R. पिस । १०. L,A. missing. ११. MT. कुरङ्गः । १२ L.A. missing.

सुवृत्त[१]काञ्चीगुणघृष्टि[२]रेखया
विदन्ति वृत्तं सुरतं वनेचराः ॥ ५० ॥

[३]उपागतोऽपि ग्रसितुं विलोचन-
प्रभानिषेकाहितमेचकद्युतिम्[४] ।
मृगीसमूहः[५] परिणामदूषितं
विशङ्क्य भूयस्त्यजतीव पल्लवम् ॥ ५१ ॥

ननु[६] विदधति पादपूरणानि
प्रथितयताव[७]चले किरातदेशाः ।
विशदमतिभिरव्ययाः[८] प्रबन्धे
रचित इवार्थवतीह विप्रहीनाः[९] ॥ ५२ ॥

दुरुत्तरं विवरमुखस्थपन्नगं
वनश्रिया परिगतमुत्प्रवालया ।
इति स्तुवन् जलधिमिवाथ भूभृतं[१०]
सुतो भुवं समवततार भूभुजः ॥ ५३ ॥

महर्षयो नरपतिपौरसंहिताः
मुखानि[११] तन्नुतिमुखराणि बिभ्रतः ।
उपस्थितश्रियमभिषेकसंभृतिं
प्रगृह्य तं नृपतिसुतं प्रपेदिरे ॥ ५४ ॥

रामो वृतो[१२] भरतलक्ष्मणतत्कनिष्ठैः
बद्धाञ्जलिर्गुरुविधेयतयैव[१३] पृच्छन् ।
वीरश्चकार हृदयं सहसा स तीव्र[१४]
व्रीलावतारविधुरं भरतस्य मातुः ॥ ५५ ॥

---

१. MT. सवृत्त । २. MT. वृष्टि; R. पृष्टि । ३. L,A. missing. ४. MT. द्युतिः; R. द्युति । ५. R. समूहं । ६. A,R. नन । ७. MT. यतापचले; L,A. रुचावचले । ८. MT. अप्यया; L A. ईर्ष्यया । ९. MT. हलिप्रहीनाम्; R. नृपार्थवती फलिप्रहीना । १०. MT,R. भूभृतः । ११. L. तत्स्तुति; A. तस्तुति ; MT. तं नुति । १२. L. राज्ये कृतो; A. राज्ये भृतो । १३. MT. विधेयकयैव । १४. R. सतीव ।

तस्यानुजद्वयकरस्थितशातकुम्भ-
कुम्भच्युतं शिरसि राक्षसनाथशत्रोः[१] ।
श्वेतातपत्रतलभाजिनि बद्धधारं
मातुर्ममार्ज भरतस्य कलङ्कमम्भः[२] ॥ ५६ ॥

दृष्ट्वा राज्यग्रहणविभवं तं महान्तं महान्तं
गत्वा रामे[३] विहितविनतिः सत्सभार्ये[४] सभार्ये ।
सिद्धैः क्रीडानुभवविधिभिर्मानितान्तं[५] नितान्तं
शैलं[६] प्रायाद्गिरिरिव निरातङ्कपीनः कपीनः[७] ॥५७॥

पारावारं[८] नयनसलिलातानमस्यन्नमस्यन्
रामं वर्णस्थितिपरिकरत्रास[९]कान्तं सकान्तम् ।
तेन प्रायात्सुररिपु[१०]पतिश्शोकसन्नः कसन्नः[११]
खेदं मा दा[१२] इति कृतसमाश्वासमुक्तः समुक्तः ॥५८॥

चक्रे देवीमुपकृतमुनि[१३]स्थानयज्ञो नयज्ञो
वृत्तौ सक्ता[१४]मवि[१५] चल[१६]गुणाभ्यास[१७]सत्यां ससत्याम् ।
क्रोधं हन्त्रीमपि बहुमतासृग्वसानां वसानां[१८]
ह्रीशौचाख्ये सततमहते[१९] वाससी तां स सीताम्[२०] ॥५९॥

ईर्ष्यामोहस्मयमदधनप्रेमहीनान् महीनान्
कृत्वा भ्रातॄन्, महति विभवे न्यस्तदासः सदासः ।
रामोऽरक्षत् कृतपरहित[२१]स्वोदयायां दयायां
स्थित्वा पृथ्वीमविचलतया तत्समः तां समस्ताम् ॥६०॥

---

१. L,A. तदिह मूर्धनि रावणारेः । २. R. अद्भ्यः । ३. MT, R. रामं । ४. A. सभाये । ५. MT, R. मानितामानितान्तं । ६. MT, R. शैलप्रायात् । ७. R. कवीनां कवीनां । ८. A. पारं पारं । ९. L, A. ग्रास; MT, R. परिकृतत्रास । १०. MT. सुरपतिरिपु; R. सुररिपुपतिं । ११. MT. कसन्ना-कसन्ना; R. कसन्नां कसन्नां । १२. L, A. मागा । १३. A. ममस्थान । १४. MT, R. सत्तां । १५. all except R. अपि । १६. L, A. कल । १७. MT. गुणाभास । १८. L, A. ध्वस्तव्रीलाविवशहृदया सेवमानावमानां । १९. R. महसे । २०. L, A. राज्ये लक्ष्मीमुपपतयशोवाससीतां ससीताम् । २१. MT. कृतपरिनिहतः ।

नित्यं सद्गुणभक्तिरिन्द्रियदमश्रीसंयतः संयतः
शस्त्रद्योतितमूर्ध्नि मुक्तहृदयोऽभीसङ्गतः सङ्गतः ।
विद्वानस्य कवेः पितार्यहृदयं धीमानितो मानितो
लङ्कैश्वर्यभुजः कुमारमणिरित्यासन्नयः सन्नयः ॥६१॥

येनारिप्रकृतिं निराकृतवता सम्मानितो मानितो
यस्य स्वाङ्गमभिघ्नतो रिपुभृशंनाशोऽभितः शोभितः ।
श्रीमेघोऽस्य कवेरसौ किल बृहद्धामातुलो मातुलो
दृष्टस्त्रासजडं द्विषामधिगतत्रासेनया सेनया ॥६२॥

श्रीमानेकः शरण्यः परिभवविपदाभाजनानां जनानां
रूपेणानुप्रयातो दिवमतिसुभगं रञ्जयन्तं जयन्तम् ।
भ्राता तन्मातुरन्यः शशिधवलयशःकारणानां रणानां
कर्ता पुत्रोऽग्रबोधिर्जनशिरसि लसद्भासुराज्ञः सुराज्ञः ॥६३॥

आदायैनं दशायां स्थितमपि तदहस्स्रस्तनाभ्यां स्तनाभ्यां
तुष्टे तस्मिन् गदानामरिहतपितृके पारयन्तौ रयं तौ ।
आत्मापत्याविशेषं पुपुषतुरहतप्रेमदान्तौ मदान्तौ
यत्सानाथ्यात्स काव्यं व्यरचयदसुरद्विण्महार्थं महार्थम् ॥६४॥

CANTO XVI

1. Having known from the door-keeper (of Rāvaṇa) that his work for the day for Rāvaṇa, the enemy of Indra, had been carried out, and having obtained his (Rāvaṇa's) permission, the Sun went to the (setting) mountain situated in the western ocean.

2. With their shapely noses bent to their necks, themselves bowed down by the reins drawn tightly by the hands of Aruṇa (the charioteer), the horses of the Sun descended down the slope of the great mountain with the rims of the chariot wheels falling on their hips.

3. With his body torn by the hosts of bees in the form of the thick darkness that was forcibly setting in, the Sun as if in fright and seeking a way out, sank into the water.

4. The Kumuda flowers, which were at first, for a while, reddish owing to Sun-set, and then occupied in the interiors by darkness, were beheld by bees from a distance with a doubt, whether they were red or blue lotuses.

5. At that evening time, in the breeze strewn with particles of waves that broke on the ruby platforms, the lotus in the garden shrank as if struck by a cold blast.

6. "Move aside quickly; the Sun is setting; the petal-doors are closing on the lotuses"—As if announcing this to the host of bees, a bee humming sweetly went round the pond.

7. When the end of the day was approaching, the tree-groves, with the birds flying away from them, with darkness enveloping, and with their tops shaking and bent, looked as if affected by old age. (When the end of one's days comes, the good part of one's life has passed, and the head has come to droop and shake).

8. When the Sun had slipped down, the sky reddened by the

spread of the evening twilight, resembled the heart of Rāvaṇa covered with wounds caused by hundreds of arrows from (his enemies) the Devas.

9. The moon that was within the waters of the sea, as if hiding himself out of fear of the Sun, appeared to stretch out his hands (rays) in the sky, to know whether the Sun has gone away or not.

10. The evening first rendered the Universe dark (made it the enemy of demon Andhaka), then gave it very ruddy stars (pupils of the eye), then united it with the moon (throwing out or comprehending the Universe through 'Kalā', one of his five śaktis[1]) and thus made it attain the form of Siva.

11. The simultaneous going down in the sky of the Sun who had been overcome by the end of the (his) day, and the coming up of the orb of the moon with his form unimpaired (full of the digits), were like those of two persons who had mounted the scales of a balance (one at the end of his days and another full of health).

12. Redness left the moon, who was leaving the rising-mountain and was becoming clear in his orb, even as it (redness) would leave a crystalline drinking cup when the wine in it was being drunk by the lips of the lady of Eastern quarters.

13. As if having found often the (wicked) Evening to be a faithless lover, the quarters with their colours changed as if in anger (with their facial colour changed) rubbed off the saffron decoration put on the breasts for the evening sport. (The saffron-like red decoration on the cloud caused by the play of twilight).

14. "Why does this lady of the 'Quarter' put on her upper-garment of darkness on her breasts (clouds) during night and throw it off at the end of night (daybreak)? —Witnessing this perverse behaviour, the lilies appeared to break into loud laughter.

1. See Introduction, chapter on "Kumāradāsa's Learning."

15. Has all the heavily enveloping darkness of the hue of the cuckoos been torn to pieces by the disc of the moon risen from the mount of Rise, and laid along with the darkness inside the cavities or has been destroyed totally ?[1]

16. "Here the (white) splendour of the moon has fallen along with bits of the (dark) colour of its deer"—Thus did the lilies in the pond along with the bees spread over them give rise to a doubt in the (minds of the) people.

17. To the moon who had just risen and who favoured (the world) with his rays cool like snow and white like (pearl) necklace, the moon-stone arch made the water-offerings of welcome (arghya) with the continuous trickle of water.

18. "Not I alone have been vanquished by the splendour of the incomparable faces of the Rākṣasa women, but this deer too has been vanquished by their glances"—Appearing thus to show to the world his deer-spot, (the moon, the lamp of the quarters, arose from the rising mountain).[2]

19. With his rays falling scattered on the Suvela mountain, in front, producing in the minds of the ladies in the city the doubt of a new water-fall and thereby great passion; (the moon, the lamp of the quarters, arose from the rising mountain).[3]

20. By his lustre, increasing the passion to a great extent in the minds of the ladies, the moon, the lamp of the quarters, white like the elephant's tusk and the abode of Kalās (splendour), rose up from the rising mountain. (The comparison is suggested here to an ivory lamp with artistic carvings which is kept in lovers' bedrooms and forms part of the surroundings that enkindle pleasant feelings).

21. When the silver pot of the moon was thrown in the lake of the sky by (the lady) Night, the densely spread darkness

1. In this verse Kumāradāsa keeps in his mind the image of a hunter issuing from a hill, slaying some dark birds like cuckoos and putting them into the holes or consuming them.

2. Refers to the last line in Verse 20.

3. Ibid.

receded like a mass of moss tossed away by the waves caused thereby.

22. The wide ocean of darkness struck by the ray of the moon as by the trunk of the (white) heavenly elephant (Airāvata), began overflowing, with an unimpeded course, the woods on the shores of the quarters.

23. When the moon had risen, the lotuses of the faces of ladies in union with their lovers were decorated by 'Night' with musk, camphor and red paint (resembling the bimba fruit); and 'Night' made lotuses of the faces of those in separation from their lovers feel fed up with the splendour of the orb of the deer-marked moon.[1]

24. The eyes of the ladies of travellers resembled only in their lustre the beauty of the rubies. But when the moon had risen they resembled by the their act (of shedding tears) the moon-stone wrapped in the moon's rays.

25. The lily creeper, with the bed of lily flowers closely covering the waters and with its colour variegated by the bees which were falling heavily thereon, appeared to have wrapped herself with the hide of a tiger.

26. When the images of the planets began to appear at night in the waters, the swan moved towards that other pond, taking it for one with lilies and singing in glee.

27. When the moon, whose rays shattered the profuse darkness, had spread his light, feelings began to show their play in the mind of cupid and in the hearts of the young.

28. Having herself painted the decorative designs (on her cheeks) which even like the mark on the moon of her face, one beloved, when the lover was delaying, wiped off the futile decoration with her tears.

1. The first line clearly indicates the twofold application with reference to those in union and those in separation and the meaning above given in the translatlon is clear, though with reference to those in separation the expression 'अलञ्चकार' is somewhat cryptic; it has to be taken in the latter case as 'अलं चकार'.

29. "(This) love (red colour) does not appear when the lover is near and in his separation it is useless"—So thinking another lady did not decorate her lip with the red paint of Yāvaka.

30. The foot-impression with its wet Yāvaka paint, forming the mark of the kick of the other beloved was not perceived by another lady on the chest of the lover, being hidden in the red lustre of the bright ruby ear-rings.

31. One lady obedient to the words of her lover, did not blow away with her mouth the particles of the fragrant powder fallen from her tremulous hair into the eyes of her lover, whose eyes were engrossed in her enjoyable limbs.

32. Even when the lamp was put out by the decorative flower on the ear, flung by the beloveds, the Rākṣasa lovers in their love-sports, did see the region of the waist whose girdle, by the lustre of its gems, dispelled the darkness.

33. Of the ladies who had been undressed and embraced, the saffron on their slender waists did not disappear, even though that on their heavy loins and breasts had fallen.

34. "That your beloved in her exceeding anger has kicked you on your head with her lotus-foot, is indeed a great blessing to you; if she should become appeased in heart, what kind of gain are you going to have ?

35. You, faithless lover ! this your lower lip which is even cut by the teeth in the impetuous kiss of the love-mad beloved, you are continuously drenching with your tears for the alleviation of the pain !

36. Why do you here talk before me, covering your mouth with your tender palm ? You are hiding the mark of the teeth of your beloved or are we the objects of such veneration ?[1]

1. The practice is that before venerable people others should speak with their palm over their mouth.

37. Thus faltering in their talk owing to anger, the Rākṣasa women spoke severe words mingled with tears to their lovers who had been released after being enjoyed by rival ladies.

38. "Has not the lustre of your lip been eclipsed by the vehement sighs, when your lover has come to your side? you have not cast your glance weighed down with sympathy, when he has fallen at your feet ?"

39. The hand (of the lover) placed on the breast has been brushed aside; when spoken to, silence has been adopted; and at his appeasement you have bitterly laughed; this is a lady's punishment to a lover !

40. "Friend ! leave off your anger, later repentence will torture your tremulous heart"—with such words from the clever lady-friend, the pride in the mind of the Rākṣasa lady was removed.

41. "My messenger-girl ! if my lover delays, why should it cause this vehement anger in you, that you impetuously bite and wound your lip ?"

42. By reason of the friendly conduct exhibited by me, by sharing with you my drinks, flowers, fragrant paste and the like, you have yourself, my friend, aggrandised a share of this pleasure of enjoying my lover too.

43. The mark of the teeth is patent, your limbs throb, and your face is drenched with perspiration—Tell me in truth —Did the lewd man (serpent) of crooked course violate (bite) you (in love) ?

44. The words that you uttered previously—"Friend ! you are not different from my own self"—are indeeed true, for what was to have been done by me with effort in respect of my lover, all that you have yourself done.

45. Thus did the words, harsh to hear and accompanied by pride and laughter, spring forth towards the lady-messenger

from the Rākṣasa lady whose fortitude had been shaken, who had become angry and who bore a face overcast with drops of perspiration.

46. The beautiful lower lip with its lustre lost due to the sighs, and the floral decorations of paint transferred to her palms (from the cheeks), bespoke the great anxiety of the Rākṣasa lady when her lover arrived late.

47. After making the messenger-ladies unsuccessful in their efforts (to bring them there), and coming and hiding behind, the lovers listened in glee to the words of their beloveds spoken with anger and pride.

48. "Let it be that the wound on the lip is due to the mango-juice that has fallen into the drink. What is the cause for this mark of the nails on the cheeks, you, who are of firm mind ?"

49. You fickle-minded man ! on your upper lip with its incipient and sparse growth of mustache, the clear collyrium-impression made by the lashes when you kissed the eyes of the lady is somehow discernible.

50. "With your eyes engrossed in the face of the lady, you are not obviously listening to my words; O ! you, lewd man (serpent), you are only apparently sweet, you whose movement is crooked ! You have surely become one that hears by the eyes (serpent)."

51. Thus did the Rākṣasa damsel, representing the young man as fickle in his love, speak with staring eyes, words of derisive laughter exhibiting her feeling of offended love.

52. "Enticing him by offering your own body and desiring to bring him here, even as a wild elephant, you, my friend, have acted like a she-elephant; indeed, only a good soul remembers the friend's mission !"

53. Friend ! to you who went to that unyielding man and submitting yourself to unbearable trouble on my behalf,

there is just this injury on the lip, while to me, however, the pain in the heart is acute !"

54. In this manner the Rākṣasa damsel with the orb of her face rendered beautiful with eyes reddened (in anger) spoke severe and wrathful words with reference to the lady-messenger who had committed treacherous offence and was being laughed at by other friends.

55. Ladies who were slothful with the infatuation of love drank the wine poured from the ruby drinking jars, doubting in their innocence that the liquid essence of the ruby jars themselves were, somehow, flowing out.

56. Having deposited in the heart, mouth and eyes of those damsels its intoxication, smell and colour respectively, the wine came out in a pure form under the pretext of the drops of perspiration on the exterior of the cheeks white like the reed flower.[1]

57. When the moon with all its digits had made the dark lily put forth its buds[2] (in the waters) its (moon's) deputy in the form of the deer spread in the drinking cup (its shade resembling) the colour of the dark lily.

58. Bashfulness, already shattered by the innumerable attractive qualities of the lover, could not, when wine was being enjoyed for long, keep its foot-hold in the heart of the lady, crowded as it was with infatuation and love.

59. By virtue of the common attractive colour, red like the disc of the newly rising Sun, the wine in the ruby cups was known by the women-folk as having been consumed, only by reason of its weight.

1. There is a suggestion of one leaving behind his defects, like mada etc. and emerging as a pure person.

2. मुकुलयति । This word is usually used in the sense of 'closing' as opposed to विकसति but is here used in a different sense. The idea of the poet is that while the white moon made the lily put forth its buds, the dark spot in the moon reflected in the drinking cup appeared verily to open out the lily buds and spread the dark colour in the wine-cups.

60. & 61. On the terrace where at the instance of the door-keeper the wind-god himself had swept off the dust, when the clouds had for a moment sprinkled water without hindering the rays of the moon, and where there was the music of celestial damsels accompanied by the lute of Tumburu, the enemy of the Gods (Rāvaṇa), surrounded quickly by ladies in love, enjoyed himself.

62. Quaffing off in haste the wine flowing from the golden pots poured before him, Rāvaṇa, with his ten mouths and the gold ornamentation fixed on all of them, appearing like shells, looked like the sea taking in the rivers flowing from the ten directions.

63. [1]That one Rāvaṇa, playing with the rows of his hands all varieties of instruments like those of string, percussion (drum) and metal (cymbal), and taking the three measures, (the slow, middling and fast) and singing with eight of his mouths, directed the dance of a lady.

64. With his row of arms on every woman and their lotus-faces brought to his ten mouths, Rāvaṇa who sported simultaneously with all his beloved women sitting around him, gave no room for anger (jealousy).

65. With his lip bit by one of the women and with all his faces consequently emitting the hissing sound of pain, the lover Rāvaṇa was struck in anger on all his other nine heads by the beloveds who had been perturbed by the force of love.

1. तत means stringed instruments like Vīṇā. Drums are usually referred to by the term अवनद्ध because they are tied over with stretched skin. For obvious reasons of metre, our poet has used here the word वितत in the sense of drum, signifying, of course, the same meaning of leather spread over the surface. घन is metal, like bronze, which is used to mark the rhythm (Tāla). The other class of instruments included by the term आद्य is सुषिर or bored ones like flutes or pipes which are to be played both by the hands and the mouth. One of the mouths should have been pre-occupied with the flute. Of the remaining nine faces only eight are mentioned as singing. And we are told that he is also conducting the dance. So his main central face might have been left out for speaking or for giving instructions. Perhaps the eight faces are mentioned to correspond to the eight Rasas which are to be portrayed in dance.

66. If my mouth is a drinking cup, O ! you wicked one, why do you suddenly bite the lip ? Having drunk the wine none but the inebriate takes pleasure in biting the edge of the cup.

67. "How can another kiss your lip that has been marked with the impressions of the teeth and sealed by one lady ?" — Thus was the King of the Rākṣasas addressed by the woman-folk with their sternly-knit brows.

68. The Meru mountain with its elated elephants residing on its slopes, decorated with wide-spread minerals and with the disc of the moon standing on its summit, frequently appeared like Śiva (the destroyer of the three cities) having snakes proud of being his armlets, adorned with the holy ash[1] smeared all over his body and having the image of the moon on his head.

69. Divine minstrels sang, approaching that intoxicated demon who was verily a disease and a fright to all the three worlds,[2] who was fearless like an elephant in rut and who bore carnivorous teeth looking like the fork of the crescent moon.

70. The moon cool like the touch of the mass of snow has gone to the summit of the Meru Mountain. The terrestrial regions have also been clearly separated from darkness by the rays of the Sun (his charioteer) and the wind blows tossing the row of bees clinging fondly to the lilies and the yonder chirping water-bird standing on the wave of the water.

1. The word 'Dhātu' is well-known in classical usage to refer to minerals and elements of the body. But in Buddhistic literature it is common to find 'Dhātu' as referring to the ashes or the relics of the body, such as worshipped in Buddhistic Stūpas. In this verse the poet uses it in the sense of 'ash' which might be taken as an indication of his acquaintance with Buddhism in his Ceylonese surroundings.

2. त्रिभुवनभयरोगदानवन्तं may be interpreted as—'one who was sheltering (अवन्तम्) the Rākṣasa hosts who were giving fright and illness to the three worlds. (त्रिभुवन-भय-रोग-दान्).

71. "The sea, reaching the time of the tidal ebb retreats from the shore. The female-birds have taken to the endless chirping at the end of the sleep; and as the faces of the quarters whiten (with day-break) yonder cluster of stars with its lustre gone has set completely.[1]

72. "When the heavy column of the bears has crossed over the bolt of the city-gate,[2] when Lakṣmaṇa son of Sumitrā who causes terror in the hearts of the enemy has also come with his arms, and when Rāma strikes, who is that superior warrior that you have on hand who can stand them? When that whole army (of Rāma) which tears the enemies is striking, wherefore are you now sleeping?"

73. Mailed and intent on the close and complete destruction of the Rākṣasas, elated with his effulgence *hetinā* and the arms bearing the formidable, divine missiles, he (Rāma) the destroyer (*pamsana*) who has come to the battle produces a shudder in our hearts and O! Protector of our honour! (you are in) this sleep, deaf to the out-cries of the city!

74. Those minstrels became silent after thus waking up in his chamber (or at day-break), quiet with the noises of the (morning) conches and drums subsided, the passionate Rāvaṇa always desirous of elaborate sexual pleasures, that timid lover who was crossing the ocean of the night with the aid of the large pots of breasts, in his sports with the love-smitten women, brought over by him in bondage (*sitānām*).

1. End of the third line and beginning of fourth—तत ताराचक्र न न श्रस्तं इतम् ।

2. All manuscripts read : परिघ उल्लंघनायां । If, however, the correct word is परिखा उल्लंघनायां we have the happier meaning of the bears of Rāma's army crossing the moat round the fort of Laṅkā.

CANTO XVII

1. Bowing then in devotion to the Creator of the[1] World, ardently performing the festive rite in honour of the Fire-God, (Rāma) the descendant of the family of[2] Aja, who took his stand on proper policy came down to the battle-field in a short while from Mount Suvela.

2. And Rāma's enemies (the Rākṣasas), desiring to establish for themselves the position guaranteeing the pride of (superior) prowess in that battle to be waged for the destruction of their foes, performed in the bright Fire-God the rites favourable to them, accompanied by the offering of oblations.

3. Then that eminent Rāvaṇa, huge (and dark) like a mountain of collyrium, who made the faces of his friends bloom, went to his court-hall and addressed the following words to the assemblage there, effulgent like the spreading fire.

4. "In the manner in which you, endowed with firmness, bear with regard to me the burden of my good, rendered lovable by your affection, in that manner a mother would not, nor a virtuous wife, a beloved son, nor even a kind father.

5. "While on the many occasions (in the past) nothing unfavourable has been done to me (by you), how is it going to be (different) in the present circumstance ? And this fame of mine, which is unimpaired in the World—thanks to your policy which safeguards me—how could it be (now) devoid of good fortune and proper policy ?

1. In Vālmīki's Rāmāyaṇa, there is no such salutation to Brahma or propitiation of fire-god mentioned on the eve of the battle.

2. The word indicating the subject is अजस्य बन्धुः which may mean both Rāma and Rāvaṇa. नये स्थितः and सुवेलात् अगात् (following the proper policy and getting down from Suvela) are the attributes which clinch the subject being Rāma.

6. "Surely you have always the vast capacity to deprive Śiva forcibly of his greatness and to strike terror in (the heart of) the Sun and yet you have not given up your goodness (towards me) in (your) pride.

7. "Who has not been beaten in the terrible field of battle by that formidable army of yours; the army on whose noise (even that) Indra mounted on his chariot, whose effulgence is not less than that of the Sun, shudders.

8. "You are as fearless in battle as in the past. Any great fear from this mortal (Rāma) does not look well. When our army stands on the battle-field, who is even that odd-eyed Śiva, the dance-master of the ghosts (to face us) ?

9. "That wicked Varuṇa who throws on the neck of the people the poisonous fetter of the serpent noose, was threatened in the battle even by your playful glance and was vanquished gradually by the fire of your imprecations.

10. "When Śiva himself with his wrath evident and his army of Gaṇas surrounding him all around is afraid of these invincible arms, who else will not get afraid of them ?

11. "In the battle which destroyed Vidyādharas and Cāraṇas, the enemy, Kumāra, son of Pārvatī, all red with the flow of blood from the elephants on the opposite (our) side, deprived of his weapon Śakti, was defeated by you with your shouts terrible like the thunder of clouds.

12. "That preceptor (of the Gods) endowed with sound policy, whom enemies conquer not in battle, and in whom rests high heroism, even him I have seen conquered and deprived of pride by you in the battle in which the bodies (of enemies) were wounded.

13. "That enemy Kubera whose rule stands always high by virtue of his power, approaching in battle our forces which have the great strength of sound policy, gives up that noble choice of his namely the vow to fight.

14. "You, who conquered Indra's city of high towers in the

battle in which the gate-way of that city was uprooted, intoxicated with your pride which infuses into you strength and power (or which destroys the strength and power—of enemies), did not (even) resort to the mace[1] that destroys the enemy.

15. "Making terrific noise[2] in the vehemence of anger, depriving Indra of his manliness in the great battle, which victor amongst you did not bring down on the Gods his huge heavy arm that struck terror in the hearts of the foes ?

16. "That boundless and collected army of the Gods, bearing a multitude of sparkling weapons, which was not vanquished even by me with my formidable weapon of Śakti, has been made by you to beg and bend low at (our) feet.

17.......................

18. "The closely-hooded army of the Nāgas (Serpents), bearing the burden of the battle, led by Vāsuki and emitting laughter along with their speed, was subdued by your army when it met (you) its enemy and was cut to pieces.

19. "By you (the enemy of the Gods) was put down the throbbing enthusiasm of that protector of the serpents named Ananta (Ādiśeṣa), who harmed his enemies with his poison and who was firmly established in (his own) unimpaired and praise-worthy power.

20. "May you, who have thus attained by reason of your prowess the position of tormentors of the enemies, conquer in battle with this army (of yours) that new man, the wicked one who has taken the sacred grass for his girdle.

21. "Which enemy in this world is to be destroyed other than this one, who is now attacking me in his pride, and at whose hands 'Khara' the crest-jewel of (our) family was lost, the wicked one who is now bearing enmity towards me ?

1. The idea is that in the pride of their strength they went forth for the battle even without equipping themselves with their arms.

2. स्वरम्, सु+अरम्

22. "In your battle which tears up the bodies of the enemy heroes, that Indra (himself) by the loss of his fame and deprived of his strong (followers) does not stand face to face; why mention (this mere) man who has collected monkeys?

23. "When my fame has suffered this first eclipse, I am not able to bear the wretchedness that has come over me owing to the loss of strength. If I do not make him (Rāma) bend before my feet, I shall offer in fire my massive hands fit to be decorated with armlets.

24. "Let that (Sītā) whose face is beset with the harassment of intoxicated bees which mistake it for a full-blown lotus and who burns my mind which is full of love (for her), see (her) husband killed along with her brother-in-law.

25. "Seeing that husband of hers killed in this big battle along with his kinsmen and friends, let Sītā who is (averse) like that towards me, strongly in love with her, go atwain, bereft of enjoyment and with her heart dried up."

26. So addressed (by Rāvaṇa), the gathering, free from any kind of suffering and shining with the armlets and dangling necklaces, then dispersed, with its tread shaking the earth and desirous of throwing the enemy-lines in disorder.

27. One (Rākṣasa) left his residence, leaving his mind with the soft-haired frontal locks of his beloved and being looked at with deep anxiety by her, who was shedding profuse tears over her lip and breast.

28. (Another) demon given excellent wine by his beloved, went from his mansion, his big chest smeared with the saffron (of the beloved whom he had embraced,) bent with an excess of drink and tugging (in his hand) his garment flowing on the ground.

29. Another, beautiful with his loins tied over with a fine garment and beautiful with his coat of mail, moved out and reached his elephant of Asura extraction, held on all sides, ready for battle and smelling with rut.

30. Then, another covered over with strong armour and intent on the battle, quickly mounted the elephant, strong with the vehemence of its own rut, and which it discharged setting at naught the will of the mahout.

31. By the advancing armies, the long column of dust enveloping the quarters and the clouds, was raised so heavily that even the imperishable row of Sun's horses came to grief with their hoofs stuck up (in that dust).

32. Issuing out of the city, then the army (of the Rākṣasas), [1]quickly reached the enemy stationed in front looking verily like the embodiment of poison, namely the king of the monkeys who was hastening for the fight taking on his hand a mountain with serpents inside.

33. With their beautiful movements, slow with intoxication, the pitiless and fearless monkeys approached (the enemies) and with trees having coral-like sprouts, struck hard the mountain-like elephants (of the enemies).

34. That army (of the Rākṣasas), fierce in battle, red with the flow of blood and resplendent with its own effulgence, moved on, — that army which by its magic warfare vanquished in battle (the demon King) Maya[2], who was free from the disease of fear.

35. Then, when one of the Rākṣasas was struck down by the (monkey) enemies with mountains full of snakes inside, all his flesh along with skin was torn and cast away and he expired, his open skeleton stood there.

36. Uprooting a banyan tree, a vertitable settlement of birds, and reaching with its branches the cloud-canopy, one (monkey) released it in the battle striking terror in the (enemy) army and making the Quarters resound with the noises of the tree.

1. तु–अरम्=Quickly. लघुक्षिप्रमरम् (Amara).

2. This presupposes a conflict between the Dānavas and Rākṣasas before Maya gave his daughter in marriage to Rāvaṇa.

37. Another successful warrior uprooted forcibly with his arms that had conquered kings, a hill with resounding stream and flinging it, smashed the mace and the body of one of the enemies and that wounded enemy fell on the ground from the side of the chariot.

38. Another, torn all around by the missiles falling from the enemy and killed lay on the ground chill with blood, bitten to pieces by the dog with its shining teeth and by the screeching birds.

39. Similarly another enemy in that battle, struck forcibly at his saffron-red neck by the enemy bearing a tree, fell on the ground in blood, confounded and deformed in his eyes.

40. Another, after felling many with his shining sword, himself fell at the hands of his fatal enemy, struck by a hill sheltering serpents and elephants in its bowers, with his skull breaking.

41. Another who had been lauded in the battle with heroic songs, lay on the ground spreading his two arms effulgent like the Sun and well-protected by their own strength (or by his own armies), having been killed by his opponent who had been victorious over the enemy.

42. Beaten thus and red with the attractive mass of the colour of the blood which was frothing and coming out with the fat, the army of the enemy of the Gods (Rāvaṇa) ran into the screaming city, with their steps imperilled with faltering on even surface too.

43. Having heard that his whole army had thus taken fright and had been routed, the proud effulgent Lord of Laṅkā, his face blazing in anger asked his son (Indrajit), the great archer, who emitted a terrible (peal of) laughter, to tear and kill in battle the Prince (Rāma) whose wife (Sītā) he had brought over.

CANTO XVIII

1. Indrajit, about to start for the battle, circumambulated the King (Rāvaṇa), seen all around and with affection with the row of eyes of the same (Rāvaṇa).

2. Then saluting with devotion, Maya (his grandfather) and finding the time appropriate, Indrajit went ahead dragging his army bespangled with banners.

3. Resounding with fully-drawn bows, shining more as it were by reason of the smell of blood, and discharging series of terrible arrows, they fought.

4. The battle was such that one could hardly look upon it, with its fighters bathed in the waters of blood released from the vessel-mouths of the elephant corps smashed by mountains[1].

5. The fire issuing out of the sheath of the tusk of the elephant struck by the stone, flashed forth and spread, dispelling the darkness created by the dust.

6. That (saḥ) enemy of Heaven (sura-āsa-ariḥ) (Indrajit), having a strong sword (sāra-asiḥ), of firm and beautiful thighs and chest (uru-su-ūru-uraḥ), having a taste for (discharging) fast showers of arrows (sa-ara-āsāra-asusū-rasaḥ) and making a noise with the firm swan-like voice (sa-sāra-sārasa-ārāsaḥ), advanced (sasāra).

7. Having come, Rāvaṇa's son bound with serpent nooses, the two heroes of Raghu's line (Rāma and Lakṣmaṇa), rendered visible by the subsiding of the dust sprinkled over with blood.

8. Then with disdain towards (the enemy) who had been bound, he (Indrajit) entered his city with a gait, the sportful and leisurely steps of which surpassed those of the elephant.

---

1. hurled by the monkeys.

9. The two princes (Rāma and Lakṣmaṇa), bearing minds afflicted hundred-fold, were seen by Sītā; but the hundred-fold splendour (of the brothers) due to the impossibility of mortal suffering (in them) was not seen by her who was beside herself (in grief).

10. That Rāma, seated with his brother, said this with a smile to the king of birds (Garuḍa) shining with splendour, who had come at the very moment he was thought of.

11............

12. The monkey-chiefs, struck with wonder at the serpents swallowed by Garuḍa, who had been addressed thus (by Rāma), shouted, the ears of (those in) the army splitting with the noises with which they struck their bodies with their arms.

13............

14. Then Kumbhakarṇa was beat on the chest and awakened with difficulty by the demons who were blown away by the wind of the severe snoring (krātha?) done by Kumbhakarṇa himself.

15. Then with the army together with its leaders (sa-inayā-senayā) and accompanied by Vibhīṣaṇa (sa-asuraḥ), the commander of the (monkey) forces (Nīla), a veritable God by virtue of his strength (sahasā suraḥ) stood at the exterior (entrance), awaiting Kumbhakarṇa.

16. That army of excellent arrows stood very near (the enemy), being free from all fear. The sorrow of the lady (Sītā) also went down; with her lord nearby (sa-inā), that virtuous lady was rid of all fear.

17. & 18. Looking at the battle over the summit of the mountainous parapet (of the city) in front of him, even as he was seated with his face distorted with anger, with the marrow of the flesh which he had taken, swallowed and masticated, flowing (about him), scattering mountains (or trees),

and demolishing towers with the impact of his feet, (Kumbhakarṇa) advanced forward with force.

19. Leaving the corners of the mouth of Kumbhakarṇa, who was grinding the heads of monkeys with a cracking sound, the blood drenched his chest.

20. Aṅgada with courage addressed the huge army of his father, such as survived those that were torn and pounded by the fall of his (Kumbhakarṇa's) trident, and had fled in the (different) directions.

21. Having overcome all distress (atiyāta-ārtiḥ) by its excel-
22. lent glory (su-bhāsā) and resplendent (bhāsurā), that (army of the enemies— 'śātravī senā' in the next verse)[1], proud (darpa-bhāvitā), strong (sārā), firm (dhīrā), endowed with glory and auspiciousness (sa-śobhā-ayā) and with enthusiasm, is marching on the battle-field; that enemy-army with Kumbhakarṇa at the head, desires to cut off the rear (tails) of you who have turned away from the battle.

23. O! you Hanumān, don't you become afflicted and go away. Fight without fear. For, fearless, towards those who fall back (skanna-a-dara), this (enemy) pitilessly and with force hits you.

24. When Suṣeṇa, the son of Dhanvantarin turns away from battle, who will bring back that frightened Suṣeṇa to his senses? (Or, who will have a taste for handling the missiles. āsa=astra).

25. Tell me, why do you, this capable person, not kill with your arm having a rock, this Rākṣasa, the wicked leader of the sinful enemy? What a wonder!'

26. Always intent on battle owing to his pride, that Kumbha-

1. The verse itself might contain a word expressive of the army. But it is not clear. Taking suggestion from a similar verbal effect employed in Māgha (XIX. 3), we may, however, suggest that the expression sārādhīrā means the army with advancing chariots.

karṇa full of power, harasses very much (even) you, my father (tatam), who has won the Gods with his prowess.

27. When your arms droop in fear, which other lion is there to protect the monkeys from being swallowed by the teeth of the Rākṣasa-crocodile.

28. ....

29. Afraid of the Rākṣasa, you fall away from prosperity. May you retain by your victory, that same impenetrable mountain-kingdom of yours.

30. ....

31. Death is very likely even in one's house and for one there may be welfare even on the field of battle; for which reason it is not proper for you to leave your master in the battle-field, out of fear.

32. ....

33. When the shafts of the enemy are freely falling on Rāma, is Lakṣmaṇa looking forward to another occasion for (the display of) his prowess ?

34, 35. ....

36. O ! King of the monkeys, unimpaired in your prowess, you do not look well in abandoning, with your army, the battle which is the ground of pure fame.

37. Rāma (on the other hand), endowed with polity and proper behaviour, free from trouble and fatigue, strong with his formidable splendour and incomparable, does not go away from the battle.

38. You do the fighting here in the battle, terrible with the clash of numberless arms; of that fighting (the fruit) is another world in the beautiful heaven (su-khe), which is all unalloyed bliss (?) (sarva-sminna-sukhe).

39. ....

40. Of you, who abandon, out of fear, at the field of battle that king (Rāma), superior in qualities, will not the fame, beautiful like the white cloud, suffer ?

41, 42. ....

43. Extensive and difficult to look at, owing to the abundance of the light from the flash of swords, blocking the ears by the noises of the hitting of resounding arrows;

44. ....

45. Our army has thus been put to distress in the battle by the weapons of the enemies surpassing the Sun in their lustre.

46. ....

47. Hearing those words (of Aṅgada) the monkeys returned from the quarters; in the matter of making one give up a wrong path, the taunt of the good one is indeed a sharp goad.

48. ....

49. Naḷa and Nīla, desirous of battle, approached Kumbhakarṇa who was creating a continuous shower of trees and hill-tops.

50. ....

51. When (Naḷa), the son of the Fire-God had been struck down and Naḷa had fallen, the Rākṣasas went forward to devour the army of the enemy.

52. ....

53. Returning then, that Sugrīva who had fainted as a result of the hit given by Kumbhakarṇa and was being carried away (by the latter), became angry and biting with his teeth severed the nose (of the latter).

54. Of that Kumbhakarṇa, who in anger, unable to disting-

uish between his own and those of the enemy, was devouring the army (śastra-mālinīm), the mountains of the limbs fell as a result of the striking of the arms of Rāma.

55. The rear (of the army) devoid of good manoeuvre and with the valour of the nearby enemies gone down, was blockaded by elephants which were like clouds, by reason of their heights and were full of bees busy taking their ichor.

56. ....

57. Rāma entered the battle-field full of arrows, enemies and monkeys and having the monkey Kumuda hit by arrow-points, even as the sylvan animal called rāma would enter in summer the lake having the śarāri birds, frogs and lilies pressed by the mouths of bees.

58. Some of the elephants of the enemy, which had rendered futile his magical missiles and other means, were deprived by him of one of their tusks and of their commanders (which had rendered futile incantations and other means of control and being deprived by him of one of the tusks were made into Gaṇeśas, i.e. ekadanta-vināyakas).

59. Some of the elephants which had a wealth of pearls, were adorned with white tusks and were dark in colour, were destroyed by him even as clouds, which had delivered themselves of their showers (mukta-āsārāḥ), adorned with white birds and were dark in colour, by autumn.

60. Hit by the forceful arrows of Rāma and driven far away, the elephants deprived of their ruttishness, wandered with their shattered backs (bones), (even as the low caste-Mātanga tribes, driven far away, become nomadic with their scattered families).

61. That mountain (Trikūṭa) having the Rākṣasa army as the trees and whose inanimate objects had been shattered by the arrows of Rāma (or, which had been hit by Rāma's arrows and rendered insensate or motionless),

became intolerable for the enemy army (i.e. Rāma's army). Mountain Trikūṭa, though the sea water (at its feet) had been thrown (far away by the arrow of (Paraśu) Rāma, did not become the Sahya mountain).

62. When the leaders of the monkey divisions girding up their
& loins with their tails and armed with trees, were standing,
63. having struck down Prahasta, Śuka, Dhūmrākṣa, Prajaṅgha, Narāntaka, Devāntaka, Vidyujjihva, Mahāpārśva, Makarākṣa, and Mahodara;

64. Having heard of the loss of Indrajit, the capable Rāvaṇa, then sallied forth, charging heaven and earth with the uproar raised by his army.

65. Then took place, Rāvaṇa's battle, harassing Lakṣmaṇa and the expanse of all the quarters being pervaded by the twang of bows and cries of victory.

66. When his bow was cut by the arrow of Lakṣmaṇa, the enraged enemy of terrible power, took up his missile named Śakti for killing the enemy (Lakṣmaṇa).

67. Then in that battle in which elephants were falling, Rāvaṇa who surpassed a great elephant in his weight, struck in anger his arms which caused terror among the enemies in the army.

68. Rāvaṇa, who put an end to the happiness of the vānaras and human beings (vānara-ka-antakārī); (naraka-antakārī), fought (raṇam cakre), shouting in the midst of his army (cakre raṇan); (similarly) Rāma, the Lord who destroyed the Narakāsura (narakāntakārī) and delighter of the monkeys (vānara-kāntakārī) fought, raising a war-cry in the midst of his army. (Or, urged his army forward raising a war-cry- raṇan, cakra-īraṇam cakre.)

69. In that battle (yuddhe), which was to be won with weapons of war (yuddh-heti-jeye), that Rāvaṇa (sa) proceeded swiftly (tarasā) against the enemy (param) (Lakṣmaṇa), who was making a war-cry and who was foremost with exceeding and invincible strength (ati-jeyetara-sāra-

santam) with the missile of Śakti, which was aimed with force and which gave rise to severe distress that deprived one who was struck by it, of his power (āhata-śakti-haītyā).

70. Seeing Lakṣmaṇa struck down and laid on the ground, looking verily like a second Sun that had set, Rāvaṇa asked his own army of multi-coloured armours to get into the forces of the prince (Rāma), which had been rendered extremely weak (su-abalam).

71. ....

72. No monkey (chief) was able in that battle to safeguard his army whose monkeys had flung away their weapons in the form of trees and rocks, whose leading ones had fled, with their tremulous eyes cast on all sides and distressed the army which, devoid of strength, was becoming a prey to the enemy of the gods (Rāvaṇa).

73. Becoming scarlet in the limbs (of the monkeys) by the flow of blood, and with the effort (of the monkeys) broken by Rāvaṇa, with their eyes reeling on their prowess being shattered and surpassing the early action of Sugrīva by reason of the fear (i.e. running in different quarters as Sugrīva did of yore when Vāli chased him), the army (of the monkeys) which was (almost) routed, went away somewhere, leaving the desire for battle.

74. Then Rāma stopped by force on the way with his resounding arrow whose bottom was hid within his palm (drawing the bow string), in that battle in which Sugrīva was afraid of the fearless Rāvaṇa, his army of monkeys bearing faces ruddy like ruby-dust, and fierce with bodies soaring high into heaven, with terrible faces and teeth and long nails.

CANTO XIX

1. Then quickly struck on the way by (the demon) Kālanemi, who resembled verily an iron discus, Hanumān somehow overpowered him and returned, bearing the summit of the mountain (of herbs).

2. The doctor monkey (Suṣeṇa) who was lauded and was full of joy, having obtained from the slopes of that mountain the great herb, removed then the fatigue of Lakṣmaṇa and made him open his eyes in a moment.

3. Then Indra's charioteer brought to the prince (Rāma) the chariot (of Indra) whose flag was fluttering in the breeze of the celestial Ganges and in between whose spokes (in the wheels) slices of clouds were sticking.

4. With his left hand holding the hand of Indra's charioteer and with his bow in the other hand, that Rāma comparable to Indra slowly mounted the chariot held before him.

5. Desirous of seeing the battle the multitude of Gods came in front of it, angrily setting aside the clouds; and the armies (of Rāma and Rāvaṇa) refraining from striking mutually stood with their eyes fixed on Rama and Rāvaṇa.

6. (Rāma) the destroyer of enemies mounted on the chariot, and playfully drawing an arrow out of the quiver approached in battle, that great warrior, the enemy of Indra who was also standing with his bow united with arrow.

7. 'Either you discharge the arrow first or take (mine)'— after these words (of Rāma), the arrows of Indra's enemy fell in the direction of Rāma, tearing his ears with their terrific noise.

8. Having hit the Prime Being in the guise of Rāma, and swept as if by that irresistible sin, the arrows of Rāvaṇa

took a downward course (attained a lower animal birth) and went in a moment to the Nether Worlds.

9. The ten-headed Rāvaṇa with his golden ornaments flashing like lightning, laughing without interruption with all his ten faces, looking verily like the deluge-cloud, spread the inter-space of the firmament with his great arrows, as if by showers of rain.

10. Thereupon that wooded area (of the battle-field) with its trees and herbs broken and bent by the gale-like (shower of) arrows, appeared like a wood on the bank (its trees) uprooted, bent and breaking by the impact of a great river.

11. The prince (Rāma), constructed a long causeway for the victory over the enemy, not only in the waters of the sea but along the path of the Sun too, with the close spread of his arrows.

12...... ......

13. The bow-string of Rāvaṇa continuously vibrating owing to the frequency of the incessant (action of) drawing and releasing, protected the demon's chest from the arrow of (Rāma), the foremost of men, which was falling with a heavy noise.

14. In the imperceptible speed of the arrows of the royal archer (Rāma), the sequence, namely the release of the arrow first and the wounding of the enemy's body later, could be known (only) by the (process of) inference.

15. 'Has the heavenly stream (Ganges) taken the form of a continuous flow of arrows and is falling with noise; or has a bridge been thrown across the path of the Sun for the coming over of the Goddess of Victory ?'

16. 'Emitting harsh sounds and hiding the rays of the Sun with their multitude, was it to strike (at the Sun) themselves, that the arrows of his (Sun's) enemy (Ravaṇa) leave his bow and soar into the sky ?'

17. 'Has a big mass of net woven with terrible arrows, obstructing the spread of the Sun's light, been cast in the sky to capture the stag lying in the moon ?'

18. 'Have the clouds converted their showers into the form of arrows and are pouring down on all sides'—Thus in that great battle the army (of Rāvaṇa), whose strength had gone down, was in great delusion for a moment.

19. The wide canopy of arrows of the two, supported by the pillars of their (Rāma and Rāvaṇa) big arms, accommodating inside all the warriors without exception and preventing the rays of the Sun, enveloped the most part of the sky.

20. Rāma severed by an arrow, at the collar bone, the arm of the enemy which was throwing arrows continuously. But every time another (fresh one) appeared at the place of the cut and held firm the falling bow.

21. Then Indra's enemy (Rāvaṇa) pierced with his arrow the shining surface of the prince's (Rāma's) forehead, which was cast over with the streak of perspiration and rolling locks of matted hair.

22. Thereupon with that arrow whose feathers shine like gold struck in between his brows, Rāma bore verily the beauty of the form of the odd-eyed Śiva, having the glowing tawny forehead-eye (pupil).

23. Prince (Rāma) slew with his arrows a head of his enemy Rāvaṇa, while yet it was half-way through its utterance of abuse. Frequently uttering the remaining part of that noise (of abuse) another head rose unimpaired.

24. The demon with (newly) risen head saw his own (old) heads with their diadems shattered by the fall of arrows and with blood flowing from the lips cut by the saw of their teeth.

25. Standing on the battle-field strewn with his own felled heads, with the huge arrows of his enemy (Rāma) sticking to them, and fighting, that Rāvaṇa exhibited in the battle his prowess, rare in the human world.

26. With vehemence Rāma and Rāvaṇa carried on that battle in which the car-drums split by the loud noise increased by the velocity of the iron-arrows which was unbearable with the serpents that fell and the Garuḍas that fell upon[1] them and which was looked upon (by the spectators) as being equal only to itself.[2]

27. Then telling prince Rāma of the mortal spot of Rāvaṇa[3] (the enemy of the Gods), Mātali gave him the arrow[4] of wonderful wings sent by Indra for his benefit and which would shatter the armour (of Rāvaṇa).

28. By virtue of being pulled, the swift missile itself in whose excellent wings and head, Wind and Fire[5] were present, reached the base of the ear (of Rāma) as if desiring itself to reveal to Rāma the mortal spot of Rāvaṇa.

29. Struck by Rāma at his life-centre in the heart, with that arrow of the weight of a big mountain and roaring terrifically, the enemy of the Gods (Rāvaṇa) fell with a terrible yell.

30. After tearing the mortal spot of the Rākṣasa king, the arrow of the great Rāma went under-ground, as if having killed the lord of the three worlds and offended him thereby, it desired to go out of sight in fear.

31. Then hit by the arrow, Earth resounding instantaneously shook as if in fear ; a shower of flowers fell on Rāma from

1. Vālmīki says that the arrows of Rāvaṇa took the form of hissing serpents and those of Rāma took the form of Garuḍas and devoured them. Ref. Vālmiki Yuddhakāṇḍa, Chapter 103, Verses 17 to 34.

2. Rāmāyaṇa : रामरावणयोर्युद्धं रामरावणयोरिव ॥

3. Mātali telling Rāma of Rāvaṇa's marma—this is not according to the Southern recension of Vālmīki's Rāmāyaṇa. But Gorresio's edition (Eastern version) refers to this. See p. 490, Canto 92, Verses 41 & 42 of that Edn.

4. According to both versions of Vālmiki's Rāmāyaṇa, Mātali is not giving the Brahmāstra to Rāma. It was from Agastya that Rāma had already received it. Vide Chapter on 'Kumāradāsa and Vālmiki'.

5. विचित्र पत्र Compare the elaborate description of the Brahmāstra in Vālmiki's Rāmāyaṇa where wind itself is said to be established in its wings. यस्य वाजेषु पवनः etc.

heaven looking verily like the fame of the enemy (Rāvaṇa) tha thad come back (from that place).

32. Maṇḍodarī[1] proceeded to the battle-field though her girdle fell at her feet and held her, as if saying: Your lord is dead; you have yourself seen the condition of those destroyed by our enemy.'

33. Maṇḍodarī noisily beat, with both her palms, her breast which did not go atwain even when Rāvaṇa (her lord) had come to grief, out of either grief (at the death of her husband) or anger (at her not following suit).

34. In a moment Rāvaṇa got that long-desired clasp of the soft arms of his queen, which had been hard to obtain even when attempted due to the quarrel caused by the abduction of Sītā.

35. 'Burning in her heart with the fire of the loss of her lord, she might go to pieces'—fearing thus her two eyes drenched continuously with the water of tears that Maṇḍodarī who was suffering in the grief.

36. Streaming with tears the loving Maṇḍodarī softly removed the accumulated dust of the ground covering the arrow-wounds of her beloved lord, her hands trembling out of fear of causing pain, though (in fact) (the body) was without life.

37. Frequently kissed and fondled in the past by her lover, the eyes of Maṇḍodarī, offered water-libation with the tears flowing from the end of the eye-lids to that Rāvaṇa who had been killed.

38. That very lip to which, most enjoyable among the features of the beloved's face, that lover (Rāvaṇa) was previously attached, trembled now in anguish, being parched with the grief of that calamity.

1. Expression in the text सुता नरेन्द्रस्य may be amended into सुता नरेन्द्रस्य or the word नरेन्द्र is to be taken generally as meaning 'king' and referring to Maya.

39. With the tears flowing from her eyes, Maṇḍodarī appeared as if to give a funeral bath, at the attainment of heaven by Rāvaṇa, to those (two) friends of his, namely her breasts resembling golden pots.

40. With grief, with her face devoid of lustre and tormented, the poor Maṇḍodarī, casting her pathetic eyes at the quarter(s), began to weep thus:

41. These limbs of the beloved lord moving though only because of being pulled by the wolves desiring flesh, rouse in me the joy of the hope (of his being alive), (and make me take them in my hands) but are thrown down again on my realising the fact (that they are lifeless).

42. Among the women of that lord of three worlds was there not even one who was endowed with those characteristics of impeccable fortune, thanks to which the celebrity of unwidowed life would have endured for long even in me devoid of such fortune ?

43. This much of subjugation is enough to place a man of self-respect at the head of the good-minded. O Gods! Save my beloved husband. For, even in a fight the good deprive one of the fame, not of life.

44. O Indra! don't you bear in mind the humiliation which he in his exceeding arrogance inflicted on you in the past; save him who has lost (all) power and has fallen at your feet, from Death's mouth.

45. O Lord (Śiva)! Remember that, for the sake of your sacrificial propitiation the resplendent lotus-faces of (Rāvaṇa) the lord of the three worlds, with their quivering petals of lips and tremulous bees of eyes were cut (by him) with the sword.

46. O Kubera! for the sake of wealth (even) a wise man picks up a quarrel with his own kith and kin and succeeds. (But) when humiliation for the family comes from a stranger, he makes common cause with his kinsman.

47. O Brahman (the Four-headed), being the grandfather

of this Rāvaṇa, who is skilled in propitiating elders, you do not see the crests of this Rāvaṇa of honour being scattered like beads on the earth by (pecking) birds."

48. When Gods showed no response to those words of very pathetic wail, the people then exclaimed that as there was no means of proof of their existence, the Gods are mere words.

49. The continuous tears from Maṇḍodarī's eyes, like a friend who knows what was to be done on that occassion, wiped off the charms of the decoration of paint and design on the pale cheeks and red lips.

50. When those that knew the procedure were doing with sacred fire, the crematory rites of that enemy of the Gods (Rāvaṇa), the kith and kin took Maṇḍodarī and led her away by force to the water-side for bath.

51. "These two different last rites namely burning in fire and immersion in the tank—is this proper for us two who have never been of different ways ? I shall quickly take to your (last fate, i.e. fire)"—Thus did Maṇḍodarī raise the cry.

52. When bending by reason of the nerves being caught by the flames, the hands of that proud Rāvaṇa were turning into clenched fists, fire (of the funeral pyre) got frightened very much and did not blaze forth fully, though Wind (the friend of Fire) had already killed (that Rāvaṇa, by rendering him breathless or dead).

53. The most ancient Being, who had become man through his mystic power, entered the enemy's city (Laṅkā), bestowed the kingdom on Vibhīṣaṇa and with the Rākṣasas showing him honour all around and for long, reached the court-hall.

54. The warriors bowed to the moon named Rāma, the repository of accomplishments (digits), accompanied by Lakṣmaṇa (having the dark mark), beneficient to the monkey Kumuda (to the lilies), who had come out from

the mouth of Indra's enemy Rāvaṇa (Rāhu[1]), and who was attended with auspiciousness (held in esteem by Śiva).

55. Sītā impelled by her love, went, surrounded by Trijaṭā and others, to see the destroyer of Rāvaṇa, seated in the palace of that enemy of Indra and resplendent in his victory.

56. Sītā, bearing a body pale and dusty in the plaite of hair, and with streaming tears, made the mind of her lover who looked at it, sad and cheerless.

57. Then, when Rāma (the foe of Rāvaṇa) out of the fear of calumny by the people, had turned his eyes away from Sītā, she spoke pitifully, the following words, faltering but shot with indignation.

58. O you hero, this bee-like eye (of yours) which throws into shade the beautiful form of the blossomed lotus,—what kind of infamy would it incur, if it is cast on me?

59. Why do you not, the self-possessed man that you are, put a stop to these tears of mine caused by not seeing you, flowing for a long time and ceaselessly increasing?

60. Sīta, who had undergone extreme and unsurmountable hardship, who had become very pale, having become subdued by penances, told Rāma who destroyed the outcome of pride and was a veritable death to the unsubdued ones, these words, free from blemish and full of merits and stood (there).

61. Hearing what she said pitifully and with tears, and in a state of extreme and endless sorrow, Rāma raised the fire fed by logs of wood, which was to purify her and to gratify the people, and (therefore) was dear to his beloved (Sītā).

1. It is just possible that as the moon will rise from behind the mountain and the mountains were once punished by Indra, the expression इन्द्रद्विषद् refers to mountain. But it is more natural and appropriate to take that word in the sense of Rāhu.

62. Then, witnessed with tearful eyes by the countless hosts of powerful monkeys, and prompted by her Kṣatriya strength to enter the fire quickly, Sītā, of truthful word, uttered the oath full of feeling.

63. "O Lord Rāma, who has destroyed the strong Rāvaṇa, if I had given quarter in this pure heart of mine, to that ten-headed Rāvaṇa, who was adorned by the celestial damsels angrily abducted by him and whose command knew no frustration, then let this humble self of mine, whose festivities had been cut short by the enemy, (but) and devoid of strength, be burnt up.

64. If that dog of a Rāvaṇa (Indra's enemy) did not sport with me even in a dream, let me not be burnt now even slightly in this big fire"—Thus did that chaste woman utter forth most pitifully and with profusely falling tears, and bound by that act of truth, Fire immediately withdrew its fierce heat.

CANTO XX

1. Then accompanied by Vibhīṣaṇa and along with Lakṣmaṇa and the monkey-chiefs, Rāma together with his wife mounted the Puṣpaka with its shining golden sides and desiring to proceed to his own city, flew up in the sky.

2. Looked at by the Rākṣasas with eyes distorted as a result of the rays escaping through the palms held on their forehead to screen the Sun, the aerial vehicle entered the skies resembling the body of the bee.

3 Himself loosening with his own hands the matted plait of her hair resembling the streak of smoke from the fire of long exile, and with tears in his eyes, Rāma embraced his beloved and spoke to her thus in private.

4. "When I think within myself that a gem of a woman like you is not obtained by one who has not done meritorious acts, I feel great self-esteem flashing in me at every step.

5. My beloved! two persons proud of the fortune of having a devoted wife abide in the two worlds,—I, the servant of yours on the Earth and the great sage, the husband of Arundhatī in the Heavens.

6. Divine lady! the demon was deprived of his power by the effulgence of your chastity and (then) was he killed; otherwise how could an arrow sent by a mere man prove effective on that victor of the three worlds.

7. Take your seat on this lap of mine; cling to my neck with your arm and often cast your eyes, with their lashes tremulous in the wind, at the quarters.

8. The Southern Quarter with her big captivating breasts (cloud) and scorching the eyes with her submarine fire; possessing like a Kinnara damsel both pleasant and unpleasant characteristics, is being guarded by Yama (by one with a stern sceptre).

9. Look as the Puṣpaka is speeding across the sky, this city of the Rākṣasas (Laṅkā) becomes smaller and smaller as if by the scorching sorrow of your separation.

10. The sea (Bay of Bengal) and the ocean (Indian Ocean)[1] though separated by the waves (of the two) rising against each other, appear to be unified. Gradually and all around, with her hills and woods the (island of) Laṅkā appears to get submerged in the sea.

11. This mountain of wide summits and possessed of peaks appears like an ant-hill wherefrom the streams flowing all around shine forth like winding serpents.

12. With the slopes (girdles) beautiful with gems, with dark tamāla groves (with a face possessed of shining dark tresses), this row of mountains resembling heaps of gold delights our heart like a beloved lady.

13. As the Puṣpaka progressively sweeps over the cloud, the orb of the hot-rayed Sun, as if afraid of itself being leapt over, waxes in size covering up the sky all around.

14. These monkeys firmly clinging by feet at the axle and hanging merrily with their bodies in the sky, touch the lightning-rings in the wall-like clouds, that come nearby.

15. This aerial vehicle, with its string of ringing golden bells, this elephant of the quarter curiously looks at, lifting his trunk in front of his tusk and holding its ears motionless.

16. This cloud which has been heated by the Sun nearby and which bears the decoration of the light (colours due to refraction) of the Sun, and which drips water, (our) aerial vehicle hits against and (getting into its) inside revolves and makes noise.

1. It is just possible that by Ratnālaya is meant also Ratnadīvpa which is a name of Ceylon; the land of Ceylon and the sea become one when looked at from that height, the only demarcation between the land and the water being the white streak of breakers.

17. This sea, though ever full of manifold gems, yet having only an ornament of palmyras in its vicinity, drags the Goddess of Wealth born of the gem-casket of Varuṇa.[1]

18. They say, when, in the sacrifice of Sagara of prowess equal to Lord Hari[2], the (sacrificial) horse was carried away, this ocean was dug by the heroic arms of Sagara's sons and deepened very much.

19. This is the causeway of rocks thrown across for your sake, which shines like the arm of Earth stretched, out of curiosity to measure the length of the sea.

20. That mass of fresh foam which has broken upon the face and body of the sea-elephant which has risen (out of the water) shines like white ash in bright stripes.

21. With its waves breaking on the coral reeds shining like the lustre of fire, the sea appears to carry as it were a second submarine fire which is however totally averse to reducing the waters.

22. The sea adorned with multitude of conches and abode of coral and gems (appears to) bear the extensive wounds with protruding bones caused by the rubbing of the edges of the revolving Mandara mountain.

23. The region of the Western Quarter adorned with the Lord of Waters (Ka-pāla, i.e. Varuṇa) distinguished by his serpent nooses (or, adorned with Varuṇa distinguished by his serpent nooses and shining with the appearance of the digit of the fresh moon), shining forth (in his hands) as he just sips the Soma juice, attains similarity with the form of Śiva which is decked with skull, marked with noose-like serpents and displays the digit of the wonderful moon.

1. The underlying imagery of the poet is that of the sea conceived as a miser who despite his riches, puts on a mean appearance and goes after further riches. *Jāla-bhūṣaṇa* refers to a scroll of palmyra-leaf thrust into the earlobe as an ornament.

2. If however the reading is हरितुल्यतेजसा the verse would then refer to the person responsible for the loss of the horse, namely sage Kapila considered to be a manifestation of Lord Hari.

24. This yonder range of mountain devoid of slopes, with the clouds rolling on its lap, with the birds falling on it and with the heavens very near to it (appear) like a very old lady devoid of girdle, with breasts dangling at her lap, teeth fallen and very near the other world.

25. Sweeping the skies, dark in its neighbourhood, with the moon above its peak and beautiful with those parts surrounded by Sun and moon-stones, this mountain Devasaha[1] bears the beauty of Śiva who has discarded his garments, bears the blue colour in the neck, has the moon attached to his head and is charming in one part of his body pervaded by his beloved (Pārvatī).

26. These men moving on the road on the surface of the Earth and very tiny in appearance owing to the great distance, look with their white dress, verily like rows of worms with particles of food in their mouths.

27. This great mountain growing extensively and forcibly closing up the Quarters, was kicked by the foot of Agastya and speedily deprived of its pride and rendered puny.

28. Always delighting those that come to it, with beautiful lotus-ponds in its lower regions, with numberless elephants (snakes) and Asana trees and bearing gold within its womb, this mountain becomes verily Lord Viṣṇu Himself, the Prime Creator, having the Nandaka sword, with his feet touched by the palms of the beautiful Lakṣmī and betaking to the serpent-seat of Ādiśeṣa.

29. ....

30. With flashing golden hue, with stars (monkey queen Tārā) approaching it, attended by hoards of monkeys and kissed on his high head by the Sun, this Mandara mountain appears like Sugrīva.

1. MT. reads गिरिर्देवसहः and a mountain named Devasaha is also known from Suśruta. But nothing more is known about this mountain from other sources.

31. Surrounded on all sides by lakes of excellent water, adorned with the moon (or swans) nearby, this mountain which has swept the skies (wears the yellow garment) resembles the form of Viṣṇu, surrounded on all sides by excellent Apsara damsels and adorned by the king of birds (Garuḍa) nearby.

32. My beloved! do you remember, here by the side of the Godāvarī in the night with the rays of the moon playing on us, in the midst of our sport, talking pleasant, we roamed on the river-bank in the neighbourhood of the sands.

33. This current of water of the river shines forth prominently in between the sea and the Vindhyā mountain as if it is the arm stretched by the sea to hold the Earth by her head namely the mountain.

34. Perfumed[1] by heaps of manifold flowers and with its Mānasa lake disturbed and tremulous with snakes (with her fickle heart excited by amorous men), this Northern Quarter is resorted to (enjoyed) by the ardent (lustful) Kubera (the bounteous one) like a courtezan.

35. With its lions (monkeys) having their fore-feet stamped on the ground flowing with the blood of elephants (or according to the other reading, moving about in the ground which gives way under the stampeed of the elephants of the Matanga forests)[2] and adorned with the gems found in its table-lands (adorned with the gems of brothers), this Himālaya appears to follow me by its qualities.

36. This Himālaya with its peaks laden with minerals (with heaps of bones) and which is the recipient of the affectionate enjoyment of Śiva, which bears all the blessed fortunes, the detached men of vows (votaries of the Śaivite Mahāvrata path) resort to for the merit of obtaining success in their penance as if it is the crematorium itself.

1. The perfume of manifold flowers is mentioned with reference to Kubera and the North, because of the vicinity of the Gandhamādana.

2. This epithet is to be understood on the basis of the monkeys being natives of the neighbourhood of Matanga forest, where, as Vālmiki describes, elephants were in profusion.

37. Struck hard on the chest of its slopes by the two seas with the energetic arms of their waves, this mountain from whose big cave mineral flow is oozing out appears as if it is vomitting blood out of its mouth.

38. Here the forest fire that had arisen from the Sūryakānta stone on its contact with the rays of the Sun and had spread, the moon puts down in the nights with the streaming fluid flowing from the moon-stone.

39. The mass of nocturnal darkness, black like collyrium getting hidden by reason of this mountain which touches the Heavens, wanders about as if afraid of the Sun of terrible lustre.

40. Even after the forest fire had been put down all around by the fall of snow that had set in, in the night, the deer with their eyes on the light of the (incandescent) herbs do not give up their fright.

41. To the daughter of this mountain who was doing penance on a peak of his, the Sun nearby displayed the soft glow of the moon, the core of his orb having been rendered dark by the thick (black) colour of her eyes.[1]

42. This slope of the Himālayas with the city of Alakā bedecked with the ardent favours of its lord Kubera, and with clouds hanging and gliding over the cave-mouths bears the beautiful appearance of Pārvatī herself, whose tresses have been decked with ardent graciousness by her lord Śiva, and whose breasts drip, being attached to the mouth of her son Guha.

43. This cave which is red with the ooze of mineral looks like the bloody depth of ulcerous wound caused by the thunderbolt of Indra on the side of the mountain, whose wings had been chopped off.

1. When as part of her penance, she started at the Sun (see Kumārasambhava, V. 20). While it is natural to speak of the dark hue of the eye with reference to its pupil, the expression may also be taken to mean brightness of Pārvatī's eyes which by outshining that of the Sun itself, may be described as throwing the Sun itself into darkness.

44. This torrent which laughs at the moon (sparkles like moon-light) and whose waters are scattered on the crystal rocks, is, though not visible, yet known by the terrible echoes of its noise caused by the caves.

45. Looking frequently like efflorescence on the tops of trees, for a time out of sight underneath the dark sides of the mountain and flashing white over crystal surfaces, this cloud is being tossed about by the wind.

46. This high cliff full of mineral being abandoned by the white clouds (hovering about it) shines like a heap of fire with its light resplendent when, by reason of the wind, the ash around it is blown away.

47 These Kinnaras who, their soles being scorched by the heat of the upward rays of the Sun, fall from the peak of this mountain (but) stand on the side of the water-laden cloud.

48. Look at this slope of the Kailāsa mountain, white like a piece of lotus-stalk, which, as the wind is dragging the cloud along the side of it, appears to release its slough.

49. Why does that moon bear the stag[1] whose head is always in touch with his (moon's) rays ? (The reason is :) This mountain itself (Himalaya) keeps white by the particles of the snowy rays of the moon which fall by the rubbing of the horn of that stag..

50. In this mountain the forest-dwellers learn of the sports of the women of the Gods and Demi-gods, that had taken place on the slabs under cover of the bower of creepers, through the lines caused by the rubbing (against the ground) of (their) circular girdles.

51. The herd of does, though it approached the sprout to eat it, gives it up as it were, suspecting on second thoughts (that this sprout) to which a dark hue had been imparted by the shine of their own eyes, had become rotten.

1. The reading कुरङ्गः in nominative in one ms. does not fit in.

52. Habitations of hunter-tribes do fill the foot of this mountain of celebrated sages even as indeclinables, vi, pra, hi, na (or which are negligible) do appear as line-fillers in the composition full of meaning, written by those of clear intellect.

53. Praising thus the mountain which was like the sea itself, difficult to cross over, with serpents at the mouths of holes (in its depths), surrounded by silvan beauty characterised by shooting sprouts (surrounded by wealth of water, with growth of coral reefs) prince Rāma descended upon Earth.

54. Great sages along with princes and citizens bearing faces eloquent with the praise of Rāma, received that son of King Daśaratha whom the fortune (of kingship) had then approached and set about the arrangements for the coronation.

55. Surrounded by Bharata, Lakṣmaṇa and Śatrughna, and making enquiries with folded arms and the obedience due to elders, the heroic Rāma immediately relieved the heart of Bharata's mother of the poignant shame that had come over her.

56. The (coronation) water pouring continuously from the pitchers in the hands of the two brothers, on the head of Rāma, the enemy of the king of the Rākṣasas, underneath the white parasol, washed off the stain (calumny) of Bharata's mother.

57. Having seen that great event of the acceptance of kingship (by Rāma) which concluded with festivities, having approached and rendered obeisance to Rāma who was accompanied by his wife and the noble men of his court, the chief of the monkeys (Sugrīva) freely assuming a huge size, verily like a mountain, went to his own mountain whose sides were highly honoured by the sports and enjoyments of the Siddhas.

58. That Rāma who protects hermitages and sacrifices and is

a knower of polity, made his queen that truthful Sītā who was attached to that good conduct which practised the quality of faithfulness, who overcame the anger of even the demons who were addicted to blood and flesh (marrow) and who was always clad in that unsoiled pair of garments called bashfulness and purity.

59. Throwing off the ocean of the flow of tears and saluting Rāma who was with his beloved and who was the death of those who endangered the established institutions of Varṇa (Varṇa-dharma), the king of the Rākṣasas (Vibhīṣaṇa) sunk in grief, rubbing[1] his body with that of Rāma) and told by Rāma consolingly 'don't you give us this torment' and given leave, left.

60. Having invested with rulership his brothers, who were devoid of jealousy, delusion, elation, haughtiness or attachment to wealth, having established his dependents in great prosperity, that Rāma, taking his stand in that compassion which did good to others and conduced to his own welfare, protected the whole Earth, himself equal to that earth in firmness.

61. Always devoted to virtues possessed of the beauty of sense-control, unassociated with any fear, (there was) Mānita a man of learning and intelligence who was the poet's father, a fighter, of sound policy, in the rear guard of Kumāramaṇi, King of Laṅkā, who engaging himself at the head of the battle flashing with arms gave up his heart (life) but entered the hearts of all noble men.

62. This incomparable and highly powerful Megha was this poet's maternal uncle, Megha who defeated the enemy people and honoured Mānita, he who striking all around himself made his complete destruction of the enemies shine all around and who was looked upon with stupefaction of fear by the enemy-army whose leader also was in fright.

1. The concluding part of line 3 having the Yamaka reads शोकसन्नः कसन्नः। The last word is split as kasan—naḥ which is again being taken as kasan meaning rubbing, i.e. closely embracing ; some authorities give the form kasa for kaṣa—vide Śabdakalpadruma.

63. Another brother of his mother was Agrabodhi son of the good king, the one refuge of the people subjected to humiliations and calamities, resembling in personality the exceedingly beautiful Jayanta who is gladdening the heaven, he who waged wars productive of fame pure like the moon and one whose command shone on the heads of (honoured by) the people.

64. Taking this (poet) in that very state when he had just been born, and overcoming the virulence of his ailments while yet he was being suckled and his father had been killed by the enemies, those two (uncles) continuously affectionate and devoid of intoxication tended him (poet) as if he was their own son; and it was with their help that the poet composed the poem of great meaning having for its subject-matter the glory of (the Lord) the enemy of demons.

APPENDIX

EXTRA VERSES IN 'L' AND 'A'

We have already stated in the Introduction (pp. 11-14) about the extra verses that are to be found in the London Manuscript and the Adyar Library Transcript. Here we shall consider in detail the nature of these extra verses and the claims if they have any, to be included as genuine verses of the author.

In canto I, we have only one extra verse which appears after the 72nd verse in the text. This appears in the description of the forest into which Daśaratha goes for hunting; it describes the lessons held by the sages of the forest and the nearby parrots repeating the discussions. It will be found on an examination of the verses before and after this, that this verse is a clear insertion by a later hand. In verse 70 the king starts for the hunt, and in 71 and 72 the king pursues a prey into the forest. In 73, having entered the dense parts of the forest, the king gets down from the horse and walks; in the next verse the incident of his mistaking the sound of the pitcher being filled with water by the hermit-boy and the consequent tragedy is introduced. Now this extra verse in 'L' and 'A' appears between 72 and 73 and thus is clearly out of place. There is no context even here for description of sylvan scenes to afford a handle for its addition. Further, the hand which interpolated this verse is obviously an inferior one, for the verse in question is a bland imitation of a well-known couplet in the popular *Śaṅkaravijaya*, occurring in the context of the debate between Śaṅkarācārya and Maṇḍanamiśra.

Coming to canto II, the extra verses here go up to six. The first occurs before the penultimate verse in the description of the Lord upon whom the Devas wait. Apart from its own subject-matter which is incongruous, even the connection of the verse with its previous and later ones is difficult. The next set of extra verses (L—20, 21, 22 and 23) occurs at the end of the praise and prayer of the Devas to the Lord. It comprises four verses which are quite in keeping with the context and free from any difficulty of *Anvaya*. While it is not very easy to dismiss them off-hand, their diction and the hackneyed refrain स नो रक्षतु

and the enumeration Keśava, Mādhava and Vāmana according to the familiar mention of the Lord's twelve names, throw doubt on their authenticity. The sixth extra verse in canto II (L—61) is indeed very clever and smacks of the skill common in later cāṭu literature. It is quite in place after verse 50, but the above-mentioned consideration should prevail against its acceptance. In this connection the following verses on the same theme found in the anthologies and *Alaṅkāra*-works may be compared:—

छिन्नेन पतता वह्नौ यन्मुखेन हठात्कृते ।
स्वेति हेति हरेणोक्ते स्वाहासीत्सैष रावणः ॥[1]

निस्त्रिंशप्रतिबिम्बितेन यदुरःकम्पेन वीरव्रत-
प्रौढिस्सेति न चन्द्रहासमधुनोत्कण्ठच्छिदापर्वणि (कर्मणि) ।
जुह्वद्यः स्वशिरांसि शङ्करपुरो हाकारवैरेण न
स्वाहाकारमुदाहरन्न स दशग्रीवो गिरां गोचरः ॥[2]

The extra verse in the London manuscript is an obvious imitation of the first of the above two verses.

Three extra verses are found in the third canto after verses 58, 67 and 72. The first is an addition to the description of the evening and despite its contextual appropriateness, we have to doubt its authenticity because it introduces a different metre, namely *Vaṁśastha*, in the midst of *Upajāti*. The second verse occurs later in the further descriptions of the beginning of the night; the main metre of the original here changes to *Vaṁśastha* but in the extra verse in question, line one is in *Upajāti*. The third verse describing the beloved ones taking wine when the moon was up is quite in place after verse 72 and except for a somewhat elliptic expression at the end, might well pass for an original verse.

In the fourth canto there are as many as 16 extra verses in 'L' and 'A'. The first set of 5 verses occurs after the fourth and is designed to swell the description of the divine gift of *Pāyasa* for the birth of the four sons to Daśaratha at the sacrifice performed by Ṛśyaśṛṅga for the king. The briefer account in MT.

---

1. *Sarasvatikaṇṭhābharaṇa*, Kāvyamālā 95, p. 158
2. *Sūktimuktāvali*, G.O.S. 82, p. 319.

is compact and self-contained and would hardly suffer if we reject all these five verses. The second set of additional verses occurs immediately after the fifth and similarly spins out the theme of the queens conceiving, their confinement and the birth of the princes. Here again the idea is clear that in the original, the important event of the birth of the princes did not deserve to be disposed off so briefly and called for some more elaboration. In fact, the fifth extra verse here (L—15) is a mere re-statement in a more explicit manner of verse 6 in MT. mentioning the actual birth of the four sons. After verse 13, there is an extra verse on the juvenile sport of Rāma which is quite in place and about whose authenticity nothing can be said.

A set of four verses is then found between 14 and 15, which apparently abruptly mention the boys' education and the sudden appearance of Viśvāmitra. These four extra verses elaborating the education of the boys and the delight of the father on seeing them are on a par with the earlier set of extra verses dealing with the birth of the princes. The last extra verse in this canto is found after 65, in the beginning of Viśvāmitra's argument for killing Tāṭakā. The original itself contains quite a number of verses on this subject and the rejection of the extra verse in 'L' would hardly affect the context.

The number of extra verses in canto V mounts to 33. They start after verse 11 when the subject of the sacrifice performed by Viśvāmitra is just introduced. In the version in MT., the sacrifice itself is not described at any length. The extra verses appearing after 11, form one continuous series of 29 verses devoted to the elaborate description of the sacrifice. This set does not require much argument to show that it is due to a desire to enlarge this context. Secondly, it is incongruous to find here mention of the *Yajamāna* and his wife. Thirdly, there is too long a parade of the details of Vedic sacrifice, in fact the longest and the most detailed in any Kāvya. Fourthly, the echoes and parallels from other poets are too patent. Fifthly a mistake like 'labhet' in *parasmaipada* occurs here. Lastly, this set of extra verses brings the performance of sacrifice to a completion before the demons come in.

After the 25th there is one verse having gaps in lines 3 and 4 which mentions the on-coming army of the Rākṣasas as seeking the two princes and pouring down blood all around. It is difficult to decide about the authenticity of this verse which is somewhat incomplete.

The context of the fight that follows between the two princes and the forces of the demons, gives scope for the next set of additional verses, the last three inserted after verse 37. This set of three verses has to be rejected, as the description of the fight is generally with reference to the whole hosts of Rākṣasas and no particular emphasis is laid here on Mārīca and Subāhu alone; and in this general description, as pointed out elsewhere, both Mārīca and Subāhu are said to have perished, making the whole situation somewhat different from that in the *Rāmāyaṇa*. But in these three verses, as in the earlier ones, the effort of the hand that added has been clearly to bring the description of the fight in line with that in Vālmīki.

The additional verses in canto VI, start with one after verse 6 ; it states the fact of the sage crossing the Ganges along with the two princes. But the verse would hardly fit in at that place where there is a series describing the two princes.

In the context of Ahalyā being rid of her curse, two verses are inserted after verse 15 to state more clearly the acceptance of Ahalyā by Gautama after the purification.

On the entry into Mithilā, the reception accorded by Janaka, which is put briefly in one verse in MT., is elaborated in four verses describing the offer of *Arghya* and *Pādya* and the kind enquiries made by Janaka.

The rest of the additional verses in this canto numbering as many as 46, form one big unit of addition inserted after verse 55. In MT. VI. 55 the fact of the messengers of Janaka having gone to Daśaratha is mentioned. The arrival of Daśaratha and his party is communicated only in VII. 32. Therefore this set of verses expatiating upon the meeting of the messengers with Daśaratha, the consequent starting of Daśaratha for Mithilā and the description of the journey itself at the end of canto VI cannot fit in.

29 verses are found additionally in 'L' in the 7th canto. The first set refers to the theme of the description of Sītā's beauty, quite a convenient context for inserting additional verses. Four verses are thus added, one after 6 and three after

8. In the first, the verbal borrowing from Kālidāsa is very plain. On the next set of three verses, the remarks called for have already been made in the Introduction.

Nine verses forming a unit appear next after verse 19, setting forth the varied observations about Rāma in the assemblage there.

The next series of additional verses refer to the reception accorded to Daśaratha on his arrival. In MT, it is only in verse 32 that the arrival of Daśaratha is mentioned. Immediately in 33 the celebration of the marriage ceremony is taken up and as already pointed out, it is this kind of brief treatment that forms the prevailing method of the original. The additional verses here in 'L' appearing after verse 30, should really appear after verse 32, for, they set forth in detail the party going out to meet Daśaratha on the way and receiving him with all due pomp. These verses number 13.

The last set of three verses appearing after 56 are clearly occasioned by the supposed gap in the original : in the original at 56, the poet just mentions Rāma's marriage and passes on to a description of the love of Rāma and Sītā. The whole of the 8th canto which immediately follows is taken up by a description of this love. When canto 9 opens, in his usual manner, the poet briefly refers to the marriage of the three brothers, while speaking about the departure of Daśaratha and party. The impatient hand which has made the addition has taken the context of Rāma's marriage itself as deficient in respect of the marriage of the three other brothers and to that effect adds three verses. The additional verses in this canto exhibit some grammatical lapses also.

A review of the extra verses in this canto would show not only the obvious spuriousness of these verses but also the characteristic way in which they are occasioned by two main circumstances : (1) Brief treatment in the original and scope for elaboration and (2) a supposed gap or omission and the supply of additional details.

When we come to canto VIII, the love sports of Rāma and Sītā afford obviously justifiable scope for the interpolator. After verse 3 in MT, there is a general observation on the universal sway of love, but as this is put in the mouth of the speaker, it does not fit in at the place.

Regarding the other verses, the suspicion is only too strong as among them there are two other well-known verses found in the anthologies over the name of Kalaśa and Mañjīra :

अञ्जलौ जलमधीरलोचना etc. and,
अन्यतो नय मुहूर्तमाननम् etc.

Fifteen verses are found extra in canto IX. The first set of these numbering seven forms a duplicate and more elaborate description of the coming out of the party of Daśaratha and his sons from Mithilā; part of this is already covered by verses in MT, and the two sets cannot be accepted without involving repetition.

The next additional verse seen after 20, just adds one more picture to the series begun in 20. Similarly that after 27 adds one more description to Paraśurāma. The verses after 55, in a context describing city-damsels rushing to see the princes entering Ayodhyā, elaborate only the usual pictures found in such descriptions ; the imagery in one of these appears in a different context in the same poem (XIX. 32) and another looks like an obvious imitation of Māgha XIII. 33. In fact Māgha seems to be the main inspirer of many of the additional verses in 'L'.

After verse 62 there are three additional verses giving three observations of the ladies who were looking on, in elaboration of the idea found in brief in the context in MT.

41 verses are found extra in the latter part of canto X. In 52, it is mentioned that Rāma reached the Ganges. Then in MT the narrative passes from Virādha straight to Pañcavaṭī. The prevailing mode adopted by the poet here is a rapid summary of the incidents in the forest. This has evidently not satisfied the assiduous adding hand which has set forth after verse 70, a detailed account of this part of the story mentioning all the sages and their hermitages visited by Rāma. Similarly, three verses are introduced to set forth the happiness on reaching Pañcavaṭī ; six verses to expatiate on the beautiful form in which Śūrpaṇakhā appeared and

some more to deal more extensively with the episode of Śūrpaṇakhā.

After 75, the next elaboration appears to make up for the extremely summary manner in which Sītā's abduction by Rāvaṇa is given. Śūrpaṇakhā's complaint to Rāvaṇa, Rāvaṇa's plan to abduct Sītā with the help of Mārīca and the whole incident of Mārīca are all found here. It has been already pointed out that Kumāradāsa has obviated the need for the Mārīca episode. Consequently, Kumāradāsa has avoided also the unpleasant exchange between Sītā and Lakṣmaṇa. But in the additional verses which follow further, the exchange between Sītā and Lakṣmaṇa is also set forth.

The last two extra verses in this canto appear in Rāvaṇa's boastful words to Sītā before lifting her, the second of which looks like a verse not belonging to this context at all.

Canto I

व्याख्यानकाले रचिता मुनीन्द्रै-
र्निशम्य वाचो मधुरस्वभावाः ।
स्वतः प्रमाणं परतोऽथवेति
शुकाङ्गना यत्र विसंवदन्ते ।। 72A, L-74

Canto II

सर्वस्य कारणं कार्यादभिन्नं परमार्थतः ।
अत एव तयोरैक्यं प्राहुः सत्कार्यवादिनः ।। 8A, L-9

यं दृष्ट्वा हृदयाम्भोजकलिकापीठमध्यगम् ।
योगिनो यान्ति निर्वाणं स नो रक्षतु माधवः ।। 18A, L-20

आद्यन्तरहितं मूर्तित्रयातीतं परात्परम् ।
यं प्राहुर्ध्येयमाम्नायाः स नो रक्षतु केशवः ।। 18 B, L-21

यस्मिन् सकृत्प्रणामो हि संसारार्णवतारणः ।
वाचामगोचरो विष्णुः स नो रक्षतु रक्षिता ।। 18 C, L-22

सगुणोऽपि गुणातीतो निर्गुणोऽपि गुणाश्रयः ।
ओङ्कारपदवाच्यो यः स नो रक्षतु वामनः ॥ 18 D, L-23

दशमेन मुखेनाग्नौ पतता स्वास्वरे हठात् ।
आश्चर्येण शिवेनोक्ते हेति स्वाहाकृतेर्दृशम् ॥ 50 A, L-61

Canto III

परस्परं चञ्चुपुटद्वयार्पितं
बिभर्ति चक्राह्वयुगं मदालसम् ।
नितान्तसंघाटनकीलकोपमां
वियोगभीत्येव मृणालनालिकाम् ॥ 58 A, L-65

महद्भिरोघैस्तमसाभिभूतो
भयेऽप्यसंमूढमतिर्भ्रमन् क्षितौ ।
प्रदीपवेषेण गृहे गृहे स्थितो
विभज्य देहं बहुधेव भास्करः ॥ 67 A, L-69

प्रसन्नमद्ये चषके निशाकरं
स्वकीयमालोक्य मुखं च भामिनी ।
ददर्श मुग्धा मुहुरात्तकौतुका
द्विचन्द्रमासीत् किमिदं नभस्तलम् ॥ 72 A, L-75

Canto IV

यजमानमुनी सहोत्थितौ
पुरुषं वीक्ष्य ततः कृताञ्जली ।
पुरुहूतमिवेन्दुभार्गवौ
रुरुचाते कृतकृत्यमानसौ ॥ 4 A, L-5

स विभण्डकसूनुहस्तयो-
श्चरुमादाय युगेऽथ पायसम् ।
नृप देहि विभज्य पावनं
महिषीभ्योऽन्तरदधादिति ब्रुवन् ॥ 4B, L-6

अथ स प्रगृहीतभाजनो
मुनिना दत्तमसौ पृथक्कृतम् ।

कृतमङ्गलवाचनं नृपः
स्ववधूभ्यः प्रददौ यथाक्रमम् ।। 4C, L-7

सुरदुन्दुभयः प्रदध्वनु-
र्दिवि गन्धर्वगणैरगीयत ।
ननृतुः कृतगानमङ्गल-
ध्वनिवाद्यानुगमं सुराङ्गनाः ।। 4D, L-8

जलधिवसुधे पुरातनः
पुरुषस्ते भविता च नायकः ।
इति वक्तुमिव प्रियं मुदा
विससाराशु तटं विलङ्घयन् ।। 4E, L-9

दिवसेषु गतेषु केषुचित्
स सखीभ्यः स्थिरगर्भसंभवाः ।
रमणीरुपकृत्य दन्तुरान् (दत्तवान्)
मणिचिन्ता (त्रा) भरणानि मेखलाः ।। 5A, L-11

प्रमदासु विलोक्य लक्षणं
सकलं गर्भमयं महीपतिः ।
मुमुदे नितरां हि चातको
नवमेका (घा) न्तमिवाभ्रसंक्रमे ।। 5B, L-12

अथ पुंसवनादयः कृता
विधिना तासु पुरोहितेन तैः ।
किल गर्भचतुष्टयं शनै-
र्ववृधे मेघजलैरिवाङ्कुरः ।। 5C, L-13

निशमय्य स सूतिकागृहं
वनिताभिश्च कटाक्षितं जया (वा) त् ।
धनधेनुपरार्बुदं तदा
प्रसवाद्वेदविदा (दो) न्यवेदयत् ।। 5D, L-14

अथ कोसलराजनन्दिनी
सुषुवे रामममपश्रयं सताम् ।

इतरा महिषी च मध्यमा
भरतं राममिवापर गुणैः ।। 5E, L-15

कलशिञ्जितरत्नकिङ्किणी-
वलयोद्भासितपादपङ्कजौ ।
अवनौ सुविकृष्टहस्तयो-
र्युगलेनाशु जगाम मन्थरम् ।। 13A, L-20

धृतशैशवभूषणः पुमा-
नधिगन्तुं धनुरागमद्गुरुम् ।
जगतां गुरु रप्युपास(द)-
द्भृगुसूनुर्विनयादिवेश्वरम् ।। 14A, L-27

सकलागमतत्त्ववेदिनो
निरवद्या गुरुतो गरीयसी ।
रघुनाथमुखं ययौ कलाः
कमलं फुल्लमिवार्कदीधितिः ।। 14B, L-28

मृगयादिषु लक्ष्मणः स्वयं
प्रणयेनानुजगाम राघवम् ।
भरतानुवशस्तथाऽपरो
युगयुग्मं प्रणयादजायत ।। 14C, L-29

अथ नोपरराम वीक्षितुं
स कुमारानुपनीतिशालिनः ।
प्रमदोदितवाष्पबिन्दुभिः
परिपूर्णोभयपक्ष्मचक्षुषा ।। 14D, L-30

प्रतिषेधविधिर्व्यवस्थितो
यदि न स्यादपरो विशेषगः ।
स्त्रियमेव मनुष्यघातिनी-
मभिहन्यादिति गीयते विधिः ।। 15A, L-82

Canto V

नियुज्य रामं क्रतुरक्षणे ततः
चकार ऋत्विग्वरणं स कौशिकः ।

वितानमध्वर्युवरः प्रचक्रमे
विधातुमग्रस्थितकार्यसन्ततिः ।। 11A, L-12

बभूव कर्तृत्वमकुर्वतः स्वयं
तपोनिधे ऋत्विजि कुर्वति क्रियाः ।
यथात्मनो ग्राहकता च गृह्णति
प्रलीनतुङ्गस्तनकुम्भजस्य ये ।। 11B, L-13

प्रसह्य मौञ्जीरशनां पिशङ्गिता-
मथोपतस्थे यजमानजाया ।
शिखीव जम्भोन्नतपीनसंहत-
स्तनद्वयाभुग्नकु(क्व)शावलग्नया ।। 11C, L-14

महत्त(त्वि)जोच्चैः स्फुटमत्र चोदितः
स सामिधेनीरथ हौत्रपाठकः ।
अघौघविध्वंसविधौ पटीयसी[1]-
रवोचदग्नीन्धनवादिनीर्ऋचः ।। 11D, L-13

हविः प्रचारेऽग्निपदादिवैष्णवे
सहार्यिहिंकारमचोदितस्स्वयम् ।
अगायदुच्चैरिह साम सामवि-
न्निरीक्षणीयः समयो हि धीधनैः ।। 11E, L-16

कृतोपहूतं विधिनैष्ठिकर्त्विजः
समं पुरोडाशमिडाभिधानिकम् ।
समन्त्रकं प्राशुरतः परस्परं
पवित्रतामीयुरिडाप्रयोगिणः ।। 11F, L-17

स दीक्षणीयेष्टयवसानदीक्षितो
मृगाजिनप्रोर्णतया सुतीवलः(?) ।
वलित्रयालिङ्गिकुरङ्गशृङ्गया
रराज तन्वा सशिरस्त्रदण्डया ।। 11G, L-18

अनेकरत्नैः पशुभिर्महावनै-
श्चकार सोमक्रयणं क्रमेण सः ।

---

1. This whole line is Māgha I. 18 c.

क्रतोस्समाप्तिर्भवितात्र केनचि-
द्ध्रुवं धनेनेति जनैः प्रतर्कितैः ॥ 11H, L-19

रथे स्थिते राजनि राजितध्वजे
परार्ध्यरत्नद्युतिपुञ्जपञ्जरे ।
स्थितोऽन्तरे यो मखनेतृनोदितः
समाजुहावेन्द्रमथेन्द्रियापरः(?) ॥ 11 I, L-20

स शीघ्रमातिथ्यमवारितातिथिः
समागतायाखिललोकसाक्षिणे ।
अतीतमूर्तित्रितयाय विष्णवे
चकार कर्तार्घ्यमतः परैः क्व वा ॥ 11J, L-21

कृतोपहूतिर्विधिनादिपूरुषः
वषट्कृतं मानयति स्म पावनम् ।
अलङ्घ्यवेदोदितकर्मगौरवा-
त्प्रभुः प्रभूणां कुरुते हि संमतिम् ॥ 11K, L-22

प्रवर्ग्यपात्रे नयनादिसंभृते
पयस्समानीय वषट्कृता स्तुतम् ।
अथोपनीयोपयमेन पावके
जुहाव हव्यं प्रतिदिङ्मुखं मखे ॥ 11L, L-23

पुरत्रयं जेतुमजय्यमीशिरे
दिवौकसो याभिरिमास्तपोनिधिः ।
जयाय तत्रोपसदः प्रचक्रमे
विनाप्यदृष्टं क्व फलाप्तिरिष्यते ॥ 11M, L-24

स्वयं क्रतूनां फलदश्शरीरिणां
जगद्विनाशस्थितिजन्मकारणम् ।
अपारसंसारसमुद्रतारनौ-
रिहाविरासीदथ यज्ञपूरुषः ॥ 11N, L-25

अथारणेर्जातमवेक्ष्य पावकं
प्रमोदवाष्पं मुमुचे स कौशिकः ।

अदृष्टपुन्नाननवन्ध्यलोचनः
पितेव सूनुं सकलार्तिनाशनम् ।। 11O, L-26

समित्समिद्धोत्तरवेदिपावके
शृतां वपामध्वरनेतृवर्गणाः ।
निधाय जुह्वामभिघार्य सर्पिषा
जुहाव मन्त्रेण वषट्कृतावसौ ।। 11P, L-27

निधाय सोमानपरे शिलामये
महाहविर्धानिपुरः प्रतिष्ठिते ।
सुविस्तरे प्रैषकृतस्स्वदिङ्मुखाः
समन्त्रकं ग्राम(व)भिरभ्यषिञ्चत ।। 11Q, L-28

महीयसि द्रोणघटेऽत्र सामगाः
पवित्रमच्छाच्छमृजीषशोधनम् ।
वितत्य सामानि जगुस्तदध्वरे
कराङ्गुलिन्यासपृथक्कृतस्वय(र)म् ।। 11R, L-29

कृथा(ता)तिदेशाहृतमन्त्रगोचरं
दुरूहमूहन्नयशास्त्रकोविदः ।
विनिश्चिकायार्थवशेन कुत्र वा
विनैव मीमांसकमर्थनिश्चयः ।। 11S, L-30

ग्रहान् गृहीत्वा प्रतिगीर्य याजको
जुहाव सोमानपदिश्य देवताः ।
ततः समागम्य सदो वषट्कृता
निपीतसोमं पिबति स्म चोदितः ।। 11T, L-31

अथोपहूयाध्वरनेतृहोतृकौ
समन्त्रकं सोमरसं रसायनम् ।
अनुत्सृजन्तौ ग्रहमैन्द्रवायवं
परस्परं भक्षयतः स्म संसदि ।। 11U, L-32

इहैकमुद्गातृपदादिमाश्रितं
सदस्समेतं चमसं सपादिनः(?)।

अभक्षयन् येन च गानकारिणः
स कामतोऽयं समयः प्ररोचते ।। 11V, L-33

हुतेषु सोमेष्वथ यज्ञदक्षिणां
मुनीश्वरः श्रौतपथप्रवर्तकः ।
अदादपर्यन्तमवाप्तदक्षिणा
यथर्त्विजामाशयमत्यशेरत ।। 11W, L-34

जगत्त्रये तादृशरत्नसञ्चयो
न कस्यचित्पुण्यजनस्य दृश्यते ।
भुवो न तावान् न पयोधिमेरुणो-
स्तपस्विनां किं न करोति वैभवम् ।। 11X, L-35

परार्ध्यचिन्तामणिनिर्मितः करः
किमेष सन्तानतरुः फलद्रुमः ।
वसिष्ठधेनुः किमभीष्टवस्तुदा
जनैर्न जज्ञे ददतस्तपोनिधेः ।। 11Y, L-36

प्रदत्तनानाविधरत्नसञ्चय-
प्रधारणस्वीकृतरामणीयका ।
तदादि नूनं स्फुटमथसंगतं
वसुन्धरा नाम दधा(धा)ति मेदिनी ।। 11Z, L-37

प्रदाय तेभ्योऽथ वदान्यताश्रयो
द्विजान्तरेभ्योऽपि ददौ स कौशिकः ।
वसून्यमूल्यानि यथेष्टमन्यथा
कथं लभेत्स्वीयपदं वदान्यता ।। 11A, L-38

ततस्तृतीये सवने समाप्लुतः
स याजमानं निरवर्तताखिलम् ।
स्वकीयमार्त्विज्यमशेषमृत्विजः
क्व वा विलम्बो भविता मनस्विनाम् ।। 11B, L-39

समाप्तयज्ञस्य मुनेरनन्तरं
न देवतातः फलमस्य दृश्यते ।

अतश्च यागादपरं फलप्रदं
वदन्ति तत्त्वार्थविदो विपश्चितः ॥ 11C, L-40

क्व तिष्ठतः कौशिकयज्ञरक्षिणौ
शिशू निशातायुधभेददुस्सहौ ।
इति ब्रुवन् ... ...
...... सेना रुधिराणि सर्वतः ॥ 25A, L-56

स शूलमुग्राग्रमरातिसूदनं
मुमोच रामं युधि जेतुमाशया ।
तमम्बरस्थं शतधा तु लीलया
शरैस्स चिच्छेद रुषा नु राघवः ॥ 37A, L-69

अथास्त्रमानार्तित(?)भानुमण्डलं
मुमोच मारीचजयाय राघवः ।
अगच्छदुग्राशनिभैरवारव-
प्रभिन्नशैलोरुदरीमुखं द्विषम् ॥ 37B, L-70

विभिन्नवक्ष क्षरदुग्रशोणित-
स्फुरत्कपालं कृतभीमविग्रहम् ।
तमस्त्रमस्तारिबलं बलीयसा
जवेन वि(चि)क्षेप सुरारिमम्बुधौ ॥ 37C, L-71

Canto VI

भागीरथीमथो तीर्त्वा कौशिकश्शोणसङ्गमे ।
तर्पयित्वा पितॄन् देवान् कुमारानुगतो ययौ ॥ 6A, L.7
ततस्तानवद्याङ्गी तपोमूर्तिमिवाश्रिताम् ।
गौतमः प्रतिजग्राह प्रभां प्रातरिवांशुमान् ॥ 15A, L-17

......तमात्मीयदुर्नयव्यञ्जिमेखलाम्(?) ।
गौतमः प्रतिजग्राह प्रभां प्रातरिवांशुमान् ॥ 15B, L.18
अर्घ्यपाद्यादिभिर्भूपः पूजयित्वा तपोधनम् ।
कुशलं सर्वगं पृष्ट्वा...............॥ 33A, L.37

.... ।
आत्मयोनेरिवामोघदर्शनं-तनोति नः ॥ 33B, L.38
अद्य मे सफलं जन्म............।

..............अद्य मानस्य भाजनम् ।
अद्य निर्विघ्नतां यज्ञः संप्राप्तश्च पवित्रताम् ।। 33C, L-39

पुत्रयोः कौशलं राजा चिरं प्रोषितयोर्मुहुः ।
............प्तमुनिनोद्वाहमशृणोद्दूतवार्तया ।। 55A, L-62

अपूर्ववदभूद्राज्ञः कौशलं च सदा श्रुतम् ।
स्नेहस्य रूपमेवेदं नूतनं यत् क्षणे क्षणे ।। 55B, L-63

स्नेहेन गन्तुकामस्य राघवौ चक्रवर्त्तिनः ।
हेत्वन्तरमभूद्दैवात् कन्यादानमभीप्सितम् ।। 55C, L-64

कौशलश्रवणोत्फुल्लप्रेमपूरादमानिव ।
प्रासादे विपुलेऽप्याशु स राजाङ्गणमाविशत् ।। 55D, L-65

स्योपत्यवदनाध्मातो(?)निस्सहायो महादरः ।
भृत्यानामाचचक्षेऽथ राज्ञो गमनमञ्जसा ।। 55E, L-66

मन्थरक्रमसञ्जातमञ्जुशिञ्जितनूपुराः ।
परिवव्रुस्त (रुण्य)स्तं कंप्रस्तनभरानताः ।। 55F, L-67

प्रयाणरुचिराकल्पास्तुरङ्गाधिरुहो नृपम् ।
तोरणाद्बहिरालोके तस्थुर्भृत्याश्च मन्त्रिणः ।। 55D, L-68

.........भेरीमृदङ्गनिर्घोषः करुणादरः (?)।
रणशब्दमधश्चक्रे....................।। 55H, L-69

.... ।
............षपूरिताभूदिन्द्रदिङ्मुखः(?)।। 55 I, L-70

आययौ मिथिलां राजा वि(हि)मानीगौरचामरः ।
पृतनां तोरणासङ्ग....................।। 55J, L-71

............................।
सद्यः कर्मफलानीव पुण्यभाजनमन्वयुः ।। 55K, L-72

राजानः स्वीयसामन्तसेविताश्चक्रवर्त्तिनम् ।
अवान्तरदिशो.........मन्वयुः ।। 55L, L-73

निरुध्य कथमप्यश्वान् सादिभिः क्षणमीक्षितान् ।
क्रीडन्तो धूलिभिः पुत्राः पथो…… ॥ 55M, L-74

………पारैरस्पृशन्त—वर्त्मगाः ।
सपक्षाश्च विपक्षाश्च पार्श्वयोः कीर्णचामराः॥55N, L-75

उरोऽवलम्बि………………… ।

…स्तं क्वापि दुर्दर्शं तत्सहासं सैन्यमैक्षत ॥ 55O, L-76

……घण्टाघणघणध्वानं शनैः……।
……वणः क्षिप्रंभारभागः(?)पलायत ॥ 55P, L-77

……………………… ।
कृतार्तं बृंहितं पद्म…तुस्तौ परस्परम् ॥ 55Q, L-78

……करिणः श्रुत्वा धावतो घर्वि(?)तारवम् ।
…………………… ॥
…………………रपत्रचित्रैरिवाबभौ ॥55R, L-79

उद्धूता तुरगैर्धूलिस्तप्ता सूर्यमरीचिभिः
……………………… ॥ 55S, L-80

……घेस्तस्य क्षेत्रमाक्रम्य गच्छतः ।
महत(:)सरमू(यू)रग्रे सीमेव क्षणमाबभौ ॥55T, L-81

……गजाः पूर्वं परितस्ता जगाहिरे ।
उत्तेरुस्तरसा…मदाम्भःप्रचुरीकृताः ॥ 55U, L-82

अतीर्यंत तुरङ्गैस्सा पारे निहितलोचनैः ।
स्फुरद्घोणाग्रमुद्गच्छन् मीनभीतैरिव क्षणात् ॥ 55V, L-83

पादैरिव मु(सु)खं लोकै (?) अरित्रैश्शीघ्रगामिभिः ।
गोगणैः सहसोत्तेरुः केचित्त्रस्तवधूजनाः ॥ 55W, L-84

भुजैः कृतसमैः क्षिप्रं क्षिपन्तो लहरीगणान् ।
हेलयातारिषुः केचित् पद्मान्युन्मूल्य कौतुकात् ॥ 55X, L-85

भुजाभ्यामुत्तरन् ...भक्षितं(तुं)ब्राह्म(ग्राह?)मागतम् ।
खड्गेन शतधा च्छित्वा चक्रे तां रुधिरापगाम् ।। 55Y, L-86

प्रासादातिशयश्रीका निवासाः पथि चाभवन् ।
विषोग्रविधुरां तनुं (?) पुरुषः पुरतो ययौ ।। 55Z, L-87

विमानैरथ सौवर्णैः मणिमौक्तिकचित्रितैः ।
महिष्यः प्रययुः शीघ्रं तरुणीगणवेष्टितैः ।। 55A, L-88

कुमारौ तुरगारूढौ मौक्तिकच्छत्रमालिनौ ।
कलमागधसङ्गीतश्राविणौ जग्मतुश्शनैः ।। 55B, L-89

वन्यद्विपमदामोददुर्धराः पथि यन्तृभिः ।
विनोदितास्तरुच्छेदैरिभा दूरेण निन्यिरे ।। 55C, L-90

उन्मील्य नयने रूक्षं शयालुत्वापदेशतः ।
सिंहः सुखमशेताहो प्रभूणामीदृशी गतिः ।। 55D, L-91

तुरङ्गमखुरोद्धूतधूलिधूसरदिङ्मुखम् ।
गण्डकां गण्डसंपर्कदूष्यतोयां बलं न्यगात् ।। 55E, L-92

पुरात्प्रभृति यद्वृत्तं राज्ञः प्रतिदिनक्षणम् ।
तत्सर्वमत्वराः प्रोचुः दूता जनकसत्रिणे ।। 55F, L-93

ततश्चक्रनदीतीरं तिरोहितमहीतला ।
ध्वजदूष्यविमानाग्रैरलञ्चक्रे महाचमूः ।। 55G, L-94

सेनानिवेशनाशंसी पटहः समहन्यत ।
प्रदध्मे शङ्खिना शङ्खो राज्ञो वेशनसूचनः ।। 55H, L-95

अवतीर्य विमानेभ्यो महिष्यः कलनूपुराः ।
विविशुः स्वीयवेश्माभिव्यजनप्रावृतातपम् ।। 55I, L-96

शाखासु कमनीयानि निधायाभरणान्यथ ।
वारमुख्याः क्षणं तस्थुरधोधो वनपादपान् ।। 55J, L-97

विपण्यैरापणिं पूर्णां विपणिस्थूलशालिनीम् ।
क्रयितप्रात (?) निर्घोषपूरिताशमकुर्वत ।। 55K, L-98

भूषणैर्भूषयित्वाशु वेश्या दूष्यपुरस्थिताः ।
चिरासीनवदाभाष्य वल्लभान् जग्रहुर्विटान् ।। 55L, L-99

दृष्टिपातक्षणे किञ्चित् कुञ्चितस्मेरलोचनैः ।।
अनुसस्रे परा यूना हर्तुं चित्तमिवाहृतम् ।। 55M, L-100

स्वजनान् दूरतो यातान् अन्यतो वीक्ष्य तत्क्षणे ।
उद्बाहुराजुहावोच्चैरेकः प्लुतकृतस्वरम् ।। 55N, L-101

अन्यामालोक्य गच्छन्तीं धावन्नुक्षिप्य सादिनम् ।
दुर्वारः सैनिकैर्वाजी चक्रे शिविरमाकुलम् ।। 55O, L-102

उन्नतोच्छ्रितदूष्यान्तं निषण्णा वारयोषितः ।
शय्यासु भेजिरे निद्रां सुखं व्यजनमारुतैः ।। 55P, L-103

तालवाद्यानुगैर्गीतैर्नर्तकीनां कलस्वरैः ।
तुरङ्गहेषितैः पूर्णस्कन्धावारो व्यरोचत ।। 55Q,L-104

ऊचुरल्पाक्षरं केचित् राज्ञश्चक्रनदीतटे ।
अजनन्दनसेनायाः निवेशनमभूदिति ।। 55R, L-105

अयोध्यापतिरस्माकं देशमिन्द्रसखः स्वयम् ।
संबन्धार्थमिहायाति कृतार्थोऽहममन्यत ।। 55S, L-106

तत्प्रेमपूरितुं नेत्रं रामे निहितमादरात् ।
न शशाक तदाहर्तुं बन्धमोक्षो हि दुस्सहः ।। 55T, L-107

Canto VII

इयं हि काष्ठा विधिकौशलानां
संकल्पसूतेरभिमानदैवम् ।
निदानमक्ष्णोरनिमेषताया
रसायनं मन्मथरोगशान्तेः ।। 6A, L-7

सोक्षण(ष्मं) प्रकृत्या कठिनं द्वयं यत्
तापं तनोति स्तनयोस्तदस्तु ।
मध्यस्थमप्येतदनिन्द्यवृत्ते-
र्वलित्रयं मां दहतीति चित्रम् ।। 8A, L-10

1. cf. Kumārasambhava III. 24c

स्तनौ न कुम्भप्रतिमौ सुदत्या
निश्शेषवक्षस्तटबद्धबिम्बौ । Found in 'N'
न्यस्तौ शरीरादतिरिक्तवन्तौ
पिण्डौ नु पीनौ नवयौवनस्य ।। 8B, L-11

अन्योन्यबाधिस्तनमण्डलस्य
मध्यस्य तन्व्या नवरोमराजिः ।
शरीरजन्मानलधूमरेखा
सीमा विभक्तेव विभाति धात्रा ।। 8C, L-12

दृष्ट्वा सदस्या मुनयो मुनीन्द्राः
प्रत्युत्थिताः संभ्रमसारनेताः(त्राः) ।
कृत्वा सपर्यां कुशलप्रणामैः
तस्मिन् निविष्टे परितो निषेदुः ।। 19A, L-24

आश्रावणानन्तरमेव होता
याज्याभिरीजे भरतः क्रमेण ।
सामानि केचिज्जगुरत्र चान्यः
पुण्यान्यधीते स्म यजूंषि यष्टा ।। 19B, L-25

एतौ कुमारौ कमनीयरूपौ
यातु (?) स्म मित्रावरुणौ किमिष्टौ ।
कामस्त्रिनेत्रावमतिं निरस्य
लब्धः शरीरे नु तपः प्रभावात् ।। 19C, L-26

केनात्र भङ्ग(भग्नं) गिरिधन्वचापं
दुर्भेदकार्कश्यगुणं गरीयः ।
पृष्टः सदस्यैरिति सर्वमूचे
वृत्तं तपस्वी समवेतवृत्तः ।। 19D, L-27

येनाकरोत्सख्यमवार्यवीर्यः
पुरन्दरोऽनीशतया विजेतुम् ।
तस्याजसूनोस्तनयो हि रामः
तस्यानुजोऽयं खलु लक्ष्मणाख्यः ।। 19E, L-28

एतेन पुत्री खलु चक्रवर्ती
भोज्या सुतो मे मखरक्षणेन(?)।
स एव चात्मीयगुणानुरूपं
लेभे सुतं वाक्पथदूरकीर्तिः ॥ (?) 19F, L-29

शैवं धनुर्भञ्जति राजपुत्रे
हासो महीशैः करतालमन्यैः ।
चक्रे परैर्मूर्च्छितमासनस्थैः
राज्ञो मुखं मेऽथ च फुल्लमासीत् ॥ 19G, L-30

एकस्त्रिलोके यजमानवर्ग-
स्त्रातायमेवेति कृतप्रतिज्ञा ।
यूपाङ्गुलं(लिं)चारु चकार रम्या-
मुन्नम्य भूमी (भूर्निर्) दिशतीव रामम् ॥ 19H, L-31

श्रुत्वा वचस्तस्य मुखं दधाना
वाष्पाम्बुसिक्तं मुनयः कराग्रैः ।
स्पृष्ट्वा शिरस्याहुतिपुण्यगन्धैः
पुत्रौ शशंसुर्नृपमेव सर्वे ॥ 19I, L-32

आयाति सुत्रामसखः ससैन्यं
राजन्नवोचन्निति दूतवर्याः।
ततः कटाक्षेण दिदेश पुत्रौ
प्रत्युद्व्रजेतं रघुवंशकेतुम् ॥ 30A, L-44

मातङ्गकुम्भस्थितशातकुम्भ-
कुम्भान् पुरस्कृत्य शिवाम्बुपूर्णान् ।
मुक्तातपत्राण्यभितो विधूत-
शुभ्रांश्च बालव्यजनाभिरामान् ॥ 30B, L-45

ततश्शशाङ्कप्रतिमातपत्रौ
सीतानुजौ पुष्यरथाधिरूढौ ।
सुमन्त्रसूताभिमुखं स्म पुर्या
निर्जग्मतुः पिङ्गलतुल्यरूपौ ॥ 30C, L-46

गम्भीरभेरीरवकर्णपूर्णे(पूर्णकर्णे)
लोकेऽसमर्थे वचनं ग्रहीतुम् ।
हस्ताङ्गुलीपल्लवचेष्टयान्ये
प्राबोधयन् प्रस्तुतवाक्यशेषान् ।। 30D, L-47

चक्रभ्रमन्नेमिसमुत्थपृथ्वी-
धूलीलुठत्केतुविराजमानैः ।
जग्मुः कुमारौ परितः स्वसूतै-
र्वेगीकृताश्वं रथिनो रथौघैः ।। 30E, L-48

आवर्तिभिस्संभृतदेशरत्नै-
र्जाज्वल्यमानैर्भृतरन्ध्रदेशैः ।
लक्ष्मीतनूजौ(जैः) विदधे धरित्री
दुर्वारवेगैरिव निम्नगेशैः ।। 30F, L-49

कुम्भीन्द्रशृङ्गाकुलितानिवार्या
तरङ्गवीचीवलया जगाहे ।
वैदेहसेना रघुनाथसैन्यं
गङ्गेव नानामुखमम्बुराशिम् ।। 30G, L-50

डिम्भौ विदेहाधिपतेश्च वीरौ
यथोचितं तस्य विधाय पूजाम् ।
अथान्वयातां नृपशेखरं तौ
धर्मापवर्गाविव पुण्यभाजम् ।। 30H, L-51

उत्तीर्य पीनस्तनहेमकुम्भ-
द्वन्द्वेन यानादवरूढरामाः ।
अथातिदूरीकृतमध्यभागं
परस्परं सस्वजुरादरेण ।। 30I, L-52

वैदेहभोज्यासुतयोरभेदं
स्नेहेन सेनायुगलेऽपि याते ।
अन्योन्यमक्षोभि मुहुर्महेभैः
क्व वा विवेकः क्व मदावलिप्ताः ।। 30J, L-53

आलोकनोत्कण्ठनकामिनीना-
मालोकनेत्राहितजाललक्ष्मीम् ।
कौसुम्भकेतूज्ज्वलराजमार्गां
मुक्तागुणालङ्कृततोरणाढ्याम् ।। 31A, L-55

द्वारेऽवरुह्याथ रथान्नरेन्द्रः
कृतावतारं भवनं विवेश ।
रामानुजाभ्यामथ कौशिकस्तं
द्रष्टुं निवेद्यागमनं प्रपेदे ।। 32A, L-57

कृत्वा स तस्यापचितिं तनूजा-
वङ्के हठादेव निवेश्य वीरौ ।
आनन्दवार्ष्पैः शिरसी निषिञ्चिन्
आजिघ्रदुत्कण्टकरोमशाली ।। 32B, L-58

कृत्वा विवाहं रचितोत्तरीयं
सिंहासनस्थं भरतं सजानिम् ।
स्थानेषु दीपानधिरोप्य चक्रुः
नीराजनं रञ्जितवारमुख्याः ।। 56A, L-83

तत्रोर्मिला वारवधूविधूत-
चन्द्राननाभासुरचामराभ्याम् ।
संवीज्यमानाथ गृहीतपाणिः
सौमित्रिणा वायुसखो ववन्दे ।। 56B, L-84

घनाम्बुबिन्दूल्लसगण्डबिम्बा
दर्भैः परिस्तीर्णसमृद्धवह्नौ ।
शत्रुघ्नहस्तेन गृहीतपाणिः
लाजानहौषीच्छबलायताक्षी ।। 56C, L-85

Canto VIII

तिर्यगादिषु जगत्पतौ तथा
कृत्यमेव मदनस्य शासनम् ।
सोऽयमीदृशविभूतिवैभवो
मा कृथाः सुरतकेलिवञ्चनम् ।। 3A, L-5

उत्तरोष्ठपुटपायिनि प्रिये
सा तदीयमधरोष्ठपल्लवम् ।
चुम्बति स्म मुहुरत्र केवलं
युक्तमेतदिति वेत्ति भामिनी ॥ 50A, L-24

मैथिलीरतयदेव(रतय एष?) निर्दयं
हुं गृहाण दृढमोष्ठपल्लवम् ।
वेधयेति यदवोचदस्फुटं
तज्जगाम कुसुमेषुसूत्रताम् ॥ 31A, L-32

क्वेयमुल्लसशिरीषकोमलौ(ला)
क्वातिपाटवमपोढलज्जितम् ।
चिन्तयन्निति रतान्तरं शनै-
रादिदेश मदनो मृगीदृशः ॥ 41A, L-36

पीवरोरुकुचकुम्भमर्दन-
क्लेशमेष सुरतेषु सोढवान् ।
मित्रमस्य वदनं नु सान्त्वने
पुष्पवृष्टिममुचन्नु कौतुकात् ॥ 44A, L-38

सा ललाटजनितश्रमोदक-
श्लिष्टकुन्तलवराग्रमञ्जरी(म्) ।
सामिमीलितविलोचना श्रियं
प्राप सौरतविरामशंसिनीम् ॥ 44B, L-39

यां सखीव दयितोपगूढया
ह्रीरमुच्यत चिरेण सीतया ।
सा रतान्तसमये हि संगता
का सहेत विरहं सखीजनैः ॥ 44C, L-40

अञ्जलौ जलमधीरलोचना
लोचनप्रतिशरीरपूरितम् ।
आत्तमात्तमभिकान्तमुक्षितुं
कातरा शफरशङ्कया जहौ ॥ 34A, L-43

कामिनीभिरभिसारवाञ्छया।
कोपजिह्मितकटाक्षमीक्षितः।
संकुचत्करमसौ शनैश्शनैर्
भीतवद्रविरुपैति पश्चिमम् ।। 54A, L-53

स्निग्धवल्लभवियोगखेदिनी
चित्तनाथमुपगूह्य निर्दयम्।
वीक्षतेऽस्तगिरिभानुमध्यमं
चक्रवाकवनिता मुहुर्मुहुः ।। 54B, L-54

दूरतश्चिरमुपेतवल्लभै-
र्यान्तुगाढपरिरम्भचुम्बनैः।
निर्वृतिं युवतयोऽस्तमेयिवान्
भानुरित्थमनुकम्पयन्निव ।। 54C, L-55

सामिमीलितसरोजलोचनाः
पद्मपाणिपुटलम्बितांशुकाः।
दीर्घमैत्रमधुराः सरोजिनीः
कृ(क)ष्टमेष सविता समुज्झति ।। 55A, L-57

देवि पश्य नलिनी कृतांहसं
भानुमन्तमवलोक्य सादरम्।
अक्षमा विरहितुं क्षणादहो
नापराधगणनप्रियाः प्रियाः ।। 55B, L-58

......तिस्सहचरी सखीव मां
सङ्गतं त्यजति वारुणाशया।
अव्यया(?)कि(मनये?)ति तां त्यजन्
मज्जतीव सविता जलाशये ।। 56A, L-62

विद्रुमद्रुमविहङ्गरोचिषा
भिद्यमानतिमिरं निशाकरम्।
पश्य मन्दमुदितं दिगङ्गना
चारुनूतननखक्षतिश्रियम् ।। 83A, L-73

चन्द्रिकाकुसुमषण्डमण्डित-
ध्वान्तजालपृथुवेणिबन्धने ।
पश्य सुन्दरि सुरेन्द्रदिङ्मुखे
चन्दनार्द्रमिव चन्द्रमण्डलम् ॥ 70A, L-75

लोलसिन्धुसलिलोन्नमानमै-
रुद्गते शशिनि गूढदर्शिते ।
कन्दुकेन कमनीयकान्तिना
क्रीडतीव पुरुहूतदिग्वधूः ॥ 79A, L-78

मन्दमन्दमुदयन्तमम्बुधे-
रिन्दुमिन्दुवदने विलोकय ।
कुन्दगौरमरविन्दवैरिणं
नन्दयन्तमधुना कुमुद्वतीम् ॥ 82A, L-82

इन्दुबिम्बमुदितं पयोनिधेः
पश्य दाडिमगुलुच्छपिञ्जरम् ।
आदिपद्ममिव फुल्लमायतं
शौरिनाभिसरसस्समुत्थितम् ॥ 81A, L8-3

पश्य चन्द्रमुखि चन्द्रमण्डलं
तापभानुविवशं जगत्त्रयम् ।
वीजितुं रहितदण्डमण्डनं
तालवृन्तमिव यामिनीधृतम् ॥ 74A, L-88

अन्यतो नय मुहूर्तमाननं
चन्द्र एष सरले कलामयः ।
मा कदाचन कपोलयोर्मलं
संक्रमय्य समतां गमिष्यति ॥ 86A, L-90

Canto IX

रराज वृत्रारिसखो महारथो
रथाधिरुढैस्तनयैस्तनूदरैः ।
चतुर्भिराशापतिभिस्त्रिलोचनो
निषेवितो मेरुरिवाथ दिग्गजैः ॥ 18A, L-18

सशङ्खभेरीरवभिन्नकाहला
कठोरसांराविणपूर्णदिङ्मुखम् ।
जगाम राजा विशिखां पृथक्कृतः
स्वचिह्नसेनापतिभिर्निषेवितः ॥ 18B, L-19

विरिञ्चवक्त्रादिव वेदराशयो
जगन्ति विष्णोर्जठरादिव क्षणात् ।
हरस्य जूटादिव जाह्नवीजलं
पुराद्ध्वजिन्यो निरयुर्निरन्तरम् ॥ 18C, L-20

परस्परं श्लिष्टमुखाग्रपीडन-
ध्वनत्खलीनैस्तुरगैरसंयुतैः ।
निरीयुरन्योन्यविषक्तजानवः
तुरङ्गिणो हेषितभिन्नगोपुरैः ॥ 18D, L-21

निरन्तरालेऽपि जनैस्सुदूरतो
विमुच्यमाने पथि हेलया गजैः ।
क्रमेण ज...रुचिपुञ्जशालिभिः
प्रदीपवृन्दैस्तमसीव दुश्छिदे ॥ 18F, L-22

क्रमादनीयन्त रथा महीतलं
जवेन यातो विनियम्य गोपुरात् ।
नियन्तृहस्ताहृतरश्मिसन्नत-
स्वकन्धरासक्तयुगं तुरङ्गमैः ॥ 18E, L-23

गृहीतवालव्यजनैर्वधूजनै-
र्धृतातपत्रैः पुरुषैश्च वेष्टिताः ।
ययुर्महिष्यः पथि वेत्रपाणिभि-
र्निरस्तलोकं शिविकाधिरोहिताः ॥ 18G, L-24

करेण कामान्धमुदग्रविग्रहं
मुहुः स्पृशन्तीं करिणं करेणुकाम् ।
विलोक्य लज्जामुकुलीकृतेक्षणा
पराङ्मुखी साऽथ बभूव मैथिली ॥ 20A, L-28

विशुष्कपङ्क्रुहबीजमालिकां
विनिद्ररक्तोत्पलशङ्कया तताम् ।
विलोचनोपान्त इवालिसन्तति
विशालवामांसतटावलम्बिनीम् ॥ 27A, L-36

निधाय काचित्कुचयोरथाञ्जनं
विलोचने लोध्ररजांसि सम्भ्रमात् ।
तमालचूर्णं चरणे समाययौ
सुवर्णपत्रं च करे निबध्नती ॥ 55A, L-64

रुरोध कस्याश्चिदुपात्तसंभ्रम-
प्रयाणवेगादियमेति वेदनाम् ।
इतीव काञ्चीकलनादकिङ्किणी
सखीव दीना विनिपत्य पादयोः ॥ 55B, L-65

अपास्य काचित् चरणं प्रसाधिका-
करोदरादेकपदेऽनुरञ्जिते ।
हरार्धगौरीव चकार भूतलं
क्रमेतरालक्तकबिन्दुचित्रिताम् ॥ 55C, L-66

जगन्ति पीत्वा निखिलानि यः पुरा
युगान्ततोये चरणाम्बुजाङ्गुलिम् ।
लिलेह सोऽयं पुरुषोऽतितृष्णया
तुतोष काचित् कुसुमानि मुञ्चती ॥ 62A, L-74

शुकाशु मामिन्द्रसखे नयेति तं
जगाद काचित्करपल्लवाश्रितम् ।
नयामि देवीति वदन्तमञ्जसा
समालिलिङ्गे कलनादशङ्कम् ॥ 62B, L-75

इयं हि लावण्यग्य(म)तीष्व(त)वाक्पथं
'जगाम रामादिति काचि(श्चि)दूचिरे ।
न वित्थकन्तैव(?)नृपस्य भूषणं
स्वपक्षपातं ब्रुवते वधूजनाः ॥ 62C, L-76

Canto X

गङ्गाजलकणोद्वाही मन्दः कुन्दवनालयः ।
मार्गखिन्नाय रामाय प्रादादिव मरुत्करम् ॥ 52A, L-53

ददर्शाथ महारण्यमण्डनं पुण्यभाजनम् ।
शरभङ्गाश्रमं श्रान्तश्रान्तिहारिमहीरुहम् ॥ 70A, L-72

मन्त्रपूतां तनुं रामो जुह्वन्तं देवतामुखे ।
विस्मितो मुनिमुद्वीक्ष्य सुतीक्ष्णाश्रममेयिवान् ॥ 70B, L-73

अग्निहोत्रं ततस्तस्य होमकाले निषेदिवान् ।
प्रसन्नवदनो रामो हविर्भागिव देवता ॥ 70C, L-74

निमीलितदृशं बाणपाणिना रचिताञ्जलिम् ।
अन्येन धृतपात्रं तं जपन्तं मन्त्रमैक्षत ॥ 70D, L-75

द्विधाकृतपुरोडाशपुण्यगन्धाधिवासितम् ।
उटजाङ्कणनिष्पन्नयवप्रसवपेशलम् ॥ 70E, L-76

पुण्याहुतिसमुत्थ(द्धूत)धूमधूम(स)रवीरुधम् ।
मण्डलीकृतपुष्पाढ्यमगस्त्याश्रममाश्रयत् ॥ 70F, L-77

दर्भासनसमासीनं तत्रागस्त्यमलोकयत् ।
निवातनिश्चलं दीपमेकाग्रमिव संयतम् ॥ 70G, L-78

पुष्पशय्यासनासीना(नां) मैथिली(लीं) मदिरेक्षणम्(णाम्) ।
दृष्ट्वाश्रमपदं रामो बभाषे प्रीतमानसः ॥ 71A, L-80

कलकण्ठकलध्वानं जृम्भमाणमनोभुवम् ।
पश्य पञ्चवटीं देवि रोचितां रुचिरानने ॥ 71B, L-81

नूनं नः शङ्करी माता यया वनमिहागताः ।
विहाय स्वां धुरं राज्ये सेव्यमिन्द्रादिभिः प्रिये ॥ 71C, L-82

आयान्तीमवलोक्यैनां रामो विस्मयमाययौ ।
बिम्बोष्ठी मृगशावाक्षी किमियं वनदेवता ॥ 72A, L-84

नूनमस्या मुखं दृष्ट्वा धावन्निन्दुजिघित्सया ।
राहुः केशभरोत्प्रेक्षी मयूराशङ्कया ययौ ॥ 72B, L-85

कृपया किन्नु विन्यस्तौ स्तनौ धात्रा मनोभुवः ।
अनङ्ग इति तन्वङ्ग्याः किमेतौ स्वयमाविशत् ॥ 72C, L-86

अस्यास्स्तनभरानम्रमध्यलावण्यमीक्षितुम् ।
नयने निर्मिते नूनं धात्रा लोकानुकम्पया ॥ 72D, L-87

दुर्वहस्तनकुम्भौ ते वोदं(ढुं)नेष्ट(ष्टे) तनूदरम् ।
इतीव कृपया काञ्ची क्रोशति प्रचुरारवम् ॥ 72E, L-88

मुखतीयैः (?) ततः साचिलोचनैर्मधुरस्मितैः ।
नेत्रानन्दकरी तस्मै तिष्ठते स्म निशाचरी ॥ 72F, L-89.

अथ रामः पतीयन्तीमवोचच्चारुहासिनीम् ।
भाविता ते सपत्नीयं कनीयांसं भजस्व मे ॥ 72G, L-90

अथोवाच वृषस्यन्तीं स सौमित्रिरमित्रहा ।
परिणेतुमहं नेशे तमेव भज मानिनि ॥ 72H, L-91

आवासः प(पा)दपावासः वल्कलं शयनं कुशाः ।
मुग्धे किं बहुना कामः क्व वयं क्व तपोधनाः ॥ 72I, L-92

तद्भृत्यं पतिमिच्छन्त्याः किञ्चानिष्टविचेष्टितैः ।
इदं च प्रार्थनीयं ते दास्यं लोकापहासितम् ॥ 72J, L-93

कामकञ्जलते वीरं भजस्व जगतीपतिम् ।
सापत्न्यं प्रायशः सह्यं दास्यं को नाम वाञ्छति ॥ 72K, L-64

प्रत्याख्यातागमत्तेन रामं तेनापि लक्ष्मणम् ।
गमनागमनादोषकलिकेवाकुलाभवत्(?) ॥ 72L, L-95

प्रत्याख्यानमनस्तापपीडितापि मनोभुवा ।
ययाचे पतिमादिष्टा कामाज्ञां तेन कुर्वते ॥ 72M, L-96

निर्गुणेष्वपि सत्त्वेषु साधवः कुर्वते दयाम् ।
आभिजात्यगुणैराढ्यां संग्राह्यां न जहीहि माम् ॥ 72N, L-97

भवल्लभादुत्वभा (?) नूनमनुरूपा सुमध्यमा ।
प्रयच्छ सुभगोत्सङ्गं संयतिस्सुलभा पुनः ।। 72O, L-98

इदमव्याजलावण्यं रूपं कान्तिरमानुषी ।
मर्त्यतामपि नैवाहुर्दूरतो राक्षसीकथाम् ।। 72P, L-99

सा देवीं भर्त्सयामास निःसाफल्यसुखोन्मुखी ।
मन्मथापूरसंपूर्णस्तनभङ्गुरमध्यमा ।। 72Q, L.100

ततस्तद्वधसंभ्रान्तचित्ता रावणपादयोः ।
पपात नासिकाकृत्ता केलके(खेलते?) कोऽयमीदृशम् ।। 75A, L-104

त्वन्मुखाम्भोजवैरूप्यं विद्धि तस्येति भामिनि ।
सान्त्वपूर्वमिदं पृष्ट्वा दशाननमुवाच सा ।। 75B, L-105

न ब्रह्मा न च वैकुण्ठो नापि मुग्धेन्दुशेखरः ।
किन्त्वयोध्यासमुत्पन्नं रक्षोघ्नं परमौषधम् ।। 75C, L-106

अस्य प्रियानवद्याङ्गी गौरीव प्रतिभाति माम् ।
मेनकाद्या दिवादीपश्रियं भेजुर्यदग्रतः ।। 75D, L-107

अथाकर्ण्य वचस्तस्याः पाणिनाश्रु परामृशन् ।
मारीचं प्रेषयामास दर्पिष्ठो वञ्चयेति तम् ।। 75E, L-108

ततस्स मणिचित्राङ्गो मृगरूपी निशाचरः ।
हरिणीयूथमध्यस्थ···वशः(?)शष्पमालिहन् ।। 75F, L-109

लिहन्तं शष्पमालोक्य मृमृ(गं)गेपि (मृग)विलोचना ।
मैथिली विपुलोरस्कमयाचत मृगाजिनम् ।। 75G, L-110

अथ व्याधवदामुक्तजटाजूटः स राघवः ।
आकर्णपूर्णमाकृष्य कोदण्डं मृगमन्वयात् ।। 75H, L-111

अनुतिष्ठति तिष्ठन्तं गच्छन्तमनुगच्छति ।
मायाविनं च मायावीच्छायेव मृगमन्वयात् ।। 75I, L-112

तेन मुक्तः शरो मार्गं मार्गान्तस्य शिरोऽहरत् ।
रक्षोभूयं गतो मार्गं मार्गं हित्वा पपात सः ।। 75J, L-113

रामे चिरयति त्रस्ता(त)मैथिलीप्रहितस्ततः ।
सौमित्रिः प्राञ्जलिर्देवीमुवाच मधुराक्षरम् ।। 75K, L-114

मायाविनां द्विषामास्ये भवतीमविवेकिनीम् ।
अवज्ञाय गुरोराज्ञां त्यजेयं कानने कथम् ।। 75L, L-115

तद्वचःश्रवणाभुग्नभ्रुकुटीकुटिलेक्षणम् ।
भर्त्सयन्ती दृशा सीता गमयामास लक्ष्मणम् ।। 75M, L-116

मामालोकय नीलनीरजदलप्रस्पर्धिना चक्षुषा
हारत्वं मम कण्ठदेशविहितं बाहुद्वयं नीयताम् ।।
उन्नामं नय सुभ्रु वक्त्रशशिनं ज्योत्स्नारसस्यन्दिनं
द्यौरिन्दुद्वयशालिनीं वितनुतां शोभामभूतोद्भवाम् ।। 88A, L-130

कूजत्कोकिलकेलिकल्पितकलक्वाणक्वथन्मानसे
प्रोद्यद्भृङ्गपुरन्ध्रिवृन्दरणितस्फारीभवन्मन्मथे ।
स्फूर्जत्पुष्पपरागपङ्क्तिधवलव्यालोलमत्तानिले
कालेऽस्मिन् रहितस्तया वद कथं प्राणेश्वरः प्राणिति ।।
88B, L-131

Canto XII

शशङ्किरे यान्तमवेक्ष्य वानराः
किमेति कृत्या कुलनाशनोन्मुखी ।
अकाण्डसंहारकृतोद्यमः स्वयं
तृतीयनेत्रं नु विधाय धूर्जटिः ।। 38A, L-39

अमरभवनकल्पं कल्पवृक्षाभिरामं
प्रसवरचितशय्यं शीतलं तोरणाढ्यम् ।
मणिगणगुणचित्रं निर्मितं वस्तुमुख्यैः
कपिकरमवलम्ब्य प्राविशन् मन्दिरं सः ।। 51A, L-53

सौमित्रिपादौ स मृशन् कराभ्या-
मादिष्टवानङ्गदमर्धदृष्ट्या ।
निर्गम्य तस्मादथ यूथनाथा-
नाहूय शीघ्रं समनीनहत्सः ।। 51B, L-54

ध्मातदरोदरनादमनोज्ञं
काहलया सहितं सहसैव ।
उच्चतरध्वनितं पटहानां
सूचयति स्म कपीश्वरयात्राम् ॥ 51C, L-55

तारातनूजमवलम्ब्य मृगेन्द्रगामी
रामानुजो निरगमद्धृतचापलक्ष्मीम् ।
जूटाटवीकलितचन्द्रमरीचिमालो
नन्दीशहस्तमिव मन्दिरतस्त्रिनेत्रः ॥ 51D, L-56

सेनापतिच्छत्रशशाङ्कबिम्ब-
व्रातावरुद्धार्कमरीचिवृन्दा ।
एकातपत्रा पृतना तदासी-
दसौ बहुच्छत्रतयानुयान्ती ॥ 51E, L-57

ऋश्यमूकमथतुङ्गि(ल?)शृङ्ग-
श्रेणिवारितदिवाकरमार्गम् ।
राममन्दिरमलोकयदद्रिं
लक्ष्मणः क्षपितवीरवियोगः ॥ 51F, L-58

अन्त्यकुलकम्—

एकत्र रूप्योपलभिन्नतोयाः
परत्र नीलोपलनीर(ल?)नीराः ।
कलिन्दकन्याजलजातलक्ष्मी-
गङ्गाश्रियो यस्सरितो बिभर्ति ॥[1] 51G, L-59

इन्द्रनीलमणिभूषितमूलं
राजताश्मधवलीकृतमध्यम् ।
हेमरञ्जितनभस्तलमुच्चैः
कुत्र च स्थितमिव त्रिपुरं तम् ॥ 51H, L-60

सौन्दर्यसीमानममन्दरोचि-
र्वृन्दोपमं सान्द्रमरीचिकुन्दम् ।

---

1. After Māgha IV. 26.

दृष्ट्वा तमद्रीन्द्रममन्दनन्दं
सौमित्रिमूचे हरिराजसूनुः ।। 51 I, L-61

अस्य प्रदीप्तस्य विचित्ररत्नै-
रुत्सङ्गभूपातुकनिर्झराणि ।
रत्नप्रदीपानि गुहागृहाणि
लभेत कोऽध्यासितुमीक्षितुं वा ।। 51J, L-62

ऊर्ध्वांशुपाशे दिननाथबिम्बे
यातोदयेऽस्तं व्रजतीन्दुबिम्बे ।
धत्तेऽयमद्रिः प्रविलम्बमान-
घण्टाद्वयाबद्धगजेन्द्रलीलाम् ।।[1] 16A, L-64

यक्षोऽयमक्षिगतपूर्णशशाङ्कबिम्बः
छायाननां हयमुखीं शिखरेऽस्य वीक्ष्य ।
काऽसौ स्फुटेन्दुवदनेति सकौतुकस्तत्
प्रान्तं विषीदति गतोऽथ वृथाप्रयासः ।। 18A, L-66

कैलासशैलमपि साभ्रगजेन्द्रचर्म-
वासोऽवकुण्ठिततनुर्गिरिशोऽधिशेते ।
अस्मिन् सदा सुखकरे निवसन् मनुष्यो
नोपैति किञ्चिदपि दुःखलवं क्रुशोऽपि ।। 19A, L-70

*आनन्दभान(ज)नमपास्तसमस्तदुःखं
निर्धूतजन्ममरणं पदमेतुकामाः ।
अस्मिन् भजन्ति भवभेदधियो मनुष्याः
वेदे यथा दुरितहारिणि गोपितार्थे ।।[2] 21B, L-75

बिम्बं निहत्य परवारणशङ्कयायं
मत्तः करी रुचिरहैमतटे स्वकीयम् ।
विच्छिन्नदन्तमवलोक्य करेणुशङ्की
भूयश्शनैः स्पृशति मन्मथपारवश्यात् ।। 28A, L-77

---

1. After Māgha II. 20.
*21A is found in the 20th canto of JH
2. Cf. Māgha IV. 37.

चुम्बन्तमोष्ठमिह किन्नरमात्मवध्वाः
सत्कुर्वते हयमुखाः मुखपानलुब्धाः ।
श्लिष्यन्तमेनमितरेऽपि तुरङ्गवक्त्रां
पीनोन्नतस्तनभरां परिरम्भकामाः ॥ 28C*, L-79

अह्नि प्रभाकरकराहतसूर्यकान्त-
निर्गच्छदग्निभिरमी परितः परीताः ।
इन्दूपलस्रुतजलोर्मिकृताभिषेका
वप्रास्तपांसि चरतां श्रियमाचरन्ति ॥ 28E*, L-81

श्रुत्वाङ्गदस्येति मधु स्रवन्तीं
वाचं प्रसन्नामथ राजसूनुः ।
आलम्ब्य हस्तं कपिराजसूनो-
रध्यारुरोहाचलमृश्यमूकम् ॥ 28G*, L-83

राजात्मजौ चरणयोः प्रणिपत्य मूर्ध्ना
धृत्वार्पितं शिरसि रामकराङ्गुलीयम् ।
श्रुत्वा तदीयवचनानि कपीन्द्रदृष्ट्या
निर्दिष्टदक्षिणदिशं हनुमान् जगाम ॥ 55A, L-88

भुजङ्गमालिङ्गितरङ्गभङ्ग-
त्वङ्गत्तिमिं शुक्तिविमुक्तमुक्तम् ।
प्रायान्महेन्द्राचलमम्बुराशिं
मत्तेभबन्धार्थमिव प्ररूढम् ॥ 55B, L-89

Canto XIII

रचितैकवेणिमथ रात्रिचरीं
परिवारितां मलिनचन्द्रमुखीम् ।
हरिवेष्टितामिव मृगीं प्रणम-
न्निदधेऽङ्गुलीयकमहं शिरसा ॥ 37A, L-28

निहतोऽङ्गुलीषु पुनरेष तया
कुचकुम्भगण्डनयनेषु मुहुः ।

---

*—28 B is found in Canto xx
*—28 D ,, ,, ,,
*—28 F ,, ,, ,,

हृदि चार्पितस्मरशरव्यथिते
स्तिमि(तं) सलज्जमनिशं ददृशे ।। 37B, L-29

कथमाहतानि पुरुहूतरिपू-
निति चिन्तयन्नहमभीष्टजयः ।
अथ निश्चिकाय वधहेतुरयं
वनभङ्ग एव दृढयुक्तियुतः ।। 37C, L-30

सदशोककाननमपास्तसुरं(र)
द्रुमशोभभूरुहकदम्बधरम् ।
सुरराजनन्दनवनप्रतिमं
सकलर्तुपुष्पनवगन्धवहम् ।। 37D, L-31

प्रियबाहुपीडननिषण्णवधू-
परिमुक्तकल्पकलताभवनम् ।
प्रविभज्य चैत्यगिरिमीक्षितवान्
विनयेन नीतमिव मेरुगिरिम् ।। 37E, L-32

द्रुतकाञ्चनेष्टकचितं शिखर-
स्थितपद्मरागरुचिरांशुचयैः ।
धृतदीपिकाशतमिवोच्चतरं
प्रतिदिङ्मुखं निहितदीपि(प)तरुम् ।। 24A, L-37

कृतबुद्धिबुद्धमुनिशास्त्रपथ-
प्रतिपाद्यवन्दननरार्थतया ।
कृतवन्दनं सुगतशिष्यजनै-
रस(व?)रुज्य तं भुवि निपातितवान् ।। 24B, L-38

अवरुग्णचैत्यतरुषण्डमिदं
प्रतिवीक्ष्य राक्षसवधार्थतया ।
अवलम्ब्यमाननवमुक्तगुणं
मणितोरणं चलपताकमगाम् ।। 24C, L-39

शकलीकृतैकवनबुद्धिरपा-
कृतचैत्यवन्दननरार्थमतिः ।

परपक्षदूषणमयात्मजयो
भवमीशवार्त्तिकपथप्रवरः ।। 24D, L-40

विहिताञ्जलिर्द्विरदकुम्भदृढ-
स्तनभारभङ्गुरविलग्नतया ।
वसनाञ्ज(ञ्च)लापिहितमुग्धमुखं
वदति स्म काचिदिति पङ्क्तिमुखम् ।। 24E, L-41

प्रमदावनं वनजराजिरुचा
रुचिरं चिरध्वनितषट्चरणम् ।
चरणोपनम्रकुसुमप्रचयं
विबभञ्ज कोऽपि कपिरूपधरः ।। 24F, L-42

किमयं हृताभ्रकुपितो मघवा
उत पुष्पकाहरणतो धनदः ।
रजताचलोद्धर(ण)भीतिचल-
न्नयनाद्रिजार्तिकुपितो नु हरः ।। 24G, L-43

जनकात्मजाविरहवह्निशिखा-
घटितो नु दाशरथिरस्तदयः ।
त्वयि चेष्टिते प्रियविधानपरो
न हि विद्म शाधि परपक्षभिया ।। 24H, L-44

श्रुतवाक्यरावणवचःप्रहितान्
प्र(पृ)तनाधिपान् समरमध्यगतान् ।
हरिणीगणानिव हरिर्नखरै-
स्तृणवत्कपाल(?)शितकुन्तमुखैः ।। 24I, L-45

अथ रामदूतनखभिन्नचमू-
पतिशोणितान्त्रभुजगप्रचया ।
जमदग्निसूनुपितृतृप्तिकरी
रुधिरापगेव वहति स्म नदी ।। 24J, L-46

अथ भीततन्मरणकोपचल-
द्दशकण्ठवीक्षितदिशास्तमुखाः ।
समराय निर्ययुरमात्यसुताः
क्रियते यथाहृदयमेव हितम् ।। 24 K, L-47

इतरेतरं स्वशिरसाभिहताः
समरे मया विपिनवह्निरुचा ।
अभजन्त मन्त्रितनयाः प्रचल-
द्रसनाग्रभीषणकृतान्तमुखम् ॥ 24L, L-48

श्रुततद्वधागतभयाकुलितः
कुलि-रिः[1], अक्षमवलोक्य जगौ ।
युधि यत्र मन्त्रितनया निहताः
सुत तत्र तं जहि हमुल्ललितम् (?)[2] ॥ 24M, L-49

मशकोऽयमीश ननु कस्य रिपु-
र्यदि वास्तु रावणरिपुः किमहो ।
अथवानयं(या?)पूतनया किमलं
द्विषतेऽहमेव युधि शाधि विभो ॥ 24N, L-50

इति शूलगर्वितमवेक्ष्य दृशा
कुटिलभ्रुवादिशदथेन्द्ररिपुः ।
स निहन्तुमस्य निरगादशनि-
प्रतिमोग्रशूलमवघूर्ण्य ततः ॥ 24O, L-51

सहसा मदीयनखलूनशिराः
निनिप(निपत ?)न्नसूनमुचदाजिमुखे ।
परिरभ्य नाकवनितामशक-
न्न विमोक्तुमेष मुखपानपरः ॥ 24P, L-52

अमरीमृषन् प्लवगभा(मा)जिभ(म)गा-
दिति बद्धबुद्धिरमरारिसुतः ।
मम वज्रभेदिशरलूनशिरः-
कपिशोणितं पिबतु भूमिरियम् ॥ 24Q, L-53

कपिलीलया निकटवर्तिशरा-
नभितो विभज्य दशनाग्रकरैः ।
प्रतिरोमसायकमुचं हनुमान्
मुमुदे निरीक्ष्य दशकण्ठसुतम् ॥ 24R, L-54

1. A word for Rāvaṇa is required here.
2. May be 'जहिहि दुर्ललितम्'

अथ कालयापनमवेक्ष्य तदा
किमनेन हन्मि ननु दृष्टिविषम् ।
व्यवसाययन्निति निगृह्य करो(रे ?)
दृढमुष्टिनोरसि जघान रिपुम् ॥ 24S, L-55

स समुद्गिरन्नुरुदरीकुहर-
प्रतिमाननेन रुधिरौघजलम् ।
निपपात मस्तकपतन्मुकुटः
समरे गतासुरसुरेन्द्रसुतः ॥ 24T, L-56

अथ रावणिः समरमेत्य शितैः
विशिखैर्बिभेद मम मर्म दृढम् ।
स शरैस्तिरोदधतमात्मवपु-
स्तमवैक्षताथ बहुमानदृशा ॥ 24U, L-57

तमवेक्ष्य दक्षिणमदक्षिणया
क्षणमक्षतं क्षितिजरूक्षदृशा ।
चरणेन मौलिमभिहत्य ततो
ध्वजमच्छिनद्विजयदर्पमिव ॥ 24V, L-58

न च हन्मि वध्यमपि शक्रजितं
दशकण्ठवीक्षणविरोधितया ।
अवलोकनं रणयतो(मरणतो ?) न भवे-
दिति तद्वधं न चकमे सुशर(क ?)म् ॥ 24W, L-59

अथ तत्कृतापजयहीनमुखः
स विरिञ्चनास्त्रमभिमन्त्र्य दृढम् ।
परिणह्य पृष्ठगतहस्तयुगं
तम[व]लोकयद्दशमुखाय सुतः ॥ 24X, L-60

अथ मां निरीक्ष्य भृशमाकुलितः
कलिता(कुलिशा)युधारिरिति शङ्कितवान् ।
किमयं शिलादतनयो भगवान्
वितथे(व्यथते ?) यदीयवचसो हृदयम् ॥ 24Y, L-61

न च शक्यमेनमभिधातुमयं
प्रणिधिर्यतोऽत्र न च दण्डविधिः ।
कृतवाननेकमपराधमतः
स्वयमेव दण्डचतरतामयते ॥ 24Z, L-62

न वियोजयाम्यसुभिरेनमयं
प्रणिधिस्तदीयमुरु पुच्छमहम् ।
करवै विरूपमिति निश्चितधी-
र्भ्रुवमुन्नमय्य भृशमैक्षत माम् ॥ 24A, L-63

अथ रावणेङ्गितविशेषविदो
मम पुच्छदण्डमदहन्नसुराः ।
स च विप्रकीर्णशिखिपुञ्जवहः
सहसोत्पपात भवनान्यभितः ॥ 24 B_1, L-64

ज्वलदग्निपुञ्जकुसुमस्तबकै
रुरुचे ममैष पृथुवालगुणः ।
कनकाद्रिकन्धरविरूढपृथु-
स्तबकोल्लसाग्रनलिनीसरसः ॥ 24 C_1, L-65

अतिसूक्ष्ममेकमपि रोम शिखी
न ददाह चित्रमिति कस्य मतम् ।
सखिसूनुरात्मतनयो हि न चेत्
स्वयमेव वेत्ति रघुनाथशरम् ॥ 24 D_1, L-66

भ्रुकुटीललाटनयनोग्रमुखः
पृथुवालदण्डचलित(चल)चापधरः ।
शिखिभिः स्मराररिव स त्रिपुरीं
सहसा ददाह दशकण्ठपुरम् ॥ 24 E_1, L-67

पुरदाहिनं नु पवनोऽनुययौ
मरुतं कृशानुरथवाऽनुचरः ।
चरतौ तु तौ सह सहायतया
न मयावगम्य तदिहापतिताः ॥ 24F_1, L-68

अधिरुह्य कुट्टिमतलं ददृशुः
परितः शिखाकवलितं भवनम् ।
अवरोधिका भयविमूढधियः
ति(स्ति)मिता बभूवुरवघूतकराः ॥ $24G_1$, L-69

अपहाय पञ्जरमिदं सरले
करकुड्मले कुरु सखी (शुकी?) तनुजम् ।
इति काप्यवोचदयमेति शिखा-
रसनावलीढभवनं दहनः ॥ $24H_1$ L-70

दयितेऽवलम्ब्य मम हस्तमितो
व्रज जीवितेश पुरतः क्रि(स्त्रि ?)यताम् ।
इति मैत्रशाट्य (ठ्य?) मवलम्ब्य मिथो
मिथुनं विपन्नमनलाकुलितम् ॥ $24I_1$, L-71

अतिशीतलाम्बुकणपुञ्जमुचा
व्यजनेन वीजनमिदं सखि मे ।
ज्वलदग्निकुण्डवसनव्यसनं
कुरुते हि कापि जहिहीति जगौ ॥ $24J_1$, L-72

विहसन् कृशानुरवलोक्य वधूं
विगलन्दु(द्दु)कूलजघनं जगृहे ।
अवलम्ब्य हस्तमुपगृह्य ततो
मधुरोष्ठमिष्टवदचुम्बदहो ॥ $24K_1$, L-73

ज्वलनावलीढललिताङ्गलता-
मवलोक्य वल्लभतमामपरम्(रः) ।
अशयिष्ट तां समुपगूह्य सुखी
स्मृततद्गुणानुभवपूर्णमनाः ॥ $24L_1$, L-74

शिशुरग्निमागतमवेक्ष्य भिया
नयने निमील्य नलिनप्रतिमे ।
शयने जुगोप गतिशून्यतया
किमतोऽत्र कृत्यमुचितं विदुषाम् ॥ $24M_1$ L-75

भवनोदरात् किमिति बोद्धुमिमां
तुमुलं बहिष्कृतपदाम्बुरुहाम् ।
तरुणीं तदेतदिति वक्तुमिव
स्वयमेव कर्णमविशद्दहनः ॥ $24N_1$, L-76

अथ काचिदङ्कमधिरोप्य निजं
मुखचुम्बनानि दिशती शिशवे ।
सुखपारवश्यहृषिताङ्गरुहा
न विवेद वह्निदहनव्यसनम् ॥ $24O_1$, L-77

अपराऽऽशुशुक्षणिमवेक्ष्य भिया
तनुजं निगृ(गृ?)ह्य विपुलाङ्कगतम् ।
आ(अप)यातुमुत्थितवती सहसा
रुरुधेऽग्निना झटझटाध्वनिना ॥ $24P_1$, L-78

नवशक्तवोपसरणे(?)त(भ?)वनं
परितः प्रदीप्तमुपवेष्टुमपि ।
इति निश्चिकाय मरणं मिथुनं
न हि कर्म शक्यमतिलङ्घयितुम् ॥ $24Q_1$, L-79

भवनेन याम्यहय(म)नेन लयं
स्वगृहे कुरुष्व तरले धिषणाम् ।
लयमेव यामि न वियोगमहं
ब्रुवती सखीति न परा निरयात् ॥ $24R_1$, L-80

दग्धे पुरेऽपि निखिले न मुमोच लङ्कां
वैरेण किम्नु दहनः सुखलिप्सया वा ।
किं वा हिरण्मयमहीधरनिर्मितत्वाद्
दोधूयमाननवधूमलताविहीनः ॥ 42A, L-83

पुनरप्यपश्यमवनीन्द्रसुतां
क्षितिधूलिधूसरितचारुमुखीम् ।
शरदच्छमेघवि(पि)हितेन्दुकलां
हिमनष्टपद्मनलिनीमिव ताम् ॥ 42B, L-84

चण्डालनीतामिव सामशाखां
वियुक्तकान्तामिव चक्रवाकीम् ।
सोमाहुतिं वा श्वमुखे पतन्तीं
ख्यातिं प्रलीनामिव नीचवाचा ॥ 42C, L-85

आज्ञातिचारो दयितानये स्यात्
स्वतन्त्रता कार्यविरोधिनीयम् ।
एवं विचिन्त्य प्रणिपत्य देवीं
सुवेलमेवागममुच्चशृङ्गम् ॥ 41A, L-91

Canto XIV

अथ जगाद कृताञ्जलिरुद्धतं
कपिपतिः क्षम देव पयोनिधिम् ।
न च तदीयनियोगपुरस्सरं
गिरिकुलं तिमिभिः खलु भक्ष्यते ॥ 52A, L-49

पटकुटीकृतमन्दिरसुन्दरं
शिविरमैक्षत लक्ष्मणपूर्वजः ।
समवलम्ब्य विभीषणमुच्छ्रित-
ध्वजविराजि विवेश निकेतनम् ॥ 83A, L-81

प्रासादतोरणबहिःस्थितकेतुयष्ट्या
रामस्य मारुतिविराजितया प्लवङ्गाः ।
स्वावासभागमधिजग्मुरशङ्कमानाः
देशं न जग्मुरपरे परितो भ्रमित्वा ॥ 83B, L-82

शत्रुं दिवे (शत्रूनिवे) भदृढकुम्भविभेददक्ष-
तीक्ष्णायुधाग्रनखरानपवार्य सिंहान् ।
अध्यासिताद्रिपृथुकन्दरमन्दिराणि
रत्नप्रदीपरुचिराण्यपरे कपीन्द्राः ॥ 83C, L-83

सुग्रीवहस्ते निहितैकपाणि
वितानशीताङ्गणभूचरन्तम् ।
आकाशलक्ष्मीपददत्तदृष्टि
विभीषणो राममिदं बभाषे ॥ 83D, L-84

कथं नु कन्यागमनापवादं
प्रक्षालयेयं जगति प्ररूढम् ।
इतीव भास्वान् परिवृद्धताप-
स्तुलां विशुद्धयर्थमिवारुरोह ॥ 83E, L-85

अम्भोजनेत्रे हसनेन किं ते
यातः प्रियो हाऽयमुदेति वैरी ।
मुञ्चाशु शोभां नयने निमील्य
स्वापं व्रजेत्याह सखीव भृङ्गी ॥ 83G*, L-87

आवेपते भ्रमति रोदिति मोहमेति
कान्तं विलोकयति कूजति दीनदीनम् ।
अस्तं हि भानुरधिगच्छति चक्रवाकी
हा जीवि(व?)तोऽपि मरणं प्रियविप्रयोगः ॥ 83H, L-88

वृद्धोऽपि वृद्धिं पुनरब्धिरेति
ज्योत्स्नाः(त्स्नां)समालिङ्गच तरङ्गहस्तैः ।
ऊर्ध्वाम्बुजो(यो)गैः पुलकैरिवोढै-
स्तन्वी विकारं न करोति केषाम् ॥ 83J*, L-90

Canto XV

ऊर्वशीकरसरोजविधूत-
श्वेतचामरविराजितदेहम् ।
किन्नराङ्गुलिविघट्टिततन्त्री
र्मण्डलक्वणितगाननिषण्णम् ॥ 2A, L-3

मेनकामधुरगानमनोज्ञ-
ध्वानवाद्यलयनाद्भुतनृत्तम् ।
वीक्षमाणमनिमेषविशालो-
त्फुल्लपक्ष्मदलपेशलनेत्रैः ॥ 2B, L-4

---

*83-F found in canto VIII.
*83-I found in canto VIII.

वंशकीर्तिमुखरैः कलनादं
तुम्बुरुप्रमुखवन्दिभिरग्रे ।
स्तूयमानगुणमैक्षत रूक्षं
भीमवक्त्रमथ रावणमेषः ॥ 2C, L-5

रत्नपुञ्जरुचिपिञ्जरमग्रे
सिंहचर्मरचितोपरिभागम् ।
अङ्गदाय सहसादित पीठं
रावणेक्षणनिरीक्षितमेकः ॥ 2D, L-6

राज्यलिप्सुरनुजोऽपि च सेव्यं
सेवते खलु तमाहितभक्तिः ।
तद्विरोधमपहन्तुमनिन्द्यं
रामपादमनिशं भज वीर ॥ 27A, L-30

वालिवालि(ल)वलयाङ्कितबाहुः
शङ्करादिपरिखण्डितमानः ।
अर्जुनेन कलितश्चिरमाजौ
वालिकालमनयाऽऽशु भजेथाः ॥ 27B, L-31

अङ्गुलीयकशिरस्स्थितरत्न-
प्रग्रहावलिकृतोन्मु(ल्मु)कचक्रम् ।
तर्जनीं मुहुरघूर्णयदण्डं
दग्धुकाम इव धूम्रपदाक्षः* ॥ 32A, L-37

वारिराशिजलपूरितपृथ्वी-
मण्डलं शिथिलिताद्रिनिबन्धम् ।
अङ्घ्रिणा खलु महीमथ कोपा-
दाजघान पुरुषान्तकनामा† ॥ 32B, L-38

सामोपायनयप्रपञ्चपटवः प्रायेण ये भीरवः
शूराणां व्यवसाय एव हि परं संसिद्धये कारणम् ।
विस्फूर्जद्विकटाटवीगजघटापीठैकसञ्चूर्णन-
व्यापारैकविनोदनस्य विजये सिंहस्य के मन्त्रिणः ॥ 60A, L-67

---

* धूम्राक्षः
† नरान्तकः

क्षुत्क्षामोऽपि जराकृशोऽपि शिथिलप्राणोऽपि कष्टां दशा-
मापन्नोऽपि विपन्नधीघृतिरपि प्राणेषु नश्यत्स्वपि ।
दर्पाध्मातगजेन्द्रकुम्भदलनप्रेङ्खन्नखाग्राशनिः
किं जीर्णं तृणमत्र(त्ति) मानमहतामग्रेसरः केसरी* ॥ 60B, L-68

Canto XVI

अधरमणिमसौ व्यखण्डयत्ते
स्पृशति शनैरुपचुम्बितो न दोषः ।
अमहदपि कृतं प्रपद्य कर्तु-
र्द्विगुणतरं विदधाति यः स साधुः ॥ 43A, L-44

विरचितप(च?)टुचारुरम्यभावं
प्रमदरसं रतिमूलमादरेण ।
मधुनिहितसरोजमङ्गनाः स्वै-
र्मुखचषकैर्दयितान्निपाययन्ते ॥ 55A, L-57

चषकमधुनि बिम्बितं प्रियाया
वदनमवेक्ष्य सरोजशङ्कयालिः ।
अधिमधु निपपात गन्धलोभाद्
विषयसुखप्रवणे कथं विवेकः ॥ 62A, L-59

दशभिरपि मुखैः सुगन्धि हृद्यं
मधु वदनैरुपनीतमङ्गनानाम् ।
बहुवदनफलं निपीय लेभे
सुररिपुरेतदहो दुरापमन्यैः ॥ 56A, L-63

करकिसलयधूननं मुखान्तः
कलमणितं नयनार्धमीलितानि ।
अविरतकलसीत्कृतं वधूनां
प्रणयिषु मन्मथदीपनान्यभूवन् ॥ 58A, L-65

अपगतविनयं यदस्तलज्जं
यदसमयं यदनिष्टमस्तधैर्यम् ।
यददयमसमाधि रागवृद्धं
रतिषु हि तत्तदभूद्गुणो न दोषः ॥ 58B, L-66

---

* found in Bhartṛhari's *Nītiśataka*.

उपरि विहरणे विलासिनीनां
कुचकलशोद्गलितं निदाघवारि ।
मनसिजमभिषिञ्चति स्म यूनां
पृथुलभुजान्तरपीठसन्निविष्टम् ॥ 58C, L-67

वदनमिदमुरोजकुङ्कुमार्द्रं
सुतनु विलोकयताद्(?)इति स्वमङ्कम् ।
सरभसमधिरोपिता तदोष्ठं
क्व नु तदिति ब्रुवती चुचुम्ब हृष्टा ॥ 58D, L-68

तरुणि तव भवामि वल्लभाहं
भव पतिरित्युदिते शिरो धुनाना ।
न हि न हि वलयं स्वकीयमेका
दयितकरे न्यधितारुरुक्षुरङ्कम् ॥ 58E, L-69

Canto XVII

ततस्स रात्रिं मदकातरं तरन्
प्रियाश्रितं सौरभवासितं सितम् ।
निशम्य सूतादिति शंसतस्ततः
ससर्ज तल्पं मणिभास्वरं स्वरम् ॥ A, L-1

उल्कामुखैरुज्ज्वलिताखिलाशैः
प्लवङ्गमा मानसमानमानाः ।
तृणीकृतारात्रि(ति)पुरं रिपूणां
देहुर्यशो मानसमानमानाः ॥ B, L-2

रामः स्थितः कुत्र चमूचखो (चरा वा ?)
क्व चापयाता इति भाषमाणाः ।
इतस्ततो निर्ययुरायुधीया
युद्धाय चक्रीकृतचारुचापाः ॥ C, L-3

समरशिरसि धौतखड्गरेखा-
रुचिपरिपि(बृं)हितकुण्डलं दधानाम् ।
त्रिशिरसमवलोक्य रामदूतो
हरिणमिवाभिययौ मृगाधिराजः ॥ D, L-4

पत्रिभिरेष बिभेद रणस्थं
राघवदूतमनिन्दितशौर्यम् ।
राक्षसलोल(क)भयङ्करमुग्रं
शैलमिवाशनिना पुरुहूतः ।। 1A, L-6

रिपुमुदारमुदाररवाकुलं
भयविमूढविमूढजयश्रियम् ।
अरिमहाहिमहाहितपन्नगं
नगसमुक्तसमुक्तसरोऽन्वितम् ।। 1B, L-7

भिन्नेऽथ शैले शितचित्रपु(ङ्खैः)-
र्मध्यं ध्वजिन्याः क्षणमेव गत्वा ।
सैन्यान्ममाथायमुपात्तकोपो
रङ्कूनिवैणाधिपतिः समन्तात् ।। 1C, L-8

अश्वानश्वैर्वारणैर्वारणेन्द्रान्
शस्त्रैश्शूरान् स्यन्दनैः स्यन्दनस्थान् ।
एको वीरः पत्तिभिः पत्तिमेवं
यावद्दृशं व्याजघानारिसैन्यम् ।। 1D, L-9

भङ्क्त्वा हस्तैरथ रथमश्वैर्गाढं
हृत्वा ··· निशितमसिं तीक्ष्णाग्रम् ।
(तेनाला)तेनालावी(त्)सतिमिति(समिति?)शिरांसि क्षिप्रं
शत्रोः शि(शी)तस्तृणमिव लीलावेगात् ।। 12A, L-11

श्रुत्वा वचः कोपविवृत्तनेत्र-
ज्वालावलीभीममुखाग्निपुञ्जः ।
सद्यस्त्रिलोकीमिव लब्धुकामात्(दग्धुकामः)
सिंहासनादिन्द्ररिपुश्चचाल ।। 2A, L-14

श्रुत्वा वाणीं पितुरिदमवदत्
शक्रारि[तु]स्तं त्वयि धृतधनुषि ।
शैलाः कम्पं विदधति चलति
क्षोणी का ते रिपुमृगगणना ।। 20A, L-19

अथ तमुद्धतमाह नरान्तको
हनुमता(दा)स्त्रभुजङ्गमसेविताम् ।
रिपुमुखाम्बुजशोणितकुङ्कुमै-
र्युधि समर्पयिता विजयश्रियम् ॥ 21A, L-21

देवान्तकोऽपि वदति स्म तमस्मदीय-
बाणावलूनरिपुशोणितशोणवाहाः ।
नद्यस्स्फुरास्त्रभुजगीगणसेव्यमानाः
संपूरयेयुरखिलं समरं समन्तात् ॥ 23A, L-23

तव यशश्शशिनिर्मलभास्वरं
कुचतटार्पितहारमनोहरम् ।
हरिकिरीटशिखामणि किं पुनः
क्षितिपसूनुरवैति भयङ्करम् ॥ 24A, L-25

आक्षिप्तैः प्रतिपक्षभूमिपतिभिः क्रुद्धो न देव त्वया
वित्रस्तैर्न महायुधानि विविधान्याविष्क्रियन्ते युधि ।
दूरावर्जितमौलये तनुभिते····केवलं
नानाकारकिरीटरत्ननिकरैरिन्द्रायुधानि क्षितौ ॥ 25A, L-27

अद्यैव पुष्पाणि पतन्ति भूमौ
द्रक्ष्यामि जित्वा रिपुमायुधीयम् ।
कृत्वेति बुद्धिं सहसारुरोह
प्रोन्नाहिताङ्घ्रिर्गजराजमेकः ॥ 26A, L-29

करतलविहिताङ्गस्फालनै(:)या(?)गृहीत्वा
चलितललितगात्राद्(न्)बद्धपल्यान(ण)वम्रा(धा)न् ।
अधिरुरुहुरनङ्गे (नेके ?) साधि(दि)नो लाघवाढ्यं
कनककुथविचित्रान् वज्रहस्तास्तुरङ्गान् ॥ 27A, L-31

नियमितजवनाश्वान् रत्नकिञ्जल्करा-त्(-रागान् ?)
कमलमुकुलरोचिः क्रीडतोरङ्ग(क्रीडितोत्तुङ्ग ?)केतून् ।
अधिरुरुहुरथैते(के) स्फारयन्तो धनुर्ज्यां(ज्यां)
करधृतकशसूतान् स्यन्दनान् श्वं ततानः(?) ॥ 28A, L-33

दन्ता न यातो (?) पुनरस्मदीय-
दृष्टे भुवं (?) बुद्धवतीव नूनम् ।
आनेतु (त्र) मार्गादनिमेषमेका
युद्धाय यान्तं मुहुरीक्षते स्म ।। 29A, L-35

निर्वर्तितो मातृवचोभिरेक-
स्तातस्त्व (तात क्व) यासीति वदन् स्वसूनुः ।
यातो रणायास्य चकर्त धैर्यं
तथ्यं वदत्ये (व) शिशुः कदाचित् ।। 30A, L-37

भेरीकटुक्वाणनिरुद्धकर्णं
भूरेणुपुञ्जावृतदृष्टिमार्गाः ।
संधाय सैन्या निरयुः स्वकेतू-
नानम्य ते तोरणमध्यभागे ।। 31A, L-39

विलोक्य दूरे सुरशत्रुसेनां
गजेन्द्रघण्टाघटिताश्वहेषाम् ।
समाजुहावेव समीरधूत-
ध्वजाङ्गुलीभिः समराय सैन्यम् ।। 18A, L-41

तिरोदधुश्शङ्ख (ङ्कु) भिरग्निकल्पै-
राकाशमम्भोभि (भिरिवो) दवाहाः ।
छिन्नैः शिरोभिः पृथिवीं कपीनां
दैत्या विनम्रीकृतभीमचापाः ।। 32A, L-43

मुखपटपिहितार्थ (क्ष?) श्चर्मंत (चामर?) द्वन्द्वग (ण्डः ?)
(म) दसलिलविवासा (सुवासः?) संभ्रमभ्रान्तभृङ्गाः (ङ्गः) ।
कठिनमुसलहस्तश्शत्रुसैन्यं विधून्वन्
जलनिधिमिव युद्धं नागभा- जगाहे ।। 19A, L-45

मुक्तामुक्तैरायुधैर्हन्यमानाः
स्थातुं सेनानीश्वरा राक्षसेनैः ।
युद्धे भीता वानरेन्द्रेण सद्यः
सह्येनेवारोधि सिन्धुः सवेगः ।। 10A, L-47

के(कौ)चित्समक्षं कुपितौ समेतौ
वेगेन पाणिग्रहमाशु कृत्वा ।
शस्त्राणि मुक्त्वा दृढमुष्टिघातै-
स्तंताप(स्तान्ताव ?)यातामथ मल्लयुद्धम् ।। 33A, L-49

मुहुरकारि हतैः कलभैरवः
पतितहस्तिपकैः कलभं रवः ।
मृधमुखं ययुरावणवाजिभि- (?)
स्तुरगिणः सहसा रणवाजिभिः ।। 33B, L-50

प्रकाशयन्तो जयमाप्नुवन्तः
क्वचिन्न सङ्गं निशिताः पतन्तः ।
अपेत्य किञ्चित्प्लवगैः कराग्रै-
र्बभञ्जिरे युद्धमुखे कलम्बाः ।। 33C, L-51

समरशिरसि कश्चित् जीवपूर्वं गृहीत्वा
निशितपरशुशूलप्रासखड्गाभि(दि ?)शस्त्रम् ।
निखिलमपि च हृत्वा प्राहिणोदक्षताङ्गं
कपिबलभि(मि)दमेव प्राभवं मानभाजाम् ।। 7A, L-53

कपीन्द्रसूनुर्बलभङ्गमुग्रै-
रुद्भिन्नखैश्चक्रतुरङ्गमारी ।
इति स्म यासीस्सुतमाह बाणै-
रुद्भिन्नखैश्चक्रतुरङ्गमारी ।। 7B, L-54

अङ्गदमाजिजये यतमानो
भीमबलाम्बुधिमध्यनिविष्टः ।
क्षोभितवानरसैन्यसमुद्रो
निर्दयमाहतवान् किल बाणै : ।। 7C, L-55

उन्मग्नलोचनयुगो हरिराजसूनु-
रामूललून इव कल्पतरुः पपात ।
जेतुं ततो···वानरराजमाजौ
कामस्त्रिणेत्रमिव साहसिकः प्रपेदे ।। 36A, L-57

रासभरासभयावहसेना
सादरसादरमायतचापा ।
वारणवारणशब्दितघण्टा
रासितरासितमाप जगाम ।। 41A, L-59

अथ जगाद पलायितमाहवाद्
बलमुपेत्य चमूपतिरन्तरा ।
इदमयुक्तमुपेत रणाजिरं
कृतमहातुमुलं हरिसैनिकैः ।। 41B, L-60

शिरांसि भिन्दन्ति चमूचराणां
खड्गैस्तदीयैस्तृणवत्प्लवङ्गाः ।
निर्वर्तिता तेन जगाम युद्धं
प्राणिक्षयक्षोभितसिन्धुवेगाः ।। 5A, L-62

कोप(कोऽपि ?)द्विपानुग्रनखैरलावीत्
कार्तस्वरापूरितरामणीयान् ।
....
....................................5B, L-63

केचिन्निशातकरवालभुजङ्गभीमा
जित्वा कपीनथ सहैव गताः कपीन्द्रम् ।
खड्गैर्विभिन्नशिरसः समरे स्वकीयै-
र्देहान् विहाय पुरुहूतपुरं प्रपन्नाः ।। 15A, L-66

सहसारणमारणप्रभावैः
समयुध्यन्त सुरारयः प्लवङ्गैः ।
सहसारणमारणप्रभावै-
र्निहताः पेतुरधोमुखं समीपे ।। 37A, L-68

हत्वा कपोले दृढमुष्टिनाग्रे
जहार कुन्तं निशिताग्रधारम् ।
तेनैव भू(भि)त्त्वा हृदयं सुरारिः
कञ्चित्क्षणं भ्रामयति स्म युद्धे ।। 37B, L-69

वृन्दं निहत्याजिभयासितानां
दित्वा कृपाणप्रभया सितानाम् ।
व्रातैर्हताघोरणतोमराणां
पुरीं ययुस्ते रणतोऽमराणाम् ॥ 39A, L-72

अरोधि नागै रिपुभिश्च सैन्यं
ततार जीमूतघटासमानैः ।
कृत्वाशुगैराशु वियोगमेषां
ततार जीमूतघटासमानैः ॥ 6A, L-77

वृत्तमेकमुपगुह्य सुरस्त्री
दक्षमिष्टमुदिता सुरसङ्घे ।
नोज्झितुं रहसि सौरत-रागा-
दक्षमिष्ट मुदितासुरसङ्घे ॥ 38B,* L-81

कृत्तं शिरश्चेति जगाद कश्चिद्
पितृव्यपेते हरिणा क्षमायाः ।
वक्तुं द्विषा वक्षसि पादघातं
पितृव्यपेते हरिणाक्षमायाम्(याः) ॥ 17A, L-86

एवं कश्चिद्बोधितो धावमानः
सेनां हित्वा भिन्नवक्षाः परेण ।
सद्यः शूलं घूर्णते(?) कालभूतं
मध्ये युद्धं प्राविशद्वीर्यशाली ॥ 8A, L-89

कृत्वैव युद्धं प्लवगैस्समीके
सेनामयोधामकरेभवाङ्कैः ।
शुश्राव कश्चित् क्रकरे समीपं
सेनामयोधामकरेभवाङ्कैः ॥ 8B, L-90

* 38-B found in canto V

रिपुवक्त्रसरोजराजितत्री (श्री?)
रुधिरापूरजलाहितोर्मिमालाः ।
करिहस्तभुजङ्गमाङ्घ्रिकूर्माः
सरितः सङ्गरतो ययुर्जवेन ।। 13A, L-93

नवविखण्डनमूरुतलोल्लस-
त्कदलिकासुरराजमहासिना ।
बलमनेन किमुद्धतमुत्पत-
त्कदलिकासुरराजमहासिना ।। 39A, L-95

समरपटहवाद्ये काहलागायिकोन्य (द्यद्)-
ध्वनितमधुरगाने राजसूनोस्समीपे ।
ननृतुरथ कबन्धा हीनचक्षुःप्रयोगा
बहलरुधिरधाराः कुङ्कुमालिप्तगात्राः ।। 39B, L-96

पुरा न भीता युधि कातरेतरे
जगद्विपत्तौ कृतसंयमे यमे ।
विजित्य जग्मुर्जितशम्भुजैर्भुजै-
र्यशस्तथैके स्तुतिमासितं सितम् ।। 39C, L-97

समरविषयसङ्गाश्शत्रवो मुक्तवार (?)
हितविषयमसङ्गैरन्तरीक्षं प्रयातैः ।
क्रमविहितपतङ्गैर्वायुवेगैर्विभिन्ना
मुहुरकृषत युद्धं दुच्चितालोकवृत्तिः (?) ।। 39D, L-98

तेनैकान्ते व्यरमत कान्ता
लोकालोकास्यान्ता जि यशसि कान्ता (?) ।
लोकानन्दा कृतरतलीला
रम्भाश्रोणिशशिलीलारम्भाः ।। 40A, L-100

Canto XVIII

छादयन्नाशुगैराजि समायोधनयोजितः ।
रामेण सहसा शूरः समायोधनयोजितः ।। 5A, L-6

द्विषतामायुधैरेवमस्मदीया पताकिनी ।
विबला चलितादित्यद्युतिभिः प्रथमं कृता ।। 46A, L-48

विव्याध सायकच्छन्नभूतलोहितकं बलम् ।
रामस्तत्र शरैः शूरभूतलोहितकम्बलम् ॥ 54A, L-57

सा तेनाहवनादश्रीपीतेनाजि निनादवे ।
भीतेनायुधिनादत्ता भीतेनाहवनादयः ॥ 63A, L-66

विश्वामित्रशतानन्ददूषणेऽस्मिन् हते बभौ ।
विश्वामित्रशतानन्दसम्मतो विजयश्रिया ॥ 63B, L-67

यातुधानैः प्रयुक्ताशीः यातु धाम दिशो गजान् ।
यातु राजिरथेन्द्रारेः यातुराज जयोऽस्तु ते ॥ 63C, L-68

नुन्नानीकानकानेको नाकिकैः कनकाननः ।
कननौकाः कनकोनो नीकिनी नकनीनिकः ॥ 56A, L71

—द्व्यक्षरम् ।

सटाच्छटाविभिन्नाभूत्तीक्ष्णदंष्ट्राभयङ्करः ।
नरसिंह इवालावीन्नखैर्वक्षस्सु विद्विषः ॥ 56B, L-72

कृताननपटैर्नागैः कटकं प्रमदालिभिः ।
साधीयो मुसलै रुग्णं कटकं प्रमदालिभिः ॥ 56C, L-73

शोकाशककृशाकाशः किंशुकांशुकशङ्कुकः ।
कौशिकाङ्कुशकोशेशः शुककाशांशुकांशुकः ॥ 56D, L-74

—द्व्यक्षरम् ।

रावणिर्मुमुदे धन्वी स्वनन्तमदमोहितः ।
गणमालोक्य युध्यन्तं स्वनन्तमदमोहितः ॥ 56E, L-75

हनुमन्निह मामेहि मानं हन्मि महाहिना ।
ननु हानीहमानेन हीनमोहमहाहनिः ॥ 56F, L-76

—त्र्यक्षरम् ।

इत्थं वदति दैन्येऽन्यो दरीपदतिसङ्गरः ।
तदास्यं पाटयामास तदास्यन्नखरै रथम् ॥ 56G, L-77

भ्रमयन् शूलमुद्भिन्ना भ्रमयन्नुन्नवानरम् ।
वानरप्रचयं त्रासयन्नासक्तमतिः(?)क्रुधा ॥ 56H, L-78

मायामयमयामेयो मायायामामयायमा ।
मायामयमयायीयो मायो यो ययुयाथमः ॥ 56I, L-79

—द्व्यक्षरमा[या]दियमकमूर्धन्यमसंयोगाक्षरं च ॥

जीवग्राहं गृहीत्वान्ये वधाग्राहोवतो वतः ।
बलं ग्राहरदानित्थमूचुर्ग्राहपरान् परान् ॥ 58A, L-81

नमनामाननामीना मामिमानमाननु ।
नममानानमीनाना मामिमानमना ननुः ॥ 58B, L-82

—द्व्यक्षरम् ।

मानवादरमायाति स्मरणादरितापदः ।
" " " " ॥ 59A, L-84

—समुद्गयमकम्

रामनामाक्षरेषूग्रैः शोणितैर्मास्तु शोणिमा ।
इतीव रिपुगात्रेभ्यो जगृहुर्जीवितं शराः ॥ 59B, L-85

सासारि सरसीसूरा रिरंसुरसुरैरसौ ।
सासारि सरसीसूरः सूरिः सारसिरासिराः ॥ 59C, L-86

—द्व्यक्षरं पादयमकं च ।

ईषत्कटाक्षविक्षेपपुरस्सरमथानुजः ।
आदेश इव रामस्य भेजे स्थानममित्रहा ॥ 59D, L-87

तयोर्युद्धमभूज्जेतुमुत्साहबलयोर्मिथः ।
मुक्तामुक्तैर्विभिन्नाभ्रं शङ्करान्त(ध)कयोरिव ॥ 6A, L-89

रुचिराचारचारार्चा चोरारी रुरुचे चरः ।
चारु चीररुचीरोचिरुच्चार्चाचिरुरुचीचरः ॥ 6B, L-90

—द्व्यक्षरम् ।

मीनेनानूनमौनूनं मिन्नमानोननून्मनाः ।
माननिम्नो नमीनानमुन्नमेनानमन्निमम् ॥ 60A, L-92

—द्व्यक्षरम् ।

निरस्यारिबलं बाणैरिन्द्रजिज्जयवाञ्छया ।
सौमित्रिहृदयं भित्वा रुरुचे विजयश्रिया ॥ 60B, L-93

नुन्ननीविनवीनेन वनिनावननाविना ।
...नेव नवान्नूना वनिनावननाविना ।। 60C, L-94
—द्वयक्षरं पादयमक च ।

तेनाच्छेदिन्द्रजित्सैन्यं सकलम्पास्सि मानवम् ।
हित्वा हृदि ततौ मौर्वी सकलं पास्सि मानवम् ।। 60D, L-95

पीतपोततपोपेतः पीततापपतीतितः ।
ततापापतितापत्तिः पत्तिः पातिततत्ततिः ।। 61A, L-97
—द्वयक्षरम् ।

ते रिपून् बिभिदुर्वर्मचित्रभानुचिताहवे ।
गणदाक्षे यथा क्रोधचित्रभानुचिताहवे ।। 61B, L-98

सहसा सहसा सेहे हे से साहस साहसा ।
साहसा सहसा सेहे हे से साहस साहसा ।। 61C, L-99
—द्वयक्षरं समुद्गयमकं पादार्धप्रतिलोमं निरोष्ठ्यम् अमूर्ध-
न्यमसंयोगाक्षरं च ।।

शरच्छिन्नगलः सूतो रणादिव निवृत्तये ।
तस्यापाते पतत्तन्वा शिरसा रावणस्य च ।। 61D, L-100

प्रत्यक्षेऽपि परोक्षेऽपि तस्यानकभयानकः ।
शिरोभारः सुराभारः तेनाङ्कुशनिरङ्कुशः ।। 61E, L-101

विषमं चक्रजालेन सर्वतोभद्रसम्भ्रमम् ।
युद्धं काव्यमिवाधीरैः दुरीक्षमभवत्तयोः ।। 61F, L-102

चक्राश्वे पत्तिभिर्भिन्ने विशदभ्रान्तमाशये ।
छद्मनारीन् जयन् युद्धे विशदभ्रान्तमाशये ।। 61G, L-103

निपतन् पत्तिमार्गेण मुक्तैरिषुभिरम्बरान् ।
भिन्नमर्मापतद्भूमौ क्षीणपुण्य इवेन्द्रजित् ।। 61H, L-104

काकुकाको कुकाकाङ्के किं ककाकिककङ्कके ।
ससाससससीसासो सासासासिससूस्ससोः ।। 61I, L-105
—एकाक्षरार्धम् ।

सद्यश्चिच्छेद बाणेन मुष्टेरुपरि कार्मुकम् ।
इन्द्रारेः सोऽपरं चापं गृहीत्वा युयुधे पुनः ।। 61J, L-106

विभीषणो जगादाथ लक्ष्मीलक्षणलक्ष्मणम् ।
लीलया कृतमिन्द्रारिं जहि वध्यं जगत्पते ।। 61K, L-107

शिञ्जिनीदीधितिप्रीतिकीर्तिश्चीरिक्षिती विधिः ।
नीतिवीधिनिधिद्वीपिकीर्तिदीपिगिरिस्थितिः ।। 61L, L-108

—इवर्णवान्

शरं रणे ज(ज्य?)या मुक्तमेघनादमनिन्दितम् ।
हन्तुं स वीर्यतो मुक्तमेघनादमनिन्दितम् ।। 61M, L-109

करिष्ये सुखमिन्द्रारेः कृत्तेन शिरसा हरेः ।
चिन्तयन्निव मुक्तेषु कण्ठं तस्याशु शिश्रिये ।। 61N, L-110

सादरं दरहन्तारं तारतारभयङ्करम् ।
करं करत्तमात्रासत्रासत्रासं चकर्त सः ।। 61O, L-111

—असवर्णवान्

लूनं तस्य शिरः कायात् पपात रुधिरारुणम् ।
सन्ध्यारागारुणं भानोः बिम्बमस्तगिरेरिव ।। 61P, L-112

रामारिर्मर्मरो रेमे मामामारुरुमारिरी ।
मारोरुमुम्मरोरीरो मेरुरामारमामरैः ।। 61Q, L-113

—द्व्यक्षरम्

युद्धे शक्रजितं वृत्तमाश्लिषत्सुरसुन्दरी ।
इभकुम्भदृढोत्तुङ्गस्तनभङ्गुरमध्यमा ।। 61R, L-114

दिव्या जगौ रणे रागादिवसाधिपराशये ।
संहतिर्मधुरं तस्मै दिवसाधिपराशये ।। 61S, L-115

शिलीमुखमुखक्षुण्णमकरन्दसुगन्धिनी ।
पपात सुमनोवृष्टिः सुमित्रातनयेऽम्बरात् ।। 61T, L-116

धूम्राक्षपतनं तेन विध्वस्तमितरं जनम् ।
श्रमोदयदिवाम्भोजं विध्वस्तमितरञ्जनम् ।। 61U, L-117

प्रजङ्घस्म(स्य?)रुषा कालादपरो हस्तिवाहनः ।
निश्चितेन हता स्वस्मादपरो हस्तिवाहनः ।। 61V, L-118

पशुघातघ्नता शूरमङ्गदेन नरान्तकम् ।
योगाद्बलीयसी रूढिरिति स्पष्टीकृतः परम् ।। 61W, L-119

किशेशशिशुकोशोककोशशङ्काशुकेशकः ।
शशाक काशकः केशाकेशिकोशः कुशेशकः ।। 61X, L-120

—द्व्यक्षरम्

वैराशंसनमालोक्य वैराशंसनमुष्टिना ।
करेण निहतो रक्षः करेण प्रमृडे(धे?) परः ।। 61Y, L-121

धीरो धीरो धराधीरोधराधरधराधरः ।
सुरसासुरसारासस्सुरसारिः ससौरसीः ।। 61Z, L-122

—त्र्यक्षरम्

पश्यत्तनुं शिरस्स्वीयामहीनां पतितामदः ।
जहौ महोदरस्याग्रे महीनां पतितामदः।। 61A, L-123

पलाशपत्रपातालं पीतमासारसस्वना ।
पलायतस्समीपात्सा सहस्तः सेन्दिरासुतैः ।। 65A, L-126

—गूढसम्बन्धः

कर्कंरार्ककराकारः करीरकरकोरकः ।
क्रूरकिङ्कररङ्कूरः करङ्ककुलकोकिकैः ।। 65B, L-127

—द्व्यक्षरम्

विभीषणमवष्टभ्य स्थितः सौमित्रिणा बभौ ।
ब्रह्मेन्द्रसहितेशानलक्ष्मीरामो रणाजिरे ।। 65C, L-128

नुन्ननानाननोनेना नन्नेनानिन्ननुन्निनो ।
नुन्नान्निनोने नानुन्ना नोनिनन्ननु···।। 65D, L-129

—एकाक्षरं यमकं च ।

सेनानीस्तस्य सावन्या समानी चतुरङ्गया ।
निर्ययौ पुरतः शृङ्गी समानी चतुरङ्गया ।। 66A, L-131

रुद्राद्रिदारदोरारदारादरदुरोदरः ।
रुरुरादरदोद्दूरे दारादरदुरोदरः ।। 66B, L-132
—द्व्यक्षरं पादयमकं च ।

कङ्कालमालया दत्तविषमांसो विभूषितः ।
कङ्कालमालया दत्तविषमांसो विभूषितः ।। 66C, L-133
—समुद्गयमकम्

रुरोध रुधिरा राधी रराधि-धराधरा ।
धुरोरेरधिधीराराधि - - - धराधरा ।। 67A, L-135

तस्या[1]**कुञ्चित**[7]**जानु**मद्रिसदृशं देहं[10] ददौ [4]**दाहिना**
सङ्ग्रा**मा**[2]ग्रम[8]**नलपराक्षसजयश्री**[11]**रञ्जितं** [5]**सर्वदा** ।
कृत्वा [3]**रक्षित**[9]**कीर्तिसाहसमपि** प्रा[12]**णं** **बलस्य**[6] क्रुधा
-ष्टयेश्वा तनुशासनोऽपि कृतयानादी तदानेकधा (?)।। 75A, L-144
(कविकाव्यनामाङ्कम्—कुमारदासस्य जानकीहरणम्)

Canto XIX

प्रपद्य तं नायकरत्नरञ्जितं
परं परार्ध्या कटकं पताकिनी ।
विभूषितेव ज्वलदङ्गदागदा
जगाम सुग्रीवविभीषणान्विता । 2A, L-3

सहस्ररश्मिद्युतिपुञ्जपिञ्जरे
रथः ससूतः पुरुहूतचोदितः ।
अथाविरासीद्दिवि दिव्यकेतनः
स विश्वरूपो भगवानिवांशुमान् ।। 2B, L-4

तमारुरोहागतमात्तकार्मुकः
करं गृहीत्वा पुरुहूतसारथेः ।
निबद्धजूटस्त्रिपुरीजिगीषया
पितामहस्येव करं त्रिलोचनः ।। 4A, L-7

रथचक्रनिवर्तनोत्थभीम-
ध्वनिभिन्नश्रवणं रथः सुरारेः ।
विधिसारथिचोदितः प्रपेदे
समरं कम्पितकेतुराजितश्रीः ।। 4B, L-8

शिताग्रमुग्रं खरनाशनं शरं
शरासनासन्नहिते विलोकयन् ।
स तेन कोपेन चिरोपसेविना
तदैव योगं व्रजति स्म रावणः ।। 6A, L-11

मुहुरध्वनदुच्चकैः सलीलं
रिपुणास्फाटि(लि)तकार्मुकं महीयः ।
प्रलयोद्धतवायुवर्धितोच्च-
स्फुटकल्पाग्निशिखासमानजीवम् ।। 6B, L-12

बहिरावरणं न चास्ति यस्य
प्रभया सर्वमिदं तिरोहितं च ।
तमहो किल साहसी पुमांसं
स तिरस्कर्तुमथाशुगैर्ववर्ष ।। 6C, L-13

विशुद्धिभाजो दधतः प्रगल्भतां
गृहीतपक्षाद् दृढयुक्तिमङ्गलान् ।
सुसंहतानेष रणे शिलीमुखान्
मुमोच शब्दानिव वादिरावणः ।। 9A, L-16

निशितैर्विशिखैः सुवर्णपुङ्खैः
पिहिते राजसुते सुरारिसङ्घाः ।
तमसां पटलेन भानुबिम्बे
बहुलेनेव निशानना ननन्दुः ।। 9B, L-17

कृतसारसनादगङ्कमुच्चैः(?)
स्फुरितज्यारुचिरं सुवर्णचित्रम् ।
ध्वनति स्म शरासनं गरीया(?)
गुरुणास्फालितमुच्चलत्पताकम् ।। 9C, L-18

कृतमावरणं परेण बाणैः
पृथुदुर्भेदमशेषसैन्यनीडम् ।
अनुमानमसिद्धसाधनाद्यैः
प्रतिवादीव निराचकार रामः ।। 13A, L-23

परितः शरजालरन्ध्रनीडे
नृपसूनोरिषुभिस्ततो निरस्ते ।
रुरुचुः प्लवगाः पयोदजाले
प्रहृते वायुवशादिवोडुसङ्घाः ।। 13B, L-24

रणशक्तिरियं नु वैष्णवीया
यदि वा पाशुपती, न मानुषी स्यात् ।
इति निश्चितधीर्विजेतुमेनं
मुमुचे स्वापनमस्त्रमस्त्रशाली ।। 23A, L-35

विरहय्य तमोऽभिराममेकं -
कपिसैन्यं रजनीमिवाससाद ।
अथ नेत्रयुगं न्यमीलदेके
समवष्टभ्य परस्परं निषण्णाः ।। 23B, L-36

द्विगुणीकृतपक्ष्ममीलिताक्षी (क्षाः?)
प्रकटस्वापशिरःप्रणामकम्पाः ।
अभवन्नपरे वसन्नभस्ताः(?)
तरुरन्यस्य पपात पुष्पपालिः ।।(?) 23C, L-37

शिथिलाग्रकराः क्षणेन मील-
न्नयना वन्यगजा इव प्लवङ्गाः।
विटपेषु महीरुहां निषेदु-
र्विपुलैरंसतटैरभिन्नधैर्याः ।। 23D, L-38

अथ मेरुतटादिवार्कबिम्बं
तिमिरोन्मूलनमूलमाविरासीत् ।
कमलद्युतिदीपिताखिलाशं
पृथुरोचिर्मनुवंशकेतुमूर्ध्नः ॥ 23E, L-39

अथ नैशमिवान्धकारमर्क-
प्रसभं(प्रभवैः?) तत्तिमिरं-र्निरासे ।
नयनानि च नै[न्]द्रपारवश्यं
जहुरादित्यगभस्तिभिः प्रसस्तैः(न्नैः?) ॥ 23F, L-40

उरगाभरणोऽपि यस्य मूर्तिः
शयनं यस्य च नागराडनन्तः ।
तमयं किल भोगिभिर्विजेतु
भुजगास्त्रं मुमुचे भुजङ्गभीमम् ॥ 23G, L-41

अथ फुल्लफणा भुजङ्गसङ्घा
रसनालीढमुखोभयप्रदेशाः ।
विषवह्निशिखा विलोलजिह्वा
गतपीडाखिललोकमाविरासन् ॥ 23H. L-42

शिरोविलम्बाहिजटास्समन्ततो
ललाटमध्यस्थविषाग्निलोचनाः ।
कृतोपवीता भुजगैः प्लवङ्गमा-
विडम्बयन्ति स्म कपालिनः श्रियम् ॥ 23I, L-43

रराज कश्चित्फणरत्नभासुरै
र्भुजङ्गमैराशिरसोऽभिवेष्टितः ।
विनिद्रपुष्पस्तबकोल्लसल्लता-
वितानसंवेष्टितभूधरश्रिया ॥ 23J, L-44

विषानलालीढमशेषसैनिकं
निरीक्ष्य चित्रप्रतिमं निरीहितम् ।
सवैनतेयं स्मरति स्म पत्रिणा-
मि(म)थाविरासन्नयुतानि पुष्करे ॥ 23,K L-45

तिरोदधे मण्डलयद्भिरम्बरं
सुवर्णसङ्घैरवधूतभास्करैः ।
मृ(यु)गक्षयक्षोभितवायुरंहसा
विभिन्नमेरोरिव शृङ्गमण्डलैः ।। 23L, L-46

अथ पत्रिपतत्रिवायुवेग-
प्रसभोन्मूलितभूधरावकाशैः ।
भयसङ्कुचितोरुदर्पनागै-
र्विविशेऽधोभुवनं विनष्टचेष्टैः ।। 23M, L-47

विनतातनयानवेक्ष्य रामः
कृतकृत्यान् कृतिनं प्रणम्य यातान् ।
कृतसंहृतिकालकालशङ्को
रिपुराग्नेयमथाजुहाव मन्त्रम् ।। 23N, L-48

सटाच्छटारूक्षशिखाभयङ्करः
कृताट्टहासस्फुटिताद्रिकन्दरः ।
अथाविरासीद्दिवि दृष्टिपाटनः
कृशानुसिंहो नवधूमवालधिः ।। 23O, L-49

इतस्ततः कीर्णशिखाग्रचञ्चल-
त्करालजिह्वाशतलीढवारिदाः ।
जगद्विनाशोन्मुखवाडवानल-
प्रभाः समस्तं स्म दहन्ति पावकाः ।। 23P, L-50

चितौ सुवर्णैरिव जातवेदसं
निरीक्ष्य कुर्वाणमशेषरोष(द?)सी ।
स वारुणास्त्रं स्मरति स्म भेजिरे
मुखानि मेघाः ककुभामनन्तरम् ।। 23Q, L-51

अवेक्ष्य विद्युन्नयनै रुषा रिपुं
बकोटमालावरणा बलाहकाः ।
इरम्मदोत्सारितराक्षसं जलै-
रकुर्वदै(तै)कोदकमुर्वरातलम् ।। 23R, L-52

तदवेक्ष्य निरस्मस्तत्रमन्यं
मुमुचे यद्यदसौ जयाय तेन ।
अथ तत्तदभेदनिर्विशङ्कं
तिमिरं भानुमतैव सूचिभेद्यम् ।। 23S, L-53

ज्वलदग्निमुखं शता[रा]ग्रमुग्रं
प्रतिसूर्यस्थितमम्बरेऽरिमुक्तम् ।
पृथुचक्रमुपासदं जिगीषोः
सकलं याति वशं विशेषतोऽस्त्रम् ।। 23T, L-54

अभिमन्त्र(त्र्य) विरिञ्चनास्त्रमुच्चै-
रथ सन्धाय धनुः कठोरमौर्व्या ।
ज्वलनं ज्वलिताहिमांशुबिम्बं
सहसाकर्षदसौ सलीलमुग्रम् ।। 27A, L-58

श्रुतमूलनिषण्णधीरमौर्वी-
दृढसक्तङ्गुलिपल्लवोऽस्य दृष्टिः ।
ददृशे खचरैः क्षणं पुरारे-
स्त्रिपुरं दग्धुमिवोन्मुखैकमुष्टिः ।। 27B, L-59

अपारशोकाम्बुनिधौ भयङ्करे
सुदुस्तरे प्राणवियोगकारणे ।
क्षणेन निक्षिप्य विनष्टचेतनां
गतः क्व दीप्तिः सहचारिणीमिव ।। 43A, L-74

त्वदेकजीवामयि दुःखमोहितां
अनन्यचित्तामशिवैकभाजनम् ।
रिरंसयाऽपास्य यतो ययापि सा
मदीयपापादिह नास्ति दुर्लभा ।। 43B, L-75

अभिक्षताया इव जीवने मणिः
पिपासिताया इव वाऽमृताञ्जलिः ।
प्रणष्टलब्धो विधिपर्ययात्पुनः
त्वमेव मे हस्तगतो विनश्यसि ।। 43C, L-76

Canto XX

लङ्काकपीशकरपल्लवधूयमानः
शुभ्राभ्रगौरगुरुचामरवीज्यमानः ।
लज्जापराङ्मुखमुखीमवलम्ब्य देवीं
अङ्के न्यवीविशदसौ निरवद्यकीर्तिः ॥ 2A, L-3

नीहारहारितपयोधरचारुमध्या
सौदामिनीकनकभूषणभूषितेयम् ।
हंसस्वनैस्तव मु[सु]खाय दिगङ्गनाशु
प्रस्थानमङ्गलगिरं कुरुते सखीव ॥ 7A, L-9

किञ्चोल्लसत्तरुणपल्लवलीयमान-
मञ्जुक्वणच्छुकशिखावलिराजमाना ।
हंसावलिव्यजनमुज्ज्वलमुन्नमय्य
त्वां वीजितुं सरभसा समुपस्थितेयम् ॥ 7B, L-10

लङ्का त्रिकूटशिखरस्थितहर्म्यशृङ्ग-
प्रत्युप्तरत्नरुचिपिञ्जरिताम्बरश्रीः ।
त्वां प्रेमतोऽनुसरतीव वियोगखिन्ना
सद्यः सखीव जवमेयुषि पुष्पकेऽस्मिन् ॥ 10A, L-15

आदाय तोयमभितो जलधिं पयोदै-
र्वेदादिवार्थमृपिभिर्विहिताः स्फुरन्तीः ।
पश्यापगाः सलिलधिं दयितेव यान्ती-
र्वेदं स्मृतीरिव महाजनसेव्यमानाः ॥ 15A, L-20

त्वङ्गत्तरङ्गजलवेगनिरस्तरुष्ट-
भोगीन्द्रनिर्ण(?)मणिमण्डितवालुकौघम् ।
पश्याम्बुधेस्तटमनेकविचित्रपुष्प-
गण्डान्त(गन्धान्ध?)भृङ्गपटलासितवृक्षषण्डम् ॥ 15B, L-21

उन्मग्नशङ्खशशिपेशलमञ्जनाभ-
मज्ञातपारमनपायमभिप्रवृद्धम् ।
मीनाकुलीकृतमुपासितगाङ्गतोयं
पश्यान्तरिक्षमिव वारिनिधिं विचित्रम् ॥ 15C, L-22

शुभ्राभ्रफेनरुचिकल्पितहंसलीलः
पश्यन् विशालशफरीनयनेन हृद्यम् ।
आलोलवीचिकरयुग्मकृताञ्जलिस्त्वां
उत्त(त्ति)ष्ठतीव जलराशिरि(र)तीव हृष्टः ॥ 18A, L-25

अस्मिन् युगान्तसमये जलराशिशय्यो
निद्राकटाक्षिनयनः श्रुतिवन्द्यमानः ।
संहृत्य लोकमखिलं क्षणमद्वितीयः
शेते पुराणपुरुषः स्म समस्तमूलः ॥ 18B, L-26

अम्भोनिधिं प्रतरतः किल वायुसूनो-
र्मैनाकभूभृदभिभूतदिगन्तरालम् ।
श्रान्तिं विनेतुमुदतिष्ठदुदग्रशृङ्ग-
मुक्तोदकावलिकृतोभयपक्षशाली ॥ 18C, L-27

जीमूततुङ्गिततरङ्गविलोलनीर-
जीमूतमञ्जननिभं निभृतं पिबन्तम् ।
ऐरावतीरुचिरमाशु विलोकयैन-
मैरावताञ्चलितशङ्खरुचः पयोधेः ॥ 20A, L-29

किञ्चिच्चलत्कुवलयावलिलोचनश्री-
रालोक्यतामलिकुलार्पितवेणिबद्धाम्(न्धा) ।
हंसस्वनैस्सरसमाह्वयतीव देवीं
चक्रांसुयोन्नतरुचा(चक्राह्वयोन्नतकुचा?) खलु ताम्रपर्णी ॥
13A, L-35

पश्योक(प)कण्ट(ठ)कमखण्डितचण्डवात-
पिण्डीभवन्मधुपमण्डलपुण्डरीकान् ।
त्वङ्गत्तरङ्गरयमुक्तसमुक्तशुक्ति-
मुक्ताफलालिकवलीकृतकच्छदेशान् 13B, L-36

एका(ला)लिङ्गित(?)चम्पकमञ्जरीक-
सम्पर्कसङ्क्रमितसौरभपूगगन्धैः ।
सीतेनुमानवनमेति(?)कुबेरकन्या
नेदीयसीति शिशिरैरपि मन्दवातैः ॥ 24A, L-38

मत्तालिपालिवनितेव समाह्वयन्ती
त्वम(त्वामु)ज्जगौ कलरवैर्यदनङ्गदूती ।
कृत्यन्त(नृत्यन्ति?) गीतमभिनेतुमिवा(व प्रवालैः?)
हस्ताङ्गुलीभिरभितो वनवृक्षमालाः ।। 24B, L-39

तीरं विलोकय मनोहरसैकतश्री-
निर्धूतशीतकिरणं मदमत्तहंसम् ।
पुष्टान्यपुष्टकलकूजितजायमान-
जीवन्(वं?)मधुव्रत(वृत)व्रततीप्रताना(न)म् ।। 24C, L-40

या गीयते मुनिवरैरपि दाक्षिणात्य-
गङ्गेति गौतमकृताखिलपापभेत्री ।
गात्राणि वीचिपवनेन शनैः स्पृशन्ती
दत्ते सुखानि जननीव करेण मह्यम् ।। 24D, L-41

विन्ध्याद्रिपादविषमोपलविप्रकीर्ण-
घात्कारभैरवमहाभ्रमपाः(भ्रमण?)प्रवाहाः (हा) ।
आवर्तनैः(ने ?)प्रसितवेगिनि मग्नवृक्षा
रेखा विभाति नरसिंहगिरिप्रसूता ।। 16A, L-47

पूर्वाम्बुधिस्तरलतुङ्गितवीचिहस्तै-
रालिङ्ग्य चुम्बति नदीरतिर्निविशङ्कम् ।
सापत्न्यकोपविवशेव नितम्बकन्या
पाश्चात्यसागरमुपैति कृतोरुवेगा ।। 16B, L-48

एकेन सप्तजलधिं चुलुकेन सद्यो
यः पीतवानकृत विन्ध्यगिरिं च नीचम् ।
चक्रे च्युतञ्च नहुषस्य पदान्मघोनः
तस्याश्रमं तरुणि लोकय कुम्भयोनेः ।। 33A, L-50

मय्यर्पितुं सकलराज्यभरं विनीतः
खिन्नो जगाम भरतो धृतराज्यलक्ष्मीः ।
प्रेमप्रपूरपरिपूरितचित्तनुन्नैः
पौरैस्सहैनमवलोकय चित्रकूटम् ।। 25A, L-52

या घर्मभानुतनयाप्यतिशीततोया
जामी यमस्य जगतामपकारकार्या (?) ।
कृष्णा विशुद्धिजननी हरिनीलशृङ्ग-
क्षोदौघनीलसलिलामवलोकयैनाम् ।। 25B, L-53

आवर्तनाभिसरसीरुहभृङ्गवेधाः
पद्मावलम्बितविशालतरङ्गहस्ता ।
तापिञ्छपिच्छनिचया धृतशङ्खचक्रा
रूपश्रियं मधुरिपोरियमेति सीते ।। 25C, L-54

पुण्याहुतिप्रभवधूमवितानगन्ध-
सम्पादिताम्बरतलं यमुनातटस्थम् ।
पश्याश्रमं श्रमहरं भवतीं प्रसूनै-
र्यस्मिन्नभूषयदृषिप्रहितानुसूया ।। 25D, L-55

सीते भगीरथनृपेण मदीयवंश-
नक्षत्रवृन्दशशिना पितृमुक्तिहेतोः ।
कृत्वा सुदुष्करतपांस्यवतारितेयं
गङ्गा विभाति भवबन्धनभेददक्षा ।। 25E, L-56

रामोऽथ मारुतिनिरुद्धकृशानुपातो
यावन्ननाम भरतः शिरसा धरण्याम् ।
आलिङ्ग्य तावदशकन्न विमोक्तुमेनं
बाष्पाम्बुबिन्दुनिचिताननवारिजश्रीः ।। 53A, L-64

अम्भोरुहोदरदलारुणदीर्घचारु-
शीताद्भुतोज्ज्वलविशालविलोचनाभ्याम् ।
पश्यत् प्रणम्य चरणौ जनकात्मजायाः
सौमित्रिमेव कृतवन्दनमालिलिङ्गे(ग)।। 53B, L-65

अन्यान्विभीषणमुखानथ वानरेन्द्रान्
प्रेम्णा यथोचितमसौ परिरम्भणाद्यैः ।
केयूरहारवलयैरपि भूषयित्वा
रामाय जैत्ररथमाशु निनाय वीरः ।। 53C, L-66

प्रस्थाप्य पुष्पकमसौ धनिने महान्त-
मारुह्य जैत्रमनुजैरथ पौरलोकैः ।
आवेष्टितः स्वपुरमाशु विवेश रामः
सर्वैः सुरैः सुरपुरीमिव देवराजः ॥ 53D, L-67

रामाज्ञया दिव्यशरीरभाजः
प्लवङ्गमा भूषितसर्वगात्राः ।
आरुह्य नागानधिजग्मुरेनं
पूर्णेन्दुबिम्बप्रतिमातपत्रम् ॥ 53E, L-68

रामोऽवरुह्य भरतं भृतभूरिकीर्तिं
हस्तेऽवलम्ब्य भवनं निजमाससाद ।
दृष्ट्वा प्रमाममुखमे(ष?)कुलप्रवृद्धाः(न्)
नाम्ना कुमारमखिलं किल पृच्छति स्म ॥ 53F, L-69

श्रुत्वाभिषेकिकमथो रघुवंशकेतो-
र्नक्षत्रमेष सकलाभ्युदयैकमूलम् ।
सम्भारमाशु समपादयदैन्द्रयाम्य-
कौबेरवारुणसमुद्रजलादि सर्वम् ॥ 53G, L-70

तत्रोत्सवोप(पा)करणं कृषिस्यं(कुरुध्वं ?)
प्रस्तिम(?)वानेष जनानयोध्या ।
नित्योत्सवा नित्यमलङ्कृते(ता ?)ऽपि
प्रायेण वेगेन हि विस्तृतासीत् (?) ॥ 53H, L-71

ऋक्सामैर्विजयमुखास्तपस्विनोऽष्टौ
सौवर्णाद(न)नुकलशान्निधाय वेद्यान्(म्) ।
इन्द्रादीनिह विधिनैव लोकपाला-
नावाह्य प्रविदधुरर्चनानि तेषाम् ॥ 55A, L-74

आबद्धप्रतिसरमासनोपविष्टं
राज्यार्थं व्रजमनुजैः(?) सजानिमार्यः ।
जाबालिप्रमुखतपोधनैर्वसिष्ठ-
स्तैस्तोयै रघुकुलनाथमभ्यषिञ्चन् ॥ 55B, L-75

प्रत्युप्तप्रचुरपरार्ध्यरत्नरोचिः-
क्षिप्तार्कद्युतिमुकुटेन भासमानः ।
सम्पूज्य द्विजमहितार्ध्यपाद्यमाल्यै-
र्विप्रेभ्यः क्षितिधनधेनुकुण्डलाद्यान् ।। 56A, L-77

श्रुतिविहितविभागस्पष्टषड्जस्वरादि-
स्फुरिबतद्दुविशेषग्रामयोर्मूर्च्छितानाम् ।
ततयुतमिव-षण् (?) मूर्च्छनां व्यञ्जयन्तीं
सरसमथ गृहीत्वा गायिकाभिः प्रगीतम् ।। 56B, L-78

तस्यातपत्रं भरतो विशालं
पूर्णेन्दुबिम्बप्रतिमं बभार ।
सुग्रीवलङ्काधिपती कराभ्यां
श्वेते स्म वालव्यजने दधाते ।। 56C, L-79

दत्वाशिषं तेन कृताभ्यनुज्ञा
जाबालिमुख्याः प्रययुर्यथैतम् ।
दृष्ट्वाभिषेकं कृतकौतुकास्तं
कृत्वा महीशाः स्वमुपायनानि ।। 56D, L-80

पद्यसूची–INDEX OF VERSES

Sanskrit page numbers refer to the Text and the English numbers to the Appendix.